Architectural Theories of the Environment: Posthuman Territory

As architects and designers, we struggle to reconcile ever increasing environmental, humanitarian, and technological demands placed on our projects. Our new geological era, the Anthropocene, marks humans as the largest environmental force on the planet. This extension of the human technological network across the globe prompts a more comprehensive, or posthuman, understanding of the actors—both human and non-human—that comprise the environment.

In this anthology, editor Ariane Lourie Harrison collects the essays of architects, theorists, and sustainable designers that together provide a framework for a posthuman understanding of the design environment. An introductory essay defines the key terms, concepts, and precedents for a posthuman approach to architecture, and nine fully illustrated case studies of buildings from around the globe demonstrate how issues raised in posthuman theory provide rich terrain for contemporary architecture, making theory concrete. By assembling a range of voices across different fields, from urban geography to critical theory to design practitioners, this anthology offers a resource for design professionals, educators, and students seeking to grapple the ecological mandate of our current period.

Case studies include work by Arakawa and Gins, Arons en Gelauff, Casagrande Lab, Natalie Jeremijenko, The Living, Minifie van Schaik Architects, R&Sie(n), SCAPE, and Studio Gang Architects

Essayists include Gilles Clément, Matthew Gandy, Francesco Gonzáles de Canales, Elizabeth Grosz, Simon Guy, Seth Harrison, N. Katherine Hayles, Ursula K. Heise, Catherine Ingraham, Bruno Latour, William J. Mitchell, Matteo Pasquinelli, Erik Swyngedouw, Sarah Whatmore, Jennifer Wolch, Cary Wolfe, and Albena Yaneva

Ariane Lourie Harrison is a critic and lecturer at the Yale School of Architecture and a principal of Harrison Atelier.

Architectural Theories of the Environment:
Posthuman Territory

Edited by Ariane Lourie Harrison

Routledge
Taylor & Francis Group

First published 2013
by Routledge
711 Third Avenue, New York, NY 10017

Simultaneously published in the UK
by Routledge
2 Park Square, Milton Park, Abingdon, Oxon OX14 4RN

Routledge is an imprint of the Taylor & Francis Group, an informa business

Library of Congress Cataloging-in-Publication Data

Architectural theories of the environment : posthuman territory / [edited by] Ariane Lourie Harrison.
      pages cm
      Includes index.
      1. Architecture--Environmental aspects. I. Harrison, Ariane Lourie, editor of compilation.
      NA2542.35.A65 2012
      720'.47--dc23   2012016341

ISBN: 978-0-415-50618-2 (hbk)
ISBN: 978-0-415-50619-9 (pbk)
ISBN: 978-0-203-08427-4 (ebk)

Publisher's Note
This book has been prepared from camera-ready copy provided by the author.

Acquisitions Editor: Wendy Fuller
Editorial Assistant: Laura Williamson
Production Editor: Siobhán Greaney

Book Design: Ariane Lourie Harrison

Printed by Ashford Colour Press Ltd, Gosport, Hampshire

Contents

Section I: Posthuman Subjects

Section II: Posthuman Assemblages

Section III: Posthuman Territory

Acknowledgements

I am grateful to Routledge: to my commissioning editor, Wendy Fuller, for her vision and encouragement for this project; to Laura Williamson and Siobhán Greaney for their steadfast editorial support.

Jean-Louis Cohen, Cynthia Davidson, Peter Eisenman, Reinhold Martin, Mark C. Taylor, and Mark Wigley provided insights that helped to shape the themes and framework of this book. Newton and Helen Mayer Harrison contributed their example as environmental artists in our ongoing conversation about the big picture.

My sincere thanks to the architects, designers, and colleagues who have graciously contributed time, insights and visual material to this project: Arnoud Gelauff from Arons en Gelauff, Marco Casagrande, David Benjamin from The Living, Jan van Schaik from Minifie van Schaik Architects, Chris Perry and Catherine Dwyer from Pneumastudio, Kate Orff and Gina Werth from SCAPE, Jeanne Gang and Alissa Anderson from Studio Gang Architects, Natalie Jeremijenko, Eléonore de Lavandeyra Schöffer, François Roche from R&Sie(n), and Madeline Gins and Joke Post for the fantastic trip to the Bioscleave House.

Much appreciation is due to the contributors of texts for this anthology: Gilles Clément, Matthew Gandy, Francesco Gonzáles de Canales, Elizabeth Grosz, Simon Guy, Seth Harrison, N. Katherine Hayles, Ursula Heise, Catherine Ingraham, Bruno Latour, William J. Mitchell, Matteo Pasquinelli, Erik Swyngedouw, Sarah Whatmore, Jennifer Wolch, Cary Wolfe, and Albena Yaneva. Many thanks are due to Martin Puchner for introducing me to the work of Ursula Heise and to Denise Bratton for her suggestion of Gilles Clément's "L'alternative ambiante" and her expert editing and guidance toward Clément's symbiotic humanity.

Profound thanks are due to the Yale School of Architecture: to Robert A.M. Stern, Dean of the School who supported my seminars on this topic, to my students during three years of "Sustainability for Posthumans" seminars, and to the many friends and colleagues have offered their insights on this topic in discussions and during reviews. The opportunity to present this material in conferences helped this book to evolve. Thanks to John McMorrough for the stimulating workshop forum provided by his *Matter of Opinion Conference* at OSU (2009) and to Jennifer Leung for her incisive comments on my paper "The Parameters of the Posthuman" for her panel "Post-Parametric Environments" at the ACSA100 (2012). Important sources of support and inspiration came from people connected to several Harrison Atelier projects: thanks to Chris Soller, Superintendant of the Fire Island National Seashore, for the posthuman territory we explored at Talisman/Barrett Beach; to Eva Franch Gilabert for her steadfast support and the opportunity to display a pharmaceutical landscape at the Storefront for Art and Architecture and to Lucien Zayan, for encouraging our work on human-animal instrumentalization at the Invisible Dog.

Finally I would like to thank my Harrison, Lourie, and Schram families. My greatest gratitude and admiration to Seth Harrison, my posthuman partner in all things.

Introduction

Charting Posthuman Territory
Ariane Lourie Harrison

I. Bodies and Natures

A *posthuman* continuum between human, nature, and technology becomes increasingly evident in the smart materials, sentient systems, and ubiquitous communication networks that populate the urban environment today. The contingency of these organic and technological categories provokes new questions for architecture. For how many different species do you design? How responsive is the envelope of your building? How does your building engage the material and discursive forces of its site? In suggesting that architectural theory can integrate these questions, this anthology aims to expand our understanding of the messy contingencies, material ambiguation, and heterogeneous audiences that posthuman theorists suggest compromise our everyday space. *Architectural Theories of the Environment: Posthuman Territory* assembles critical texts and case studies that establish continuities rather than new dialectics to characterize the dynamic between architecture and the environment in the Anthropocene period. In doing so, this anthology beckons the discipline of architecture to recognize that its once familiar terrain is now bristling with new hybrids.

The term *posthuman* operates in a largely hidden territory, making only a brief appearance in architectural criticism as an unexplained adjective—except perhaps to gesture toward a hazy, technologized future. *Posthuman* and its related terms (*posthumanism, posthumanist*) conjure almost as many different theoretical positions as they would seem to portend new species along a continuum of human, animal, and digital life.[1] The posthumanist vocabulary for architecture also differs from the discourse of formalism, which maintains a conceptual separation (if not an operational divide) between critical-representational goals internal to architecture and its ambitions to engage the political and social complexities of the world at large. In this sense, the posthuman challenges the long-standing conception of the building as an object autonomous from its environment and governed by disciplinary interiority.

1. The terms *posthuman, posthumanist,* and *posthumanism* are related among the writings on this body of thought. Andy Miah provides a useful analysis of the dialogue between cultural and philosophical approaches to posthumanism. See Andy Miah, "Posthumanism: A Critical History," in B. Gordijn and R. Chadwick, eds., *Medical Enhancements and Posthumanity* (New York: Routledge, 2007), 1–24. See also Neil Badminton, *Posthumanism* (2000) and Cary Wolfe, *What is Posthumanism?* (2010). Yet many texts that intertwine scientific and cultural studies rely instead on the term *posthuman*, such as N. Katherine Hayles's *How We Became Posthuman* (1999), Judith Halberstam and Ira Livingstone's *Posthuman Bodies* (1995) and Elaine Graham's *Representations of the Post/Human* (2002). This anthology uses the terms *posthumanism* and *posthumanist* to reflect the philosophic critique of humanism; and it adopts the term *posthuman* used in cultural and literary theory to discuss the materiality of the body and the interconnections between human, animal and machine.

Perhaps the most common references for the posthuman rely on a techno-transcendent vision of the future, fueled by breakthroughs in biotechnology and debates on human enhancement as forms of posthumanity. Yet between the polarized positions of rival futurists—Francis Fukuyama's *Our Posthuman Future* (2002), which decries the "dehumanizing" effect of biotechnological advancement, versus Ray Kurzweil's *The Singularity is Near* (2005), which promotes a positivist merger of human intelligence with technology by 2050—lies a posthuman territory that reflects the entangled and co-constitutive relation of human, technology and environment. Not simply a biotechnological harbinger of the new, the posthuman is also grounded in the nineteenth-century philosophical project that questioned the foundational myths of human identity, associated since the Enlightenment with reason, free will, and self-consciousness. Mining this line of thought, the late 1960s pitted humanist disciplines against new human sciences that revealed man's technologies to be fundamental supports. Michel Foucault emphasizes that, "As the archaeology of thought easily shows, man is an invention of recent date. And one perhaps nearing its end."[2] Many aspects of these two positions—the posthuman as disciplinary revisionist versus the posthuman as techno-transcendent—blend as we come to understand what posthumanism offers for an architectural theorization of the environment.

Bodies

Posthuman perspectives in cultural and science studies highlight that human embodiment remains in flux, unlike the static harmonies of the Vitruvian figure or Le Corbusier's Modulor Man. The notion of the machinic body, articulated as early as 1748 in La Mettrie's *L'homme machine*, yields, by 1948, to the image of a networked body described by Norbert Wiener in *Cybernetics: or communication and control in animal and machine*. The term *cybernetics* derives from the Greek word for "steersman" and describes the manner in which devices with tracking systems can absorb stimuli and govern responses to their environments. In exploring how systems organized themselves to achieve stability or a functional optimum, postwar cybernetics sought to understand how information between entities was exchanged, rather than focusing on the properties of the entities themselves. This idea took physical form when research scientists Manfred Clynes and Nathan Kline coined the term *cyborg* (cybernetic organism) in their 1960 article in *Astronautics Magazine* to describe an organism-machine system that "deliberately

2. Michel Foucault, *The Order of Things: An Archaeology of the Human Sciences* (New York: Random House, 1994), 387.

Lourie Harrison

incorporates exogenous components extending the self-regulatory control function of the organism in order to adapt it to new environments."[3] The authors announced one of the first cyborgs "to be a rat equipped with an osmotic pump;" a prototype for equilibrating human bodies for space and a first step towards "adapting man's body to any environment he may choose."[4] The animal-machine hybrid would help man colonize new territories, "permitt[ing] man's existence in environments which differ radically from those provided by nature as we know it."[5] Already this first cyborg embodied major themes for the posthuman: human-animal exchanges, networks, bodily enhancement, and designed environments.

Feminist theorist Donna Haraway later popularized the term in her 1985 "A Cyborg Manifesto," invoking the cyborg as a sophisticated blend of body and machine that challenged the organic composition of the human while embodying its particular political and economic context. Haraway summarizes the concept in her introduction to *Simians, Cyborgs, and Women* (1990):

> Cyborgs are post-Second World War hybrid entities made of, first, ourselves and other organic creatures in our unchosen "high-technological" guise as information systems, texts, and ergonomically controlled labouring, desiring, and reproducing systems. The second essential ingredient in cyborgs is machines in their guise, also, as communications systems, texts, and self-acting, ergonomically designed apparatus.[6]

Haraway intends her cyborg to frame a sly critique of feminism in allying a feminist reading of alterity with military technology. The cyborg becomes an "ironic political myth," the subversive humor of which registers the discrepancy between the essentialist "nature" attributed to gender through biology and the lived experience of nature as a technology-infused construction. Indeed, the Promethian possibilities of the body, represented as alien, cyborg or animal-hybrid, brings identity politics into closer dialogue with technology and undermines narrow associations of the body with nature. Haraway's cyborg voices a need for culture and its critics to accept the dissolution of humanist hierarchies and contend with the effects of technology. Whether or not the cyborg remains descriptive of contemporary network culture—or as N. Katherine Hayles asks in her contribution to this anthology, "is it networked enough?" for today's world—is an ongoing question for architectural research that now integrates fields as diverse as artificial intelligence, the bio-digital and DIY biotech.

3. Manfred E. Clynes and Nathan S. Kline, "Cyborgs and space," *Astronautics* (September 1960): 27.

4. Ibid.

5. Ibid., 26.

6. Donna Haraway, *Simians, Cyborgs, and Women: the Reinvention of Nature* (New York: Routledge, 1990), 1.

The hybrid status of the body—its interpenetration by and translation into patterns of information—is not new, but is closely bound to mid-century cybernetic research. This history is mapped by N. Katherine Hayles in her integrative book *How We Became Posthuman* (1999).[7] In this meticulous study of the complex development of cybernetics, Hayles traces the growth of three models of information within cybernetic theory—instrumental language, reflexive language, and emergent systems—and demonstrates the political and social stakes embodied in each model of information in the postwar period. This dynamic history of information models parallels a cybernetic strain in postwar architecture and is worth understanding in detail.

According to Hayles, a first wave of cybernetic theory flourished between 1945 and the early 1960s. This movement was led by Norbert Wiener, the theorist who first explored the concepts of environmental feedback that led to pioneering cybernetics research, and Claude Shannon, the mathematician and engineer whose research laid the foundations for modern information theory. This initial conceptualization of cybernetics promoted a binary (signal/noise) concept of information that focused primarily on the sender and receiver of information. This is a dematerialized view of information, one that regarded consciousness itself as a pattern independent of the material world. Hayles' later work argues that such a perspective leads to futuristic visions of transcendent humanity: the complete removal of human consciousness from its biological substrate popularized by Hans Moravec, Nick Bostrum, and Ray Kurzweil.

A second wave of cybernetic theory, launched in the late 1960s by Francisco Varela, Humberto Maturana, and Gregory Bateson, expands the cybernetic system to include the observer and his/her effects on the system in question. The self-reflexive network fosters a more complex, autopoetic informational system. This concept of *autopoesis*—that an organism simultaneously maintains an openness to energetic and environmental stimuli and a formal closure within its environment—views information in its specific and material context, and in this sense, it challenges the binary model (signaler/receiver) studied by Wiener and Shannon. Despite its nuance, this embodied view of information has also been interpreted in a reductive fashion to justify the politically conservative stance, popularized by Fukuyama, that human consciousness is preserved in a human body that exists in the current-species form and that biotechnological transformation of the human body will eradicate human values.[8]

7. N. Katherine Hayles, *How We Became Posthuman: Virtual Bodies in Cybernetics, Literature and Informatics* (Chicago: University of Chicago Press, 1999).

8. N. Katherine Hayles, "Flesh and Metal: Reconfiguring the Mindbody in Virtual Environments," *Configurations* 10, no. 2 (Spring 2002): 297.

Lourie Harrison

A third and current interpretation of cybernetics developed by Rodney Brooks, Eugene Thacker, and Hayles addresses the context and physical nature of networks: the material substrate for data is integral to its informational structure, apparent in new methods for processing data through machinic and organic matrixes in the fields of artificial intelligence, biotechnology, and nanotechnology. This third position argues that the human body in its current form is not a sacrosanct vessel for human consciousness, a perspective that envisions humans and machine intelligences co-developing in various degrees of interdependency. The relationality of this third wave of cybernetics is posthuman. "In the posthuman," writes Hayles, "there are no essential differences or absolute demarcations between bodily existence and computer simulation, cybernetic mechanisms and biological organism, robot teleology and human goals."[9] Cybernetics is therefore an important theoretical model for the posthuman approach, because it is an interdisciplinary discourse concerning systems in general, yet it does not address the full social and ethical spectrum of the posthuman. Hayles reminds us: "What it means to be human is finally not so much about intelligent machines as it is about how to create just societies in a transnational global world that may include in its purview both carbon and silicon citizens."[10]

The posthuman is equally a product of the late twentieth-century's globally networked subjectivity, one represented by a postmodernity for which architecture served as a primary reference. Architectural theorist Reinhold Martin suggests that the architectural "endgame" of postwar corporate modernism is a "'postindustrial' or even 'posthuman' subject, a subject immersed in and constructed by data flows and patterns."[11] Martin's *The Organizational Complex* (2003) demonstrates the corporate organization of media and material in response to shifting patterns of information, architecture becoming one element in this feedback system as a medium in and of itself. The organizational aesthetic resonated in the visual feedback between the grids of curtain wall, floor plan, and computer screen, habituating its subjects to interaction with, if not dependency on, the patterned flows of information across capital networks. This mesmerizing flicker of information is conceived as being substrate-independent, linking the first wave of cybernetic thought to a posthuman subject.

K. Michael Hays locates a posthumanist subject for architecture even earlier in the 1920s work of Ludwig Hilberseimer, which addresses a dispersed subject: "called upon to take multiple and contradictory subject-positions," in moving beyond "an arrogant

9. Hayles, *How We Became Posthuman*, 3.

10. N. Katherine Hayles, "Computing the Human," *Theory Culture and Society* 22 (2005): 148.

11. Reinhold Martin, *The Organizational Complex: Architecture, Media, and Corporate Space* (Cambridge, MA: MIT Press, 2003), 12.

bourgeois humanism" to a "new post-individualist framework."[12] This networked conception of the subject, while predating cybernetics, strikes Hays as a posthuman sensibility. Christopher Hight examines the cybernetic underpinnings of modern architectural discourses on proportion in his *Architectural Principles in the Age of Cybernetics* (2008). He locates the blurred contours of Le Corbusier's Modulor Man in post-structuralist and phenomenologist architectural theory as well as in contemporary proliferations of blob, mutant, and prosthetic forms. Yet his statement that "cybernetics and the cyborg stand in contemporary theory for the post-human" oversimplifies the scope of the posthuman project and favors its formal interpretation over its programmatic manifestations in postwar and contemporary architecture.[13] Posthuman bodies and their networked subjectivities nevertheless do emerge in postwar architectural precedents.

Natures

Posthuman theory extends the cyborg metaphor beyond the body and into the built environment, imagining designed space itself as a prosthetic and producing new understandings of a "nature" that itself can no longer be conceived as an originary or neutral ground. Fields ranging from sociology to geography have explored the political implications of extending the human body into the environment through science and technology, fueling the debate over the status of nature. Nature is further dismantled by the field of Science and Technology Studies (STS), a body of research initiated in the 1970s and developed by Latour, Hayles, Michel Callon, and Manuel De Landa, among others. STS situates scientific activity in a social and cultural context and grants agency to nonhumans; the formerly "neutral" environment becomes a space crowded by human and non-human actors.

Latour argues that the "modern" urge to distinguish the social from the natural is characteristic of the desire to divide the world into neat categories of subjects and objects and that the teleological impulse to separate modern present from primitive past has never matched the reality of our hybrid assemblages. By this logic, we are "non-modern" if accept that even the most mundane gesture reveals the co-constitution of technology and environment:

> Press the most innocent aerosol button and you'll be heading for the Antarctic, the University of California at Irvine, the mountain ranges of Lyon, the chemistry of inert gases and then maybe to the United Nations, but this fragile thread will be broken into as many segments as there are pure disciplines.[14]

12. K. Michael Hays, "Inscribing the Subject of Modernism: the Posthumanist Theory of Ludwig Hilberseimer," *Strategies in Architectural Thinking,* eds. John Whiteman, Jeffrey Kipnis and Richard Burdett (Cambridge, MA: MIT Press, 1992), 126.

13. Christopher Hight, *Architectural Principles in the Age of Cybernetics* (New York: Routledge, 2008), 189.

14. Bruno Latour, *We Have Never Been Modern,* trans. Catherine Porter (Cambridge, MA: Harvard University Press, 1993), 3.

Lourie Harrison

In *Politics of Nature* (2004), Latour differentiates the posthumanist politics of "collectives" from the humanist politics of nature which enforce a static conception of nature versus man: it prescribes a limited set of objectifying and exploitative interactions between man and his surround. Refusing to reduce objects of knowledge to discrete entities (politics, objects, or discourse), Latour reveals their status as composites, as quasi-objects/quasi-subjects after Michel Serres, meriting a "non-modern" politics capable of "represent[ing] the associations of humans and nonhumans through an explicit procedure, in order to decide what collects them and what unifies them in one future common world."[15] The argument follows to describe a "crisis of objectivity," in which the understanding of "facts" as discretely bounded objects of knowledge gives way to an appreciation of their rhizomatic and complicated status; objective "facts" become subjective "matters of concern." "Nature" too is in need of revision, given that "nature is what makes it possible to recapitulate the hierarchy of beings in a single ordered series. Political ecology is the destruction of that idea of Nature."[16] Latour recommends a pragmatism translated to politics that can only be applied site-specifically. This pragmatist approach is meant explicitly to encode the operating principles of an ecology: the integration of as many elements present in a given place or situation at a moment in time, and the generation of as full an understanding of their interactions as possible.

Most posthuman approaches therefore address the term *nature* with some suspicion and underscore the constitutive role of technology in various aspects of the environment. One reasonably comprehensive articulation of this claim is that of Paul Crutzen and Eugene Stoermer, who coined the term *Anthropocene* to describe the present geological era, one in which man (*anthropos*) has become the most significant factor affecting global environmental change.[17] Other efforts to qualify the posthuman continuum between humanity, technology, and nature include Damian White and Chris Wilbert's anthology *Technonatures* (2009), a work that translates the Anthropocene concept from the geological and evolutionary to the ethnocultural level. They describe how various human social groupings utilize technologies to construct their own versions of nature, which the authors term *social natures*.[18]

Architecture is undeniably implicated in such revisions, as the editors of *Verb Natures* (2006) demonstrate. This compendium of over twenty contemporary firms examines how each deploys organic materials, modes of assembly based on organic structures,

15. Bruno Latour, *Politics of Nature: How to Bring the Sciences into Democracy* (Cambridge, MA: Harvard University Press, 2004), 41.

16. Ibid, 25.

17. Paul Crutzen and Eugene Stoermer, "The Anthropocene," *IGBP Newsletter* 41, (May 2000): 17–8. While the term anthropocene was coined relatively recently, Crutzen and Stoermer locate the beginnings of the Anthropocene period to the 19th century's innovations in industrial production.

18. Damian White and Chris Wilbert, "Inhabiting Technonatural Time/Spaces," in *Technonatures: Environments, Technologies, Spaces, and Places in the Twenty-first Century*, Ed. Damian White and Chris Wilbert (Waterloo, Canada: Wilfrid Laurier University Press), 6.

and organic metaphors; the book explores how the "fusion of natural and artificial matter produce[s] new architectural organisms, new environments, new natures."[19] While useful as a collection of provocative projects, *Verb Natures* refrains from questioning whether such new organicisms produce new discursive structures for the discipline. In his book *Subnatures* (2009), David Gissen delves deeper into the historical and theoretical underpinnings of what he similarly identifies as an organic material-aesthetic in contemporary architectural practices, emphasizing their uses of "peripheral and often denigrated forms of nature."[20] The *subnatural* becomes manifest in overlooked materialities—smoke, dust, pigeons, weeds—selected by Gissen to challenge the instrumental value to which nature tends to be relegated in the contemporary city, from the docile greenways of landscape urbanism to the green-washed facades of eco-cities. Gissen's term *subnatural*, like Latour's term *non-modern*, references a hybrid "nature" which harbors a political agenda in its capacity to inspire new collectives: "forc[ing] us to consider how architects might employ the crowd's socionatural chemistry in an era in which the transformative aspects of the crowd appear momentarily suspended."[21]

Architectural historian Antoine Picon offers another possible trajectory towards the posthuman proliferation of hybrid natures. In a body of research that spans *La ville territoire des cyborgs* (1998) to *Digital Culture in Architecture* (2010), Picon describes the longstanding effects of science and technology on architectural culture: cyborg networks, computational aesthetics, diagrams of complexity, and data-driven urbanism intertwine to create architecture's "digital culture." Rather than focusing on materiality and sensory effects produced by this digitalization of architecture, Picon explores the dialogue between architectural, scientific, and social discourses; he duly critiques the parametric naturalization of the environment as a flexible matrix of digitally-coded objects. Picon does not emphasize the term but rather alludes to a posthuman approach: "Digital architecture is trying to express this new condition that differs radically from the humanistic conception of man."[22]

Such recent qualifications of architecture's environment as *subnatural* or *technonatural* or even *socio-natural*, deviate from the conventional attempts to preserve "nature" as an other to architecture; these new terms mark our changing relationship to nature and point to an emerging architectural imagination of posthuman hybridity.

19. *Verb Natures* ed. Irene Hwang, Tomoko Sakamoto, Albert Ferré, Michael Kubo, Noorie Sadarangani, Anna Tetas, Mario Ballesteros and Ramon Prat (Barcelona: Actar Press, 2006), 5.

20. David Gissen, *Subnatures: Architecture's Other Environments* (New York: Princeton Architectural Press, 2009), 22.

21. Ibid, 200.

22. Antoine Picon, *Digital Culture in Architecture* (Basel: Birkhäuser, 2010), 13.

Lourie Harrison

II. Toward an Architecture for Posthumans

Architecture's potential for networked interactivity took form as the postwar discourse on cybernetics penetrated the spatial imaginaries of postwar European, American, and Japanese architects. Skeptical of modernism's romance with the image of technology—from the factory aesthetic to Le Corbusier's house as a "machine for living"—these postwar architects explored the implications of technology for program rather than form. Projects sought to materialize the network as a geometric organization that promised to unify a stratified postwar society. This aspiration drew on both the "biotechnic" future advanced by Lewis Mumford in *Technics and Civilization* (1934) and the environmental "equipoise" with which Sigfried Giedion concluded *Mechanization Takes Command* (1948); both texts set forth historical frameworks for the integration of humanity, technology, and environment into a new social model. In projects from the 1950s to the 1970s, the network took many forms but mined several themes consistently: the power of cybernetic technologies to produce novel environmental effects; the translation of an abstract network into a geometrical array of similar units; and the new forms of mobility inspired by a network's capacity to relay information across distance. Some projects combined all of these tendencies in attempting, in Mark Wigley's terms, to create a "visible aesthetic for an invisible net."[23]

The postwar era produced a rich chronology of architecture's deployment of network models. The following paragraphs chart these efforts as precedents for contemporary formulations of a networked, responsive— or even posthuman—architecture.

Cybernetic Atmospheres

In exploring architecture's potential as a responsive medium, postwar artists and architects, often in collaboration, adapted cybernetics, semiotics, and communication theories to justify their attempts to animate physical constructions and buildings. If, in phenomenological terms, space could be considered an environment that is activated through the perception of its subjects, then the use of technology to stimulate the senses would theoretically heighten this effect: it would awaken the body and catalyze new modes of inhabitation.

Early efforts involve kinetic constructions, such as the fifty-meter high Spatiodynamic Tower (1954) by French-Hungarian sculptor Nicolas Schöffer.[24] With vibrating cantilevered bars and cables, panels and perforated surfaces tilting with prevailing winds,

23. Mark Wigley, "Network Fever," *Grey Room* 04 (Summer 2001): 111.

24. I have provided the titles of projects in English but am making reference to the following works by Nicolas Schöffer: *Tour Spatiodynamique* (1954), *Maison à Cloisons Invisibles* (1957), and *La Ville Cybernétique* (1969).

and a mechanized soundscape, Schöffer's Spatiodynamic Tower created a field of sensory effects that were environmental in scale, distinct from the local effects produced by appliance-sized devices, such as cybernetician Gordon Pask's Musicolor Machines (1953).

Fig. 1.1 Nicolas Schöffer, Spatiodynamic Tower at the Parc de St. Cloud, France, 1954 (courtesy of Eléonore de Lavandeyra Schöffer).

Schöffer's House with Invisible Walls (1957) demonstrated that technology networks could even replace conventional architectural enclosures. Here Schöffer apposed two environmental conditions—one heated, sonorous, and colored with infra-red light and the other cool, silent, and bathed in blue-fluorescent light—to create a threshold or "invisible wall" without constructing a physical separation. Schöffer's exploration of sensory apparatus into the environment frames the body as an active node within the cybernetic construction of space. Yet, with what Schöffer termed his first "cybernetic sculpture" in 1956, the body would need to engage an environment populated by robotic species as well. Schöffer proposed CYSP-1: an eight-foot tall mobile construction, distinguished by its actual spatial autonomy and its "electronic brain" developed by Philips engineers. Microphones in CYSP-1's base detected sounds while photoelectric cells sensed color, enabling CYSP-1 to respond to ambient stimuli. For example, the

Lourie Harrison

color blue or silence prompted agitated movements from CYSP-1: it rapidly rolled backwards and forwards; it made quick turns; it spun its sixteen polychrome plates. In environments bathed in warm hues and loud noises, CYSP-1 appeared to "calm down."

Fig. 1.2 Nicolas Schöffer, CYSP-1, at the Cité Radieuse, Marseilles, 1956 (courtesy of Eléonore de Lavandeyra Schöffer).

Making its debut as a "robot-dancer," CYSP-1 performed with Maurice Béjart's ballet dancers in several venues including on the rooftop of Le Corbusier's Cité Radieuse in Marseilles. An admiring press noted that the element of indeterminacy in CYSP-1's movements "gives [it] a life and an almost organic sensibility."[25] Trying to deploy such kinetic constructions for an urban scale, Schöffer and the architect Claude Parent envisaged a radically networked city. Their Cybernetic City (1969) dotted Paris with towers following the model of the realized Cybernetic Tower for Liège (1961) but was capable of generating "programmed climates." Electronic management of all the Cybernetic City's systems, from its Scientific Research Centers to its Center for Sexual Recreation, reiterated the vision that responsive networks could not only refashion the city but also connect city-dwellers on the most intimate levels.

Few works integrated cybernetics into program as famously as the project for the Fun Palace (1961–64) by architect Cedric Price with

25. Gerard Cottin, "CYSP-1 danseuse-etoile est un robot," *Science et Vie* (September 1956): 65. See www.cyberneticszoo.com for other articles on CYSP-1 from the 1950s.

theater director Joan Littlewood, and cybernetician Gordon Pask. Envisioned as an open steel structure, serviced by moving gantry cranes that reassembled each of the building's elements (walls, platforms, catwalks, steerable escalators and mobile screens), the Fun Palace would provide a dynamic scaffold for leisure activity:

> Its form and structure, resembling a large shipyard in which enclosures such as theatres, cinemas, restaurants, workshops, rally areas, can be assembled, moved, re-arranged and scrapped continuously. Its mechanically operated environmental controls are such that it can be sited in a hard dirty industrial area unsuited to more conventional types of amenity buildings.[26]

Provisional spatial divisions such as sky-blinds, vapor zones, and optical screens replaced fixed programmatic enclosures, while circulation proliferated as temporary catwalks, escalators, and ramps. In addition to proposing an architecture flexible in siting, program and form, Price argued that the discipline of architecture needed to follow this example. His interest in interdisciplinary collaborations helps us to better understand his integrating cybernetic and game theory systems into the Fun Palace's program. Joining the project in 1963, Pask launched a Committee for Fun Palace Cybernetics Theater and integrated informational networks into a project that Price had envisioned initially only in terms of mechanical mobility. The Fun Palace would also have a "mind of its own," constituted of machines that did not "get bored:" Pask argued that architecture is "only meaningful as a human environment. It perpetually interacts with its inhabitants, on the one hand serving them and on the other hand controlling their behaviour."[27] To effect this idea, theater seats, among several elements of the Fun Palace's program spaces so equipped, would relay audience feedback to a computer, which in turn would convey the information to actors on stage, who would adapt their performance to this constant flow of information; elsewhere, closed circuit TVs and surveillance systems would communicate to Fun Palace goers the images of themselves learning to "play" with the instruments of computer culture.

Conceived without a specific site, the Fun Palace proposed to integrate human with mechanical and informational systems within the envelope of the building, yet it did not explore how its systems could engage the environment to the same degree as Price's contemporaneous Aviary for London's Regents Park Zoo (1960–63). The Aviary also embraced a provisional aesthetic: lightweight aluminum mesh, held aloft by masts and tension cables,

26. Cedric Price memorandum, (1964), document cited by Stanley Matthews, *From Agit-Prop to Free Space. The Architecture of Cedric Price* (Berlin: Black Dog Press, 2007), 73. See also Mary Lou Lobsinger, "Cedric Price: An Architecture of the Performance," *Daidalos* 74, (2000): 22–29.

27. Gordon Pask, cited by Matthews, *From Agit-Prop to Free Space*, 75.

Lourie Harrison

sequestered maximum flying space for birds. Like the Fun Palace, the Aviary dematerialized spatial separations. Yet within its network of tented forms and elevated walkways, human and animal were drawn into a shared space. It is important to note the difference between Price's approach to human–animal environments and that of Tecton's Penguin Pool (1934), which Picon cites as demonstrating the impact of ecological thought on architecture.[28] I would argue that the animal in Tecton's building is framed as passive object, certainly able to inhabit a modernist ramp as comfortably as any other zoo-scape, yet ultimately framed for human viewing. The walkways of Price's Aviary reverse this relationship and guide the human through an environment that seems to prioritize the birds' needs for flying space over humans' desire to view.

Such experiments toward a "living" building galvanized British architects to design new modes of interaction between human, machine, and building. The young Archigram group synthesized Price's concepts with sci-fi imagery, biomorphic shapes and London fashion to propose interactive architectures at various scales: from the Living City (1963), to the room-sized Living Pods, to the body-sized Cushicles (1966). Archigram's prosthetic extension of the human body promised to radicalize the experience of space: Archigram described the user of the Cushicle as having: "a complete environment on his back. It inflates out when needed. It is a complete nomadic unit—and it is fully serviced"; technology's role in providing the servicing is implied in the statement.[29] At a much larger scale, their Plug-In City (1964) lodged cybernetic dwelling units within a computer-controlled city. Technology's ubiquitous and liberatory presence as envisioned by Archigram reiterates Reyner Banham's prognosis in "The City as Scrambled Egg" (1959): the spread of communication technology had shattered the shells of European cities and mandated new visions for the networked city.

That the computer underwrote this complete requalification of man and his environment—and that it could engender new forms of creativity—permeated the architectural discourse in spheres that ranged from university pedagogy to architectural publications. As points of reference, it is worth noting the launch in 1967 of both the Center for Land Use and Built Form Studies at the University of Cambridge and the Architecture Machine Group established by Nicholas Negroponte at MIT: both programs embraced information sciences by advocating architectural design by computer. Likewise, information theorist Abraham Moles brought the insights of his important book, *Information Theory and Esthetic Perception* (1958),

28. Picon, *Digital Culture in Architecture*, 32.

29. *Archigram*, ed. Peter Cook, Warren Chalk, Dennis Crompton, David Greene, Ron Herron, and Mike Webb (New York: Princeton Architectural Press, 1999).

to bear on his design courses from 1961 to 1968 at the Hochschule für Gestaltung at Ulm. Exhibitions framed design as examples of the newest forms of "computer art," for example the ICA's exhibition "Cybernetic Serendipity" (1968), which included constructions by Pask and Schöffer. And attempts to reconcile the biological and computational models for technology filled the pages of *Architectural Design*: the September 1969 issue, with articles such as Pask's "The Architectural Relevance of Cybernetics" and Negroponte's "Towards a Humanism through Machines," pointed the way towards further integrating computer systems, cultural theory, and devices.

The global reach of this cybernetic vision for architecture found its expression in Montreal's Expo '67, which promoted "the plastic and technological mutation of the urban setting," and Osaka's Expo '70, which realized a futuristic landscape of robot-buildings.[30] Under the aegis of Kenzo Tange and Uzo Nishiyama, Expo '70 materialized many of the technological dreams of the prior decade under the theme "Progress and Harmony for Mankind." The building-sized Osaka Demonstration Robot by Metabolist architect Arata Isozaki emitted light, sound and smoke in response to various forms of data collected from its environment, in a manner reminiscent of Schöffer's CYSP-1; Kikutake's Landmark Tower gave form to Metabolist principles as a plug-in megastructure. Experiments in Art and Technology's (E.A.T.) Pepsi Pavilion, a collaboration of artists, engineers and scientists under the direction of Bell Labs engineer Billy Klüver and artist Robert Rauschenberg, transformed a preexisting geodesic dome into an electronic cloud. For its opening, the dome was enveloped by Fujiko Nakaya's water vapor cloud, its entry buzzing with the electronic activity of Robert Breer's sonorous "Floats" and bouncing colored lights. Inside the pavilion, a ninety-foot spherical mirror magnified the effects of laser light and sound displays. The interior program, ultimately deemed too expensive by Pepsi, would have allowed viewers to "shap[e] their own reality from the materials, processes, and structures set in motion by its creators:" the totality producing what E.A.T. would exuberantly describe as a "living" responsive environment.[31]

The historical impact of such cybernetically-charged atmospheres can be gauged by their return in contemporary architecture. For the Swiss Expo 2002, Diller+Scofidio (now Diller, Scofidio+Renfro) proposed the cloud-like Blur building, replacing the building enclosure with a vapor envelope maintained by a network of nozzles, environmental sensors, and water systems. The light and sound effects of E.A.T.'s Pepsi Pavilion are here collapsed

30. Georges Patrix, "The Triumph of Prospective Architecture in Montreal," cited in Larry Busbea, *Topologies: The Urban Utopia in France 1960–1970* (Cambridge, MA: MIT Press, 2007), 151.

31. Randall Packer, "The Pepsi Pavilion: Laboratory for Social Experimentation," in *Future Cinema: The Cinematic Imaginary after Film*, ed. Jeffrey Shaw and Peter Weibel (Cambridge, MA: The MIT Press, 2003),145.

Lourie Harrison

into a "braincoat"—a raincoat studded with sensors—with which to navigate the foggy environment. The cybernetic interface staged by the Blur building materializes a number of posthuman themes as Cary Wolfe demonstrates in his contribution to this anthology. The cybernetic atmospheres created by Schöffer, Price and E.A.T are revisited as a sensory landscape of temperature and fragrance in Philippe Rahm's Gulf Stream projects (2008). Rahm's vision of "an architecture freed from formal and programmatic preconceptions; one open to meteorological and seasonal variations,"[32] informs his projects for residences devoid of walls but divided into different climactic zones. These contemporary examples remind us that the dream of dispensing with architecture's physical divisions and instead embedding the body in an environment of technological effects, such as what Schöffer achieved with relatively primitive means in 1957, has only intensified in architecture today.

Space-frame Landscapes
Another paradigmatic manifestation for the network is the space frame: its near ubiquity in French progressive circles has been powerfully documented by Larry Busbea in *Topologies: the Urban Utopia in France, 1960–1970* (2007) and demonstrates the extent to which the spatial culture of postwar France was defined by efforts to design networks linking human, technology and environment. Numerous urban schemes deployed enormous space-frames to create megastructures: for Paris, Yona Friedman's Spatial City (1960) and Paul Maymont's Circular City (1965); for Tokyo, Kenzo Tange's Tokyo Bay project (1961) and Buckminster Fuller's Tetrahedral City (1968); for London, Archigram's Plug-In City (1964) among many others. Nature's somewhat neglected position in these examples reflects the architects' focus on large-scale housing. Friedman floated a gridded megastructural housing project above one of Paris's largest parks, the Bois de Boulogne, emphasizing that the new layer of housing would not demolish the city's historical buildings; yet he did not fully examine the effect of a park perpetually darkened under the shadow of the megastructure. Paul Maymont, in his Paris Sous la Seine (1964), envisaged a linear city with highways, extensive parking and open spaces under the Seine. While this gesture rendered the megastructure largely invisible, it treated the river as a surface rather than a three-dimensional system. In such projects, we find echoes of the logic of Fuller's Dome over Manhattan (1960), a two-mile wide geodesic dome over mid-town Manhattan that promised a perfectly

32. Philippe Rahm, "Interior Weather," in *Gilles Clément–Philippe Rahm: Environ(ne)ment* (Milan: Skira/CCA, 2006), 126.

conditioned environment, albeit one disconnecting this part of the city from its regional ecosystem.

These projects from the 60s and 70s connect to a recent history of buildings enclosing or draped in vast landscapes. Massively scaled environmental systems allowed Kevin Roche's Ford Foundation Building (1968) and John Deere Headquarters (1975) to sustain significant interior gardens while Cesar Pelli's World Financial Center (1985–88) enclosed a new neighborhood. The frustrated ambition to create an entirely enclosed ecology following Biosphere 2 (1987–91) led to solutions with increasing porosity, for example Nicholas Grimshaw's Eden Project (2001)proposing a cluster of semi-permeable geodesic domes. Corporate structures are garbed in green technology-infused surfaces, from buildings such as SITE's BEST showrooms (1978–80), Ken Yeang's Bioclimactic skyscrapers (1980s), Emilio Ambasz's Fukuoka Prefectural Hall (1992) and Patrick Blanc's green walls for Berlin, Paris, and Melbourne shopping centers (2004–8). Current formulations of the eco-tech aesthetic in Norman Foster's important body of work, from the Willis Faber Headquarter's green roof (1975) to Masdar's ecological city (2007–present), demonstrate the increasing scale and ambition of environmental "sustainability" in buildings that integrate alternative energy systems and construction materials capable of optimizing the building's energetic performance.

Yet the role of the animal within this environmental matrix, a topic that features significantly in this anthology, makes a limited appearance in these new landscape-sized buildings. Outside of the bounded format established by urban zoos, few buildings adopt the programmatic focus on interspecies exchange of John Lilly's St. Thomas Dolphin Laboratory (1960–68) or Ant Farm's Dolphin Embassy (1973–87), the latter departing from laboratory typologies to propose an aquatic residence simultaneously inhabited by human and animal.

Among the most powerful materializations of artificial environments directly aligned with the posthuman is Philip Beesley's Hylozoic Ground (2010). A suspended geotextile provides the symbolic substrate for an interactive environment: its acrylic fronds and whiskers become the antennae of a synthetic organism that responds to viewers' movements and harvests the air-born particles stirred by motion to create its own "hylozoic" soil.[33] This incremental activity—the harvest of minute particles—also occurs at the nano-scale: the installation includes suspended beakers of protocells that secrete what Rachel Armstrong, a collaborator in the

33. Philip Beesley, *Hylozoic Ground: Liminal Responsive Architecture* (Cambridge, Ontario: Riverside Architectural Press, 2010).

Lourie Harrison

project, envisions as the biological building material of the future. Hylozoic Ground marks the distance between the literal rendering of networks—as structural tubes or rigid conduits forming a matrix into which all forms of nature would be housed—and today's understanding of networks as potentially animate constructions.

Projects such as pneumastudio's 2011 Spirabilis anticipate the further integration of biotechnological networks at a landscape scale. Spirabilis allies NASA research on CELSS (Controlled Ecological Life Support Systems) with an architectural vision of the "home of the future:" domesticated technologies such as the water-filtering "Living Machine" are radically transformed to provide infrastructure for a landscape-cyborg.[34]

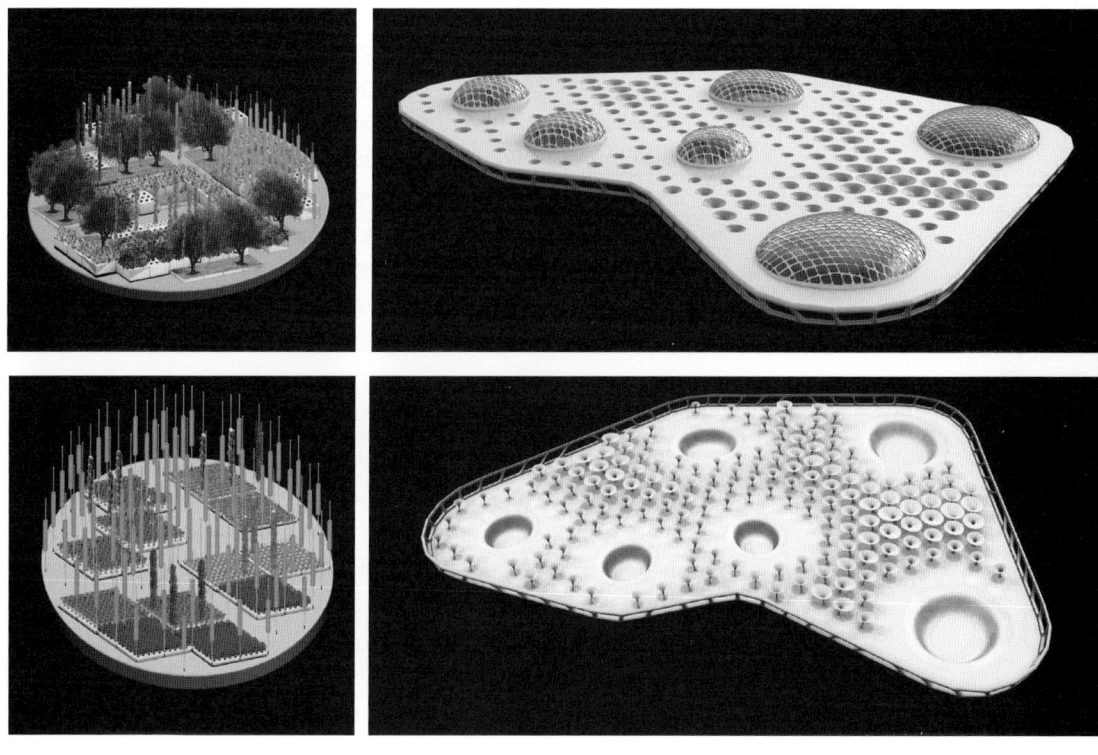

Less a utopian project than the visualization of an experimental prototype based on existing technologies, Spirabilis aligns with the post-war ethos of anticipatory design: "a fundamentally extrapolative approach to design that looks to the technological advancements of the twenty-first century as a means of providing new trajectories for the future of architecture."[35] Integrating the technophilic aesthetics of the 1960s with a present-day ecological imperative, Spirabilis envisions that the performance of architecture

Fig. 1.3 *Spirabilis*, by pneumastudio, 2011. Aerial view with six "phytotrons;" floorplate with infrastructural column field for rainwater collection; and phytotrons (courtesy of pneumastudio).

34. Chris Perry, "Fast Company," *Bracket 2: Goes Soft* (2012): 78.

35. Chris Perry, "Interview," *Constructs* (Spring 2010): 4.

itself can become responsive on a massive scale: its "respiratory" machinery engages a common concern of the twenty-first century laboring under a cloud of environmental risk.

Mobile Subjects

A final trajectory links the postwar understanding of the mobility afforded by technology networks and the discourse of prosthetics that envisions architectural extensions of the body. In the postwar imagination, it was easier to envisage the mechanization of man than the responsivity (or humanization) of machines, if the exhibitions at London's Institute of Contemporary Art—"Growth and Form" (1951), "Man, Machine and Motion" (1955), and "This is Tomorrow" (1957)—offered any indication. Staged by the Independent Group (a multi-disciplinary collaboration involving artists Eduardo Paolozzi, John McHale, and Richard Hamilton; architects Peter and Allison Smithson, photographer Nigel Henderson; critic Lawrence Alloway and affiliated critic Reyner Banham), "This is Tomorrow" offered visual evidence that the human senses were being reshaped by contemporary technologies. Appliances and media transformed the home in Hamilton's collage, *Just What is it that Makes today's Homes so different, so Appealing.* In parallel, the Smithson's anthropological catalogue of urban detritus brought the machined street into the home (and onto the roof) of their *Patio and Pavilion* installation. And the science fiction of robotics came to life in the animated figure of Robby the Robot, official greeter of the exhibition.

Technology's lifestyle-enhancing power also underwrote the domestic freedom and urbane pleasures advertised the year prior in the Smithson's House of the Future (1956). Living spaces resembled bubbles, space cabins, and pods: forms that connoted the future, especially when made of molded plastic. The House of the Future was not actually made of plastic, but its curved surfaces and rounded corners effectively conveyed the impression of a futuristic plastic environment in which every conceivable convenience (a self-cleaning bath, remote controlled lighting, air conditioning and radiant heating) was lodged in a space of its own.[36] The Smithsons dispensed with conventional partitions to produce an interactive space of flexible and amorphous room divisions, a program in which the futuristically-attired inhabitants of the House of the Future could explore less conventional couplings once freed from the domesticity of rooms.[37] Technology, in these examples, or in Schöffer's House with Invisible Walls, did away with

36. Beatriz Colomina, "Unbreathed Air 1956," *Grey Room* 15 (Spring 2004): 28–59.

37. Ibid., 41.

Lourie Harrison

the rigid demarcations of architectural program in favor of more fluid and indeterminate human usage. This technological substrate promised complete liberation of the human body, even from clothing; Banham article "A Home is not a House" (1965) advertised such freedom with François Dallegret's collages of Banham naked and happily ensconced in a bubble of technology. The pod aesthetic, as Busbea demonstrates, spoke to youth, leisure, and mobility: Ionel Schein proposed portable plastic vacation pods (1957) while Archigam's Capsule Homes (1964), Gasket House (1965) and Living Pods (1966) could "plug in" virtually anywhere. Capsules and pods almost uniformly presented a highly tailored environment and in this sense championed a "designed" lifestyle in full acceptance of technology-enhanced consumer culture.

The risks of this technological future were not ignored, however. For the cover of a 1957 *Architectural Review*, John McHale produced "Machine-made America:" a human torso conceived as a motley assembly of machine parts and industrialized food products. His description of the work on the flyleaf elaborates—with the ambivalence evident in uninflected prose—the mix of technology and mobility that comprises the American dream: "[it] reflects the world of infra-grilled steak, machine tools, power mixers, parkways, ticket tapes, sparkplugs and electronics."[38] The extension of man through his technological prosthetics, as Wigley describes, "necessarily leads to networks of overlapping technological systems that will, in the end and probably quite quickly, envelope the entire globe as a single system."[39] The totalizing effects of technology were also critiqued by members of the Situationist International: writer Guy Debord and painter Asger Jorn produced *The Naked City* (1958)— more a polemical collage than map—cutting simultaneously through the social and urban fabric of the city. The working class neighborhoods of Paris became fragments linked across the page only by arrows. These arrows evoked the Situationist *dérive* or drift through the city as feedback loops: meandering lines of individual perception that contravened the real-estate logic of urban blocks. Archigram's exuberant rendering of the technological lifestyle also fueled an ironic critique by Italian radical architects: the sprawl of electrical appliances in Archizoom's No Stop City (1969) or the arid grids of Superstudio's Continuous Monument (1969). Homogenized by uniform fluorescent lighting, ever-present air conditioning, and boxy gadgets, urbanity risked losing its meaningful architectural boundaries, argued the Italian radicals, in the wake of ubiquitous technological networks.

38. Mark Wigley, "Recycling Recyling," *Interstices* 4 (1996): 7.

39. Ibid, 3.

Other critics of the network aesthetic returned the focus to the body rather than its technological envelope. Architecture Principe, founded in 1966 by architect Claude Parent and theorist Paul Virilio, found fault with the very premise of mobile architecture: "[I]t is circulation which was to become inhabitable and not mobile architecture. We come back full circle to topology, choreography, and return to the body."[40] Theorizing the "function of oblique," Architecture Principe deployed inclined planes to stimulate bodily interaction with architecture. No longer reliant on the comfort of orthogonal surfaces, the body would combat imbalance with every step and inhabit sloping planes. Awakening the body, "the natural dynamic of this situation will achieve what social theories failed to accomplish: the invention of a new society."[41] Architecture Principe's architecture rejected the rhetoric of plastic surfaces and designer pods: their use of heavy materialities—concrete sloped floors and hunkering forms ("bunker architecture")—insisted on a phenomenological approach, one privileging an unmediated and tactile experience of the environment. Elsewhere in Europe, radical architectural practices turned the pod aesthetic against itself in staged episodes of urban activism.

Fig. 1.4   Coop Himmelb(l)au, *Hard Space*, 1970 (courtesy of Coop Himmelb(l)au, © Gertrud Wolfschwenger, Wien).

40. Paul Virilio and Sylvère Lotringer, *Crepuscular Dawn* (Los Angeles: Semiotext(e): 2002), 38.

41. Ibid, 13.

In Vienna, Coop Himmelb(l)au's Soft Space (1970) filled a street with soap bubbles; their Hard Space (1970) deployed cybernetic devices enabling a heartbeat to trigger explosions. In Berkeley, Ant Farm's pneumatic Clean Air Pod (1970) challenged the viability of the atmosphere. Despite technology's ability to foster a new degree of mobility, its constraints—ecological and political—became increasingly apparent in such architectural manifestations.

Lourie Harrison

The trajectory of this discussion of precedents for posthuman architecture follows a programmatic rather than a formal bias. If Anthony Vidler suggests that program merits a "radical interrogation of the ethical and environmental conditions of specific sites, which are considered as programs in themselves,"[42] then few works do so with the power of Rem Koolhaas's Bordeaux House (1998), for which the bodily constraints of his wheelchair-bound client provoked the reciprocal liberation of the room from its walls and its reconstitution as a mobile platform. Rather than limiting the subject's movement to a single level surface, the design features an elevator room which punctures the core of the three-level house, multiplying its user's experience of space: the kitchen and living areas secreted into the hillside, a glazed library on the middle floor open to the landscape and a private upper level with porthole views of the Garonne valley. The elevator, a longstanding object of Koolhaas's research, here becomes a prosthetic for the body, one already harnessed to other machinic supports. The film *Koolhaas Houselife* (2008) demonstrates how, through the eyes of the house-cleaner, the cyborg-house transforms the role of its inhabitants.

An extension of this radical interrogation of program might for example seek integrations beyond the physically-challenged human, to incorporate the ontological and ethical status of non-humans. In this way, posthuman architecture would make explicit, as it were, the total contemporary subject.

Fig. 1.5   OMA, Maison à Bordeaux, France, 1998 (courtesy of OMA, © Hans Werlemann).

42. Anthony Vidler, "Towards a Theory of Architectural Program," *October* 106 (Fall 2003): 59.

III. Architectural Theories of the Environment

This anthology assembles critical texts that look beyond sustainability and green building to relate contemporary architecture to a posthuman theorization of the environment. Through texts, projects, and built examples, we will come to understand how architecture comprises complex assemblages, which, when connected to a sphere of political action, begin to frame a territory. A posthuman territory emerges from the entanglement of a built or projected work, its hybrid subjects and its designed environment.

Throughout this anthology we will ask three questions to address the elements comprising a posthuman territory. The first question draws on poststructuralist interpretations of subjectivity: as agency becomes increasingly distributed among human and non-human life forms (including the digital), how does architecture address what are increasingly hybrid subjects? The second question draws on cybernetic interpretations of the posthuman: as biological substrates enter the material palette of architecture, and as the boundaries of living and non-living in building materials are broached, how does the resulting material assemblage factor into architecture? The third question develops from Science and Technology Studies: how can architecture engage an ecological sphere of action rather than a static geographical unit?

Each of the three sections of this anthology takes up one of the above questions and is respectively titled: "posthuman subjects," "posthuman assemblages," and "posthuman territory." The sections are organized in increasing scales to interrogate how architecture can be viewed from a posthuman perspective at the level of the body, building, and environment, yet these scales prove to be intertwined. Each section includes texts that emphasize critical ideas from posthuman discourse. By design, certain positions reinforce one another; others diverge, so as to maintain a spectrum of opinions—which, as will be seen, is essential to the posthuman approach. In keeping with the posthuman interest in hybridization and diversification, the anthology assembles texts from multiple disciplines, including urban political ecology, literary criticism, human geography, biomedicine and of course architectural theory. Certain shared themes, such as the entanglement of human and animal in cities, point to multiple interpretations and effectively provoke varied architectural responses in this anthology. Case studies focus on architectural projects as examples of the themes developed in each section, but each building or project gives rise to independent dialogues across the sections of the anthology.

Section I: Posthuman Subjects

The first section of this anthology addresses a posthuman subjectivity encompassing human and nonhuman hybrids. It is indebted to the concepts of alterity, emergence and becoming other in post-structuralism. The politics of such concepts take form in advocacy movements for disability, ethnicity, and gender that reveal the breadth of the human "norm". In cultural studies, the posthuman other reveals itself to be an anti-hero whose uncanny proximity to the human figure provides, in Marshall McLuhan's terms, a *counter-environment*: embodying transformative technologies that highlight the limits of the subject.[43] Posthumanist theory also examines the relationship of humans and animals, challenging established claims for the instrumentality of animals. While a number of the projects and essays included in this anthology engage the animal as an environmental subject—an approach that differs from the tendency to treat animals as relatively inconvenient factors at a site—it is important to understand how thinkers such as Jacques Derrida, Gilles Deleuze, Giorgio Agamben, and Jean Baudrillard locate the animal as a mainstay of Western anthropocentrism.

In his essay, *The Animal That Therefore I Am* (1997), Derrida confronts the humanistic tendency to view the animal as a generality, arguing instead for the concept of the animal as a multiplicity. According to Derrida, the indifferent grouping of numerous species into one category, "the animal," marks a violent apex of humanistic thought. Shifting the understanding of animal from a singular term to one that harbors its plurality, Derrida argues that the relationship between that which we call "animal" and that which we call "human" is not a clear demarcation but a thick and undecidable network of interactions:

> Everything I'll say will consist, certainly not in effacing the limit, but in multiplying its figures, in complicating, thickening, delinearizing, folding, and dividing the line precisely by making it increase and multiply.[44]

Derrida's string of participles gives grammatical form to a nondialectical and non-transcendental approach that Deleuze had earlier termed the "becoming animal" in *A Thousand Plateaus* (1980). Becoming animal in this sense does not involve representation, a relation requiring a human to stand in for the animal, but instead suggests the interpenetration of subject and object. In his analysis of Deleuze and Guattari, Lawlor suggests that "becoming [animal] consists of a zigzag structure: we

43. Marshal McLuhan, "The Invisible Environment: the Future of an Erosion," *Perspecta* 11 (1967): 163–67.

44. Jacques Derrida, *The Animal That Therefore I Am* (New York: Fordham University Press, 2008), 29.

become animal so that animal becomes, not human, but something else."[45] In *Homo Sacer* (1998), Agamben finds the status of the animal to reflect the political implications of a life that is neither explicitly included in nor excluded from the political realm; it occupies a zone of exception in which any legal or moral rights are suspended. In *The Open: Man and Animal* (2004), Agamben further traces the effects of this idea in the operations of what he terms the "anthropological machine"—a conceptual function distinguishing man from animal and thereby buttressing the instrumental logics of anthropocentism. While animal social hierarchies, territorial habits and competitive dynamics have often been used to naturalize human gender and race conventions, the posthuman usage of the "animal" often undermines these reactionary practices and tendencies.[46] Yet the French philosopher Jean Baudrillard, in his essay, "The Animals: Territory and Metamorphoses," warns against the counter-tendency to ignore animal territoriality and indulge in a sentimentalized anthropomorphization. Donna Haraway is perhaps the best known theorist promoting a radical revision of the human-animal relationship, characterizing the human instrumentalization of the animal in medical research and industrialized agriculture as a dependency. Lab rats, feedlot cattle and guide-dogs become "companion species" because they are locked into an "obligatory, constitutive historical, protean relationship with human beings,"[47] yet also have agency and subjectivity. The disruption of humanist hierarchies makes way for new categories of hybrid subjects.

The first section of this anthology focuses on how architecture confronts the hybrid subjects of posthumanism. N. Katherine Hayles' thoughtful history of the relationship between information and its substrates helps to frame the limits of the cyborg metaphor for the posthuman subject. Architectural theorist Catherine Ingraham proposes a "post-animal" subject that "denotes animal human life after its animal aspect has… been put under the supervision of science and psychology."[48] She challenges architectural modes of representation to ask how architecture's "set of historical relations to animation, existential being and movement play themselves out in this new milieu" of post-animal life.[49] Biotechnologist, designer and writer Seth Harrison examines the aging subject—made cyborgian in his or her intimate ties to longevity-extending technology—and describes new programmatic areas for architecture in dialogue with the gerontologist Dr. Caleb Finch. Architect and theorist Francisco Gonzáles de Canales discusses the filiation of media and ecology as a new environmental model for architecture—a "society-nature"

45. Leonard Lawlor, "Following the Rats: Becoming-Animal in Deleuze and Guattari," *SubStance* 117 no. 37, (2008): 178.

46. Jennifer Wolch, Sarah Whatmore, Jody Emel and Kay Anderson address the political, economic and cultural positioning of the animal in *Animal Geographies: Place, Politics and Identity in the Nature-Culture Borderlands*, Jody Emel and Jennifer Wolch, eds., (London: Verso, 1998).

47. Donna Haraway, *The Companion Species Manifesto* (Chicago: Prickly Paradigm Press, 2006), 12.

48. Catherine Ingraham, *Architecture: Animal, Human: the Asymmetrical Condition* (New York: Routledge, 2006), 16.

49. Ibid, 328.

Lourie Harrison

for which he locates precedents in art and architecture. Concluding this section's essays, media theorist Matteo Pasquinelli establishes an expansive framework for subjectivity, addressing the "digital parasitivism" of the city as interpreted through a techno-progressive lens: an urban subject entrained in an "ecosystem of excess."

Case studies in the first section propose design for posthuman subjects. Arakawa and Gins' Bioscleave House (1999–2008) destabilizes the residential interior by requiring that occupants continually adjust to the "wildness" of the house— adjustment and flexibility seen as contributing to physical longevity. The technological extension of human lifespan thematizes Arons en Gelauff's Plussenburgh retirement housing (2001–6), a building that interweaves medical assistance with an active community for "new aging" populations in Rotterdam. R&Sie(n)'s Paris residence, I'm Lost in Paris, (2008) everts the green components of the stereotypical ecological house to create a vegetal assemblage that binds users and organic material together in an urban landscape. Each case study establishes a dialogue between the building and the hybrid subjectivities of its users.

Section II: Posthuman Assemblages
The second section of this book explores networks as heterogeneous assemblages. Deleuze and Guattari describe the dynamic role of an assemblage organizing its surrounding space, if only temporarily:

> We will call an assemblage every constellation of singularities and traits deducted from the flow—selected, organized, stratified in such a way as to converge (consistency) artificially and naturally; an assemblage in this sense is a veritable invention.[50]

The concept of the assemblage derives from ecology, yet has occupied the margins of architecture since the early twentieth century; evidence of this borrowing can be found as early as Patrick Geddes's *Cities in Evolution* (1915) and Ian McHarg's *Design with Nature* (1970). These works describe ecosystems as flexible networks that foster the adaptive organization of resources. From these ecosystems, form evolves as the result of external (environmental) stimuli and internal (cultural) pressures. Even somewhat controversial evolutionary models such as Lynn Margulis's theories of species fusion from her *Symbiotic Planet* (1999) prompts architecture to consider new models for biomimicry; Margulis's fused assemblages offer an important reference point for contemporary architects such as Greg Lynn. Architectural critic Helene Furjan also draws on the concept,

50. Gilles Deleuze and Felix Guattari, *A Thousand Plateaus: Capitalism and Schizophrenia*, tr. Brian Massumi (Minneapolis: University of Minnesota Press, 1987), 406.

conceiving architecture as a gradient of fused assemblages that establish the building–environment relationship as a loose network. She suggests that "a concept of performativity [is] rigorously tied to material dynamics, environmental parameters, urban and social organizations (as infrastructural parameters rather than socio-political representations) and ambient conditions."[51]

Actor-Network-Theory (ANT) offers additional nuance to the term *assemblage*. If any entity (human, non-human, scientific, architectural) can be conceptualized as both an actor and a network, then ANT questions the circumscribed attribution of specific capacities to specific things, proposing that such capacities may in fact be distributed widely among networks of human and non-humans. As Latour demonstrates in *Assembling the Social: An Introduction to Actor-Network-Theory* (2005), the relation among actors in a network determines a provisional form, which is nevertheless contained in a larger matrix of relations and of distributed agency:

> It is the thing itself that has been allowed to be deployed as multiple and thus allowed to be grasped through different viewpoints, before being possibly unified in some later stage depending on the abilities of the collective to unify them.[52]

By this approach, it becomes more difficult to refer to an entity as a discrete object and more productive to find precise ways to describe the relations between entities. It is also important to note that ANT relationality challenges the (somewhat architectural) notion of hierarchically-ordered or nested scales, linking the body to the cosmos in a chain of being. Instead, the scale of interaction is produced by the actor. The specificities of network elements in ANT may not be distinguished, and to some, ANT presents a tightly interconnected if not totalizing matrix for the environment: ANT critic Timothy Newton suggests that to "see that everything is interconnected . . . is the ecological thought."[53] The problem for Newton among other object-oriented philosophers is to avoid the holistic view of nature as a totalizing network and to instead propose a mode of thought that addresses the particularity of relationships forged between specific network objects. Yet in its applicability to architecture, it could be argued that ANT helps to reveal the specificities of the architectural object by means of its connectivity to and function as an actor. ANT uses specialized vocabulary, of which the term *translation* is important in describing what actor-networks do: the interests of each actor must be communicated to every other actor in the terms (or translations) comprehensible to

51. Helene Furjan, "Eco_Logics," in *Softspace: from a Representation of Form to a Simulation of Space*, Eds. Sean Lally and Jessica Young (New York: Routledge, 2007), 124.

52. Bruno Latour, *Assembling the Social: An Introduction to Actor-Network-Theory* (Oxford: Oxford University Press, 2005), 116.

53. Timothy Newton, *The Ecological Thought* (Cambridge, MA: Harvard University Press, 2010), 1.

Lourie Harrison

all, hence the focus on "making visible" each actor in the network. Architectural theorist Albena Yaneva applies ANT methodologies to architectural criticism, challenging the tendency to interpret architecture as a by-product of disciplinary objectives or social forces, and she instead proposes that architectural critics "map controversies" to understand the building within a nexus of forces, resources, and concerns (all of which are actors).[54] In the posthuman understanding of architecture, discursive and material networks combine, as a number of the essays in this anthology suggest, to create spaces for new collectives.

Essays included in this second section consider how architecture functions as an assemblage. Latour and Yaneva's "An ANT's View of Architecture" critiques architectural representation using actor-network theory. Yaneva and Latour focus on two aspects of the architectural process: the scale at which architects represent their buildings at various stages in the process of design; and the parallel and evolving network of conversations among designers and clients/users. The authors challenge architects to develop tools to visualize buildings at multiple scales simultaneously, i.e., as actor-networks. Similarly, second-order cybernetic systems provide literary theorist Cary Wolfe with terms—*autopoeisis and self-reflexivity*—to describe the cultural and technological feedback mechanisms that he finds in Diller+Scofidio's Blur building. Bodies are, of course, part of the architectural assemblage, yet as philosopher Elizabeth Grosz demonstrates, these transform under technology's pressure. Her chapter "Futures, Cities, Architecture" identifies spaces that harbor diverse imaginations of the body and that therefore blur the distinction between the architectural discipline and spatial figurations from other disciplines. Simon Guy's "Pragmatic Ecologies" sets forth a fluid space of interrelation for sustainable design—offering a number of innovative and realized architectural examples—that can address a spectrum of socio-technical issues.

Shifting to an urban scale, the architectural and media theorist William Mitchell examines the profound impact of global communication, information, and computational networks in his book *Me++: The Cyborg Self and the Networked City*; his chapter "Against Program," included in this anthology, focuses on the programmatic fluidity of the networked city and the nomadic and dematerialized spatial practices of its users. Urban geographer Erik Swyngedouw's "Metabolic Urbanization" excavates the cyborgian materiality of urban infrastructure in describing how "cities are constituted through dense networks of interwoven socio-

54. Albena Yaneva, *Mapping Controversies in Architecture* (Surrey: Ashgate, 2012).

ecological processes that are simultaneously human, physical, discursive, cultural, material, and organic."[55] In this dynamic framework, he identifies a "metabolic" exchange that begins to describe the uneven texture—in social and environmental terms— of urban natures.

The case studies in this section examine the architectural assemblage of human/nonhuman subjects, hybrid materialities and new programs. The 2006 Australian Wildlife Health Center by Minifie Nixon (now Minifie van Schaik Architects) transforms the spatial experience of the veterinary hospital by establishing complementary programs of treatment and observation of treatment, thereby assembling animals and humans under the same technological network of care. The Living's 2009 Living Light pavilion broadcasts information related to air quality, communicating this data as illuminated registers that are integrated within the building envelope and disseminated through Seoul's telecommunications network. Here the architectural assemblage incorporates technological and formal strategies to communicate air quality information to a diverse public. Studio Gang Architects' Ford Calumet Environmental Center in Chicago (2004–present) integrates human observers and the animals indigenous to the proposed Calumet site. Recently made an important component of Chicago's Millenium Reserve Initiative, the project makes visible the interplay of industrial activity and wetland preserve, producing an assemblage from multiple networks.

Section III: Posthuman Territory

The third section expands from urban to regional—and in some cases planetary—scale according to a dynamic concept of territory. Rather than define territory by geographic boundary or physical feature, the writers in this section use the term to refer to spheres of action, building on Foucault's lectures, *Security, Territory, Population, 1977–78*. Foucault described how abstract systems, such as the census, land surveys, and legislation embed a control logic to allocate finite resources among populations, yet as Elden suggests in his analysis of Foucault: "Territory is more than merely land, but a rendering of the emergent concept of 'space' as a political category: owned, distributed, mapped, calculated, bordered, and controlled."[56] We can return to Baudrillard's "The Animals: Territory and Metamorphoses," to insist on territory's relational quality: "The territory is the site of a completed cycle of parentage and exchanges—without a subject, but without exception: animal and vegetal cycle, cycle of goods and wealth, cycle of parentage

55. Erik Swyngedouw, "Metabolic Urbanization: the Making of Cyborg Cities," *In the Nature of Cities*, Eds. Nik Heynen, Maria Kaika and Erik Swyngedouw (New York: Routledge, 2006), 20.

56. Stuart Elden, "Governmentality, calculation, territory," *Environment and Planning D: Society and Space* 25 (2007): 578.

Lourie Harrison

and the species, cycle of women and ritual—there is no subject and everything is exchanged."[57] Architectural historian Antoine Picon builds on this metabolic quality of the territory to formulate what he calls the "territorial city": "It appears simultaneously like a continuous fabric and like a chaotic assemblage of infrastructure and building . . . It is not easy to understand the multiple ties which link such very different entities as a network while at the same time remaining aware of the deep fractures of such a new urban morphology."[58] Focusing on the relevance of this concept in his special issue of *Architectural Design*, titled *Territory: Architecture Beyond Environment* (2010), architectural historian David Gissen demonstrates by citing numerous architectural projects—several of which have been included in this anthology—that the term *territory* can be understood as a location temporarily secured by the constitutive forming of architecture and site.[59] Gissen identifies the term *environment* to imply a neutral, if not fictional, exterior. This anthology, however, locates the territorializing assemblage of architecture within an ecological and political perspective, which extends well beyond the building to engage multiple disciples—landscape, geography, and ecology—for which the word environment retains a political charge.[60]

The essays in this section extend the conceptual and physical manifestations of the urban network framing territorial assemblages. Urban geographer Matthew Gandy charts the shift from the nineteenth-century "bacteriological city" to the contemporary "cyborg city" to reveal how the overlap of systems—urban networks and architectural typologies, discursive constructs, and their material effects—create "zones of indistinction," in which different forms of spatial and political marginality are interwoven. Jennifer Wolch's "Anima Urbis" explodes the premise of cities as specifically human environments, proposing in its place a trans-species urbanism to better accommodate existing animal networks into the urban fabric. Wolch outlines a research agenda for the urban geography of human–animal relations that effectively expands the "urban moral landscape." In a selection taken from her book *Hybrid Geographies: Natures, Cultures, Spaces*, geographer Sarah Whatmore combines feminist and environmental theory to redefine urban geography as a spatial register of distributed agency and proposes that we consider "relational ethical praxes by either 'embodying' or 'enlarging' the company of ethical subjects."[61]

The final essays focus on the political stakes raised by the concept of the Anthropocene for the built environment. Challenging

57. Jean Baudrillard, "The Animals: Territory and Metamorphoses," in *Simulcra and Simulation*, trans. Sheila F. Glaser (University of Michigan Press, 1994), 139.

58. Antoine Picon, "Le temps du cyborg dans la ville territoire," *Les Annales de la Recherche Urbaine* 77 (December 1997): 72–7.

59. David Gissen, "Introduction: Territory: Architecture Beyond Environment," *AD Territory: Beyond Environment* (June 2010): 8–13.

60. See Kay Anderson and Bruce Baun, eds., *Environment: Critical Studies in Human Geography* (Surrey: Ashgate, 2008).

61. Whatmore, Sarah. "Hybrid Cartographies for a Relational Ethics," *Hybrid Geographies: Natures, Cultures, Spaces* (London: Sage Publications, 2002), 163.

landscape design to engage ecological science and promote biodiversity, horticultural engineer and gardener Gilles Clément has framed his teaching and works within a series of theoretical propositions on the relationship between humans and the environment.[62] In his work, Clément effectively grows a nested set of ecological concepts which he roots in his landscape practice.[63] The first proposition, the *jardin en movement* (dynamic garden), extrapolates Clément's observations of his own garden into principles for working "with and never against nature:" adapting an economy of means and fostering biodiversity with minimal human interference. The second, the *jardin planetaire* (planetary garden) meditates on the political stakes of ecology, and recommends a minimally intervening human stewardship: monitoring ecosystems, observing the *brassage planetaire* (global mixing) of species and resisting conservative or nativist environmental politics. His third proposition, the *Manifeste du Tiers Paysage* (*Manifesto on the Third Landscape*) proposes a third landscape as the residuum of urban development: third landscapes are abandoned, post-industrial, or transitional spaces that represent the seeding ground for biodiversity, "a territory of biological invention."[64] For this anthology, I have translated Clément's fourth proposition, "The Emergent Alternative," in which he proposes "symbiotic humanism:" simultaneously a critique of and remedy for the social and environmental cost of sustainable development. Concluding the anthology, Ursula Heise, in a selection from her book, *Sense of Place, Sense of Planet,* calls for realignment of political sensibilities of eco-cosmopolitanism and in the process proposes a global reconceptualization of territory in posthuman terms.

The case studies suggest that human and nonhuman elements regarded as irreconcilably disparate in a humanist frame of reference integrate in a posthuman one. The Living's 2009 collaboration with Natalie Jeremijenko for the installation Amphibious Architecture assembles piscine, human, and media ecologies into a floating network on New York's East River. SCAPE's 2010 Oyster-tecture extends the filtering properties of mollusks to create a marine infrastructure with cultural as well as ecological benefits; the ongoing pilot project integrates the remediative capacities of oysters within an active industrial harbor in Brooklyn, NY. A final case study, Marco Casagrande and C-Lab's Ruin Academy (2010–present) in Taipei, hybridizes ecological programs, anarchist culture, and indigenous farming offering a radical approach to ecological education.

62. Gilles Clément and Louisa Jones, *Une écologie humaniste* (Paris: Aubanel, 2006).

63. Denise Bratton, "An Interview with Gilles Clément," *Log* 12 (Spring/Summer 2008), 83.

64. Gilles Clément, *Manifeste du Tiers Paysage* (Paris: Éditions Sujet/Objet, 2004), 53. See Gilles Clément, *Manifesto on the Third Landscape* (MIT Press, forthcoming), translation and introduction by Denise Bratton.

Conclusion

Posthuman architecture engages the paradox of the Anthropocene period: the absorption of the environment into the realm of human technology invites a renewed appreciation for the diversity of actors and networks that share this envelope of consideration. To theorize the environment in posthuman terms might begin by reiterating the three questions that I posed at the outset: as agency becomes increasingly distributed among biological and digital life forms, how does architecture address its increasingly hybrid subjects? As biological substrates enter the material palette, and even the boundaries of living and non-living building materials are breached, how does the resulting hybrid material assemblage factor into architectural discourse? How can architecture engage an ecological network, conceptualized as a sphere of action rather than as a static geographic boundary? Many of the architectural case studies herein address such questions by expanding the field's subject beyond the human, by incorporating hybrid materials that may be assemblages of seemingly disparate elements, and by siting built work and theory within an multi-scale territory which includes the consciousness of its environmental politics.

This anthology brings texts from numerous disciplines together with actual buildings and pilot projects to demonstrate that a posthuman approach to the designed environment is underway and generating powerful forms and programs for architecture. Rather than a claim for the new, the posthuman both highlights the ongoing dynamics of humanist thought in architecture and offers alternative theorizations for the discipline. This usage draws on the manner in which the architect Peter Eisenman formulated "post-functionalism," as a negation of what he considered to be the humanist biases of functionalism. Post-functionalism is not only an important critique of humanist conventions in architecture, but it also deploys the prefix *post* to offer "certain positive theoretical alternatives—existing fragments of thought which, when examined, might serve as a framework for the development of a larger theoretical structure."[65] It is my hope that addressing architecture within a posthuman framework similarly stimulates existing thought, prompting practitioners, theorists and students to hybridize methods from multiple bodies of knowledge as we work towards an architecture that is responsive to the precariousness and potential of human and nonhuman collectives.

65. Peter Eisenman, "Post-functionalism," (1976) in *Eisenman Inside Out: Selected Writings 1963-1988* (New Haven and London: Yale University Press (2004), 87.

Section I

Posthuman Subjects

Unfinished Work: From Cyborg to Cognisphere
N. Katherine Hayles

Donna Haraway's "A Manifesto for Cyborgs" (1985) has become a legend of late 20th-century scholarship. Cited thousands of times and translated into a dozen languages, it has achieved monumental status, especially when juxtaposed against statistics from the Citation Index indicating that well over 90 percent of articles in the humanities are not cited even once.[1] While Haraway's own interests in the last few years have turned away from the cyborg and toward companion species, the project she outlined in "A Manifesto for Cyborgs" remains vitally important, perhaps even more so than in 1985, the original publication date. The issues have morphed in significant ways, but the ethical drive and social commitment that galvanized readers then were never more necessary. With the hindsight of twenty years later, the wonder is not that the article appears dated but rather that it remains remarkably prescient in many of its concerns.

Written in the last years of the Cold War, the article was in part a provocation to feminists who wanted to position women in alliance with nature and against technology. As Haraway says in her interview in this issue, "My feminist friends and others in 1980 thought the cyborg was all bad."[2] Deeply connected to the military, bound to high technology for its very existence and a virtual icon for capitalism, the cyborg was contaminated to the core, making it exquisitely appropriate as a provocation. In the years since, new technologies have sprung up from the same nexus of forces that gave birth to the cyborg, most notably the Internet and the world wide web, along with a host of networked information devices, including cell phones, sensor networks (including "smart dust") yielding real-time data flows, RFID (Radio Frequency Identification) tags, GPS networks and nanotechnology. For those interested in exploring the implications of these developments, the cyborg no longer offers the same heady brew of resistance and co-option. Quite simply, it is not networked enough. Although Haraway associated it with the "informatics of domination," the cyborg's shock value came mostly from the implication that the human body would be modified with cybermechanical devices.[3] Although research on implants continues, contemporary formations are at once more subtle and more far-reaching than the figure of the cyborg allows.

1. Donna Haraway, "Manifesto for Cyborgs: Science, Technology and Socialist Feminism in the 1980s," *Socialist Review* 15, no. 2 (1985): 65–107. (Reprinted in revised form as "A Cyborg Manifesto: Science, Technology, and Socialist-feminism in the Late Twentieth Century," in *Simians, Cyborgs, and Women: The Reinvention of Nature* (New York: Routledge, 1991), 149–81.

2. See Nicholas Gane and Donna Haraway, "When We Have Never Been Human, What Is to Be Done?: Interview with Donna Haraway," *Theory, Culture & Society* 23, no. 7–8 (December 2006): 156.

3. Gane and Haraway, "When We Have Never Been Human," 135.

At the center of these formations, transforming the conditions of life for millions of people, are networked and programmable media, and they are impacting everything from sensorimotor functions and non-conscious cognitive processing to national political discourse and transnational economies. Given the complexities of these dynamics, the individual person—or for that matter, the individual cyborg—is no longer the appropriate unit of analysis, if indeed it ever was. At issue now (and in the past) are distributed cultural cognitions embodied both in people and their technologies. As Haraway reminds us, the smallest unit of analysis is the relation. With this I wholeheartedly agree, but I would go on to ask, "What relations should be foregrounded?"

In her recent work, Haraway has chosen to emphasize companion species, in relation to which she locates the cyborg as a "junior sibling." The technoscientific networks that succeed the cyborg may be "junior" to nonhuman animals in historical progression, but not necessarily when viewed in terms of contemporary global impact on the people who live enmeshed in the networks. Moreover, if the focus expands to technology, the co-evolutionary spiral between the *Homo* genus and technology may well have preceded and enabled the co-evolutionary dynamic between humans and companion species. Since the Paleolithic era, tool-making has been an essential component of human evolution. In the contemporary moment, this dynamic is intensified as the time required to effect significant change compresses and technologies become more pervasive and interconnected. Clearly a full exploration of contemporary dynamics requires attention to technoscientific networks as well as to biological organisms. Now, as in the past, the human, the animal and the technological are joined in shifting configurations of value. In her companion species work, Haraway interrogates those relations in part through the concept of "species," which, as she convincingly shows, is less an inevitable taxonomy than a series of contingent categories whose boundaries are in flux and whose substance is not essence but dynamic relationality.

My own work has a similar intent but a different focus. In *How We Became Posthuman* (1999), I argued that a shift was under way from the human to the posthuman. I regard the posthuman, like the "human," as a historically specific and contingent term rather than a stable ontology. Whereas the "human" has since the Enlightenment been associated with rationality, free will, autonomy and a celebration of consciousness as the seat of identity, the posthuman in its more nefarious forms is construed as an informational pattern that happens to be instantiated in a biological substrate. There are, however, more benign forms of the posthuman that can serve as effective counterbalances to the liberal humanist subject, transforming untrammeled free will into a recognition that agency is always relational and distributed, and correcting an over-emphasis on consciousness to a more accurate view of cognition as embodied throughout human flesh and extended into the social and technological environment.

The three historical formations that I discussed, marked by first-order cybernetics from 1945 to 1960, autopoiesis or second-order cybernetics from 1960 to 1985, and virtuality or third-order cybernetics from 1985 to 1995, have now progressed to a fourth stage that, in my recent book *My Mother Was a Computer* (2005), I call the Regime of Computation. The characteristic dynamic of this formation is the penetration of computational processes not only into every aspect of biological, social, economic and political realms but also into the construction of reality itself, where "reality" should be understood, as Haraway says in a different context, as "made" but not necessarily "made up."

The claim that reality is fundamentally computational is for me like the posthuman in that I regard it as a formation to be interrogated rather than something simply to be believed or disbelieved, accepted or rejected. Like the posthuman, the Regime of Computation has aspects that I think we should resist; like the posthuman, it also offers opportunities to re-think and re-position traditional concepts that, as Marx poignantly put it, lie like a nightmare on the minds of the living. In highly developed and networked societies such as the US, human awareness comprises the tip of a huge pyramid of data flows, most of which occur between machines. Emphasizing the dynamic and interactive nature of these exchanges, Thomas Whalen (2000) has called this global phenomenon the cognisphere.[4] Expanded to include not only the Internet but also networked and programmable systems that feed into it, including wired and wireless data flows across the electromagnetic spectrum, the cognisphere gives a name and shape to the globally interconnected cognitive systems in which humans are increasingly embedded. As the name implies, humans are not the only actors within this system; machine cognizers are crucial players as well. If our machines are "lively" (as Haraway provocatively characterized them in the "Manifesto"), they are also more intensely cognitive than ever before in human history.

The shifting boundaries between human and machine cognition and the increasing roles that machines play in cognitive constructions are illustrated by the details now emerging about the surveillance programs that the Bush administration authorized to spy

4. Thomas Whalen, "Data Navigation, Architectures of Knowledge," paper presented at the Banff Summit on *Living Architectures: Designing for Immersion and Interaction*, Banff New Media Institute, 23 Sept. (2000).

on US citizens. James Bamford, author of two books on the National Security Agency,[5] estimates that the NSA's computer takes in two million pieces of communication *per hour*, sifting through them for names, numbers and words previously identified as suspicious. Most of this data is not seen by humans; only when patterns reach a certain level of perceived threat do they come under human scrutiny. The automated nature of the searches has raised questions about whether computer surveillance is covered under the Fourth Amendment prohibiting unlawful search and seizure. According to an article in the *Boston Globe*, Alane Kochems, a national security analyst at the conservative Heritage Foundation, said, "I don't think your privacy is violated when you have a computer doing it as opposed to a human. It isn't a sentient being. It's a machine running a program."[6] But this reasoning is surely specious, since in the first place it was humans who designed the machine. Moreover, if the material is on file, it is always available for human scrutiny. Human and machine cognitions have now become so intertwined that distinguishing between the two in the context of surveillance makes no sense. The *Boston Globe* quotes Yale Law School Professor Jack Balkin making precisely this point when he notes that if a legal distinction between human and computer surveillance was allowed to stand, the police "could simply use robots to do their dirty work."[7]

Scary as NSA's surveillance program is, the cognisphere has had many positive effects as well. Increased communication, access to databases around the world, communal knowledge-building through wikipedias and other data collection projects, and the ability to find and form networks with like-minded people in the US and abroad are only some of the forms of collective action and democratic potential made possible by the world wide web. More subtle are the changes in subjectivity that the cognisphere is bringing about. Shifts in reading practices suggest a movement from deep attention to hyperattention; incorporation of intelligent machines into everyday practices creates distributed cognitive systems that include human and non-human actors; distributed cognition in turn is linked to a dispersed sense of self, with human awareness acting as the limited resource that artificial cognitive systems help to preserve and extend.

As intelligent machines become more important in the cognisphere, the resulting re-evaluations of human agency, rationality, and affective capacities catalyze re-evaluations of human–animal relations as well, to which Haraway's (2003) work on companion species makes a valuable contribution.[8] Understanding that humans and animals have co-evolved together is entirely consistent with the

5. James Bamford, *The Puzzle Palace: Inside America's Most Secret Intelligence Agency* (New York: Penguin, 1983) and James Bamford, *Body of Secrets: Anatomy of the Ultra-secret National Security Agency* (New York: Anchor, 2002).

6. Charlie Savage, "Wiretaps Said to Sift All Overseas Contacts: Vast US Efforts Seen on Eavesdropping," (2005) Boston.com. (Accessed July 2006):http://www.boston.com/news/nation/washington/articles/2005/12/23/wiretaps_said_to_sift_all_overseas_contacts?mode=PF.

7. Ibid.

8. Writing about why she has moved away from the figure of the cyborg, Haraway observes that: "the cyborg and companion species are hardly polar opposites. Cyborgs and companion species each bring together the human and non-human, the organic and technological, carbon and silicon, freedom and structure, history and myth, the rich and the poor, the state and the subject, diversity and depletion, modernity and postmodernity, and nature and culture in unexpected ways." See Donna Haraway, *The Companion Species Manifesto: Dogs, People, and Significant Otherness* (Chicago: Prickly Paradigm Press, 2003), 4. Nevertheless, she asserts that the cyborg can no longer do meaningful work at the present moment and has accordingly turned to companion species.

contemporary but nevertheless potent phenomenon of humans and machines co-evolving together. Indeed, given the technologies of genetic engineering, implants and bio-silicon hybrids created from a variety of life forms ranging from cockroaches to lampreys, it is clear that humans, animals and intelligent machines are more tightly bound together than ever in their cultural, social, biological, and technological evolutions.

At the same time, advances in cognitive science, neurology, and related fields of brain science are clarifying the neurological basis for human perception and subjectivity, leading to the possibility, articulated by Evan Thompson and Francisco J. Varela in their forthcoming book *Why the Mind Isn't in the Head*, that the subject–object split institutionalized by the birth of modern science can at last be addressed by a cognitive science powerful enough to begin to explain the physical and psychological bases for human constructions of reality.[9] These results validate Haraway's (1988) call for "situated knowledges," demonstrating that there is no way to know the world except through the subjectivity that precedes and grounds our objective accounts.[10] We are at home in the world, as Haraway's work throughout her career has implied in generous and life-enhancing ways, because the world we understand is also the world we make, in both literal and figurative senses. As she has repeatedly pointed out, such world-making practices imply responsibility for their construction.

The conclusion that came out of my work on the Regime of Computation points in a similar direction. Computation, in this sense, is not restricted to any given medium. It is a relational process that can run in the brain, with gears, disks, balls, cylinders, and levers, in electro-mechanical and silicon devices, as well as other media not yet discovered or in nascent developments such as quantum computers. Imagining the world as the result of massive, interlocking and continuing computations, researchers such as Stephen Wolfram (2002) and Ed Fredkin (2001) see computation as the means by which physical reality is produced.[11] For those who champion computational models, this is a ground-breaking insight that promises to revolutionize a wide range of fields, from the study of complex systems to particle physics. To the cultural critic, by contrast, the Regime of Computation is apt to appear as an over-determined metaphor. Much as the eighteenth century saw the world as a clockwork mechanism, so our computationally intensive culture would naturally be inclined to envision the universe as a giant computer.

Parsing the situation as a conflict between means and metaphor might suggest that we should cast our votes with one side

9. Evan Thompson and Francisco J. Varela, *Why the Mind Isn't in the Head: The Lived Body in Biology, Cognitive Science, and Human Experience* (Cambridge, MA: Harvard University Press, forthcoming).

10. Donna Haraway, "Situated Knowledges: The Science Question in Feminism as a Site of Discourse on the Privilege of Partial Perspective," *Feminist Studies* 14, no. 3 (1988): 575–99.

11. Stephen Wolfram, *A New Kind of Science* (New York: Wolfram Media, 2002) and Edward Fredkin, "Introduction to Digital Philosophy," (2001), http://www.digitalphilosophy.org (consulted July 2006).

or the other, as if choosing were the issue.[12] However, this binary division between means and metaphor misses something crucially important: that means and metaphor are dynamically interacting with each other. The computational metaphor is potent because networked and programmable devices are so fast, powerful and interconnected; if the technology did not exist, the metaphor would not have the traction it does. For its part, the belief that the universe is fundamentally computational feeds back into the development of the technology, pursued among other reasons because it is perceived to mirror nature's own methods.

One of the important insights that has emerged in science studies in the last twenty years is the realization that scientific models are underdetermined with respect to empirical evidence (or, to put it another way, that multiple models may be consistent with prevailing knowledge). Cultural beliefs, or more accurately cultural presuppositions, play important roles in determining which models will be proposed and which will succeed. In *How We Became Posthuman* (1999), I demonstrated this dynamic at work through my analysis of information-theoretic models. The Shannon–Weaver version of information theory triumphed over Donald MacKay's conceptually richer embodied version for practical reasons (largely because it could be reliably quantified). However, the Shannon–Weaver model then rapidly traveled to other fields where quantification was impossible (such as semiotics and communication theory) because of its "scientific" cachet, whereas MacKay's model would have been more appropriate. The adaptation of a disembodied view of information spread so pervasively, I argued, because it fitted well with existing preconceptions about a separation between a material body and an immaterial essence, which of course was a subtext for a disembodied view of information in the first place.[13]

To sum up these complex interactions between means and metaphor, I offer in *My Mother Was a Computer* (2005) the following formulation, which has become central for me in understanding the contemporary situation as well as historical precedents: "What we make and what (we think) we are co-evolve together."[14] If we leave aside for the moment the parenthetical "we think," the statement would find enthusiastic agreement among anthropologists, who have long accepted, for example, that tool use and bipedalism co-evolved together. Bipedalism facilitated the use and especially the transport of tools; tool use in turn bestowed such decisive fitness advantage that it had the effect of accelerating bipedalism. This co-evolutionary spiral involved both cultural and biological changes, including for example

12. In her interview, Haraway comments, "It's not so much about choice. I don't think we sit down and decide what's important very much. I think we somehow come to terms with what's going on, and the method of working is relentlessly collaborationist." See Gane and Haraway, "When We Have Never Been Human," 155.

13. For a full discussion of Shannon and Weaver's information theory and the competing embodied theory of Donald MacKay, see N. Katherine Hayles, *How We Became Posthuman: Virtual Bodies in Cybernetics, Literature, and Informatics* (Chicago: University of Chicago Press,1999): 50–112.

14. N. Katherine Hayles, *My Mother Was a Computer Digital Subjects and Literary Texts* (Chicago: University of Chicago Press, 2005).

Hayles

the opposable thumb and the skeletal transformations that bipedalism brought about. Stanley Ambrose, an anthropologist at the University of Illinois, has demonstrated a similar dynamic at work in the practice of fashioning compound tools (tools with more than one part that have to be assembled in sequential order, such as a stone ax with a handle, bindings and a stone insert).[15] Evidence indicates that compound tools were contemporaneous with the accelerated development of Broca's area in the frontal cortex, the part of the brain involved in language use. Ambrose speculates that the sequential and hierarchical ordering required in the fashioning of compound tools co-evolved with language because language, like compound tools, requires the sequential ordering of reproducible and discrete units. In this scenario, the trait often identified with the essence of the human—our ability to use complex languages—was bound up at the dawn of *Homo sapiens* with the emergence of a relatively sophisticated technology (i.e. compound versus simple tools), initiating a co-evolutionary spiral in which what we made and what we became co-evolved together.

How does that formulation change if the parenthetical "we think" is put back into the picture? Cultural beliefs and practices are part of this co-evolutionary dynamic because they influence what tools are made and how those tools are used, which in turn affects who we are as biological organisms, which then feeds back into the co-evolutionary spiral. Haraway's insistence that the world is "relationality all the way down" applies as much to technology as to companion species.[16] In the contemporary period, computation emerges as a crucial aspect of the entwined dynamical hierarchies that structure and energize relational dynamics. As inhabitants of globally interconnected networks, we are joined in a dynamic co-evolutionary spiral with intelligent machines as well as with the other biological species with whom we share the planet.

That the cyborg is no longer the most compelling metaphor through which to understand our contemporary situation should not blind us to the fact that much urgent and pressing work remains to be done. The cognisphere takes up where the cyborg left off. No longer bound in a binary with the goddess but rather emblem and instantiation of dynamic cognitive flows between human, animal and machine, the cognisphere, like the world itself, is not binary but multiple, not a split creature but a co-evolving and densely interconnected complex system.

15. Stanley Ambrose, "Paleo-lithic Technology and Human Evolution," *Science* 291 (2001): 1748–53.

16. Gane and Haraway, "When We Have Never Been Human," 141.

Post-Animal Life
Catherine Ingraham

This is a slightly altered chapter taken from *Architecture, Animal, Human: The Asymmetrical Condition*, published in 2006. It was difficult to resist making changes—although I ended up making only a few—because I am now writing another book on the subject of architecture and biological life, more specifically on second order systems theory and biomodernity. *Architecture, Animal, Human*'s aspiration was to re-pose and re-vivify the question of life in architecture because life, per se, is now a radically different cultural-biological complex than it was even fifty years ago. Our assumptions about both the figure and fact of life in our work are based on humanist paradigms that date back to the Renaissance. The purpose of admitting animals into the room, so to speak, was not to pass beyond humanism into some post-humanist condition that emancipates us from these paradigms. Instead, it was to trouble architecture with animate forms—animals—that could not be easily assimilated into these traditions, which define so much about architectural work. Animals occupy the existential place of all that we desired to leave behind in our human dominions and this has drastically delimited our understanding of biological life. The book attempted a suggestive critique of the relation of architecture to new theories of nature and life.

Post-animal life is a description of life that both links and slips between architectural and human/animal "life" history. It takes note, as a description, of the changes in the status and value of human and animal life from the Renaissance to the present and also makes the supposition that ontological shifts in the meaning of life affect, and are affected by, shifts in the meaning of architecture. As is evident, I have adopted the much disputed, but arguable, view that modernity for architecture begins in the Renaissance, whereas modern human and animal life do not begin until the late eighteenth century. This may seem like an impossible genealogy, given that architecture is a distillation of human thought and culture; it is a human production. Yet many human productions and technologies could be said to have pursued an evolutionary path that unfolds almost independently of the human culture within which they are located. Architecture "becomes modern" when the architect

Brunelleschi invents perspectival representation in the Renaissance, which claims space as an homogeneous and mathematically abstract entity. Human beings "become modern" when they are able to establish themselves scientifically as a separate species, *Homo sapiens*, in the late eighteenth century. If this idea of a slipped history can be held provisionally, it is a way of stating the problem of post-animal life and architecture as simultaneously diachronic, i.e. historical, and synchronic, a state of existence.

By the early nineteenth century, to be "human" means to have been finally, and definitively, separated from animals. To be a non-human animal during the same period means, in effect, to have been divested of psychological autonomy and power in such a way that continued existence in the world becomes increasingly precarious. One could say that the animal, and animality, recedes from modernity as the human advances toward it and is, indeed, defined by it. Many of the things that happen during the eighteenth and nineteenth centuries—the usual things we are familiar with from reputable histories about architecture's relation to the industrial revolution, to the formation of cities and legal-juridical structures, as well as the explosion of science—result from the sudden convergence of an already modern and mathematical architecture with an emerging modern human being, autonomous, individualized, and secularized. During the same period, architecture also continues to house what could be called ongoing atavistic bestial life, in the form of the disappearing animal inside the human. This sentence, no doubt, would seem strange to those reputable historians. The "dispersal of the subject," or "post-humanism," of the late twentieth century, which subsequently dismantles ideas of human autonomy—an idea of autonomy that dates back only several hundred years, to the moment "humanness" found its place in the world—might have calculated some of the cost of the loss of human autonomy in terms of what we knew already in the eighteenth century about the loss of animal autonomy.[1] But this is a later story.

Architecture captures objects in the world in the Renaissance by means of spatial coordinate systems, which eventually, in Panofsky's skillful words, enable the "claim of the object to meet the ambition of the subject." Part of the ambition of the subject, to which Renaissance history routinely testifies, is to universalize and "make academic" architectural principles in a way that accounts for almost everything about architectural objects: their meaning, construction, placement on a site, design, authority as artistic objects and status as theoretical objects. Part of the claim of the object in the

1. K. Michael Hays, *Modernism and the Posthuman Subject: The Architecture of Hannes Meyer and Ludwig Hilberseimer* (Cambridge, MA: MIT Press, 1992), 273. Post-humanism means, among other things, the "dispersal of the subject."

Renaissance is, in a manner of speaking, to be mathematically "known" in space. The definitive separation between animate and inanimate objects based on bio-ontological differences—life and death, movement and stasis, biological and astronomical time, generative and reproductive capacities—are not yet in place in the Renaissance, but one beauty of the invention of perspective is that it treats all objects in its domain, living or non-living, as equally available for representation, and all space in its domain as capable of being filled.

Beginning in the late eighteenth century, architecture captures, specifically, human life, which is, as initially stated, in the process of gaining biological autonomy from animal life. Architecture captures this life in sophisticated structures composed in the midst of theories of time and space that have been both expanded and deepened by seventeenth and eighteenth century science. In subsequent eras, human life biologically consolidates what had been, since antiquity, its philosophical and theological centrality. Human life, as it is understood to be more biologically complex, analytically matches and in some cases replaces its historic intellectual and spiritual privilege with biological privilege. Some of these developments are registered in architecture through the secularization and formalization of public space and the development of historical epochs and typologies that are modeled after the natural sciences. Architecture also registers these developments by becoming desirous—the euphemism is perhaps too laden—of the intricate motion, depth, and organization of the body it houses and increasingly understands. From the other direction, "life's" direction, the constancy and variability of human life is formalized into ways of life, lifestyles, that impose new types of order and disorder on architecture. With the opening of representational and taxonomic spaces between beings and things, human and animal, in the eighteenth century, the distance between architecture and human biological life, paradoxically, begins to narrow. One of Giorgio Agamben's points in his short book *The Open*, which takes little account of space or architecture, is, nevertheless, the same. He remarks that the human body has always been thought to be a combination of natural and divine, or natural and social—part animal, part something else. Instead, Agamben argues, humanness "results from the practical and political separation of humanity and animality."[2] This separation is particularly potent in the post-animal age when the animal is withdrawn from the human scene in the Enlightenment, "liberating" humanness into its various modern humanities and inhumanities.

2. Giorgio Agamben, *The Open: Man and Animal,* trans. Kevin Attell (Palo Alto: Stanford University Press, 2004). See editor's remarks on book cover.

When the architectural historian Sigfried Giedion traces this same history, a large segment of his scholarly focus is brought to bear on how architecture contends both with the movement and space augmented by mechanization (*Mechanization Takes Command*), and with the movement and space increasingly implied by modern theories of time (*Space, Time and Architecture*). Alongside the deep technical interests that architecture has in moving structures and in structures that must sustain movement, and the philosophical and scientific fascination with time and space, are the issues of biological movement in space and time. Post-animal human life moves more freely in the world and claims, for itself, vast territories and resources formerly left to animals. In this modern human life, architecture confronts a number of manifestations that cannot be easily assimilated into static physical space: first, an increasingly mobilized body, outer life, and a more profound human psyche, inner life.

In the nineteenth century, the unconscious, the dark protector of contemporary human consciousness, is theorized by Freud as an inaccessible domain that lies beneath the accessible space in the mind. To gain access to this space, great care must be taken not to disturb the conscious mind with revelations that bear on the conduct of daily life in every respect. Rosalind Krauss' virtuoso critique of modern painting was to penetrate its claims for immediacy and purely surface effects by constituting the eye—more aptly, the gaze—as an "optical unconscious." The eye brokers what is seen in the external world with the restless constructive motion of the unconscious, which is the motion of desire. Architecture, which for the most part assumed that human life was, for architectural purposes, primarily a visible body in visible space, generally sidestepped the complex skein of developments that understood human movement to be evidence of a particular kind of mind, not a particular kind of body. For architecture, the perfect occupant has been, and to some degree still is, a living being chiefly identified by means of its form and the (limited, encaged) movement of its body, the humanized animal, or "human-animal" of the post-animal world. It is not, of course, as if humans were given any choice as to what kind of consciousness they have, nor do they have much say over their form. It is simply that the restraint that architecture places on human bodies in architectural space is almost purely formal and external. The form presented by architecture both to itself (a crucial part of the story) and to its human occupant is, for the most part, easily managed in terms of the movement of the body. Movement's relation to form are essential to our conception of architecture and the modern architectural program. Human consciousness, however, is not, although it would be impossible to design, build, or live in architecture without such a consciousness.

Psychological life, in architectural terms, remains naive. The nineteenth-century architectural subject is, thus, definitively human in form, its "needs" are known, and it has human privileges (it can enter and leave enclosures as it pleases), but it remains closer to what the animal has become than what the human, in other parts of its life, has become. Prior to the eighteenth century, for example, animals were understood to have magical powers (analogous to psychological powers), and these begin to evaporate once taxonomic sciences become more precise about the divisions between different kinds of life. In architectural terms, both animal and human, in the post-animal age, are increasingly understood as physical forms uniquely amenable to capture; that is, the newly discovered human and the reformed animal of the nineteenth century do not offer any psychological resistance to the act of being housed or caged; in fact, the reverse. The interior of the house comes to stand as a metaphor for the interior life of the human—it makes metaphoric, in some sense, the space of interiority that the human psyche claims for itself when it leaves the surrogate interior of the house. To be permanently "outside a house" is, at the same time, a pathological life, a homeless life.

There are, of course, reservations on all sides. As I suggested earlier, human and animal retain reserves of "wildness." For animals, we have only this word and its slippery meaning; for humans, there are numerous words—schizophrenia, legendary psychasthenia, claustrophobia, the uncanny, all the spatial phobias and aphasias such as autism, agoraphobia, attention deficit disorder, many of which had their origins in the nineteenth century clash of human life with mechanization and industrialization but all of which raise the specter of the animal and the animal caught by space. I do not want to romanticize these terms or the conditions of resistance they imply. I simply want to mark the possibility of a reserve that cannot be fully assimilated by an account of post-animal architectural life. We are familiar with the argument that this reserve or wildness is human consciousness itself, the part of the human mind that is unable to be housed by architecture and thus acts as a wild card. But I also think this reserve belongs not to the human mind, as Freud imagined it, but to the human mind as it exists inside an animal body. This is not the rat of the Ratman or the wolf of the Wolfman, nor the rat and the wolf as they might play the role of the "other," but the rat and the wolf as they are unknown, rather than known, by humans.

The particular balance between form and restrained movement that defines the animal in the post-animal world describes, almost perfectly, an ideal architectural occupant. Using, again, Heidegger's problematic but provocative terms, the "open" and "disconcealedness" of human consciousness, and much that it contains—the various humanisms and "world-making" of its history—humans thus find, specifically in architecture, a foregone animal identity that they make contemporary with themselves. Post-animal human life in architectural space is thus the paradox of an "open captivation." Architecture sustains and defines some aspect of the animal in the human long after it has been, apparently, eradicated by science, and long after the human political and social being has been brought into the fully separate place of humanness.

I also do not mean to say that architecture should, somehow, be more human, or more humane, than it is. Perhaps it should, and could, be. But the extreme difficulty, even the impossibility, of any direct reference, on the part of architecture, to the self-conscious aspect of human life—in spite of the obvious fact and paradox that architecture is designed by self-conscious human beings—is not necessarily meant to indicate a dire condition that needs correction. Instead, it is a kind of explanation for many facets of architecture that we have tried to account for in terms of life and, above all, in terms of a felt disjunction or asymmetry between life and architecture. From Renaissance harmonic proportions that were meant to make buildings and human bodies commensurate to Daniel Libeskind's obtuse architectural lines of concordance with human history, such disjunctions are, in fact, more the constitutive than exceptional to what we define as architectural. Perhaps having such a view changes, at the very least, the way certain images are read. One might notice more acutely, for example, how images of human and animal life are almost always missing from architectural images, or, when they do appear, how heavily stylized they have become. In early Renaissance drawings of building interiors, there is no Photoshopped human figure to give scale to the buildings; "giving scale" to buildings is what human figures, as a humanist ideal, were meant to do.[3] Notable exceptions are, as always, Le Corbusier and his inheritor, Rem Koolhaas, who craft their figures of life as if they were characters in a movie, stylized, backs turned, beautifully dressed, highly formal, profoundly unenigmatic. Beatriz Colomina reads Le Corbusier's images of human figures as if they are actors inside

3. Wolfgang Lotz, "The Rendering of the Interior in Architectural Drawings of the Renaissance," *Studies in Italian Renaissance Architecture* (Cambridge, MA: 1981), 13.

architectures that act like camera lenses—an "architecture as mass media" that breaks the distinction between the public and the private.[4] Koolhaas inexplicably includes an animal, a giraffe, in his photograph of the Villa dall'Ava in Paris, a house with two "apartments."

Fig. 3.1 OMA, Villa Dall'Ava, St. Cloud, Paris, 1991 (Courtesy of OMA, © Hans Werlemann).

4. Beatriz Colomina, *Privacy and Publicity: Modern Architecture as Mass Media* (Cambridge: MIT Press, 1994).

Why a giraffe? The giraffe is poignant in the photograph. It is a scaling diagram, like the modular, but also contributes traces of its characteristic posture to the structure of the house, which rides on splayed pilotis, and traces of its characteristic pattern to the stone wall. Perhaps the giraffe is a figure of lost human grace or a symbol of a wild captivity that marks post-animal life. The giraffe was young and relatively small.

It was brought to the site in a horse trailer, with its neck bent down to fit, for a fashion shoot. Perhaps, given what the animal lays on the table, we will eventually have to look at some other kind of story.

Fig. 3.2 OMA, Villa Dall'Ava, St. Cloud, Paris, 1991 (Courtesy of OMA, © Hans Werlemann).

Koolhaas' work is attuned to diverse aspects of somatic life sublimated in metropolitan and domestic architectures. The expansiveness of SMLXL, which records these somatic architectures and their "splendors and miseries" is laden with narratives and images from a human planet that lies open to an animal interior; thus a building can be carried on long spindly legs.

The Next Subject: A Conversation With Dr. Caleb Finch
Seth Harrison

Seth L. Harrison, MD, is a founding partner of Harrison Atelier, a multidisciplinary design firm, and the founder and managing partner of Apple Tree Partners, a life-sciences investment firm. Dr. Harrison has over twenty years of experience in developing biotechnology, pharmaceutical, and medical device companies, often from start-up, many of which focus on age-related diseases. It was in the process of working on one such company, beginning in 1995, that Dr. Harrison met Dr. Finch. The two developed what has become a long-standing dialogue on medicine and aging that focuses on the social and cultural implications of extended longevity.

Dr. Caleb C. "Tuck" Finch is Professor of Gerontology and Biological Sciences, and a founding member of the Departments of Molecular Biology and Neurobiology at the University of Southern California. He also holds adjunct appointments in the Departments of Psychology, Physiology, and Neurology at USC, and is one of twelve University Distinguished Professors. Dr. Finch has been studying the molecular physiology of aging for over forty years. He has written extensively on aging and longevity. In 1990, he published a major intellectual synthesis of aging entitled, *Longevity, Senescence, and the Genome*, as part of the John D. and Catherine T. MacArthur Foundation Series on Mental Health and Development. In 1995, Dr. Finch and Robert Ricklefs published *Aging: A Natural History* (Scientific American Library Series), which has been translated into five languages. In 2000, Dr. Finch co-authored with Thomas Kirkwood Chance, *Development and Aging* (Oxford Press). His most recent book is *The Biology of Human Longevity. Inflammation, Nutrition, and Aging in the Evolution of Lifespans* (Academic Press). He has published over 450 scientific papers.

SH: Would it be fair to say that one of the major shifts in our attitudes toward aging that occurred during your career was the emergence of the study of aging as a molecular discipline?

CF: Without any question, the molecular technology of the 1970s and 1980s finally allowed us to get fundamental information about aging.

SH: Can you give us a sketch of your career?

CF: My start in thinking about aging was in 1957, an undergraduate at Yale in the biophysics department, where there was high excitement about fundamental approaches to biology from a physicist's perspective. We were riding on the surge of excitement about the remarkable DNA structure of Watson and Crick announced in 1953. I was thinking about studying embryonic development, but one of my faculty mentors, the great Carl Woese said "but if you really want to do something new, why don't you think about the biology of aging—almost nothing is known and nobody with any brains is working on it." So that stuck in my mind when I graduated from Yale in '61, and was fortunate to get invited to join Rockefeller University's graduate program, where eventually I wound up picking a thesis project in the developmental biology lab of Alfred Mirsky.

I began to think of aging as a product of functional, interacting changes across the organs, in which the brain and the pituitary might have a particular role as the seat of physiological regulation. I did my Ph.D on a topic related to neuroendocrine mechanisms in aging, and then I did a year post-doc in comparative pathology at Rockefeller, because it was clear that chronic disease was a fundamental part of studying aging. Then I took my first faculty job at Cornell Medical College in 1970 as an Assistant Professor working on the molecular physiology of aging.

SH: So you've been studying aging for four decades.

CF: I've been working on it since 1965.

SH: Can you describe how aging became a molecular discipline during that time?

CF: Well, the emergence of biotechnology in the 1970s laid the foundations for the mutational analysis of long-lived worms, flies and mice, which led, in the late 1980s and early 1990s, to the discovery of gene mutations that could increase lifespan. But there was another area of aging research that really didn't depend upon molecular biology: the biochemistry of oxidative damage through which we recognized that DNA and proteins are oxidatively damaged by glucose in our body fluids. Also, aging would never have been understood at a molecular level in flies and worms without the background of developmental biology. The two fields—developmental biology and aging—really have developed like Siamese twins. Aging would never have emerged as a molecular discipline without the hundreds of superb developmental biology studies of mice, flies, and worms during the 1960s through the 1980s.

SH: You have quite forcefully argued that there is a huge difference in lifespan between people who take care of themselves, taking certain over-the-counter medicines, having regular check-ups, participating in screening and prevention, and people who either do not or cannot. Can we say definitely that old age is extending in industrialized nations?

CF: As the urban environment and sanitation began to improve in the nineteenth century, long before germ theory was understood, and as transportation networks grew that enabled better food distribution, all of this—from 1800 to 1900—reduced early mortality and increased life expectancy at later ages. Pasteurization of milk began to lower tuberculosis and other diseases. And then soon came vaccination against childhood diseases. In the 1950s, antibiotics became generally available. The next phase was the recognition of the role of high blood pressure in causing heart attacks and strokes. When Eisenhower had his heart attack, it was considered normal by the family physician that with each year of age after forty, your blood pressure would go up one or two points. Now, of course, that age changes quite aggressively when treated. The general conclusion is that the blood pressure intervention has accounted for most of the reduction of heart attacks, quite possibly more than the lipid lowering drugs.

SH: Untreated, blood pressure trends up after forty; treated it does not. So this becomes a perfect example of how in industrialized nations we're extending lifespan. Do we know why blood pressure goes up?

CF: Unmanaged blood pressure does go up progressively each year because of the loss of elasticity in our arteries, which is an outcome of biochemical aging damage.

SH: That is another example of how we are converting what has been thought of as an anatomical/mechanical model to a biomolecular model.

CF: Nice way of putting it.

SH: Most of the early longevity gains in industrializing nations came from hygiene and antibiotics?

CF: Hygiene, antibiotics, immunization and year-round access to decent food, which was not possible before national transportation networks. You couldn't get oranges up in Scandinavian countries before 1900. Or in northern Minnesota, where my great-grandparents came from.

SH: Today in industrialized nations it's a hobby to control, or supposedly control, one's longevity. Is it true that by staying fit and controlling one's blood pressure, you actually do have an impact?

CF: Oh, absolutely. The reduction of life expectancy at any age is measured in years if you're obese, have high blood pressure, have a bad lipid profile and if you don't exercise. And what's good for your heart is good for your brain on all studies that I know.

SH: What is it on the molecular level that exercise does for us that is so good?

CF: Exercise reduces the load of oxidized proteins and lipids. Exercise is also anti-inflammatory. And it stimulates stem-cell formation.

SH: So does lipid lowering do anything?

CF: It contributes to a lower inflammatory load, but at least in this past decade, 2000–2010, the blood pressure and anti-coagulant medications have been the champion effect. One can imagine, if there will some day be drugs to reduce cancer incidence or, in a not-unimaginable future, slow Alzheimer's processes, those would also have huge benefits. Cancer has been really resistant.

SH: We chip away at that. We get certain ones. Certain blood cancers, certain rarities, certain monogenic diseases tend to respond to biotechnology nicely, but we are very careful before we'll invest in an oncology project because it's so complex. Cancer seems straightforward when you get a response in relatively early clinical trials but this response tends not to be predictive. In fact, it can be the opposite.

CF: Cancer—it's a long grind. But obviously if we don't do the research, we will not get there.

SH: We've talked about cancer, heart disease, stroke, technological interventions for all of which, some effective, others not, are continually being developed. Would you argue that technology constitutes an evolutionary pressure that has extended human lifespans?

CF: Well, no: in the industrial age where lifespan began to increase as living conditions improved, natural selection had nothing to do with that, so it isn't a question of evolution in that widely understood sense of natural selection.

SH: Can you elaborate on that?

CF: Infections are the major cause of mortality in primate populations, and they were the major cause of mortality in humans before 1900. Essentially, we have almost eliminated infections as a cause of death; infections now account for less than 1 percent of deaths after the age of twenty in the industrial countries. This means that the main force of natural selection which operated prior to 1900 has essentially disappeared. Our world is post-Darwinan.

SH: As you take out those microbes with whom we co-evolved for millions of years, haven't human pressures themselves filled in that void? Some people say that humans evolving under the evolutionary pressure of humanity itself—and by this I mean, principally, technology and the by-products and lifestyles generated by industrialized society—we are, some would argue, becoming "post-human."

CF: How are we different in our perceptions than we were 200 years ago?

SH: By humanism, I don't mean some universal perception of what it means to be a member of *Homo sapiens*. I am referring to a period in western culture between, say 1450–1750, perhaps with one-century error bars. If I might define the term for our purposes: humanism is a style of thinking, according to which an organized chain of being hierarchically inscribes man at the center of Nature. Man harvests or exploits that world around him. That world is given to him. He does not create that world; he creates from that world. That's an essential difference between humanism and post-humanism. Post-humanism recognizes that man, through his technology, his evolutionary pressure, if you will, not just on himself but on other species and on the very planet, in fact creates the world and therefore gains a responsibility not to take from it but to manage the globe's resources.

CF: But I'm not so sure that our time is unique. How about the Neolithic era? When we started to live in towns and we didn't have to worry about wild animals any longer and we had a steady supply of food. Didn't all that back then also change the relation of human to the natural world, the same ballgame as now?

SH: But I think that the difference between today and the Neolithic era, is that despite the disruption that living in cities represented, no technology existed that operated on a planetary scale. Today we have those, and I don't want to say only those, but there are quite a few technologies that are like that. Today we know that we are capable of disrupting the underpinnings of species.

CF: The global aspect is certainly new to our era.

SH: The post-human argument is that our era no longer supports an idea of an exterior. The output of *Homo sapiens* has become the primary planetary change-force. This means that you can no longer think that the world exists for you, the human, simply to depict, enjoy, or exploit. On the contrary, you must accept responsibility to all the living things and even the objects and the dead things of this world, because you have essentially assumed the place of nature. Post-humanism or the post human-centered perspective coincides with the emergence of technologies with which humans can literally sculpt the globe and the genomes of its inhabitants, all those entities that we before considered "natural."

CF: Scientifically speaking, I think that the main thing that has come into the twenty-first century is that individuals can claim some control over their health destiny in later years. This is the radical idea that you don't have a foreordained number of heartbeats chosen for you in some holy predestination. Most people think now that they have some degree of control over their health status and their wellbeing, that allows them to consider their own longevity as a sort of a project in their lives.

SH: So is aging a disease or an inevitable process?

CF: Aging begins before birth. The ovary has a fixed number of cells. No new egg cells are formed after birth. The ovary clock is ticking away. Our arteries have microscopic loci of inflammatory cells and oxidized lipids at birth. There's a lifelong accumulation beginning prenatally of damage in our arteries. Dividing cells inevitably accumulate DNA mutations through normal processes of cell division that are irreducibly imperfect in DNA fidelity. This build-up of mutations ultimately leads to cancer cells. Everyone has pre-malignant cells—in their colon, in their prostate, in their uterus, in their ovaries, in their breasts. These accumulate as an outcome of random damage during the processes of life. Aging is built into our aerobic metabolism.

SH: So you answer is that aging is not a disease. It is a process that cannot be changed.

CF: It can be changed, and does change. Evolution manifestly has made the rates of aging slower or faster in different species.

SH: But am I hearing you correctly, Tuck? Are you saying that aging itself evolves? I thought that the maximal lifespan encoded in our genomes was somewhere around 120.

CF: Yes, aging does evolve—we are the longest lived primate. But given our present genes, without changing the rate of acceleration in mortality, we're not going to live much over 120. I know not everyone agrees with me on that!

SH: By acceleration in mortality, you mean—

CF: The Gompertz mortality acceleration. It looks like a "lazy J." It starts out higher in neonates, then dips down to a plateau between ages ten and thirty, and then it starts to accelerate, doubling about every eight years after the age of forty. The slope of that curve, in laboratory animals can be made slower or faster depending upon particular mutations. In humans, the Gompertz acceleration rate of aging does not seem to be able to be changed: mortality in human populations everywhere doubles about every eight years after the age of forty. There's no doubt that life expectancy at any later age is greater now than it was ten years ago. But we are, our calculations show, hitting a wall because we cannot reduce the background mortality any further, while the mortality rate is accelerating at a steeper rate now than it was fifty years ago. So we are reaching the maximum gains as the epidemiology of aging is currently understood and the only way that we will have further gains is by making the slope of mortality shallower. This can be done with genetic mutations in mice, worm and flies, but there is nothing like that yet for humans. Looking broadly at the biology of aging across species, yes, lifespans can range widely and there does not seem to be an intrinsic age limit; but, observing human demography, I think we are hitting a limit of about 120.

SH: The lifespan limit itself—this is the product of evolution?

CF: There's no question about that. Every biogerontologist agrees on that. The lifespan does evolve, and in a given branch of mammals there are short-lived and long-lived species. Humans live twice longer than their closest ancestors, the chimpanzee. In whales, the bowhead whale most likely lives more than 200 years, while other short-lived cetaceans may live only twenty years. So, the capacity to evolve very slow aging patterns is recurrent across every type of organism you look at.

SH: Have people hypothesized as to why human lifespans are longer than those of most animals? You have said that longer lifespans of humans are the result of evolutionary workarounds of great complexity. Care to elaborate?

CF: What's distinctive about our line of primates is that, going back at least 20 million years, we have one kid at a time and maturation is slow, as late-puberty may be at age ten or twelve in chimpanzees. But even then, full adult social status for male chimps may not be achieved until nearly twenty, not too different from humans. So the time it takes for us to mature is longer than the lifespan of many short-lived primates. Great apes and humans also share enormous maternal investment in raising one kid at a time, plus having kids spaced out by up to five to ten years. What this actually means is that our genetic architecture of slow development and slow aging may have completely different underlying molecular mechanisms than the very short lived flies, worms and mice we study because of their fast breeding and short generation. Even so, short-lived, high-turnover models, such as worms, flies and mice are informative about the genetics of aging, up to a point.

SH: What are the long-lived, low-turnover, high-maternal-investment animal models that molecular gerontologists can work with today?

CF: There are none besides humans. There are no active breeding programs for captive chimpanzees in the US and the NIH recently suspended new grants for biomedical research, including aging studies.

SH: How does the field deal with that?

CF: They ignore it because most research has focused on the short-lived species. I'm in a little bit of a lonely place in saying that we need a new approach.

SH: What is that approach, do you think?

CF: I'm taking head-on the fact that human aging has evolved in a dirty, complex, germ-laden world; whereas we study aging in short-lived animal models, in clean, simplified, sterilized environments, totally unlike the environments in which humans evolved their long lifespans. These clean animal models have served us well. But now we need to open the door to let real world dirt in, if we want to understand future human aging in an increasingly degraded environments.

SH: Sort of a fascinating confrontation of medicine with the limits of its models. What about caloric restriction (CR)—isn't all the molecular evidence that CR extends lifespans developed from short-lived, high-turnover animal models that are studied in clean, simplified, sterilized environments?

CF: It is. And caloric-restricted mice are more vulnerable to infections and heal wounds more slowly. And that's why I'm absolutely unconvinced that CR is valid for humans. It even turns out CR does not increase longevity in half of the strains of mice studied. So CR benefits to longevity have narrow validity and depend upon many environmental factors. No critical pathway has been identified in caloric restriction that is applicable to humans. In fact, human centenarian studies have shown that the CR pathways identified in worms, flies and mice have a very limited association with great human longevity.

SH: How plastic is aging? Or is a fixed maximum lifespan something that humans must accept?

CF: You can get a sense of the plasticity of aging from the evolution of different lifespans in short- and long-lived primates, which is due to genetic differences, the huge effects of environment in human lifespans: Aging happened much faster to humans 150 years ago.

SH: So you're saying that the potential we have today is to turn public attention to the use of technologies in the way that you would use mutations in the lab in highly controlled animal populations so as to change the Gompertz Curve for certain segments of human populations?

CF: That's a good synthesis. It's exactly what my good friend Aubrey de Grey would argue.

SH: The trans-humanist idea—

CF: Why do you say trans-humanist? That's a name that Aubrey does not use to describe himself.

SH: The trans-humanist position seems to advocate that through technology, longevity, health and sentience can be extended. In some cases, even immortality is implied.

CF: I don't want to get into a discussion of terms that I don't understand. But De Grey has a useful role, in my opinion, in that he is propagating a more public agenda for the plasticity of aging that will be increasingly accessible with additional technology. The huge opportunity we now have to study human aging has come from imaging technology and rapid clinical chemistry that allows an enormous amount of individual data to be gathered longitudinally. We're getting a glimpse of the socio-economic differences in outcomes of aging and gender differences and ethnic differences that are really extremely informative about the plasticity of aging processes and the huge role of environment and lifestyle. But the real experiments are being done inadvertently with the various drugs and lifestyle recommendations that are now being implemented at the level of primary care physicians with a preventive medicine outlook. So, with the various drugs used to lower cholesterol and lower blood pressure, blood thinners, and nutritional recommendations with a sufficiently large population, you can get sub-groups that are balanced against each other. Really important findings are emerging that will continue to emerge about what aspects of lifestyle drugs and over the counter prescriptions are influencing life expectancy and different stages of aging. In the next five to ten years we will understand the number of different alternate pathways to health and morbidity from human population studies.

SH: All of our interventions are maximizing the time on which any individual stays on that slope—at least as we currently understand science—but we don't know how to change the slope.

CF: I think that is correct.

SH: And if you were taking a long view of when our interventions might be able to change the rate of aging, would you think we would be able to make progress in ten, twenty, or even fifty years?

CF: It's completely unknowable at this time. To change the mortality rate slope would requires intervention at the population level, which seems a fantasy.

SH: You're talking about longitudinal studies that are multi-center, funded by governments, that are retrospective or prospective, studies that enroll hundreds of thousands of people, and follow them over long periods.

CF: A minimum of ten years, I would say. And, of course, nothing stays the same during that time. People often modify their lifestyles; change the proportions of what they eat and drink; also new factors come into the environment. Individual lifestyle differences are already large and are going to become increasingly so.

SH: Let's take the optimistic view that someone will attempt these studies, and that we will continue to apply science to extend our longevity, and even, perhaps, that we will succeed in, as you put it, reducing the slope of the Gompertz curve, what kinds of new products will become popular or necessary as we undergo this shift in lifespan?

CF: The bottom line is that technology will support an even more prolonged phase of morbidity. Most particularly—and this is really important—after the age of eighty, the risk of Alzheimer's-type cognitive impairment goes up towards 50 percent. That's huge! If life expectancy got towards ninety, that would mean that a third of the people who reached ninety would have difficulty in living independently due to cognitive limitations, even if they didn't have clinical Alzheimer's.

SH: So, assisted living really transforms, in a life-extended era, into an environmental design attitude that permeates almost every space that people occupy. Design might function as a cognitive enhancer.

CF: That's exactly right.

SH: Though, until we have the perfect cognitive enhancement drug, we need an environment that is designed to help do that job. Perhaps we can conclude our dialog on extended human longevity as it implicates architecture today, in our post human era, by stating: The design of any place should serve as a cognitive enhancer or cognitive support.

CF: Yes, that sounds like a fine conclusion for our purposes here. I just want to add that I'm optimistic that we will continue to develop new drugs and new interventions that will enable us to live healthier longer. Therefore, so long as we continue to advance as a civilization, there will be an absolute requirement that the architects of our physical and mental spaces take a full accounting of the avalanche of infirmities that will set upon all aging populations as lifespans continue to increase, even if the maximum human lifespan does not increase beyond 120 years.

Approaching a New Biotope
Francisco González de Canales

During the last few decades, Science Studies has tried to redefine the concept of nature according to our present period, its knowledge and technologies.[1] This task has not only meant a reshaping of our understanding of scientific disciplines related to nature, like biology or physics, but it has also provoked some social, cultural and political debate. In general terms, we could consider that these consequences have been channeled through two main perspectives, one that can be labeled as "global" or "totalizing," and another one that can be understood as "particular" or "differential."[2] However, constructing the argument from the opposite perspective, it is also true that most of the socio-cultural preoccupations posed by Science Studies have been reflected in contemporary society. If Michel Serres or Edgar Morin posed the question of constructing a consciousness of the unity of the Earth, its ecological biodiversity and our anthropo-biophysical status within it (what they call the becoming of the Planetary Age and our terrestrial destiny), then nothing fuels these perceptions more than the social consciousness of totality inspired by our Digital Culture—from the data transmission during the Cold War to mass media and the Internet.[3] Likewise, if Donna Haraway or Peter Sloterdijk have posed the question of redefining the contemporary subject and its environment in terms of human and non-human being, then the present anxieties of the contemporary subject—with his or her techno-scientific consciousness dissolved in fluxes of data, genes and memes—feed this contemporary metaphysics.[4]

Obviously, architecture, as socio-cultural and political construction, faces these determinant cultural events and confronts the collapse of culture and nature proposed by the authors above, which revises the external referents on which modern and classical architectural discipline were founded. Deeply immersed in the digital culture of the image, the architectural discipline confronts this question not only as a general principle of reorganization, but also as a matter of sensibility. That is, the idea of nature will evolve towards a new definition of materiality that will reconfigure our way of looking at our environment. If the question of nature has been approached from global/local perspectives, the question of materiality will also suggest two possible answers in architecture. On the one hand,

1. Science Studies is an interdisciplinary and critical research area that seeks to situate scientific activity in a social, political or philosophical context. It is concerned with the history of scientific disciplines and the interrelationships between science and society. See Manuel De Landa, *Intensive Science and Virtual Philosophy* (New York: Continuum International Publishing Group, 2002); Donna Haraway, *The Companion Species Manifesto: Dogs, People, and Significant Otherness* (Chicago: Prickly Paradigm, 2003); Bruno Latour, *Politics of Nature*, trans. Catherine Porter (Cambridge, MA: Harvard University Press, 2004); Edgar Morin and Anne Kern, *Homeland Earth: a Manifesto for the New Millennium* (Cresskill: Hampton Press, 1998); Ilya Prigogine and Isabelle Stengers, *Order Out of Chaos: Man's New Dialogue with Nature* (New York: Bantam Books, 1984); Michel Serres, *The Natural Contract*, trans. Elizabeth MacArthur (Ann Arbor: University of Michigan Press, 1995). Although noting that these authors have very different backgrounds and expertise, I have found the recent term "Sciences Studies" very useful in connecting this intellectual production. Probably we could also add Peter Sloterdijk—who has worked from metaphysics, or Felix Guattari—from psychoanalysis. The latter popularized the term "Ecosophy," which refers to philosophies which have a predominant eco-centric or bio-centric perspective such as eco-feminism, social ecology, and deep ecology. These works are complementary to Science Studies.

2. Although it may sometimes be difficult to disengage these two trends, we could roughly describe them with these short statements: first, the unity of the ecosystem in which we live; and second the dissolution of the particles of the subjects we used to be.

this new material realm could be understood as an expansion of our bodies through the natural-artificial infrastructure that configures our present world, redefining our place in it. Our common sense of "in-touch-ment" in a single collective (nature, artifacts, and society) promises to reconfigure our present construction of ethics. On the other hand, the digital world magnifies the experience of this new environment, exaggerating all physical sensations. Therefore, the attempt to enjoy a purely sensual world, absolutely informal and fluid, illustrates most of our contemporary fantasies. The actions of engaging our environment as an ethic and of expanding our pure material sensation as a projection provide two main guidelines for realigning our architectural thinking according to the new conceptions of this society-nature.[5]

Finally, these two orientations can be organized around a new figure of action, or in other words, a new symbolic metaphor of the subject. Humans are moving toward an integration into a new ecosystem derived from the redefinition of a society-nature, one in which animals figure as a space of interaction, testing and experimentation. Animals and animal life would evoke the pureness of that sensibility, both sensual and absolutely immersed in its own environment. In our present imagination, the boundaries between man and animal begin to blur. The worrying humanized animals designed by Patricia Piccinini, the animalized symbolism of the artist Matthew Barney in his *Cremaster Cycle* or the biological hybrids in films like David Cronenberg's *Existenz*, populate a new sophisticated bestiary. However, this issue can also be understood as a broader cultural phenomenon in and of itself. As Steve Baker has written on the presence of animals in contemporary art: "a familiar feature of the rhetoric of much recent art and philosophy has been the characterization of the human self or body as impure, hybrid or monstrous, in contrast to the allegedly uncreative propriety of modernist and humanist accounts of subjectivity. Neither the aesthetics of modernism nor the philosophical values of humanism, it is believed, can cope easily with hybrid forms which unsettle boundaries, most especially the boundaries of human and not human."[6] Somehow, the presence of biological monsters, man-animal hybrids, and transgenic hominids has been fostered by a society that considers transculturation and multiculturalism as positive and desirable values. But the idea of a transgenic flux from man to animal, from animal to plant proposes to hybridize different cultures and social conceptions; it also proposes a deeper concern about hybridizing different natures. In a world where culture and nature are collapsing, the collective no longer construes

3. Morin and Kern, *Homeland Earth: a Manifesto for the New Millennium*; Serres, *The Natural Contract*.

4. Haraway, *The Companion Species Manifesto*; Peter Sloterdijk, "El hombre auto-operable", translated by Fernando Lavalle, in *Sileno*, Madrid, (December 2001): 80–91.

5. I will call socio-nature the collective assembly of machines, nature and people (or humans and non-humans), and its common recognition, values, orders and institutions. An idea of common assembly, or in other words, the non-necessity of an exterior to define the things, has been clearly proposed by Latour in *Politics of Nature* and Serres in *The Natural Contract*.

6. Steve Baker, *The Postmodern Animal* (London: Reaktion Books, 2000), 99.

González de Canales

itself as a society in a single nature. In other words, we could say that traditional monoculturalism yields to multiculturalism in the same way that a traditional conception of universality—the singular nature of modernism—opens to the idea of a pluriverse.[7] We could say that the openness that relates man-culture to transculturation also relates human-nature to animalization. Nevertheless, we should also point out that the culture—which confuses subject and infrastructure, which envisions mixture in positive terms, and which fosters the pluralism of natures—is no other than the digital culture that exists within our own cybernetic condition. The biological hybrid has to be understood within that culture as an advanced cyborg, or even as a post-cyborg presence. Could it be that the advent of an age of the digital culture has inevitably led us towards a whole process of human animalization?

Each period relates its own architecture to the very specific subject that represents its intended inhabitant. Hence, modern architects used to build for their ideal subject; the postwar architects wanted to build for the ordinary person; post-modern architects invoked angels; later humans would be recast as cyborgs. Now it seems that the transgenic monster has become the contemporary inhabitant. The old cyborgs have to be updated. Haraway wrote: "I begin with stories, histories, ecologies, and technologies of the space-faring NASA machine-organism hybrids named cyborg in 1960. Those cyborgs were appropriated to do feminist work in the Reagan's Star Wars period of the mid-1980s. By the end of the millennium, however, cyborgs could no longer represent the problematics necessary for serious critical inquiry."[8] However, the common man did not actually displace the ideal man, nor did the angel displace the cyborg. The transgenic animal has assimilated new attributes since the collapse of modernity. As a consequence, it will retain something of the ideal, but also maintain a proximity to the ordinary; it will keep the aura of the angel and the weak confusion of the cyborg. Nevertheless, before entering into the logic of the contemporary transgenic hybrid, two concepts that have qualified the human-animal relationship must be addressed. These two concepts, characteristic of the second half of the twentieth century, are humanism and identity.

Beyond Humanism: Post-History and Post-Human
In the chapter "Animalization" of *The Open*, Giorgio Agamben writes:

> It was in some ways already evident starting with the end of the First World War that the European nation-states were no longer capable of taking on historical tasks and that peoples themselves were bound to disappear. We completely misunderstand the nature of

7. Latour, *Politics of Nature*. 43. *Ed. note*: see also Bruno Latour, *Assembling the Social: An Introduction to Actor-Network-Theory* (Oxford University Press, 2005),116.

8. Donna Haraway, "Cyborgs to Companion Species: Reconfiguring Kinship in Technoscience," in *The Haraway Reader* (New York: Routledge, 2004), 307.

the great totalitarian experiments of the twentieth century if we see them only as carrying out of the nineteenth-century nation states' last great tasks: nationalism and imperialism. The stakes are now different and much higher, for it is a question of taking on as a task the very factual existence of peoples, that is, in the last analysis, their bare life. Seen in this light, the totalitarisms of the twentieth century truly constitute the other face of the Hegelo-Kojevian idea of the end of history: man has now reached his historical *telos* and, for a humanity that has become animal again, there is nothing left but the depoliticization of human societies by means of the unconditioned unfolding of the *oikonomia*, or the taking on of biological life itself as the supreme political (or rather apolitical) task.[9]

Although the end of the history has already been exploited by our contemporary "post" fever anxieties, this concept takes us to French existentialism, and in particular to Alexandre Kojève, who popularized it among others such as Sartre, Merleau-Ponty or Bataille. Kojève re-read Hegel from an anthropological point of view in which the "end of history" implies the end of the obstacles which until now interposed between the man and the control of its own destiny. However, resituating this concept from the perspective of contemporary biopolitics, Agamben poses another interesting historical point: Could we say that totalitarian biopolitics and the total management of biological life is the consequent result of the failure of modernism and its great collective tasks? In other words, when the traditional disciplines of poetry, religion and philosophy become cultural diversions, the "total management" of biological life becomes a focal point.

For a long time the main task of the human collective was to distinguish itself from other realities. To become human was to separate from the animal nature of man, thus to differentiate human from nature. Classical ontology is based on this distinction of man, in this caesura that is extended to all categories: man and animal, nature and history, life and death. The fall of the great tasks is the fall of the collective, but it is also the liberation of the animal nature of man. In light of these reflections, it seems that all the intellectual attempts of recovering the spirit of humanism after the "animalization" of World War II are prone to misinterpretation. What was most wrong about Nazi's animalization was not the animalization itself (the re-introduction of the biological life), but the unleashing of a totalizing management of this animal life. The intellectual problem after World War II was not how to be human again—how to retrieve humanism—but rather how to bring the collective together again maintaining the animal nature of man. Neither Sartre nor Heidegger

9. Giorgio Agamben, *The Open: Man and Animal*, trans. Kevin Attell (Stanford: Stanford University Press, 2004), 76.

González de Canales

seemed to understand this. Peter Sloterdijk has pointed out this misunderstanding in revising the concept of humanism. According to Sloterdijk, it is ridiculous to continue maintaining the humanist dream, which Heidegger wanted to defend for the last time with his letter on humanism, and all he achieved was the masking of an irreversible situation for longer. It is not, therefore, as Heidegger would say, in the waking up of the being.[10] Humanity has to let humanism go. It is time for the reconciliation between men and animals, human and nature.

Co-existing: Hybridizing Natural Identities

Where does one body end and where do the others begin? In our daily life we share vapor and air, microbes, bacteria, and all kind of microorganisms that move from body to body, from men to animals. It is difficult to say, for instance, that the intestinal flora living within us is not part of our body, although according to the old categories of objects and subjects it had to be considered as an alien living organism. The same occurs when someone suffers a xenotransplantation. Is the man who received a pig pancreas more animalized? In a project called Utility Pets, Elio Caccavale asked himself this same question of how to reorganize the relationship between a man and his potential donor pet.[11] For Donna Haraway, this world of biological exchanges have altered our consciousness about ourselves. Following the pig example, every animal would resemble a potential donor, or more exactly, as a prosthetic in which their organs could be considered an extension of our organs. But that does not have a utilitarian meaning. Contrary to cyborgs, cats, pigs, and dogs are neither a projection nor a realization of a human intention. They are just what they are: cats, pigs, and dogs. Her definition of "companion species" has to do with that extension of the human body towards a sort of animalism.[12] In fact, if we try to identify the boundaries of our contemporary subject the question then would be: could we really separate this subject from the others (artifacts, nature, people) if we really want to construct an accurate definition of his identity?

The issue of animalization raises a deep metaphysical problem. Genetic technologies demonstrate the indiscernible boundary between man and animal. Seen in the light of genetics, the question of the definition of the human self changes from the objective spirit in which classical ontology was based (object–subject, culture–nature) to the principle of information (genes). In the genetic fluxes man becomes something like "a vector of forces, a concentration, a possibility of composition."[13] Nevertheless, although the problem of genetics is recent, the question of transcending the classic ontology

10. Peter Sloterdijk, *Notas para el parque humano* (Madrid: Siruela, 2000), See English publication Peter Sloterdijk, "Rules for the Human Zoo: a response to the Letter on Humanism," *Environment and Planning D: Society and Space* 27 (2009): 12–28.

11. In a near future, Caccavale imagines how people will be given a piglet with their own DNA engineered into it when they are born, something like a life assurance. Elio. Caccavale, "Utility Pets" in *Bioland*, ed. Anthony Dunne and Fiona Raby (London, 2003) http://www.dunneandraby.co.uk/content/projects/403/0. There are other interesting projects about man–animal identity in Caccavale's work like *My Bio* (2004) or *Hybrids* (2005)

12. Referring to that relation Haraway writes: "companion species is about a four-part composition, in which co-constitution, finitude, impurity and complexity are what is," Haraway. "Cyborgs to Companion Species," 302.

13. See for example the metaphysical explanation in Sloterdijk, "El hombre auto-operable," 80–91.

was posed long before the arrival of transgenic realities. In fact, could we even ask whether the pure subject of modernity had ever existed? In other words, could it be that man had always been a hybrid?

Different scholars have tried to prove this same hypothesis from different perspectives. Haraway, for instance, has researched the history of human–animal co-habitation through the lens of evolutionary Darwinism. As domestic animals were integrated into human life, their presence could be more accurately situated in human evolution as a co-constitutive element. In fact, this extended cohabitation has shaped the reciprocity between man and animal today. According to Haraway, this shared history, "makes humans and dogs companion species from the beginning. There is like some kind of co-evolution and co-constitution of man and animal."[14] A parallel occurs between man and his artifacts. It would not be strange to suggest that humans have always been cyborgs. Certainly, they have always carried tools and artifacts, which are co-constitutive with man, throughout his biological evolution. From the perspective of a revised evolutionary Darwinism, man has never appeared isolated, pure, and alone; rather his own constitution has much to do with the animals and artifacts raised alongside him.

From another point of view, Bruno Latour has turned to comparative anthropology in order to search for a model of human–nature cohabitation, what he calls the new task of political ecology. But his research has nothing to do with finding natural values in exotic societies. Latour clarifies: "If comparative anthropology offers a helping hand to political ecology, it is once again for a reason that is precisely the opposite of the one advanced by popular ecology. Non-western cultures have never been interested in nature; they have never adopted it as a category. On the contrary, Westerners were the ones who turned nature into a big deal, an immense political diorama, a formidable moral gigantomachy, and who constantly brought nature into definition of their social order."[15] Comparative anthropology offers a model in which humans and non-humans are not separated. The problem for Latour is that once we have accepted that the world is not constituted by this separation of subject from object and nature from society, we have to look for new means of maintaining the new collective of humans and non-humans. "We cannot simply bring objects and subjects together, since the division between Nature and Society is not made in such a way that we can get beyond it. We have to consider that the collective is made up of humans and non-humans capable of being seated as citizens, provided that we proceed to the apportionment of capabilities."[16] Latour cites other non-western

14. Haraway, "Cyborgs to Companion Species," 305–6.

15. Latour, *Politics of Nature*, 43.

16. Ibid., 232.

González de Canales

cultures that have maintained a hybrid collective. Probably, as he asserts in his first works: "if we have never been modern—at least in the way criticism tells the story—the tortuous relations that we have maintained with other nature-cultures would also be transformed."[17]

The Becoming Animal

We have seen that humanism wanted to preserve the old dichotomy of classical ontology, which prevented the reintroduction of biological life into the human orders (Agamben). Likewise, in the light of the fluxes of genes (Sloterdijk), the consciousness of co-evolutions (Haraway) and the assumption of new collectives of humans and non humans (Latour), the traditional preoccupation of identity has become irrelevant. However, to propose an inhabitable environment, one which would close the gap between man and animal, will not be so easy. The question returns: how could we nowadays inhabit with or as animals again? And what are the settings for this cohabitation? The human who opens to the animalism that modernity had repressed is also open to his biology and his physical reality, to his flesh and body. Gilles Deleuze has written about the concept of becoming animal in relation to Francis Bacon's paintings: "This is not an arrangement of man and beast, nor a resemblance; it is a deep identity, a zone of indiscernability more profound than any sentimental identification: the man who suffers is a beast, the beast that suffers is a man."[18] Furthermore, according to Deleuze, Bacon's art confronts man as the suffering piece of flesh that he is, a condition closer to man's animal reality. The artist explores an uncertain and unspeakable zone between human and animal, a new fleshly realm in which spirituality remains: "It is not a lack of spirit; it is a spirit that is body, a corporeal and vital insufflations, an animal spirit. It is the animal spirit of man: a pig-spirit, a buffalo-spirit, a dog-spirit..."[19] For Deleuze, the logic of sensation brings the animal spirit together with a way of painting in which the sensation is neither a simple play with light and color nor a sentimental expression; instead, it is a way of acting-presenting (more than representing) which directly addresses the body as a piece of flesh. Bacon's paintings can be said to directly affect the nervous system, triggering different sensations. "Between a color, a taste, a touch, a smell, a noise, a weight, there would be an existential communication that would constitute the 'pathic' (non representational) moment of the sensation."[20]

Bringing together the concepts of "becoming animal" and the "logic of sensation," Deleuze addresses an artistic production that could provide us with insights as to the animalized environments

17. Bruno Latour, *We have Never Been Modern*, trans. Catherine Porter (Cambridge, MA: Harvard University Press, 1993), 11.

18. Gilles Deleuze, *Francis Bacon, The Logic of Sensation*, trans. Daniel Smith (Minneapolis: University of Minnesota Press, 2003), 22.

19. Deleuze, *Francis Bacon*, 19.

20. Ibid., 37.

for animal-human hybrids. This logic applies to contemporary designers such as Diller+Scofidio, Pipilotti Rist or Petra Blaisse. In the paradigmatic Blur building designed by Diller+Scofidio, a blurred architecture can be understood as a group of molecules floating in the air, moving from body to body, dissolving the self in the logic of the inapprehensible cloud.

On the other hand, the work of the intriguing artist Pipilotti Rist explores the potentiality of unusual and exaggerated relations between forms and colors. The fragments and spots that we perceive in her video-installations seem to connect us directly with deep corporeal and visceral sensations, as overwhelming experiences that can not be processed by the brain. In her most recent work, she expands this logic to multi-screen performances, which wrap us into a fully hyper-sensorial environment. Something similar could be said about the designer Petra Blaisse, who has recently mastered the augmentation of the material properties in the interiors of some OMA's buildings. In her case, the extensive use of sensual curtains and digitally modified materials also brings us closer to this animal ideal of a purely sensitized environment. Finally, at the beginning of the twenty-first century, the sensual path towards animalization is definitively open, bringing us to face our unavoidable becoming animal.

The Biosphere of Machines: Enter the Parasite
Matteo Pasquinelli

The Living Energy of Machines and the Surplus

Behind technology, there is always energy—a surplus of living energy. Despite a few studies on the "materialist energies" that constitute "media ecologies,"[1] media theory today is predominantly the science of digital machines as a universe apart. The digital has become a hegemonic meta-model directed at organizing and arranging the whole of knowledge; the "language of new media" has been articulated and software finally has gained its Software Studies. Nevertheless, an *energetic* understanding of the media economy remains absent from this theoretical trend. A focus on the *outside* of media is missing, as they tend to be described only through internal languages and endogenic categories. It is not simply a McLuhanesque situation: we shape our tools and thereafter our tool shape us. After decades of digital colonization, our tools have now begun to impose their own internal language to describe themselves. Establishing an energetic interpretation of media, on the contrary, means to provide a description of the external energies traversing the machine, and in particular, a renewed concept of *surplus*. Any system should be defined by the excess of energy operating it. Here, surplus is understood as the general form of all the types of energy related to technology in its most fluid and turbulent state: electricity, data, information, knowledge, labour, money, desire.

An important clarification, however, is needed to avoid misinterpreting this notion of surplus as simply another weak version of the philosophy of desire. If on one side of media studies we have the new philologists of digital code, on the other, we encounter sociologists who celebrate the network as a "space of flows."[2] *Code* and *flow*—essentially, the debate around media and networks can be summarized as a dialectic between these two concepts, reminiscent of those other terms from contemporary philosophy: *representation* and *production*. The notion of code inherits the modern gnosis of collective intelligence and the postmodernist cult of the simulation (think of The Matrix, where Baudrillard is cast as the philosopher of hackers). Conversely, the notion of flow is the bastard

1. See Matthew Fuller, *Media Ecologies: Materialist Energies in Art and Technoculture* (Cambridge, MA: MIT Press, 2005).

heir of French post-Structuralism; specifically, the philosophy of Deleuze and Guattari (despite the fact that Manuel Castells originally defined the "space of flows" from the perspective of urban theory).[3] *Flow* becomes—like *code*—an endless and abstract space of linear expansion; it is a cheap form of Spinozian ontology. Between *code* and *flow*, however, resides surplus. Surplus is the excess of energy, but also its accumulation. Most importantly, it always implies asymmetry, friction, and conflict.

A new interpretation or contemporary revision of surplus is needed; a reading consistent with the classical definitions provided by Marx and Bataille, if something like a canonical tradition of the concept can be said to exist. In modern thought, the notion of surplus has been associated with both vitalism (as in excess of energy, desire and *élan vital*) and Marxism (as in surplus-value extorted from the workers and then capitalised). A general figure of surplus, however, can simply refer to different forms of energy traversing the machine. Contrary to the notion of flow, the concept of surplus can never be separated from its consumption, accumulation or sacrifice. Surplus includes its *negative*, rather than being an isolated *positive* process. A surplus of energy does not flow eternally—it is temporary like life, it breaks. If the academic interpretation of Deleuze and Guattari's philosophy of desire is still used to idealize network society as a space of endless flows, it is absolutely necessary today to illuminate the dystopian reality of this energy surplus.

In *The Accursed Share*, Bataille described society as the management of excessive energies, which are constantly being reincarnated as new forms of the state and economy.[4] From his perspective, even the contemporary mediascape can be framed as an ecosystem driven by the outgrowth of natural energies. Media are indeed feral habitats, whose underworld is navigated daily by large torrents of pornography and whose surface is the battlefield for geopolitical warfare. Media are fed by the same excess energy that shapes economic and social conflicts. But has this media energy surplus ever been effectively described? If not, what understanding of energy is unconsciously utilized by traditions of media criticism? Bataille would perhaps be a perfect guide for an exploratory tour of the mediascape, but only after freeing him from the *academic expenditure* and *leisure subcultures* that have worked to neutralise his thought. Indeed, Bataille's vision of the world is not an accommodating one: he consistently maintained that living organisms manifested more energy than what was required to preserve a normal life.

2. "Space of flows" is a concept introduced by Manuel Castells and means a new type of space, enabling synchronicity and real-time interaction without physical proximity. It was first mentioned in: Manuel Castells, *The Informational City: Information Technology, Economic Restructuring and the Urban-Regional Process* (Oxford: Blackwell, 1989).

3. Manuel Castells, *The Rise of the Network Society, The Information Age: Economy, Society and Culture,* Vol. I, (Oxford: Blackwell, 1996), 412: "Our societies are constructed around flows: flows of capital, flows of information, flows of technology, flows of organizational interactions, flows of images, sounds and symbols. Flows are not just one element of social organization: they are the expression of the processes dominating our economic, political, and symbolic life. ... Thus, I propose the idea that there is a new spatial form characteristic of social practices that dominate and shape the network society: the space of flows. The space of flows is the material organization of time-sharing social practices that work through flows. By flows I understand purposeful, repetitive, programmable sequences of exchange and interaction between physically disjointed positions held by social actors."

4. Georges Bataille, *The Accursed Share, Vol. I* (New York: Zone Books, 1988).

Neither growth nor reproduction would be possible if plants and animals did not normally dispose of an excess. The very principle of living matter requires that the chemical operations of life, which demand an expenditure of energy, be gainful, productive of surpluses.[5]

An excess of energy (or wealth in the case of society) is intended for collective growth, but if the system can no longer grow, it is condemned to consume the excess "gloriously or catastrophically."[6] What is the role of technology in contemporary production, consumption and the sacrifice of energy? To pose the question from a different angle: how can media culture be reconceived starting from a radical understanding of surplus? What is the place of surplus theory today and who are the radical thinkers capable of articulating these concerns?

To zoom out from the computer screen, the scenario appears vast and nebulous. The relations of surplus and excess are wide-ranging. The general economy of media is immersed in an accumulation of profits, capital and flows of surplus-value, but also energy consumption and crisis, media violence and Internet pornography, the exploitation of online labour and digital alienation, massive file sharing and the entropy of blogs. There are multiple dark sides to the *technological contract,* but they appear as missing links in today's sanitized media debate.[7] Even contemporary radical thought prefers accommodating descriptions and analysis of the real, with no room for uncontrollable energies. For this precise reason, Bataille's notion of "general economy" is useful as a theoretical framework for considering the broad field of forces beyond traditional economic laws. Fluxes of money, workers, and commodities should not be analyzed from a quantitative point of view alone. Bataille recognized the productive forces behind the real economy, but to avoid any neo-romantic or conservative vitalism, he described them as "biochemical energy." Tearing media away from their abstract destiny in a digital matrix, communication can be re-inscribed into the metabolism of this biochemical paradigm. There is no "Second Life," no autonomous cyberspace—all machines belong to the *bios.* Take the machinic exoskeleton of a car: it still requires biological energy to run, a fossil fuel. *Biochemical energy* or *living energy* is an anti-analytic concept that illuminates the unpredictable hypertrophy of media. *Living energy* as in *living labour*—to bridge the distance between (good) vitalism and Marxism, and break with any natural idealism.

5. Bataille, *The Accursed Share,* 27.

6. Ibid., 21.

7. The idea of a technological contract inspired by Rousseau's social contract means the unconscious and implicit pact we subscribe with technological artefacts. Technological contract is the "complicity" and the consensus around technology that are never discussed and culturally elaborated.

The notion of living energy must be defended from simplistic readings of *biopolitics* (hyper-Foucauldian interpretations of Foucault), especially approaches that identify all forms of life with paranoid concretions of power. More importantly, living energy must be defended from the recent trend of *bioart*, an emerging field innocently supporting a dominant technological paradigm that reduces life to genetic and digital code. Academia and art circles honestly believe that life and technology can be progressively or critically merged while they play with DNA under the framework of popular genetic technologies. Interestingly, here the word *life* points always to *code* (the *logos*) but never to *energy* (the *bios*, in my interpretation). As life is trapped into a set of instructions, radical thought cannot escape the cage of a *born-again digital* scientism. "Data made flesh" is both an artistic and neoliberal gnostic credo.[8] The argument must be reversed to avoid both neo-scientism and obscurantism: how did the flesh start producing data? How did human evolution embrace the digital? Where does the living energy of machines flow? Some basic questions are necessary to inaugurate a "general economy" of machines, and hopefully, a new field of investigation for media culture and art.

More precisely, what kind of surplus are we looking for? Surplus of energy, libido, value, money, or information? Machines are systems that accumulate energy surplus and consume, transform, and dissipate it. According to alternative media discourse, Bataille could only be enrolled to justify a sort of *digital potlatch*, a furious but ultimately sterile mass reproduction of digital copies. On the contrary, keeping with his theory of general economy, we must actually acknowledge how energy is maintained inside machines, crossing and feeding a multitude of devices. In *The Accursed Share*, Bataille himself considers labour and technology as an extension of life that accumulates energy and provides conditions for an enhanced reproduction of the species. Like "tree branches and bird wings in nature," technology opens new spaces to be populated.[9] Coincidently, at the same time as Bataille's writings, anthropologist André Leroi-Gourhan began to consider biological evolution as a model for technical development.[10] *Anthropogenesis* necessarily implies *technogenesis*, as Bernard Stiegler reminds us, in a sort of "zootechnological determinism."[11] But there is something more: technology accompanies the double movement of the excess of life—production and dissipation. It must be said, however, from the greasy engines of early industrialisation to the aseptic minimal design of the latest personal media, the living materiality

8. See Robert Mitchell and Phillip Thurtle eds., *Data Made Flesh: Embodying Information* (New York: Routledge, 2004).

9. Georges Bataille, *The Accursed Share*, 36: "The space that labor and technical know-how open to the increased reproduction of men is not, in the proper sense, one that life has not yet populated. But human activity transforming the world augments the mass of living matter with supplementary apparatuses, composed of an immense quantity of inert matter, which considerably increases the resource of available energy."

10. See: André Leroi-Gourhan, *L'Homme et la matière* (Paris: Albin Michel, 1943) and André Leroi-Gourhan, *Milieu et techniques* (Paris: Albin Michel, 1945). See also Deleuze and Guattari, *A Thousand Plateaus* (Minneapolis: University of Minnesota Press, 1983), 499: "Leroi-Gourhan has gone the farthest toward a technological vitalism taking biological evolution in general as the model for technical evolution: a Universal Tendency, laden with all of the singularities and traits of expression, traverses technical and interior milieus that refract or differentiate it in accordance with the singularities and traits each of them retains, selects, draws together, causes to converge, invents."

11. Bernard Stiegler, *La technique et le temps, 1: La faute d'Epiméthée* (Paris: Galilée, 1994), translated in English as *Technics and Time, 1: The Fault of Epimetheus,* (Palo Alto: Stanford University Press, 1998).

Pasquinelli

of technology has been removed by "Machinic Studies"—it has become but an unconscious companion of the everyday life of the human libido.

What happens when information technologies and especially digital networks enter the mediascape and biosphere? What kind of energy do digital machines incarnate? Just a further extension of biochemical energy like the classical technologies that Bataille had in mind? My hypothesis is that digital machines are a clear bifurcation of the *machinic phylum*: the semiotic and biologic domains represent two different strata of evolution, and the digital machine a further bifurcation compared to analogue technologies. The energy of semiotic flows is not equivalent to the energy of material and economic flows. The separation of the digital stratum from the analogue was not a smooth transition. Digital technology developed an *intensive* scale of depth and a meta-modelling language that was completely missing in the analogue world.[12] From a political point of view, that separation implies that any attempt to directly translate the digital into the social only produces partial effects and confusion, if not disaster. Of course, the two spheres interact, but not in the symmetrical and specular way that digital culture is regularly conceived—an ideology that will be introduced as *digitalism*.

Michel Serres and the Cybernetic Parasite

Energy always flows in one direction. For those acquainted with the scenario of the network society and its celebration of the *space of flows*, a safari with Bataille along the ecosystems of excess is useful for rediscovering the dystopian nature of capitalism. In Bataille, economic surplus is strictly related to a libidinal excess, enjoyment, and sacrifice. Yet between endless fluxes and their "glorious expenditure,"[13] a specific explanatory model for the accumulation of surplus is still missing. Attuned to the undercurrents of French vitalism, Michel Serres captures the asymmetry of universal life in the conceptual figure of the *parasite*. In his influential book of the same title, Serres describes how the exchange of energy between organisms is never equal, but always constituted by a parasite stealing energy and feeding on another organism. From this basic premise, Serres builds a new universal economy.

> The parasitic relation is intersubjective. It is the atomic form of our relations. Let us try to face it head-on, like death, like the sun. We are all attacked, together.[14]

12. Science fiction has explored the different evolutions of the couple digital-analog with the opposition of the two genres cyberpunk and steampunk.

13. See: Georges Bataille, "The Notion of Expenditure" in *Visions of Excess,* (Minneapolis: University of Minnesota Press, 1985).

14. Michel Serres, *Le parasite* (Paris: Grasset, 1980), translated in English as *The Parasite* (Baltimore: Johns Hopkins University Press, 1982), 8.

Cellular dystopia: at the dawn of the computer age (*Le Parasite* was originally published in 1980), the concept of the parasite becomes the pioneer of a materialistic critique of all the forms of thought based on a binary model of energy. For Serres, the elementary link is always ternary, involving a third element affecting the other two. Weirdly, the "semiconductors" of Serres steal energy instead of computing:

> Man is a louse for other men. Thus man is a host for other men. The flow goes one way, never the other. I call this semiconduction, this valve, this single arrow, this relation without a reversal of direction, "parasitic."[15]

The dimension of energy excess can be either positive or negative, depending on the point of observation. If Bataille identifies the expenditure of energy after production, Serres demonstrates how "abuse" has always been at work since the beginning of accumulation. "Abuse appears before use"—with Marxist connotations, an *abuse-value* is introduced as preceding both *use-value* and *exchange-value*. In the language of Serres' energy analytics, "it is the arrow with only one direction." An asymmetrical arrow that absorbs and condenses energy in a natural continuum passing through organisms, animals and human beings: "the parasite parasites the parasites," the mantra repeats.

In the early 1980s, the parasite made its appearance like a dystopian version of Deleuze and Guattari's desiring machines: an endless exploitation of surplus is posited as a counterpart to the endless production of desire. The parasite is the molecular odd side of nature, society, economy and technology. It actually represents quite a serene account of human existence, despite Serres' description of *The Parasite* as "the book of evil." Serres places the human at the top of the parasitic hierarchy of ecology and environments, while society itself is inscribed within an implicit civil war of parasites.

> History hides the fact that man is the universal parasite, that everything and everyone around him is a hospitable space. Plants and animals are always his hosts; man is always necessarily their guest. Always taking, never giving. He bends the logic of exchange and of giving in his favour when he is dealing with nature as a whole. When he is dealing with his kind, he continues to do so; he wants to be the parasite of man as well. And his kind want to be so too. Hence rivalry.[16]

15. Serres, *The Parasite*, 5.

16. Ibid., 24.

Serres describes society and economics as an extension of natural forces. His language even favours living figures to technological metaphors. Recognizing the Leviathan of both the collective and micro-parasites, Serres inaugurates a zoomorphic democracy. His philosophy is directed toward "reversing anthropomorphism" and proposing "an organic model for the members of a society," but without promoting a new totality through naturalistic nostalgia.

> We parasite each other and live among parasites. Which is more or less a way of saying that they constitute our environment. We live in that black box called the collective; we live by it, on it, and in it. It so happens that this collective was given the form of an animal: Leviathan. We are certainly within something bestial; in more distinguished terms, we are speaking of an organic model for the members of a society. Our host? I don't know. But I do know that we are within. And that it is dark in there.[17]

In the end, are we confronted finally with a global scenario of pure parasitic life? Somehow, for Serres, the parasite is more a technical or neutral concept with no inherent political connotations. Parasites produce life: "Everything ferments; everything rots. Everything changes." In his history of humankind, the "alliance with the parasites" is understood as being a constituent element of the process of anthropogenesis and the history of civilization (for instance, with food processing and health care: bread and wine are fermented and purified by "good" parasites such as yeast). Symbiosis with other organisms is a complex relation. Serres reveals how endo-colonisation is a common practice of the relation between humans and nature.

> Our relation to animals is more interesting—I mean to the animals we eat. We adore eating veal, lamb, beef, antelope, pheasant, or grouse, but we don't throw away their "leftovers." We dress in leather and adorn ourselves with feathers. Like the Chinese, we devour duck without wasting a bit; we eat the whole pig, from head to tail; but we get under these animals' skin as well, in their plumage or in their hide. Men in clothing live within the animals they devoured. And the same thing for plants. We eat rice, wheat, apples, the divine eggplant, the tender dandelion; but we also weave silk, linen, cotton; we live within the flora as much as we live within the fauna. We are parasites; thus we clothe ourselves. Thus we live within tents of skins like the gods within their tabernacles. Look at him well-dressed and adorned, magnificent; he shows— he showed—the clean carcass of his host.[18]

17. Serres, *The Parasite*, 10.

18. Ibid.

The symbiosis with machines is complex too. Serres shares the same vitalism of Bataille, but additionally provides a revolutionary punctual model of the relation between material and immaterial, biologic and semiotic, economy and media. The organic model of the parasite is also embraced as the core concept of a new (organic) understanding of media ecosystems.[19] Indeed, prophetically, Serres introduced cybernetics (and its extension, the network) as a late manifestation of the parasitic food chain.

> The parasite invents something new. He obtains energy and pays for it in information. He obtains the roast and pays for it with stories. Two days of writing the new contract. He establishes an unjust pact; relative to the old type of balance, he builds a new one. He speaks in a logic considered irrational up to now, a new epistemology and a new theory of equilibrium. He makes the order of things as well as the states of things—solid and gas—into diagonals. He evaluates information. Even better: he discovers information in his voice and good words; he discovers the Spirit in the wind and the breath of air. He invents cybernetics.[20]

After depicting the "information revolution" as a truly emancipatory movement for decades, it is quite difficult to acknowledge its parasitic side. Furthermore, Serres applies the same parasitic model to intellectual labour and to the network itself (as *techné* is an extension of the deceptive nature of *logos*): "This cybernetics gets more and more complicated, makes a chain, then a network. Yet it is founded on the theft of information, quite a simple thing."[21]

Serres' opportunistic relation between intellectual and material production may sound traditionalist, but even when Negri and Lazzarato began to describe the "hegemony of intellectual labour," the exploitative dimension of capital over mass intellectuality was clearly apparent.[22] Today, the *immaterial parasite* (as the symbiosis of digital networks and immaterial labour can be interpreted) has become endemic—everyone is carrying an intellectual and cybernetic parasite. What then happens to the notion of multitude, intended as the self-organization of the general intellect into an antagonistic subject, when the parasite of intellectual labour enters the political arena? What happens to Free Culture, digital commons and peer-to-peer paradigms when the network infrastructure is itself portrayed as a vampiric tentacular creature? From this perspective, it is finally necessary to reintroduce a sharp asymmetry between the semiotic and the social, the technological and the biological levels —between the material and the immaterial. If network technology

19. Jussi Parikka offers an example of "parasitic media analysis" but focusing only on "(nonorganic) ways of network life": Jussi Parikka, "Contagion and Repetition: On the Viral Logic of Network Culture," *Ephemera: Theory and Politics in Organisation*, volume 7, no.2 (2007): 287-308. Web: www. ephemeraweb.org/journal/7-2/7-2parikka.pdf

20. Serres, *The Parasite*, 36.

21. Ibid., p. 37.

22. Maurizio Lazzarato and Antonio Negri, "Travail immatériel et subjectivité," in *Futur Antérieur*, n. 6 (Summer 1991), Paris.

Pasquinelli

must be recognized as a new socio-political form, this can only be done on the basis of a dynamic and tactical alliance with an asymmetrical and dystopian economy.

The parasite re-orientates the energetic relation between machines and life. Without trying to rewrite the history of communication in one line, media have routinely been described according to particular recurring models: information channels, body prostheses, mimetic devices, desiring machines, virtual worlds, autonomous devices and, more recently, cooperative and social networks. Cyberpunk and cyborg subcultures (respectively, online and offline hybrid organisms) represented the founding mythologies of the new techno-multitudes, but their dystopian and parasitic nature has gradually been sanitized and flattened out through a progressive technological fetishism. Deleuze and Guattari's concept of desiring machines has found a similar destiny, even if it represented a rigorous conceptualization of the machinic colonization of the biosphere against both vitalism and mechanisms. And a *binary representation* of the machine is still maintained today by legions of media artists and academics following this tendency. The binary model of the cyborg can be stressed as the real subtext of media culture since its foundation, binary because the notion of cyborg is ultimately synthesized through a dualistic exchange of energy.

The challenge is not to perpetuate anthropocentrism and techno-fetishism, but to reveal which understanding of surplus is unconsciously inscribed in these models of media. The founding figure of the cyborg does not provide any economic understanding of the biochemical energy exchanged through technology. To understand the parasitic dimension of the network, it is more useful to refer to Deleuze and Guattari's *apparatus of capture* developed in *A Thousand Plateaus*. For this concept, surplus is extracted according to the "trinity formula" of rent, profit, and taxation, however, the third age of technical machines also carry along their own unique forms of *machinic enslavement* and *social subjection*.[23] "If motorized machines constituted the second age of technical machines, cybernetic and informational machines form a third age that reconstructs a generalized regime of subjection."[24]

A decade before in *Anti-Oedipus*, Deleuze and Guattari introduced three types of surplus value: code surplus, flow surplus and machinic surplus. Machinic surplus, in particular, is the surplus extracted by a machinic assemblage (freely composed by

23. Deleuze and Guattari, *A Thousand Plateaus*, 490.

24. Deleuze and Guattari, *A Thousand Plateaus,* 505.

humans, tools, animals, etc). The merit of Serres is to encapsulate these conceptual elements in an elegant formula: the parasite.

After three decades of "machinic" literacy, a move towards a dystopian *zoology of machines* must be established—even if only to rescue Deleuze and Guattari's thought from becoming a technical language or an academic *procedural knowledge*. However, this new "animal" model for digital culture is also needed to fight the combinatory model of genetics that has become the dominant toolbox whenever life is approached. Following Deleuze and Guattari's *geologism* and De Landa's *new materialism* of morphogenesis, more efforts should be focussed on a *new organicism*.[25] A partial or open organicism is required as an affective approach to the world of machines positioned against the dominance of *digitalism* (as I define the cult of the *code* against the materiality of *energy*). Organicism does not mean a new vitalism, but an acknowledgement of the dystopian reality driven by unstable cycles of surplus, entropy, and negentropy. Capital, machines, and organisms need surplus to breed. A natural or artificial ecosystem is never generous. There is always an asymmetrical arrow crossing it, an asymmetrical tension dividing the political field.

By the conceptual figure of the immaterial parasite, I name the transformation and exploitation of the *bios* through the technological and semiotic domain. Material energy and economic surplus are not simply absorbed or consumed by new semio-technologies; they are also reallocated in favour of specific nodes of the machinic network. Like a natural form of life, the immaterial parasite runs efficiently, and consumes less energy than what it accumulates to function. The immaterial flow extracts surplus from material energies through continuous exchanges and assemblages between different domains. Electricity turns to data, data to communication, communication to desire, desire to money, money to knowledge, knowledge to technology, and so on. The media economy is a symbiosis of different strata, a continuum of horizontal and vertical exchanges, but it is certainly not a flat market based on purely cooperative exchanges.

The immaterial parasite initially functions as a spectacular device. Simulating a fictional world, building a collaborative environment or simply providing communication channels, the immaterial parasite forms a symbiosis of desire with its host. The biological definition of parasite is crucial since it always implies an *alliance* and *non-hostile* relation: the parasite never desires the death of its host. The parasite is not a vampire, but a symbiont.

25. See chapter 3 "The Geology of Morals" in: Deleuze and Guattari, *A Thousand Plateaus*, 553: "The strata are extremely mobile. One stratum is always capable of serving as the substratum of another, or of colliding with another, independently of any evolutionary order... Above all, between two strata or between two stratic division, there are interstratic phenomena: transcodings and passages between milieus, intermixings". See also: Manuel De Landa, *A Thousand Years of Nonlinear History* (New York: Zone Books, 1997).

Pasquinelli

In this sense, the relation between the machine and the human is a relation of mutual desire, of seduction and fetishism. Similarly, even the economy of the immaterial parasite is not based on direct exploitation and profit extortion. On the contrary, economic rent becomes the dominant form of metabolism. The immaterial parasite always belongs to a diverse family and can survive in different kinds of habitat. Its tentacles, for instance, can innervate the metropolis (real estate speculation through the "creative cities" hype), the mediascape (rent over material infrastructures and online space monopolies), the software industry (exploiting Free Software to sell proprietary hardware), the knowledge economy (revenue on intellectual property), the financial markets (stock exchange speculation on collective behaviour) and many other potential spaces.

Bioscleave House (Life-Span Extending Villa)
Arakawa and Gins

Architect:
Arakawa + Gins

Design and construction:
1999–2008

Location: East Hampton, NY

Project Manager:
Joke Post

Detailing Architects:
Lawrence Marek, Aryeh Siegel

Engineering:
Dewhurst, MacFarlane and Partners

Size: 2,700 sq ft.

Client: Angela Gallman

The Bioscleave House, drawing its name from how an organism cleaves to its surroundings, challenges the behavioral norms of dwelling on many levels simultaneously, as is suggested by the house's title: "Life-Span Extending Villa."[1] The Bioscleave House (1999–2008) is the first realized residence in Arakawa and Gins' important body of work that extends from the mid-1960s puzzle-paintings, to literary works and installations, to buildings such as the Site of Reversible Destiny (2005), Yoro Park, in Gifu, Japan and the Reversible Destiny Lofts (2007) in the Tokyo suburb, Mitaka. The Bioscleave House proposes a radical defamiliarization of domesticity by placing the dweller in a constant state of imbalance and disorientation. Bioscleave's sloping floors and pin-wheeling array of self-similar rooms extract from architecture a new set of spatial experiences; in this building, Arakawa and Gins offer a posthuman reformulation of the dynamic between body, environment, and technology.

In an introduction to the Arakawa and Gins special issue of *Interfaces*, Jean-Michel Rabaté observes of the architects that "Their revisionist re-definition of man in this post-human(istic) state is tantamount to launching a scientific revolution, if not a revolution tout court. [...] For Arakawa and Gins, the revolution that matters is a revolution in thought, and it will ineluctably be brought about by the creation of a new logic of sense and the senses."[2] Rethinking requires terms that are not burdened by conventional usages and that can point to new relational logics outside of disciplinary confines, hence we find in terms such as *biocleave* the echoes of both scientific and cultural vocabularies. Arakawa and Gins use the term to define a starting point for architecture:

> Start by thinking of architecture as a tentative constructing towards a holding in place. Architecture's holding in place occurs within and as part of a prevailing atmospheric condition that others routinely call biosphere but which we, feeling the need to stress its dynamic nature, have renamed biocleave.[3]

Fig. 7.3, 7.4 Elevations from south-east (© Ariane Lourie Harrison).

Fig. 7.5 Ground plan of Bioscleave House (courtesy of Arakawa and Gins).

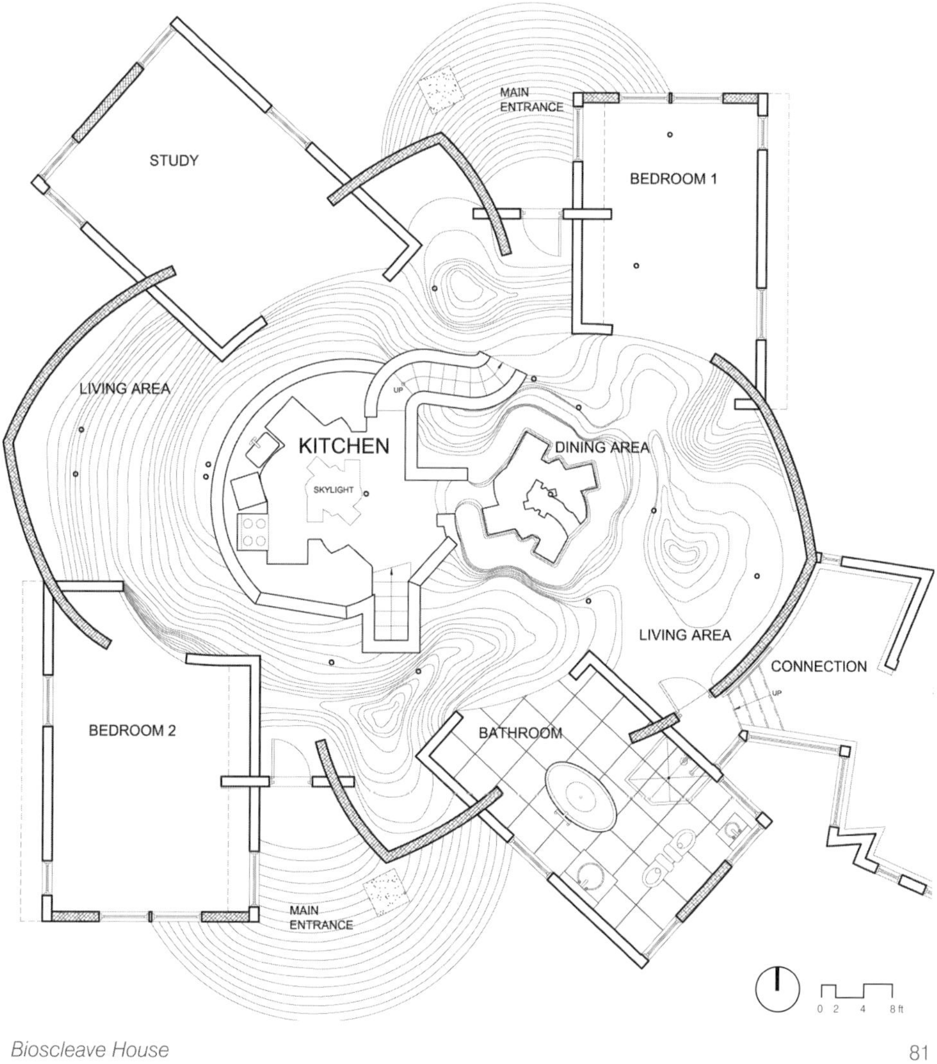

STUDY

MAIN ENTRANCE

BEDROOM 1

LIVING AREA

KITCHEN

SKYLIGHT

DINING AREA

LIVING AREA

CONNECTION

BEDROOM 2

BATHROOM

MAIN ENTRANCE

0 2   4   8 ft

In their book *Architectural Body* (2002) Arakawa and Gins describe the dynamic and performative engagement—physical and conceptual— with the subject that architecture must provide. Rather than a static construction, architecture becomes "a constructing towards a holding in place."[4] The individual subject is replaced with the ecological idea of "organisms that person": to person is a species-specific behavioral descriptive verb, and likewise it is possible, in Arakawa-Gins' language, to "dog, giraffe or cockroach the world."[5] This linguistic approach becomes a means of replacing the lexicon of form with an ecology of new concepts: *biocleave*, *landing sites*, *procedural architecture*, and *architectural body* are terms that interlock, charting a sensitive ("tentative" to use the architects' word) relation between humans and the environment through the medium of architecture. Pragmatic *biocleave* replaces Platonic *biosphere*. The word *cleave* appears frequently in Gins and Arakawa's texts and is carefully chosen. *Cleave* is an auto-antonym: it holds together the contrasting impulses to join and divide; it is a Janus-faced figuration that engages a pragmatic ambivalence within the world rather than ideal transcendence of it. *Biocleave*, in ecological terms, can be understood as a continuous adaptive fit that organism and environment make to each other. Fitness takes physical form as a *landing site*, a term meant to challenge the given view of an architectural site as a static and clearly defined area. A landing site is a temporary space defined by actions: "perceiving," "imaging," and "dimensionalizing."[6] A landing site is a situation, and as a term it encourages situational awareness within the "organism-person-environment," the constellation that Gins and Arakawa privilege.

The *architectural body* is term that describes Arakawa and Gins's central idea that the body is a physical place rather than a time-based identity. Starting from the philosophical observation that the meaning of life is constructed around a concept of time— questions of origin and progress are time based, as is that of mortality—Gins and Arakawa suggest that this centrality of time creates a focus on the individual subject as center of consciousness, that time constructs identity, free will, and the rational idea of destiny. Reversing this time-based ontology, Gins and Arakawa propose a space-based or procedural architecture approach, which involves "a continual anticipating, self-guarding, accommodating, allowing, bypassing . . . all bodily dynamics."[7]

The dynamic condition produced by the design, layout and materiality of the Biocleave House offers one way to experience procedural architecture. Its undulating and uneven floor surface keeps the body in disequilibrium; its windows disrupt conventional horizons and create disorientation. Even the enclosures that spin off from the central living-kitchen area, without closing off as private rooms, echo each other across the central living space. The architectural body links architectural space and bodily space as an embodied awareness. For Arakawa and Gins, it is also critical that the subject maintain an ecological awareness of his or her constant interconnectedness with the architecture; this requires a constant physical engagement, which contrasts dramatically with the desire for comfort of conventionally defined inhabitation. If comfort can be defined as the least possible expenditure of effort, then the Biocleave House thwarts this convention. Destabilization and effort are the necessary costs of a larger social agenda in which conceptual and physical complacency are considered by the architects to be a "totally mad and relentless wasting of life."[8] Gins and Arakawa propose biocleaving not only as a conceptual architectural engagement but also as a concrete strengthening of the body and

Lourie Harrison

Fig. 7.6 Interior overlooking kitchen countertop, north east bedroom, area 1 (© Ariane Lourie Harrison).

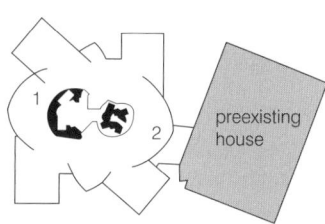

Fig. 7.7 Interior overlooking kitchen table, southeast view, area 2 (© Ariane Lourie Harrison).

Fig. 7.8 Interior, skylight (© Ariane Lourie Harrison).

Fig. 7.9, 7.10 North-west bedroom and interior view facing north (© Ariane Lourie Harrison).

mind: constant discomfiture defies physical and perceptual atrophy. The fundamental provocation of Gins and Arakawa's work—that architecture can challenge the time-based ontology of mortality—registers on both metaphoric and practical terms:

> If you want to do the impossible, should you be desirous of tilting at windmills, why not build to your own specifications the windmills at which you wish to tilt? . . . And further still, why not build windmills that tilt back toward you knowingly and informatively?[9]

The penetrating logic of this proposal cuts through architectural conventions of orthogonal windmills and of humans adapting to architecture, asking in plain terms, why not build an architecture that is more responsive to human physicality and that joins itsef to humans (if not to other animals) as a body—an architectural body?

The transformation of the domestic interior into a destabilizing landscape is one of the Bioscleave House's most didactic proposals, yet its execution remains allied with several architectural discourses of place. Forming half of a U-shaped complex around an entry courtyard, the Bioscleave House is attached by a corridor to a preexisting structure on its East Hampton site. This enframed organization is repeated at the smaller scale of the Bioscleave House, which organizes four rectangular rooms around a free-form living space defined by translucent polycarbonate walls and an undulating rammed-earth and cement floor. In the initial conception of the Bioscleave's floor as a rammed-earth construction, and even in its final form of a mix of concrete and foam, its interior stages a topographic condition that disrupts domestic comfort. The undulating floor surface is dotted with smaller mounds or footholds: each step in this house must be tentative (literally), yet each step instills the primal pleasure of physically sensing one's space, echoing Kenneth Frampton's discussion of the tactile pleasure of Aalto's brickwork stairs.[10] The interior landscape metaphor incorporates the mounded floor as well as the forest of vertical poles—ready handholds to enable the inhabitant to offset the destabilization of every step, provided the effort is made. Windows positioned either high under the roof or hugging the floor obscure the horizon line and reinforce the sense of spatial disorientation established by the almost dizzying effect of centripetally-organized, self-similar rooms. The mounded floor surface spills out of two entrances to literally connect the interior topography to that of the outdoors.

If the disorienting quality of the Bioscleave House is one aspect of its immersive capacity; another is the remarking of body and space that it performs with diagrammatic precision by repeating the figure of the floorplan. The tabletop of the kitchen tends to

Lourie Harrison

be the first physical encounter with the shape of the Bioscleave House's floorplan, albeit inverted and at a reduced scale. A second image of the plan hovers above, cut away from the ceiling as a skylight. The kitchen floor materializes a third instance of the house plan, perceptible only as the play of void against the kitchen counter edge. A final iteration of the plan was envisioned (though not built) as a garden labyrinth, comprising nested plans made of vegetation.[11] These materializations of the house plan locate the body in a space that is both physical and diagrammatic, while reiterating the idea that "architecture must be made to fit the body as a second, third, fourth . . . skin."[12] For Arakawa and Gins, procedural architecture offers an emergent response to sustaining, in their terms, "the very viability the species."[13] Species survival requires the spatial intertwining of biology and topology—synthesized in a term by Gins and Arakawa as *biotopology*—in overcoming the limitations of the physical body. According to Gins and Arakawa, "A bio-topologist produces and lives within a multidimensional interactive diagram which she forms in relation to a work of procedural architecture."[14]

Fig. 7.11 Exterior, north entrance (© Ariane Lourie Harrison).

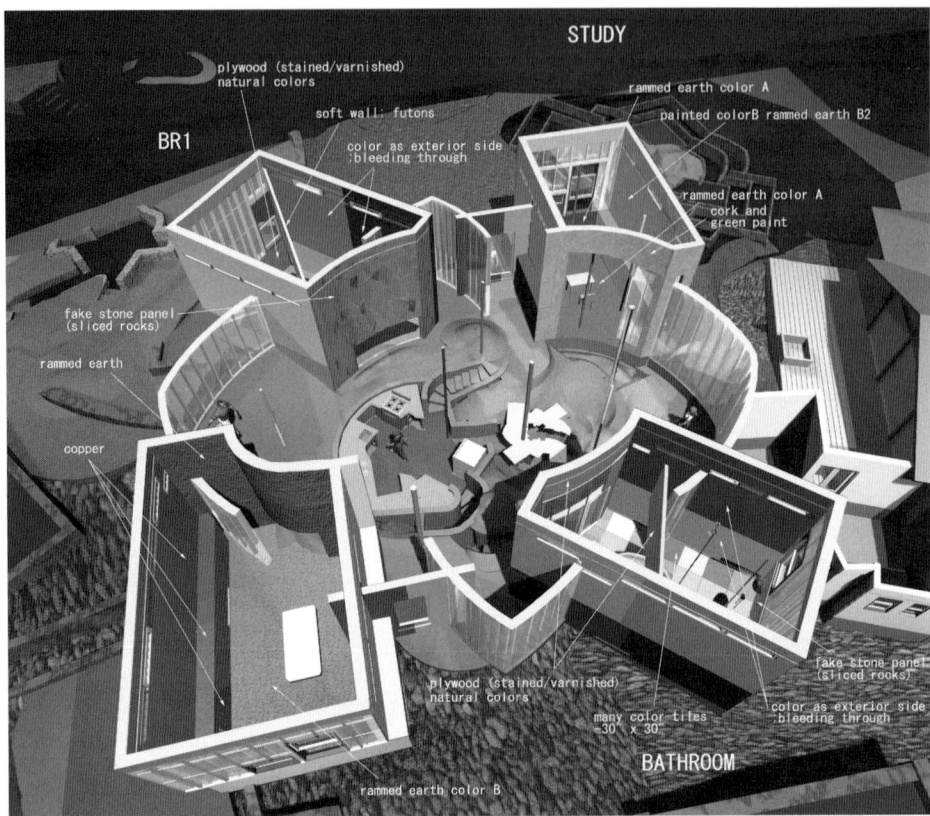

STUDY

plywood (stained/varnished)
natural colors

rammed earth color A

soft wall: futons

painted colorB rammed earth B2

BR1

color as exterior side
;bleeding through

rammed earth color A
cork and
green paint

fake stone panel
(sliced rocks)

rammed earth

copper

plywood (stained/varnished)
natural colors

fake stone panel
(sliced rocks)

many color tiles
~30" x 30"

color as exterior side
;bleeding through

BATHROOM

rammed earth color B

Fig. 7.12 Rendering of Bioscleave House, interior, view to north (courtesy of Arakawa and Gins).

Arakawa and Gins' efforts to locate architecture within a dialogue shared by other disciplines led them to found the Architectural Body Research Foundation in 1987 as an interdisciplinary platform for collaboration with practitioners of experimental biology, neuroscience, quantum physics, experimental phenomenology, and medicine. Like the postwar architects and artists exploring cybernetic exchanges between body and space, Arakawa and Gins believe that "it is desirable to keep the body in a state of imbalance for as long as possible. The actions, the range of actions, possible to the body for righting itself and regaining its balance will both define and reveal the body's essential nature."[15] This sense of circulation as a tentative process recalls the idea of inhabitable circulation put forward by Claude Parent and Paul Virilio in the mid 1960s; the effort required to navigate the Bioscleave House's sloping floors reiterates Parent's intention that inclined planes and the oblique function incite movement and self-directed change.

While the Bioscleave House awaits its certificate of occupancy (the Mitaka Lofts meet code and are viewed as a prototype for mass constructed housing), it confronts building code with the desire to animate space beyond architectural convention yet within a pragmatic understanding of physical atrophy, particularly in the aging. "People, particularly old people, shouldn't relax and sit back to help them decline. They should be in an environment that stimulates their senses and invigorates their lives."[16] Arakawa and Gins' stress that the environment for the aging adult should be structured so as to create adversity, offering obstacles around which the inhabitant must navigate in order to accomplish the normal tasks of living maintains the body in a constant state of exercise.

That architecture might present a means of extending human lifespan has struck some as dubious,[17] yet Arakawa and Gins' proposal maintains a rational link to the now established science that treats regular exercise as an age-retardant. Harrison and Finch describe how mobility and exercise counter aging on a molecular level: reducing the load of oxidized proteins and lipids in the body, stimulating stem-cell formation and serving as an anti-inflammatory.[18] New molecular models for aging remain in the forefront of contemporary research and are part of the technological substrate according to which human life has dramatically extended its limits. Yet these models reiterate the role of the active body in resisting rapid aging. The architectural body, as conceived by Arakawa and Gins participates in this process. In this sense, while not scientifically proven nor even tested, the Bioscleave House creates a compelling representation of the architectural surround as an embodied response to our posthuman environment.

NOTES:

1. http://www.reversibledestiny.org/Reversible_Destiny_-_Arakawa_and_Gins_-_We_Have_Decidede_Not_to_Die/Bioscleave_House.html#grid (Accessed 2/14/2012).
2. Jean-Michel Rabate, "Introduction to the Arakawa and Gins Special Issue," *Interfaces* 21/22 (2003): 5.
3. Madeline Gins and Arakawa, *Architectural Body* (Tuscaloosa: The University of Alabama Press, 2002), 48.
4. Gins, *Architectural Body*, 23.
5. Ibid., 1.
6. Ibid., 5–22.
7. Ibid., 53.
8. Ibid., 95.
9. Ibid., xix.
10. Kenneth Frampton, "Towards a Critical Regionalism: Six Points for an Architecture of Resistance," in Hal Foster, ed., *The Anti-Aesthetic: Essays on Postmodern Culture* (Bay Press, 1983), 28.
11. Jondi Keane, "A Bioscleave Report: Constructing the Perceiver," in *Architecture and Philosophy: New Perspectives on the Work of Arakawa and Madeline Gins,* ed. Jean-Jacques Lecercle and Françoise Kral (New York: Editions Rodopi, 2010), 152.
12. Gins, *Architectural Body*, xv.
13. Madeline Gins and Arakawa, *Making Dying Illegal* (New York: Roof Books, 2006), 60.
14. Gins, *Making Dying Illegal*, 73.
15. Madeline Gins and Arakawa, *Architecture: Sites of Reversible Destiny* (London: Academy Edition, 1994), 18.
16. Fred Bernstein, "A House Not for Mere Mortals," *New York Times*, April 3, 2008.
17. Ibid.
18. Seth Harrison, "The Next Subject," see Section I of this anthology, 54–5.

Fig. 8.1 View from east (courtesy of Arons en Gelauff).

The Plussenburgh
Arons en Gelauff

Architect:
Arons en Gelauff, Floor Arons and Arnoud Gelauff

Landscape Architects:
Inside Outside, Petra Blaisse

Location:
Rotterdam IJsselmonde, NL

Competition: 2001

Construction: 2004–6

Client:
SOR (Stichting Ouderenhuis-vesting Rotterdam)

Size:
104 apartments, 250 m² in recreational space, parking

Awards:
nomination NAI award 2006; nomination Mies van der Rohe award 2007

The posthuman approach foregrounds the fact that technology has penetrated into virtually all aspects of the global environment and has played a significant role in extending the human lifespan. Most would attest that basic technologies alone (hygiene, pasteurization, assured food supply) have contributed to the increase in longevity within industrialized nations by some thirty years during the past century. Experts debate the extent to which the battle against disease waged by the medical research complex, deploying the more sophisticated technologies of biotechnology, will be able to extend human lifespans further. But the clear impact of technology on human longevity has led to questioning long held assumptions regarding how to design environments for older persons. Aging is increasingly understood to be a contingent mixture of genetic, economic, social, and technological factors. These produce an array of lifestyle expectations that defy common perceptions of aging as a condition of retreat and isolation. If the posthuman deployment of technology is partially responsible for increased human longevity, then it may also be possible that the posthuman approach to

Lourie Harrison

Fig. 8.2 West elevation (courtesy
of Arons en Gelauff).

Fig. 8.3 Ground floor and site plan
(courtesy of Arons en Gelauff).

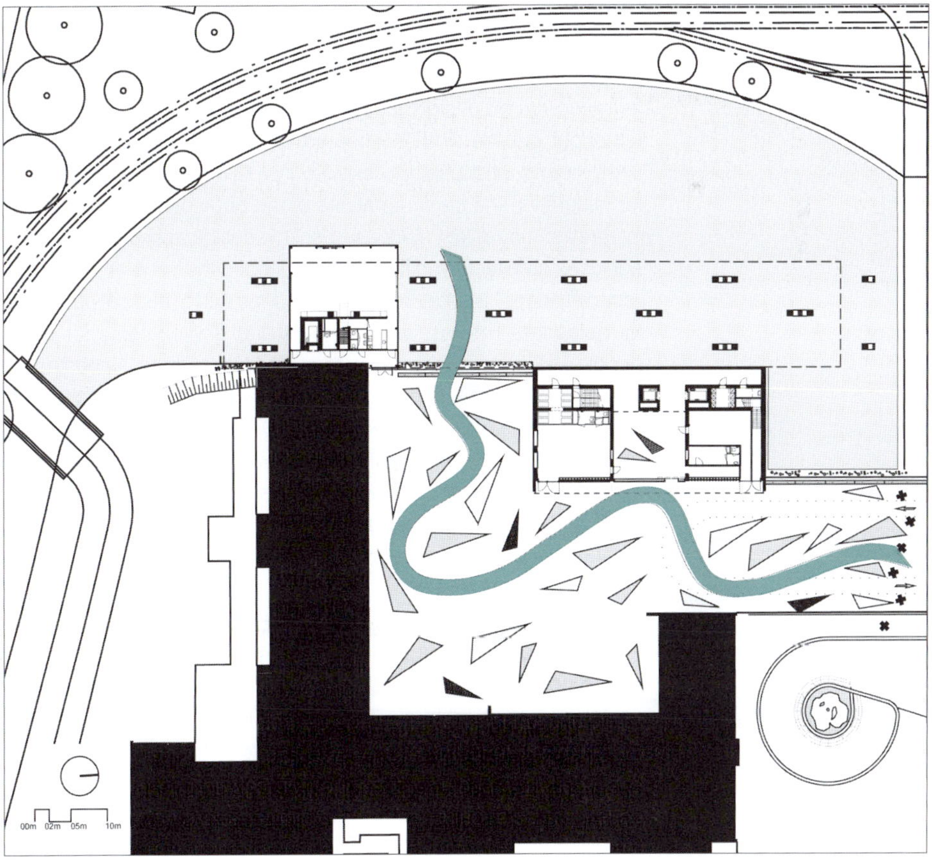

Fig. 8.4 Entry hall (courtesy Arons en Gelauff © Jeroen Musch).

architecture makes aging visible in its complexity and as an important program for design. By extension, spaces for aging are being rethought outside of the accepted ergonomic, medical, or functional norms, and begin to explore instead a variety of programs for integrating the transformations of the body over time. The term *integration* may in fact mark a key shift in design approaches for the aging. As architecture in the 1970s broached the issue of aging as a "special needs" market, initial solutions turned to medical protocols for guidance. The resulting products and environments for older people stigmatized their users through standardized, unaesthetic, and even ineffective design. Contemporary design initiatives, such as those tracked by "New Aging and Design," a 2009 conference at University of Pennsylvania, demonstrate the range of options for what we might call a non-institutionalized and non-medicalized approach to aging, one that embraces the change wrought by technology and that aims to that integrate rather than segregate older subjects.

The Dutch architecture firm Arons en Gelauff has, in its considerable body of work, considered design for the aging from this posthuman vantage point. Arons en Gelauff argues that aging, for a "hippie" generation born during the demise of modernism, is no longer a condition of retreat and retirement.[1] Similarly, their design approach refrains from marginalizing the aging, a philosophy that becomes evident in many of Arons en Gelauff's

Lourie Harrison

housing projects over the last decade. Several of the architects' projects demonstrate their attempts to integrate assisted living and medical facilities into urban and suburban residential complexes: the Oosterhoogebrug project in Groningen combines an assisted living facility for Alzheimer patients with an apartment complex; the Rokade in Groningen (2007) connects a dense residential complex to a neighboring nursing facility; and the Blijvenburg in Rotterdam (2009) incorporates elder care into a residential complex intended for young families. In each of these works Arons en Gelauff counter the prevailing logic that the aging subject should be assigned to calm and pastoral environments (regardless of their degree of isolation); they expose this logic as a quarantine strategy. Instead, Arons en Gelauff integrate the aging into a vision for an age-diverse community.

The Plussenburgh, a senior residence with 104 living units, exemplifies the integrative logic of architecture for the "new aging." The Plussenburgh was initiated with a 2001 invited competition for a senior housing project of architectural quality to further the

Fig. 8.5 Common area (courtesy of Arons en Gelauff © Jeroen Musch).

Fig. 8.6 Main entrance with colored path and landscaping by Inside / Outside (© Ariane Lourie Harrison).

Fig. 8.7 Garage (courtesy of Arons en Gelauff).

redevelopment of the Rotterdam suburb, IJsselmonde.[2] The neighborhood had undergone some development in the 1970s, characterized by cement and brick low scale "accessible" blocks around a medical nursing complex. The competition was sponsored by Harry Rietveld, director of the Housing Corporation for the government-subsidized developer Stichting Ouderenhuisvesting Rotterdam (SOR), the agency that has built over 4,000 housing units for Dutch seniors. The competition site flanks the IJsselmonde nursing home, medical center and hospice. Envisioning that a new senior housing facility could become a revitalizing element of IJsselmonde, SOR requested an architectural—if not iconic—design that could nevertheless maintain several functional ties to the neighboring nursing complex. For example, the hospice enjoyed a view onto the nearby canal and the competition brief requested that proposals preserve this visual relationship. Arons en Gelauff's proposal addressed the brief with flair and exuberance, earning them the commission.

The Plussenburgh playfully subverts the architectural conventions of retirement homes, many of which are apparent in the senior housing complex that surrounds the completed project. Asserting the sensibility of a new generation that Arons en Gelauff describe in their recent monograph, *Anything but Grey* (2011),[3] the Plussenburgh introduces imposing vertical and horizontal block forms to create one of the tallest structures in the immediate area, bringing an urban density to the suburb. This is achieved with a small footprint, which secures a park for its inhabitants along with access to the canal. Its rectangular horizontal volume—elevated eleven meters over a shallow pool—is supported on canted beams, maintaining the hospice's untrammeled view of the water. Otherwise, linkages to the nursing facilities are made deliberately hard to discern. Arons en Gelauff's strategy of "stealth-care architecture" involves hiding the visual and programmatic markers of aging: an inconspicuous

elevator connects the new residence to the medical facility and accommodates continuous and specialized medical attention for all residents. A bold color palette replaces the muted tonalities of conventional retirement institutions: 200 shades of reds, oranges, and pink glazing capture the gaze as one of the dominant notes of color in the area (and is surprisingly cheerful against the storm clouds that dogged my visit in summer 2011). The pixelated effect of the glazed facades nods to the "boomer" generation's embrace of technology. The exuberant facades, illustrating what Arons en Gelauff describe as their target market's desire for differentiation, are matched by the flexibility of the Plussenburgh's five typical plans,[4] and create spaces that range from colorful corridors to common rooms overlooking IJsselmonde's fields and low-rise structures. Other spaces in the building—the accommodating lobby with a view of the water, or the community rooms on the ground floor—create relatively free and unprogrammed spaces for sociability.

The landscaping strategy developed by Petra Blaisse and her firm Inside Outside further explodes the logic of sequestration with its interweave of interior and exterior. A bright orange footpath marks the entry of the Plussenburgh, snaking across black asphalt, leading from the street to the main doorway on the side of the complex. The path weaves under the northeast building to extend out over the canal creating a dramatic view platform. The wavy path and its terminus over water oppose the ergonomic norms for older people, supplementing the experience of walking with delight and discovery. A textured garden covers the underground parking lot below, while the verdant theme continues indoors with the grassy carpet in the recreation space and the bamboo-textured patterns set into concrete walls; both bring the outdoors into the space yet also subtly replace the conventional handrail or non-slip flooring with visually charged and tactile design elements. Gonzàles de Canales suggests that

Fig. 8.8 Garage (courtesy of Arons en Gelauff).

Fig. 8.9 Southeast view facing medical facilities adjacent to the Plussenburgh, with colored path and landscaping by Inside / Outside (© Ariane Lourie Harrison).

Fig. 8.10 Balconies on west facade (courtesy of Arons en Gelauff).

Petra Blaisse, in her "augmentation of the material properties," appeals to "corporeal and visceral sensation" and produces sensory effects that transcend conventions of "age appropriate" settings.[5]

This idea dovetails with Arons en Gelauff's conception of the Plussenburgh's public spaces: "In housing for the aged the private realm shrinks in size, but it should grow in quality and be supplemented by possibilities for collectivity and high quality, buzzing public space around."[6] The ideas that animate the Plussenburgh reflect our increasing understanding how architecture can not only buffer but also capacitate the aging subject. As Seth Harrison notes in his discussion with gerontologist Caleb Finch, a major shift in the last decades involves understanding the plasticity of aging.[7] If an extension of average life expectancy to ninety years could create a society in which, according to Dr. Finch, "a third of the people who reached ninety would have difficulty in living independently due to cognitive limitations, even if they didn't have clinical Alzheimer's,"[8] then we can understand the importance of new aging programs for residential space. Buildings such as the Plussenburgh engage the post human interdependency between the aging, the built environment and medical-therapeutic technologies.

Fig. 8.11 Common area (courtesy of Arons en Gelauff © Jeroen Musch).

NOTES

1. http://www.aronsengelauff.nl/, (accessed 1/25/2012).

2. Nico Saleh, "de Plussenburgh / Arons en Gelauff Architecten," ArchDaily. (28 Jul 2008). http://www.archdaily.com/3959, (accessed 3/14/2012).

3. AronsGelauff Architects, *Anything but Grey* (Amsterdam, 2011).

4. *Kleurrijk wonen in De Plussenburgh*, Stichting Ouderenhuisvesting Rotterdam (2005), I was not able to access individual apartments during my visit July 2011.

5. Francisco González de Canales, "Approaching a New Biotope," *The International Journal of The Arts In Society*, 2, no. 2 (2007): 36.

6. AronsGelauff Architects, *Anything but Grey*, 4.

7. Seth Harrison, "The Next Subject," see Section I of this anthology, 52–60.

8. Dr. Caleb Finch in discussion with Seth Harrison, "The Next Subject," see Section I of this anthology, 65.

Fig. 9.1 View from northwest (courtesy of R&Sie(n)).

I'm Lost in Paris
R&Sie(n)

Architect: R&Sie(n)

Creative team:
François Roche,
Stephanie Lavaux, Jean Navarro

Completion date: 2008

Location: Paris, France

Size: 130 m^2

Hydroponic system:
designed by R&Sie(n)

"Humans and animals retain reserves of wildness. For animals we have only this word and its slippery meaning; for humans there are numerous words—schizophrenia, legendary psychasthenia, claustrophobia, the uncanny . . . all of which raise the specter of the animal and the animal caught by space."[1]

As if drawing on Catherine Ingraham's meditation on architecture's residual "wildness," the architectural firm R&Sie(n), founded by François Roche and Stephanie Lavaux in 1989, explores the charged spatial dynamics instigated by phobias, anxieties, and personality disorders. This line of interest materializes in the firm's considerable body of work: from Shadow and Light (1990), a project that stages the split personality "between Shinto and manga" of a Japanese Art Foundation, to a Tokomashi parking structure/exhibition space (2003) that materializes the fear of earthquakes.[2]

R&Sie(n)'s 2008 Parisian residence, titled I'm Lost in Paris, foregrounds the phobias embedded in the seemingly benign concepts of sustainable design; the conventions of passive cooling, natural ventilation, and green roof are made lushly dangerous, overtaking the entire structure and function of the home. In I'm Lost in Paris, the house becomes a host for a parasite: a matrix of over one thousand hydroponic ferns wraps and effectively hides the residence. Today's equivalent to the modernist "machine for living," R&Sie(n)'s ecological experiment occupies its urban setting as a vegetal cyborg.

Lourie Harrison

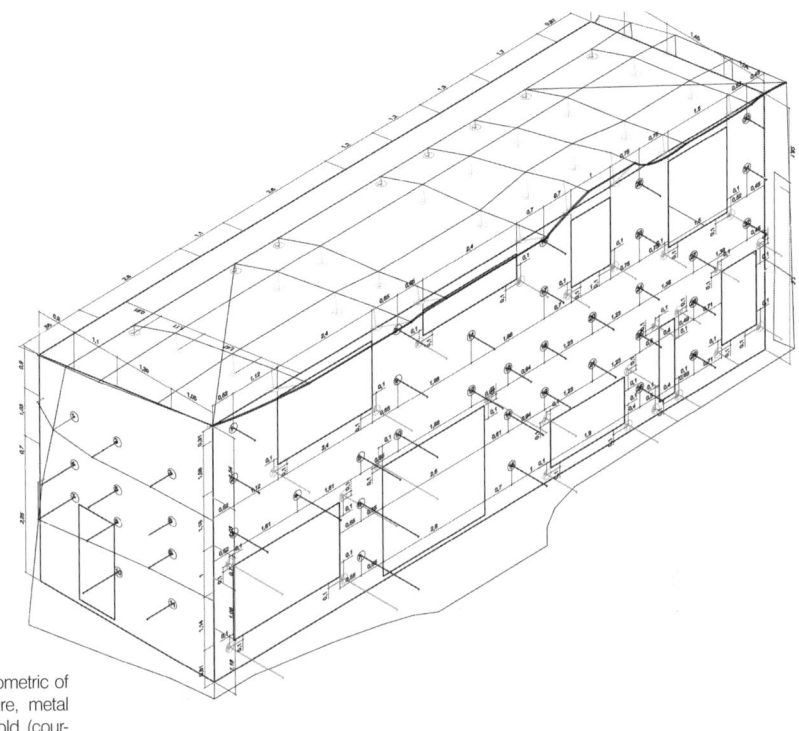

Fig. 9.2 Axonometric of concrete structure, metal and mesh scaffold (courtesy of R&Sie(n)).

Fig. 9.3 Aerial view (courtesy of R&Sie(n)).

I'm Lost in Paris

Fig. 9.4 Construction (courtesy of R&Sie(n)).

I'm Lost in Paris threatens, like kudzu colonizing roadside spaces, to transform human infrastructure into a landscape of shaggy green monsters. This overgrown Parisian residence fits in with other hybrid environments built by R&Sie(n): structures that defy the parametric sensibility despite their computational design; structures that are mischievous, deviant, and uncannily tuned to trigger human anxieties. R&Sie(n)'s design strategy here hybridizes home, laboratory, inhabitation, and infrastructure in an assemblage that constitutes a new urban "nature," exemplifying what Elizabeth Grosz describes as the corporeality of the connections between body and city:

> Cities have always represented and projected images and fantasies of bodies, whether individual, collective, or political. In this sense, the city can be seen as a (collective) body-prosthesis or boundary that enframes, protects, and houses while at the same time taking its own forms and functions from the (imaginary) bodies it constitutes.[3]

In I'm Lost in Paris, reanimating the imaginary body—the connection between city, residence, and the architectural subject—begins with the selection of the site, a Parisian courtyard in the 5th Arrondissement. "Building in a Parisian courtyard is problematic at the best of times as planning laws require two–thirds of surrounding residents to approve construction," notes architectural critic Catherine Slessor in her discussion of the project's five-year construction period.[4]

Lourie Harrison

The Parisian courtyard also symbolically records the bureaucratic imposition of spatial order in seventeenth-century Paris: courtyards absorbed the asymmetry of the medieval city, hiding it behind a systematic order of regular facades.[5] The courtyard today registers the contemporary politics of property, featuring protected views, prized sunlight, and common areas typically guarded by a surly concierge.

Into this regulated space of Parisian apartments, R&Sie(n) inserts a tuberous appendage. I'm Lost in Paris is essentially covert, or what the architects describe as "a private laboratory/duck blind cabana."[6] An outer green skin, made up of a metal armature and tensile supports for the hydroponic infrastructure, becomes protective camouflage for the new residence—a two-story concrete structure, wrapped in a thin plastic shell and polyurethane coat for insulation and hidden within an architectural ectoderm of ferns. The wrapper is as ideological as it is playful, as Roche describes:

> To territorialize architecture is certainly not to drape it in the cheap finery of a new tendency, of a style which is by nature as out of sync and "separate" as those that have just been consumed. To territorialize architecture, so that the site reweaves a social, cultural and aesthetic tissue, is to enshrine it in what it was preparing to destroy, it is to extract from the landscape, urban or otherwise, the substance of a construction, not only in comparison to the physical spaces inhabiting it but also the climate, materials, perceptions and effects.[7]

In the two main spatializations of nature in the city—the park and the waterfront—vegetation remains within the boundaries delineated by planners, designers, and architects. Yet R&Sie(n)'s I'm Lost in Paris intentionally overwhelms its site with vegetation in order to create an urban incongruity that suggests both fecund and regenerative primeval forest and overgrown ruin. The building simultaneously announces the arrival of new life and delivers the gloomy prognosis of the memento mori: that latent within each well groomed Parisian lot is potential (and eventual) decay. A house for cybernetic vegetation might recall projects such as John Hejduk's houses for the suicide and for the mother of the suicide, architecture that plays off of the anxiety provoked by the "undesirable neighbour" yet that protects the heterogeneity of urban subjects. The hybrid subject produced by the city, following Grosz's description of a collective body prosthesis, is an assemblage that ties the occupant to a network of scales, from property-line controversies to urban ecology.

Site is inscribed in R&Sie(n)'s work not through the regionalist discourses of place but rather through the provocative interpretation of "indigenous" materials, with a focus on the animate qualities that can transform these indigenous materials into important (if often overlooked) actors when deployed in an assemblage. What is indigenous to the Parisian courtyard? R&Sie(n) retrieves unexpected materials from French culture: artisanal traditions of glass blowing, the ostensibly French innovation of green walls (patented by French horticultural engineer Patrick Blanc), and the medicinal qualities of the *Dryopteris filix-mas* fern, common to Northern Europe but promoted by Louis XV as an anthelmintic (a remedy for expelling parasitic worms).[8] The fern "acts" two parts simultaneously in the historical drama developed from the site and played out in its materials: the human residence becomes the host for a vegetal parasite (the ferns), the curative properties of which include the evacuation of intestinal parasites. Yet the fern's acting of two parts simultaneously also provides a contemporary register of a schizoid quality, which Gilles Deleuze and Félix Guattari describe in terms of a subversive inhabitation between the categories that organize capitalist society.[9]

If pollution in other examples of R&Sie(n)'s work provides a contemporary register of site-specific or indigenous materials, in I'm Lost in Paris, the fern instead registers the toxicity of its urban environment.[10] Deployed in the NASA's Skylab as a method to reduce the level of VOCs in the sealed chambers of the large satellite, the hardy fern is often used to remedy Sick Building Syndrome inside the home, chemically fixing in soil the common pollutants trichloroethylene, benzene, and formaldehyde. Yet there is no "sick" interior nor even soil in R&Sie(n)'s fern network: its hydroponic apparatus establishes the ferns in a liquid or sponge-like matrix, into which a nutrient-enriched rainwater—made visible in glass beakers—is piped, drop by drop. Excess liquids are captured and recycled, nutrients rebalanced. This liquid, "fermented," in Roche's terms, symbolizes the mix of filtered toxins and anthelmintics.

Roche describes the performative aspect of the entire ensemble: "The neighborhood is both attracted by the green aspect and repulsed by the brewage and the process to produce it."[11] For a contemporary Paris in which the green walls of Patrick Blanc symbolize the public conception of urban ecology (yet provide little or no ecological benefit),[12] R&Sie(n)'s creation of an aggravated, resonating "green wall" undermines what Roche describes as the "green alibi" of sustainable design:[13] "[Architecture's] capacity for laying hold of a territory without enslaving it has to do with the troubled identity developed there, with the 'at odds' nature of the implementation, with the ambiguity of the process of extraction/transformation of which the materials are by-products."[14]

Rather that stabilizing identity, the building excavates the "troubled identity" of the human-environment assemblage. The fern envelope in R&Sie(n)'s work has the disturbing potential to encroach or unbuild the functionality of the human residences organized around the courtyard. While Javier Arbona has thoughtfully interpreted the objective of this green wrapper as being to provoke anxiety,[15] we might observe that the ferns of I'm Lost in Paris equally provoke wry ecological commentary. Since this commentary is delivered by the ferns, we might say that R&Sie(n) has responded to Latour's challenge to create architecture enabling non-humans to speak. The ferns parody the conditions of humans in the city, in that the façade installation relies on feed-lines to supply energy and to siphon off waste. The ferns are monstrous monoculture, one that, while not foreign to Parisian climes, aggressively multiplies across the building facade. It parodies nativist ecological agendas by replicating the "domestic" fern in unnatural quantities and conditions, and it conscripts its human inhabitants into an extensive caretaking role.

Fig. 9.5 West facade, interstitial space (courtesy of R&Sie(n)).

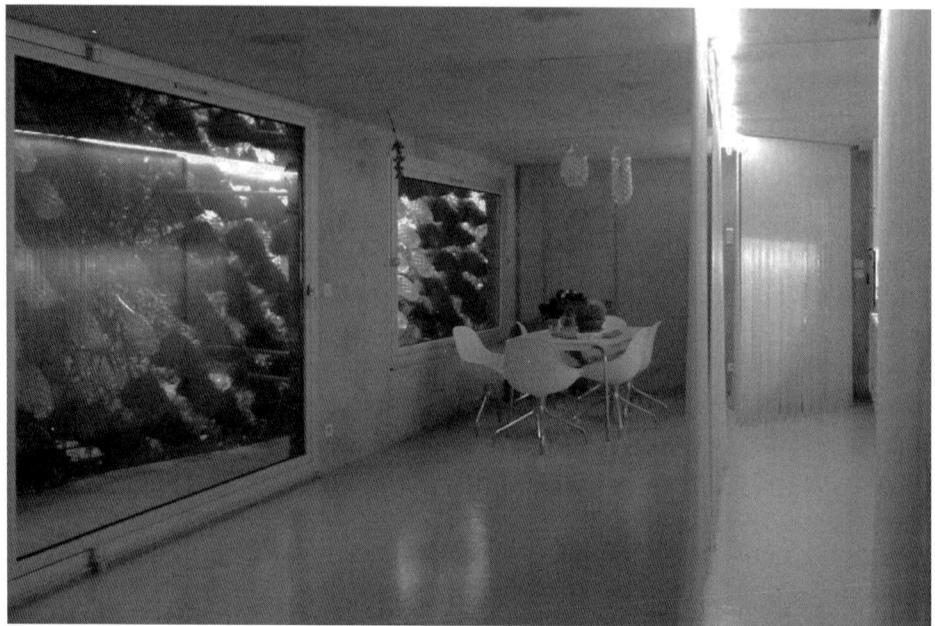

Fig. 9.6 Interior (courtesy of R&Sie(n)).

The fern becomes a cyborg, yet one whose facture mixes high technology and artisanal technologies, undermining the critical role of technology as advanced in Donna Haraway's "Cyborg Manifesto" (1985). In addition to pipes, tubes, and wires, 300 glass bulbs are part of the infrastructure sustaining the plants. These glass vessels contain a liquid mix of nutrients and assiduously harvested rainwater in a further nod to sustainability. Resembling giant glass berries, these glass vessels are individuated, blown by hand,[16] a clear reference to artisanal manufacture that folds into R&Sie(n)'s critique of the economizing imperatives of sustainability. Such allocation of labor and luxury for a non-human subject (a fern) reiterate the logics of Bataille's 1949 *The Accursed Share*, a text that set forth an ecological vision of a "general economy" within which surplus energies (sexual and sensual) remain outside of the restricted economy.[17] These surplus energies, "cursed," outside of conventional usage, nevertheless fuel species' growth. As Pasquinelli describes, "Bataille recognized the productive forces behind the real economy, but to avoid any neoromantic or conservative vitalism, he described them as 'biochemical energy'."[18]

The anemic vision of society configured by modernist efficiency, parametric optimization, or corporate greenwash ignores the persistence of behaviors that engage this economy of excess. Inverting the morality of the typical "sustainable house," R&Sie(n)'s Parisian residence simultaneously signals the hybrid subjectivity of its vegetal cyborg and that of the contemporary city as "a topography of spectacular energy expenditure."[19]

Lourie Harrison

Fig. 9.7 Glass beakers
(courtesy of R&Sie(n)).

NOTES:
1. Catherine Ingraham, *Architecture, Animal, Human: The Asymmetrical Condition* (New York: Routledge, 2006), 86.
2. R&Sie(n) Architects, *Corrupted Biotopes*, *Design Documents 05* (Korea: DADMI, 2004),163.
3. Elizabeth Grosz, *Architecture from the Outside* (Cambridge, MA: MIT Press, 2001), 48.
4. Catherine Slessor, "I'm Lost in Paris House," *Architectural Review* (Oct. 2009), http://www.architectural-review.com/buildings/im-lost-in-paris-house-by-rsien-paris-france/8600688.article, (accessed 3/15/2012).
5. Pier Vittorio Aureli, *The Possibility of an Absolute Architecture* (Cambridge, MA: MIT Press, 2011), 150.
6. R&Sie(n) Architects, http://www.new-territories.com/lostinparis.htm (accessed 1/12/2012).
7. François Roche, DSV and Sie., "Situation," *Quaderns* 217 (1997): 97.
8. Abel Tennant Stafford, *Vegetable Materia Medica: The Vegetable Materia Medica and Practice of Medicine* (Batavia: DD Waite Printer, 1837), 370.
9. Gilles Deleuze and Félix Guattari, *Anti Oedipus: Capitalism and Schizophrenia* (Minneapolis: 1983 University of Minnesota Press, 1983).
10. Andreas Ruby, "Hyperlocality: On the Archaeology of the Here and Now in the Architecture of R&Sie… ," *Spoiled Climate* (Basel: Birkhäuser, 2004), 68.
11. http://www.new-territories.com/lostinparis.htm (accessed 3/15/2012).
12. Matthew Gandy, "The Ecological Facades of Patrick Blanc," *AD Territory* 80, no. 3 (2010): 33.
13. François Roche, "Bodies without Organs—BwO," *AD Neoplasmatic Design* 78, no. 6 (2008): 68.
14. Roche, DSV and Sie., "Situation," 98.
15. Javier Arbona, "Its in Your Nature: I'm Lost in Paris:" *AD Territory* 80, no. 3 (2010): 46–53.
16. R&Sie(n) Architects, http://www.new-territories.com/lostinparis.htm (accessed 1/12/2012).
17. Allan Stoekl notes in Bataille's work, "there is a heterogeneous matter whose very virulence presents its exclusion in any 'closed economy' of use, practicality or recuperation." Allan Stoekl, *Bataille's Peak: Energy, Religion, and Postsustainability* (Minneapolis: University of Minnesota Press, 2007), 18.
18. Matteo Pasquinelli, *Animal Spirits: A Bestiary of the Commons* (Rotterdam: NAi Publishers, 2008), 56.
19. Stoekl, xix.

I'm Lost in Paris

Section II

Posthuman Assemblages

Give Me a Gun and I Will Make All Buildings Move: An ANT's view of Architecture
Bruno Latour and Albena Yaneva

Our building problem is just the opposite of Étienne–Jules Marey's famous inquiry into the physiology of movement. Through the invention of his "photographic gun," he wanted to arrest the flight of a gull so as to be able to see in a fixed format every single successive freeze-frame of a continuous flow of flight, the mechanism of which had eluded all observers until his invention. What we need is the reverse: the problem with buildings is that they look desperately static. It seems almost impossible to grasp them as movement, as flight, as a series of transformations. Everybody knows—and especially architects, of course—that a building is not a static object but a moving project, and that even once it is has been built, it ages, it is transformed by its users, modified by all of what happens inside and out side, and that it will pass or be renovated, adulterated and transformed beyond recognition. We know this, but the problem is that we have no equivalent of Marey's photographic gun: when we picture a building, it is always as a fixed, stolid structure that is there in four colors in the glossy magazines that customers flip through in architects' waiting rooms. If Marey was so frustrated not to be able to picture in a successive series of freeze-frames the flight of a gull, how irritating it is for us not to be able to picture, as one continuous movement, the project flow that makes up a building. Marey had the visual input of his eyes and was able to establish the physiology of flight only after he invented an artificial device (the photographic gun); we too need an artificial device (a theory in this case) in order to be able to transform the static view of a building into one among many successive freeze-frames that could at last document the continuous flow that a building always is.

It is probably the beauty and powerful attraction of perspective drawing that is responsible for this strange idea that a building is a static structure. No one, of course, lives in Euclidian space; it would be impossible, and adding the "fourth dimension," as people say— that is, time—does not make this system of coordinates a better cradle for "housing," so to speak, our own complex movements. But when you draw a building in the perspective space invented in the Renaissance (and made more mobile but not radically different by computer assisted design), you begin to believe that when dealing

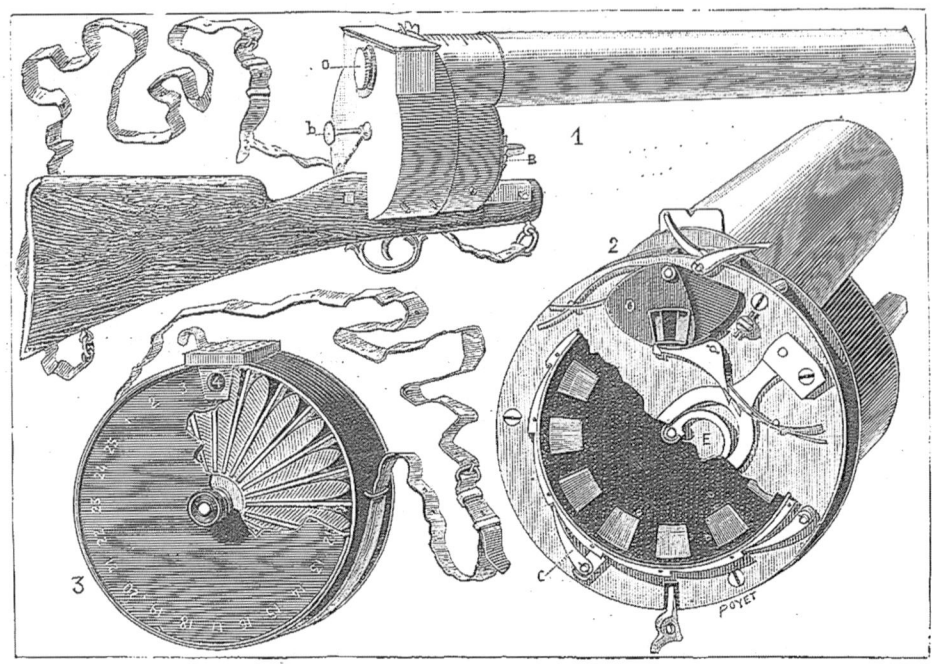

Fig. 10.1 Étienne–Jules Marey, "Photographic Rifle," *La Nature* (April 22 1882), 289, Engraving by Louis Poyet (courtesy of La BIU Santé, Université Paris Descartes).

with static objects, Euclidian space is a realist description. The static view of buildings is a professional hazard of drawing them too well.

This should not be the case, since the 3D-CAD rendering of a project is so utterly unrealistic. Where do you place the angry clients and their sometimes conflicting demands? Where do you insert the legal and city planning constraints? Where do you locate the budgeting and the different budget options? Where do you put the logistics of the many successive trades? Where do you situate the subtle evaluation of skilled versus unskilled practitioners? Where do you archive the many successive models that you had to modify so as to absorb the continuous demands of so many conflicting stakeholders—users, communities of neighbors, preservationists, clients, representatives of the government, and city authorities? Where do you incorporate the changing program specifics? You need only to think for one minute, before confessing that Euclidian space is the space in which buildings are drawn on paper but not the environment in which buildings are built—and even less the world in which they are lived. We are back to Marey's problem in reverse: everyone agrees that a dead gull cannot say very much about how it flies, and yet, before time lapse photography, the dead gull was the only gull whose flight could be studied; everyone agrees that the drawing (or the photography) of a building as an object does not say anything about the "flight" of a building as a project, and yet we always fall back on Euclidian space as the only way to "capture"

Latour and Yaneva

what a building is—only to complain that too many dimensions are missing. To consider a building only as a static object would be like gazing endlessly at a gull, high in the sky, without being able ever to capture how it moves.

It is well known that we live in a very different world than that of Euclidian space: phenomenologists (and psychologists of the Gibsonian school) have never tired of showing that there is an immense distance in the way an embodied mind experiences its surroundings from the "objective" shape that "material" objects are said to possess. They have tried to add to the "Galilean" bodies rolling through Euclidian space, "human" bodies ambling through a "lived" environment.[1] All this is very well, except it does nothing more than to reproduce, at the level of architecture, the usual split between subjective and objective dimensions that has always paralyzed architectural theory—not to mention the well-known split it has introduced between the architectural and engineering professions (and not to mention the catastrophic consequences it has had on philosophy proper). What is so strange in this argument is that it takes for granted that engineering drawings on a piece of paper and, later, projective geometry offer a good description of the so-called "material" world. This is the hidden presupposition in the whole of phenomenology: we have to add human subjective intentional dimensions to a "material" world that is well described by geometric shapes and mathematical calculations. The paradoxical aspect of this division of labor envisioned by those who want to add the "lived" dimensions of human perspective to the "objective" necessities of material existence is that, in order to avoid reducing humans to things, they first had to reduce things to drawings. It is not only the architects, his or her clients, de Certeau's pedestrians, Benjamin's *flaneurs* that do not live in Euclidian space—it is also the buildings themselves! If there is an injustice in "materializing" human embodied experience, there is an even greater injustice in reducing matter to what can be drawn. Matter is not "in" Euclidian space for the excellent reason that Euclidian space is our own way of accessing objects (of knowing and manipulating them) and making them move without transformation (that is, maintaining a certain number of characteristics); it is definitely not the way material entities (wood, steel, space, time, paint, marble, etc.) have to transform themselves to remain extant. Descartes's *res extensa* is not a metaphysical property of the world itself, but a highly specific, historically dated and technically limited way of drawing shapes on blank paper and adding shadows to them in a highly conventionalized way.

1. Dalibor Vesely, *Architecture in the Age of Divided Representation: The Question of Creativity in the Shadow of Production* (Cambridge, MA: MIT Press, 2004); Steven Holl, Juhani Pallasmaa and Alberto Pérez-Gómez, *Questions of Perception: Phenomenology of Architecture* (San Francisco: William Stout, 2006).

To press the (admittedly philosophical) point further, it could be said that Euclidian space is a rather subjective, human-centered or at least knowledge-centered way of grasping entities, which does no justice to the ways humans and things get by in the world. If phenomenology may be praised for resisting the temptation to reduce humans to objects, it should be firmly condemned for not resisting the much stronger and much more damning temptation to reduce materiality to objectivity.

But what is even more extraordinary is that this famous Euclidian space, in which Galilean objects are supposed to roll like balls, is not even a good descriptor of the act of drawing a building. The best proof of this is the necessity for an architect, even at the very early moments of a project, to produce multiple models—sometimes physical models—and a great many different types of drawings in order to begin to grasp what he or she has in mind and how many different stakeholders can simultaneously be taken into account. Drawing and modeling do not constitute an immediate means of translation of the internal energies and fantasies of the architect's mind's eye, or a process of transferring ideas from a designer's mind into a physical form,[2] from a powerful "subjective" imagination into various "material" expressions.[3] Rather, the hundreds of models and drawings produced in design form an artistically created primal matter that stimulates the haptic imagination,[4] astonishes its creators instead of subserviently obeying them, and helps architects fix unfamiliar ideas, gain new knowledge about the building-to-come, and formulate new alternatives and "options," new unforeseen scenarios of realization. To follow the evolution of drawings in an architectural studio is like witnessing the successive exertions of a juggler who keeps adding more and more balls to his skilful acrobatic show. Every new technique of drawing and modeling serves to absorb a new difficulty and add it to the accumulation of elements necessary to entertain the possibility of building anything. It would be simply inappropriate to limit to three dimensions an activity that, by definition, means piling on more and more dimensions every time, so as eventually to "obtain" a plausible building, a building that stands. Every time a new constraint is to be taken into account—a zoning limit, a new fabric, a change in the financing scheme, a citizen's protest, a limit in the resistance of this or that material, a new popular fashion, a new client's concern, a new idea flowing into the studio—it is necessary to devise a new way to draw so as to capture this constraint and make it compatible with all the others.

2. Tom Porter, *How Architects Visualize* (New York: Van Nostrand Reinhold, 1979).

3. Akiko Busch, *The Art of the Architectural Model* (New York: Design Press, 1991).

4. Horst Bredekamp, "Frank Gehry and the Art of Drawing," in *Gehry Draws*, eds. Mark Rappolt and Robert Violette (Cambridge, MA: MIT Press, 2004), 11–29.

Latour and Yaneva

So, during its flight, a building is never at rest and never in the shape of this Euclidian space that was supposed to be its "real material essence," to which one could then add its "symbolic," "human," "subjective," or "iconic" dimension. Very often models and drawings and the building stand side by side, and are amended and improved simultaneously. Under the pressure of construction, and in front of the eyes of astonished workers and engineers, architects constantly move back and forth between the building-in-construction and its numerous models and drawings, comparing, correcting and updating them. Architectural drawings, transformed into engineering blueprints and from there into the many pieces of paper used by the workers on site (glued to the walls, folded into attaché cases, smeared with coffee and paint) are still undergoing a bewildering number of transformations, none of them respecting the limits of what is described in only "three" dimensions. When a worker signs a drawing to prove that he or she has understood the workflow, is this in length, in height or in depth? When quasi-legal standards are added to the tolerance margins, which Euclidian dimension is this? The flow of transformations does not stop there, since once the building has been built, another problem of description arises: the building is now opaque to the eyes of those who are supposed to serve and maintain it. Here again you need completely new types of diagrams, new flow charts, new series of boards and labels, so as to archive and remember which part is where and how to access it in case of accident or the need for repair. So, at no time in the long succession of transformations through the cascade of many writing devices that accompany it during its flight, has a building ever been in Euclidian space. And yet we keep thinking of it as if its essence was that of a white cube translated without transformation through the *res extensa*.

What could possibly be the advantages of abandoning the static view of buildings in order to capture them (through a theoretical equivalent of Marey's photographic gun) as a flow of transformations? One advantage would, of course, be that the divide between the "subjective" and "objective" dimensions could be abandoned. The other would be that justice could at last be paid to the many material dimensions of things (without limiting them in advance to the epistemological straight jacket of 3D spatial manipulations.) Matter is much too multidimensional, much too active, complex, surprising, and counter-intuitive to be simply what is represented in the ghost-like rendering of CAD screen shots.[5] Architectural design embraces a complex conglomerate of many surprising agencies that are

5. Albena Yaneva, "How Buildings 'Surprise': The Renovation of the Alte Aula in Vienna," *Science Studies: An Interdisciplinary Journal of Science and Technology Studies*, special issue "Understanding Architecture, Accounting Society," (2008): 21.

rarely taken into account by architectural theory. As William James said, we material entities live in a "pluriverse," not in a universe. Such accounts of design would reveal to what extent architects are attached to non-humans such as physical models, foam and cutters,[6] renderings and computers.[7] They can hardly conceive a building without being assisted and amplified by the motor potential of many thinking, drawing, or foam-cutting, hands. And that is what makes them so materially interesting. Thus, the smallest inquiry into architectural anthropology, the tiniest experiment with materials and shapes shows to what extent an architect has to be equipped with diverse tools—aids of imagination and instruments of thinking tied to the body—in order to carry out the simplest procedure of visualizing a new building. Another advantage would be that at last, humans' many various demands could be fit into the same optical space as the building they are so interested in. It is paradoxical to say that a building is always a "thing" that is, etymologically, a contested gathering of many conflicting demands and yet, having said that, to be utterly unable to draw those conflicting claims in the same space as what they are conflicting about. Everyone knows that a building is a contested territory and that it cannot be reduced to what is and what it means, as architectural theory has traditionally done.[8] Only by enlisting the movements of a building and accounting carefully for its "tribulations" would one be able to state its existence: it would be equal to the building's extensive list of controversies and performances over time, i.e. it would be equal to what it does, to the way it resists attempts at transformation, allows certain visitors' actions and impedes others, bugs observers, challenges city authorities, and mobilizes different communities of actors. And yet we either see the uncontested static object standing "out there," ready to be reinterpreted, or we hear about the conflicting human purposes, but are never able to picture the two together! Almost four centuries after perspective drawings and more than two centuries after the invention of projective geometry (by Gaspard Monge, a compatriot of Marey from the little Burgundian city of Beaune!), there is still no convincing way to draw the controversial space that a building almost always is. It is hard to believe that the powerful visualizing tools we now possess are still unable to do more than Leonardo, Dürer, or Piero.[9] We should finally be able to picture a building as a navigation through a controversial datascape: as an animated series of projects, successful and failing, as a changing and criss-crossing trajectory of unstable definitions and expertise, of recalcitrant materials and building technologies, of flip-flopping

6. In the practice of Rem Kool-haas, see Albena Yaneva, "Scaling Up and Down: Extraction Trials in Architectural Design," *Social Studies of Science* 35 (2005): 867–94.

7. In the practices of Kengo Kuma; see Sophie Houdart, "Des multiples manières d'être réel– Les représentations en perspective dans le projet d'architecture," *Terrain* 46 (2006): 107–22.

8. Juan Bonta, *Architecture and Its Interpretation: A Study of Expressive Systems in Architecture* (New York: Rizzoli, 1979). Charles Jencks and George Baird, *Meaning in Architecture* (London: Barrie & Rockliff, The Cresset Press, 1969). Robert Venturi and Denise Scott Brown, *Architecture as Signs and Systems* (Cambridge, MA: Belknap Press of Harvard University Press, 2004).

9. Bruno Latour, "The Space of Controversies," *New Geographies* 1, no. 1 (2008): 122–36.

users' concerns and communities' appraisals. That is, we should finally be able to picture a building as a moving modulator regulating different intensities of engagement, redirecting users' attention, mixing and putting people together, concentrating flows of actors and distributing them so as to compose a productive force in time–space. Rather than peacefully occupying a distinct analogical space, a building-on-the-move leaves behind the spaces labeled and conceptualized as enclosed, to navigate easily in open circuits. That is why as a gull-in-flight in a complex and multiverse argumentative space, a building appears to be composed of apertures and closures enabling, impeding and even changing the speed of the free-floating actors, data and resources, links and opinions, which are all in orbit, in a network, and never within static enclosures.[10]

But one of the other advantages of taking a gull-in-flight view of buildings would be that context could be done away with. "Context stinks," as Koolhaas so famously said. But it stinks only because it stays in place too long and ends up rotting. Context would not stink so much if we could see that it, too, moves along and flows just as buildings do. What is a context in flight? It is made of the many dimensions that impinge at every stage on the development of a project: "context" is this little word that sums up all the various elements that have been bombarding the project from the beginning—fashions spread by critiques in architectural magazines, clichés that are burned into the minds of some clients, customs entrenched into zoning laws, types that have been taught in art and design schools by professors, visual habits that make neighbors rise against new visual habits in formation, etc. And of course, every new project modifies all the elements that try to contextualize it, and provokes contextual mutations, just like a Takamatsu machine.[11] In this sense, a building project resembles much more a complex ecology than it does a static object in Euclidian space. As many architects and architectural theorists have shown, biology offers much better metaphors for speaking about buildings.[12]

As long as we have not found a way to do for buildings the reverse of what Marey managed to do for the flights of birds and the gaits of horses, architectural theory will be a rather parasitical endeavor that adds historical, philosophical, stylistic, and semiotic "dimensions" to a conception of buildings that has not moved an inch.[13] That is, instead of analyzing the impact of Surrealism on the thinking and design philosophy of Rem Koolhaas, we should rather attempt to grasp the erratic behavior of the foam matter in the model-making venture in his office; instead of referring to the

10. See the project MACOSPOL, www.macospol.eu and www.designinaction.eu).

11. Félix Guattari, "Les machines architecturales de Shin Takamatsu" *Chimères* 21 (Winter 1994): 127–41.

12. Antoine Picon and Alessandra Ponte, *Architecture and the Sciences: Exchanging Metaphors* (New York: Princeton Architectural Press, 2003).

13. Anthony Douglas King, *Buildings and Society: Essays on the Social Development of the Built Environment* (London: Routledge & Kegan Paul, 1980). Neil Leach, ed. *Rethinking Architecture* (London and New York: Routledge, 1997). Ian Borden and Jane Rendell, eds., *Inter Sections: Architectural Histories and Critical Theories* (London: Routledge, 2000).

symbolism implicit in the architecture of the Richards Medical Research Laboratories in Pennsylvania as a scientific building, we should follow the painstaking ways its users reacted to and misused the building after the fact of its construction, and thus engaged in thorny negotiations with its architect Louis Kahn, with glass and daylight; instead of explaining the assembly building in Chandigarh with economic constraints or with the trivial conceptual repertoire of Le Corbusier's modernist style and his unique non-European experience in master planning, we should better witness the multifarious manifestations of recalcitrance of this building, resisting breezes, intense, sunlight and the microclimate of the Himalayas, etc. Only by generating earthly accounts of buildings and design processes, tracing pluralities of concrete entities in the specific spaces and times of their co-existence, instead of referring to abstract theoretical frameworks outside architecture, will architectural theory become a relevant field for architects, for end users, for promoters, and for builders. That is, a new task for architectural theory is coming to the fore: to find the equivalent of Marey's photographic gun and tackle the admittedly daunting task of inventing a visual vocabulary that will finally do justice to the "thingly" nature of buildings, by contrast to their tired, old "objective" nature.

Lose the Building: Systems Theory, Architecture, and Diller+Scofidio's Blur
Cary Wolfe

"The work of art is an ostentatiously improbable occurrence."[1]

The Blur building designed by the New York architectural team of Ricardo Scofidio and Elizabeth Diller—a manufactured cloud with an embedded viewing deck, hovering over Lake Neuchatel in Switzerland—seems to have enjoyed nearly universal acclaim from the moment it opened to the public in October of 2002 as part of media Expo '02. The reasons for this are not far to seek; they range from what a Swiss newspaper reviewer characterizes as the liberating effect of the zany cloud on "the crotchety Swiss"—"What a crazy, idiosyncratic thing! How deliciously without purpose!" he exclaims— to Diller+Scofidio's knowing deployment of the relationship between public architecture, the history and function of the exposition as a social form, and the manufacture and use of spectacle in relation to both.[2]

The project went through many different elaborations, enhancements, and embellishments between July of 1998, when Diller+Scofidio was invited to participate, and the closing of the Expo in October of 2002. Almost all of these were, for various reasons, unrealized in the final project. At one point, the cloud was to house an "LED text forest" of vertical LED panels that would scroll text—either from an Internet feed (including live "chat" produced by visitors to the structure) or, in a later version, produced by an artist such as Jenny Holzer (*Blur,* 163, 324). Another idea early in the project was to build an adjacent "Hole in the Water" restaurant made of submerged twin glass cylinders with an aquarium layer in between, in which diners would sit at eye level with the lake and eat sushi (*Blur,* 100–1); another, to have an open air "Angel Bar" embedded in the upper part of the cloud, in which patrons could select from an endless variety of the only beverage served there: water—artesian waters, sparkling waters, waters from both glacial poles, and municipal tap waters from around the world—"tastings can be arranged," we are told (*Blur,* 146–55). Yet another elaborate idea, rather late in the project's evolution, involved the distribution of "smart" raincoats—or "braincoats"—to visitors to the cloud, which would indicate, through both sound and color, affinity or antipathy to other visitors on the basis of a preferences questionnaire filled out upon entry to the cloud (*Blur,* 209–51).

1. Niklas Luhmann, *Art as a Social System,* trans. Eva M. Knodt (Stanford: Stanford University Press, 2000),153.

2. Diller+Scofidio, *Blur: The Making of Nothing* (New York: Abrams, 2002), 372, 92, 162 (hereafter cited in text as *Blur*).

Fig. 11.1 Diller+Scofidio, Blur building, Swiss Expo 2002, Yverdon-les-Bains, Switzerland (courtesy of Diller, Scofidio and Renfro).

As even this brief list suggests, the project went through many permutations. But in the end—not least for reasons of money—what we are left with in Blur is the manufactured cloud with the "Angel Deck" (now, not a water bar but a viewing deck) nestled at its crest. For reasons I will try to explain by way of contemporary systems theory, the fact that these permutations and sideline enhancements were not realized in the end is not entirely a bad thing, because it rivets our attention not only on what has captivated most viewers from the beginning, but also on what makes the project a paradigmatic instance of the way contemporary architecture responds to the complexities of its broader social environment in terms of its specific medium—and that is, as Diller+Scofidio put it, "the radicality of an absent building," the remarkable, audacious commitment to a building that was not a building at all but a manufactured cloud: "the making," as they put it, "of nothing" (*Blur*, 15). This core commitment was sounded by Diller+Scofidio early and often; at the core of the project, as it were, was no core at all, but a commitment to something "featureless, depthless, scaleless, spaceless, massless, surfaceless, and contextless" (*Blur*, 162). And this overriding concern was reiterated at the end of the design phase, about a year before the Expo opened, in a very important communiqué from Diller:

> BLUR is not a building. BLUR is pure atmosphere, water particles suspended in mid-air. The fog is a dynamic, phantom mass, which changes form constantly . . . . In contradiction to the tradition of Expo pavilions whose exhibitions entertain and educate, BLUR erases information. Expos are usually competition grounds for bigger and better contradiction to the tradition of Expo pavilions whose exhibitions entertain and educate, BLUR erases information. Expos are usually competition grounds for bigger and better technological spectacles. BLUR is a spectacle with nothing to see.

Wolfe

Within BLUR, vision is put out-of-focus so that our dependence on vision can become the focus of the pavilion (*Blur*, 325).

Fig. 11.2 Diller+Scofidio, Blur building, Swiss Expo 2002, Yverdon-les-Bains, Switzerland (courtesy of Diller, Scofidio and Renfro).

And, she adds in bold type: "The media project must be liberated from all immediate and obvious metaphoric associations such as clouds, god, angels, ascension, dreams, Greek mythology, or any other kitsch relationships. Rather, BLUR offers a blank interpretive surface" (*Blur*, 325). But not quite blank, as it turns out. In fact, the architects thought the perceptual experience of the Blur building would either metaphorize or, conversely, throw into relief a larger set of concerns about electronic media and how we relate to it. Midway through the project, in a presentation to a media sponsor, they characterized it this way:

> To "blur" is to make indistinct, to dim, to shroud, to cloud, to make vague, to obfuscate. Blurred vision is an impairment. A blurry image is the fault of mechanical malfunction in a display or reproduction technology. For our visually obsessed, high-resolution/high-definition culture, blur is equated with loss . . . . Our proposal has little to do with the mechanics of the eye, but rather the immersive potential of blur on an environmental scale. Broadcast and print media feed our insatiable desire for the visual with an unending supply of images . . . [but] as an experience, the BLUR building offers little to see. It is an immersive environment in which the world is put out of focus so that our visual dependency can be put into focus (*Blur*, 195).

At a different stage—one in which the LED text forest played a central role—the experience of the cloud figures "the unimaginable magnitude, speed, and reach of telecommunications." As Diller+Scofidio put it, "unlike entering a building, the experience of entering this habitable medium in which orientation is lost and time is suspended is like an immersion in 'ether.' It is a perfect context for the experience of another all-pervading, yet infinitely elastic, massless medium—one for the

Lose the Building

transmission and propagation of information: the Internet. The project aims to produce a 'technological sublime' . . . felt in the scaleless and unpredictable mass of fog."[3]

There are some interesting differences between these versions of the cloud, of course. In the first version, the resonance of the project falls on the iconographic and visually based forms of mass media; in the second, it is the ephemeral yet pervasive presence of electronic, digital forms of telecommunication generally that is in question. In the first, the point of the cloud is that it deprives us of the unproblematic visual clarity, immediacy, and transparency that the mass media attempt to produce in its consumers; in the second, the cloud's water vapor metaphorically envelopes us in the electronic ether that we inhabit like a medium in contemporary life, but deprives us of the information that usually accompanies it and therefore distracts us from just how immersed in that medium we are. I am more concerned here, however, with what the two accounts have in common: that this particular form has been selected by Diller+Scofidio, and selected, moreover, to represent the unrepresentable—hence the notion of the "technological sublime" upon which both accounts converge.

We ought not, however, take this notion of the sublime (or the term "representation," for that matter) at face value. In fact, resorting to the discourse of the sublime here can only obscure the specificity of the project's formal decisions—why it does what it does how it does—and how those decisions are directly related to the ethical and political point that the project is calculated to make. At its worst, it leads down the sorts of blind alleys we find in the July 2002 issue of *Architecture*, where one reviewer reads the project in terms of the symbolic significance of clouds and of Switzerland in Romantic literature (Mary Shelley's Frankenstein, among others) and painting (J.M.W. Turner, among others), all of which is supposedly mobilized in Blur's rewriting of the sublime as a "cautionary tale about the environment."[4] And all of which recycles exactly the sorts of "immediate and obvious metaphoric associations" and "kitsch relationships" that, as we have just seen, Diller rightly rails against.

It might seem more promising, at least at first glance, to pursue more theoretically sophisticated renderings of the sublime in contemporary theory, most notably in the work of Jean-François Lyotard (though other recent renditions of the concept, such as we find in Slavoj Žižek's conjugation of Kant and Lacan, might be invoked here as well). In Lyotard—to stay with the most well-known example—the *locus classicus* is a certain reading of Kant.

3. Edward Dimendberg, "Blurring Genres," in *Scanning: The Aberrant Architectures of Diller+Scofidio*, ed. Anderson, Laurie, Aaron Betsky, and K. Michael Hays (New York: Whitney Museum of Art, 2003), 79.

4. Ned Cramer, "All Natural," *Architecture* 91.7 (July 2002): 53.

The sublime is rendered as a kind of absolute outside to human existence—one that is, for that very reason, terrifying. At the same time, paradoxically (and this is true of Žižek's rendering as well), that radically other outside emerges as a product of the human subject's conflict with itself, a symptom of the Enlightenment subject running up against its own limits. In Lyotard's famous rendering of the Kantian sublime in *The Postmodern Condition*, it emerges from the conflict between "the faculty to conceive of something and the faculty to 'present' something."[5] "We can conceive the infinitely great, the infinitely powerful," he explains, "but every presentation of an object destined to 'make visible' this absolute greatness or power appears to us painfully inadequate. Those are ideas of which no presentation is possible. Therefore they impart no knowledge about reality (experience)."[6] And the entire ethical stake of modern art for Lyotard is "to present the fact that the unpresentable exists. To make visible that there is something which can be conceived and which can neither be seen nor made visible."[7] But how to do this? Here, Lyotard follows Kant's invocation of "'formlessness, the absence of form,' as a possible index to the unpresentable," as that which "will enable us to see only by making it impossible to see; it will please only by causing pain."[8] The sublime, then, is a "feeling" that marks the incommensurability of reason (conception) and the singularity or particularity of the world and its objects (presentation). And it is an incommensurability that carries ethical force, for it serves as a reminder that the heterogeneity of the world cannot be reduced to a unified rule or reason. And this incompleteness in turn necessitates a permanent openness of any discourse to its other, to what Lyotard calls, in a book by the same title, the "differend."

Lyotard's rendering of the Kantian sublime would seem to be useful in approaching Blur, and Kant's invocation of "formlessness" as the sublime's index would seem doubly promising. But its limitations may be marked by the fact that Kant's sublime remains tethered to "something on the order of a subject" (to use Foucault's famous phrase)—hence it remains referenced essentially to the language of phenomenology, to the affective states of a subject-supposed-to-know who, in experiencing her non-knowledge, experiences pain, and thus changes her relation to herself. What I am suggesting, then, is that in Lyotard's rendering of the sublime— and it would be far afield to argue the point in any more detail here—the price we pay for a certain deconstruction of the subject of humanism (one that will be traced from Kant to Nietzsche in *The Postmodern Condition*) is that the subject remains installed at the

5. Jean-François Lyotard, *The Postmodern Condition: A Report on Knowledge*, trans. Geoff Bennington and Brian Massumi, (Minneapolis: University of Minnesota Press, 1984), 77.

6. Lyotard, *The Postmodern Condition*, 78.

7. Ibid.

8. Ibid.

center of its universe, only now its failure is understood to be a kind of success.[9] Moreover, the fact that this failure is ethical—is the hook on which the ethical rehabilitation of the subject hangs in its forcible opening to the world of the object, the differend, and so on—is the surest sign that we have not, for all that, left the universe of Kantian humanism. For we must remember that the ethical force of the sublime in Lyotard's Kant depends upon the addressee of ethics being a member of the community of "reasonable beings" who must be equipped with the familiar humanist repertoire of language, reason, and so on to experience in the addressee of ethics being a member of the community of "reasonable beings" who must be equipped with the familiar humanist repertoire of language, reason, and so on to experience in the ethical imperative not a "determinant synthesis"—not one-size-fits-all rules for the good and the just act—but "an Idea of human society" (which is why Kant will argue, for example, that we have no direct duties to non-human animals).[10] And this in turn re-ontologizes the subject/object split that the discourse of the sublime was meant to call into question in the first place.

In contrast to this, Diller+Scofidio insist that their work be understood in "post-moral and post-ethical" terms.[11] This does not mean I think, that they intend their work to have no ethical or political resonance—that much is already obvious from their comments on Blur—but rather that they understand the relationship between art, the subject, and world in resolutely post-humanist terms. In Diller+Scofidio, the human and the non- or anti- or a-human do not exist in fundamentally discrete ontological registers but—quite the contrary—inhabit the same space in mutual relations of co-implication and instability. This boundary-breakdown tends to be thematized in their work in the interlacing of the human and the technological (as in, for example, the multimedia theater work Jet Lag, the Virtue/Vice Glasses series, and the EJM 2 Inertia dance piece); it is also sometimes handled even more broadly in terms of the interweaving of the organic and the inorganic, the "natural" and the "artificial" (think here not only of Blur, but also of projects like Slow House and The American Lawn). Sometimes those unstable relations are funny, sometimes they are frightening, but almost always the signature affect in Diller+Scofidio is radical ambivalence—an ambivalence that, in contrast to the sublime, isn't about a clear-cut pain that becomes, in a second, pedagogical moment, pleasure, but rather an ambivalence from the first moment of our experience of the work. This ambivalence is often tied to the

9. Lyotard, The Postmodern Condition, 77.

10. Jean-François Lyotard and Jean-Loup Thèbaud, Just Gaming, trans. Wlad Godzich (Minneapolis: University of Minnesota Press, 1985), 85.

11. Dimendberg, "Blurring Genres," 79.

Wolfe

difficulty of knowing exactly what is being experienced (as in works that intermesh real video surveillance with staged scenes, such as the Facsimile installation at the Moscone Convention Center in San Francisco), or, if we do know, how we should feel about it (think here of Jump Cuts or, again, Blur). All of which leads, in turn, to the ultimate question: namely, who is doing the experiencing? Who—in phenomenological, ethical, and political terms—are "we," exactly? In this light, Diller+Scofidio (like Lyotard's Kant) show us how questions of ethics are just that: *questions*; but they do so (unlike Lyotard's Kant) without recontaining the force of that radical undecidability in terms of a humanist subject, an all too familiar "we"—a "reasonable being" directed toward an "idea of society"— for whom, and only for whom, those questions are.

What this suggests, I think, is that a move beyond an essentially humanist ontological theoretical framework is in order if we are to understand the Blur project or, indeed, Diller+Scofidio's work as a whole. We need, in other words, to replace "what" questions with "how" questions (to use Niklas Luhmann's shorthand).[12] Here, recent work in systems theory—and particularly Luhmann's later work—can be of immense help, not least because it gives us a theoretical vocabulary for understanding the sorts of things that Diller+Scofidio have in mind when they suggest that in Blur "our objective is to weave together architecture and electronic technologies, yet exchange the properties of each for the other" (*Blur*, 44). For the fundamental postulate of systems theory—its replacement of the familiar ontological dichotomies of humanism (culture/nature and its cognates: mind/body, spirit/matter, reason/feeling, and so on) with the functional distinction system/environment—is indispensable in allowing us to better understand the sorts of transcodings that Diller+Scofidio have in mind, because it gives us a common theoretical vocabulary that can range across what were, in the humanist tradition, ontologically discrete categories. Moreover, systems theory will allow us to explain not only how those transcodings are specific to particular systems—how art and architecture, for example, integrate electronic technologies *as art*—but also how, in being system-specific, they are paradoxically paradigmatic of, and productive of, the very situation to which those systems respond.[13] That situation is "hypercomplexity," created by what Luhmann calls the "functional differentiation" of modern society (what other critical vocabularies would call its specialization or, more moralistically, its fragmentation), which only gets accentuated and accelerated under post-modernity.[14]

12. Niklas Luhmann, *Art as a Social System*, trans. Eva M. Knodt (Stanford: Stanford University Press, 2000), 89 (hereafter referred to as *Art*).

13. It should be noted here— and it is abundantly clear in the catalog, *Scanning*, that accompanied the retrospective of Diller+Scofidio's work at the Whitney in New York—that the distinction between "art" and "architecture" is of relatively little moment for Diller+Scofidio, and indeed their body of work is calculated to blur it (if the expression can be allowed in this context) beyond recognition. The same is true for Luhmann, who treats architecture as a subspecies of art, even while addressing here and there its differences from, say, painting or literary art.

14. It should be noted that the term "postmodern" is one for which Luhmann has no use. For him, the postmodern is merely an intensification of features already fully present in modernity. On this point, see his essay "Why Does Society Describe Itself as Postmodern?" in *Observing Complexity: Systems Theory and Postmodernity*, ed. William Rasch and Cary Wolfe (Minneapolis: University of Minnesota Press, 2000), 35–49.

For Luhmann, the social system of art—like any other autopoietic system, by definition—finds itself in an environment that is always already more complex than itself, and all systems attempt to adapt to this complexity by filtering it in terms of their own, self-referential codes which are based on a fundamental distinction by means of which they carry out their operations. The point of the system is to reproduce itself, but no system can deal with everything, or even many things, all at once. The legal system, for example, responds to changes in its environment in terms of—and only in terms of—the distinction legal/illegal. In litigation, decisions are not based—and it is a good thing too—on whether it is raining or not, whether you went to Duke or to Rice, if you are wearing a blue shirt or a white shirt, whether or not you're a vegetarian, and so on. One might well object that this ignores, say, the obvious influence of the economic system on the legal system, but for Luhmann this is simply evidence of the need for the legal system to further assert its own differentiation and autopoietic insularity. The determination of the legal by the economic system would be a symptom, to use Raymond Williams's well-worn distinction, of the undue influence of a residual, premodern mode of social organization (center/periphery or top/bottom), in which one system dominates and determines the functions of the others, on the dominant, yet incompletely realized, mode of functional differentiation that characterizes modernity.

Two subsidiary points need to be accented here. First, it is by responding to environmental complexity in terms of their own self-referential codes that subsystems build up their own internal complexity (one might think here of the various sub-specialties of the legal system, say, or for that matter the specialization of disciplines in the education system, particularly in the sciences); in doing so, systems become more finely grained in their selectivity, and thus—by increasing the density of the webwork of their filters, as it were—they buy time in relation to overwhelming environmental complexity. As Luhmann puts it in *Social Systems*, "Systems lack the 'requisite variety' (Ashby's term) that would enable them to react to every state of the environment . . . There is, in other words, no point-for-point correspondence between system and environment . . . The system's inferiority in complexity [compared to that of the environment] must be counter-balanced by strategies of selection."[15] But if the self-reference of the system's code reduces the flow of environmental complexity into the system, it also increases its "irritability" and, in a very real sense, its dependence on the environment. As for this latter point, it is worth noting that systems theory in general and the theory

15. Niklas Luhmann, *Social Systems*, trans. John Bednarz, Jr. with Dirk Baecker (Stanford: Stanford University Press, 1995), 25.

of autopoiesis in particular are often criticized for asserting a kind of solipsism separating the system from its environment. What this rather ham-fisted understanding misses is that systems theory attempts to account for the complex and seemingly paradoxical fact that the autopoietic closure of a system—whether social or biological—is precisely what connects it to its environment. As Luhmann explains, "the concept of a self-referentially closed system does not contradict the system's *openness to the environment*. Instead, in the self-referential mode of operation, closure is a form of broadening possible environmental contacts; closure increases, by constituting elements more capable of being determined, the complexity of the environment that is possible for the system."[16] And this is why, as Luhmann puts it in *Art as a Social System*,

> [A]utopoiesis and complexity are conceptual correlates . . . .
> Assuming that the system's autopoiesis is at work, evolutionary thresholds can catapult the system to a level of higher complexity—in the evolution of living organisms, toward sexual reproduction, independent mobility, a central nervous system. To an external observer, this may resemble an increase in system differentiation or look like a higher degree of independence from environmental conditions. Typically, such evolutionary jumps simultaneously increase an increase in system differentiation or look like a higher degree of independence from environmental conditions. Typically, such evolutionary jumps simultaneously increase a system's sensitivity and irritability; it is more easily disturbed by environmental conditions that, for their part, result from an increase in the system's own complexity. Dependency and independence, in a simple causal sense, are therefore not invariant magnitudes in that more of one would imply less of the other. Rather, they vary according to a system's given level of complexity. In systems that are successful in evolutionary terms, more independence typically amounts to a greater dependency on the environment . . . . But all of this can happen only on the basis of the system's operative closure (*Art,* 157–8).

Or as Luhmann puts it in one of his more Zen-like moments, "Only complexity can reduce complexity."[17] The information/filter metaphor already invoked is misleading, however, on the basis of the second subsidiary point I mentioned above: because systems interface with their environment in terms of, and only in terms of, their own constitutive distinctions and the self-referential codes based upon them, the "environment" is not an ontological category but a functional one; it is not an "outside" to the system that is given as such, from which the system then differentiates itself—it is not, in other words, either "nature" or "society" in the traditional

16. Luhmann, *Social Systems*, 37.

17. Ibid., 26.

sense—but is rather always the "outside" of a specific inside. Or as Luhmann explains it, the environment is different for every system, because any system excludes only itself from its environment.[18] All of this leads to a paradoxical situation that is central to Luhmann's work, and central to understanding Luhmann's reworking of problems inherited from both Hegel and Husserl: What links the system to the world—what literally makes the world available to the system—is also what hides the world from the system, what makes it unavailable. Given our discussion of the sublime and the problem of "representing the unrepresentable" this should ring a bell—but a different bell, as it turns out. To understand just how different, we need to remember that all systems carry out their operations and maintain their autopoiesis by deploying a constitutive distinction, and a code based upon it, that in principle could be otherwise; it is contingent, self-instantiated, and rests, strictly speaking, on nothing. But this means that there is a paradoxical identity between the two sides that define the system, because the distinction between both sides is a product of only one side. In the legal system, for example, the distinction between the two sides legal/illegal is instantiated (or "re-entered," in Luhmann's terminology) on only one side of the distinction, namely the legal. But no system can acknowledge this paradoxical identity of difference—which is also in another sense simply the contingency—of its own constitutive distinction and at the same time use that distinction to carry out its operations. It must remain "blind" to the very paradox of the distinction that links it to its environment.

That does not mean that this "blind spot" cannot be observed from the vantage of another system—it can, and that is what we are doing right now—but that second-order observation will itself be based on its own blind spot, the paradoxical identity of both sides of its constitutive distinction, and so on and so forth. First-order observations that deploy distinctions as difference simply "do what they do." Second-order observations can observe the unity of those differences and the contingency of the code of the first-order observer—but only by "doing what they do," and thus formally reproducing a "blindness" that is (formally) the same but (contingently) not the same as the first-order system's. And here, as I have suggested elsewhere, we find Luhmann's fruitful reworking of the Hegelian problematic: Hegel's "identity of identity and non-identity" is reworked as the "non-identity of identity and non-identity"—and a productive non-identity at that.[19]

The source of a distinction's guaranteeing reality lies in its own operative unity. It is, however, precisely as this unity that the distinction cannot be observed—except by means of another

18. Luhmann, *Social Systems*, 17.

19. Cary Wolfe, *Critical Environments: Postmodern Theory and the Pragmatics of the "Outside"* (Minneapolis: University of Minnesota Press, 1998), 67–8.

Wolfe

distinction which then assumes the function of a guarantor of reality. Another way of expressing this is to say the operation emerges simultaneously with the world which as a result remains cognitively unapproachable to the operation. The conclusion to be drawn from this is that the connection with the reality of the external world is established by the blind spot of the cognitive operation. Reality is what one does not perceive when one perceives it.[20]

Or as Luhmann puts it in somewhat different terms, the world is now conceived, "along the lines of a Husserlian metaphor, as an unreachable horizon that retreats further with each operation, without ever holding out the prospect of an outside" (*Art*, 92).

The question, then—and this is directly related to the problems raised by the topos of the sublime—is "how to observe how the world observes itself, how a marked space emerges [via a constitutive distinction] from the unmarked space, how something becomes invisible when something else becomes visible." Here, we might seem far afield from addressing the Blur project, but as Luhmann argues, "the generality of these questions allows one to determine more precisely what art can contribute to solving this paradox of the invisibilization that accompanies making something visible" (*Art*, 91). In this way, the problems that the discourse of the sublime attempts to address can be assimilated to the more formally rigorous scheme of the difference between first- and second-order observation. Any observation "renders the world invisible" in relation to its constitutive distinction, and that invisibility must itself remain invisible to the observation that employs that distinction, and can only be disclosed by another observation that will also necessarily be doubly blind in the same way" (*Art*, 91). "In this twofold sense," Luhmann writes, "the notion of a final unity—of an 'ultimate reality' that cannot assume a form because it has no other side—is displaced into the unobservable . . . If the concept of the world is retained to indicate reality in its entirety, then it is that which—to a second-order observer—remains invisible in the movements of observation (his own and those of others)" (*Art*, 91). This means not only that "art can no longer be understood as an imitation of something that presumably exists along with and outside of art," but more importantly for our purposes, "to the extent that imitation is still possible, it now imitates the world's invisibility, a nature that can no longer be apprehended as a whole" (*Art*, 92). "The paradox unique to art, which art creates and resolves," Luhmann writes, "resides in the observability of the unobservable" (*Art*, 149). And this is a question of form.

It is in these terms—to return to Diller+Scofidio—that we might best understand the uncanny effect of Blur's manufactured

20. Niklas Luhmann, "The Cognitive Program of Constructivism and a Reality that Remains Unknown," in *Selforganization: Portrait of a Scientific Revolution*, ed. Wolfgang Krohn et al. (Dordrecht: Kluwer, 1990), 76.

cloud hovering over a lake, with the point being, we might say, not that the cloud is not a cloud but rather that the lake is not a lake, precisely in the sense that art can be said to imitate nature only because nature isn't nature (an insight that is surely at work as well in Diller+Scofidio's Slow House project)—which is another way of saying that all observations, including those of nature, are contingent, and of necessity blind to their own contingency. To put it in a Deleuzean rather than Luhmannian register, we might say that Blur virtualizes the very nature it "imitates," but only, paradoxically, by concretizing that virtualization in its formal decisions—an "imitation of nature" that formally renders the impossibility of an "imitation of nature." As Luhmann puts it, in an analysis that is thematized, as it were, in the blurriness of Diller+Scofidio's project (and in the critical intent they attach to it), "Art makes visible possibilities of order that would otherwise remain invisible. It alters conditions of visibility/ invisibility in the world by keeping invisibility constant and making visibility subject to variation" (*Art*, 96). And here I think we can bring into the sharpest possible focus (if the metaphor can be allowed in this context!) the brilliance of the project's "refusal" of architecture and its strategy of focusing on "the radicality of an absent building." In this context, the strength of Blur's formal intervention via à vis the medium of architecture is precisely its formlessness, because it is calculated to show how "the realm officially known as architecture" (to borrow Rem Koolhaas's and Bruce Mau's phrase)[21] can no longer "keep invisibility constant and make visibility subject to variation." "Official architecture" renders the invisibility of the world invisible precisely by being too visible, too legible. And in so doing, as art, it might as well be invisible.

Here, we might recall Luhmann's suggestive comments about Christo's and Jeanne-Claude's wrapping of architectural structures. In an earlier moment of the "postmodern" in architecture, "quotation" of historical styles and elements attempts, as Luhmann puts it, "to copy a differentiated and diverse environment into the artwork," but this in turn only raises the formal problem of "whether, and in what way, the work can claim unity, and whether it can assert itself against its own (!) 'requisite variety'" (*Art*, 298–9). "How," as Luhmann puts it, "can the art system reflect upon its own differentiation, not only in the form of theory, but also in individual works of art?" (*Art*, 299). Christo's and Jeanne-Claude's response to this problem, he suggests, is "particularly striking: if objects can no longer legitimize their boundaries and distinctions, they must be wrapped" (*Art*, 400 n.220). From this perspective, we might think of Blur as a wrapped

21. This phrase was used by Koolhaas and Mau in their presentations of their Tree City project for the Downsview Park competition in Toronto in 1999-2000. For an overview, see Marco Polo, "Environment as Process," *Canadian Architect* 45.10 (Oct. 2000): 14-9.

Wolfe

building with no building inside. Or better yet, as a wrapped building in which even the wrapping has too much form and begins to obsolesce the minute form is concretized.

But what can it mean to say that an architectural project is concerned primarily with having little enough form? Here—and once again the otherwise daunting abstraction of systems theory is indispensable—we need to understand that when we use the term "form," in no sense are we talking about objects, substances, materials, or things. Nor are we even, for that matter, talking about "shape." As Luhmann explains,

> The word formal here does not refer to the distinction, which at first guided modern art, between form and matter or form and content, but to the characteristics of an indicating operation that observes, as if from the corner of its eye, what happens on the other side of form. In this way, the work of art points the observer toward an observation of form . . . . It consists in demonstrating the compelling forces of order in the realm of the possible. Arbitrariness is displaced beyond the boundaries of art into the unmarked space. If . . . one transgresses this boundary and steps from the unmarked into the marked space, things no longer happen randomly (*Art*, 147–8).

In this way, form stages the question of "whether an observer can observe at all except with reference to an order" (*Art*, 148),"and it stages the production of the unobservable (the "blind spot" of observation, the "outside" of any distinction's "inside") that inevitably accompanies such observations (*Art*, 149). As Luhmann will put it (rather unexpectedly), "the world displays all the qualities that Nicholas of Cusa ascribed to God: it is neither small nor large, neither unity nor diversity, it neither has a beginning nor is it without beginning—and this is why the world needs forms" (*Art*, 150).

> From this vantage we can say then that the function of art, one could argue, is to make the world appear within the world—with an eye toward the ambivalent situation that every time something is made available for observation something else withdraws, that, in other words, the activity of distinguishing and indicating that goes on in the world conceals the world . . . . *Yet a work of Art is capable of symbolizing the reentry of the world into the world because it appears—just like the world—incapable of emendation.*[22]

With regard to this "reentry," two related points should be highlighted here to fully appreciate the specificity of Blur's formal innovations. First, form is in a profound sense a temporal problem (if for no other reason than because of the contingency of any constitutive distinction); and second, formal decisions operate on two levels, what we might call the "internal" and "external"; they

22. Luhmann, *Art as a Social System*, 149, author's emphasis.

operate, that is, in relating the formal decisions of the artwork itself to the larger system of art, but also in relating the artwork as a whole to its larger environment, of which the subsystem of art is only a part.

> What is at stake, operatively speaking, in the production and observation of a work of art is always a temporal unity that is either no longer or not yet observed. In this sense, the artwork is the result of intrinsic formal decisions and, at the same time, the metaform determined by these decisions, which, by virtue of its inner forms, can be distinguished from the unmarked space of everything else—the work as fully elaborated "object" (*Art*, 72).

Even more forcefully, one can say that here we are not dealing with objects at all but rather with what systems theory sometimes calls "eigenvalues" or "eigenbehaviors," recursive distinctions that unfold—and can only unfold—over time, even as they can only be experienced in the nano-moment of the present.[23] From this vantage, "objects appear as repeated indications, which, rather than having a specific opposite, are demarcated against 'everything else'" (*Art*, 46). In fact, Luhmann suggests that we might follow Mead and Whitehead, who "assigned a function to identifiable and recognizable objects, whose primary purpose is to bind time. This function is needed because the reality of experience and actions consists in mere event sequences, that is, in an ongoing self-dissolution" (*Art*, 46).

These terms, it seems to me, are remarkably apt for understanding how Blur's significance as a work of art under conditions of postmodernity goes far beyond the mere thematizations we can readily articulate. Indeed, in its unstable shape, shifting constantly in both density of light and moisture, this building that is not a building could well be described as epitomizing "a temporal unity that is either no longer or not yet observed": a something that is also, to use Diller+Scofidio's words, a nothing—in short, a blur. At the same time, paradoxically, as a "metaform," one could hardly imagine a more daring and original formal decision that dramatically distinguishes itself from "the unmarked space of everything else."

When we combine this understanding of the artwork as what Luhmann (following Michel Serres) calls a "quasi-object" with attention to the double aspect of its formal decisions outlined above, we can zero in on the fact that, paradoxically, the "shapelessness" of the Blur building is precisely what constitutes its most decisive and binding formal quality—and not least, of course, with regard to adjacent formal decisions in architecture. Its "refusal" of architecture and its dematerialization of the architectural medium paradoxically epitomize the question of architectural form from a Luhmannian

23. As Luhmann puts it, "Objects are therefore nothing but the eigenbehaviors of observing systems that result from using and reusing their previous distinctions." Niklas Luhmann, "Deconstruction as Second-Order Observing," *New Literary History* 24 (1993): 768.

perspective; the shape-shifting, loosely-defined space of *Blur* only dramatizes what is true of all architectural forms. As the shifting winds over Lake Neuchatel blow the cloud this way and that, the joke is not on Blur, but rather on any architectural forms that think they are "solid," real "objects"—that have, one might say, a compositional rather than systematic understanding of the medium. In this light, one is tempted to view those moments when the winds at Lake Neuchatel swept nearly all the cloud away to reveal the underlying tensegrity structure of Blur—leaving, as one reviewer put it, the view of "an unfinished building awaiting its skin"[24] —as the most instructive all, insofar as THE BUILDING (as object), "official architecture," is revealed to be precisely not "the building" (as form).

And as we have already noted, the effectiveness of these formal decisions is only enhanced by the fact that they are smuggled inside the Trojan Horse of the work's savvy play with the "art imitates nature" theme. From a systems theory point of view, the joke is not on those who think that art imitates nature, but rather on those who think it doesn't—not in the sense of "an imitation of something that presumably exists along with and outside of art," but rather in the sense that "it now imitates the world's invisibility, a nature that can no longer be apprehended as a whole" (*Art*, 92). Another name for this fact, as we have already noted, is contingency—namely, the contingency of the distinctions and indications that make the world available and that, because contingent, simultaneously make the world unavailable. And it is against that contingency that the artwork and its formal decisions assert themselves. To put it succinctly, the work of art begins with a radically contingent distinction—a formal decision that could be otherwise—and then gradually builds up, through recursive self-reference, its own unique, non-paraphrasable character—its internal necessity, if you like. As Luhmann explains,

> The artwork closes itself off by reusing what is already determined in the work as the other side of further distinctions. The result is a unique, circular accumulation of meaning, which often escapes one's first view (or is grasped only "intuitively") . . . . This creates an overall impression of necessity—the work is what it is, even of meaning, which often escapes one's first view (or is grasped only "intuitively") . . . This creates an overall impression of necessity—the work is what it is, even though it is made, individual, and contingent, rather than necessary in an ontological sense. The work of art, one might say, manages to overcome its own contingency (*Art*, 120).

But here (and this is a crucial point), the recursive self-reference of form—and not the materiality of the medium per se—is key; as Luhmann puts it, "in working together, form and medium

24. Ashley Schafer, "Designing Inefficiencies," in *Scanning: The Aberrant Architectures of Diller+Scofidio* (New York: Whitney Museum of Art, 2003), 93.

generate what characterizes successful artworks, namely, improbable evidence" (*Art*, 119). The genius of Blur from this vantage is that submits itself to this contingency in the vagaries and malleability of its shape, its "loose" binding of time (to recall Whitehead and Mead's definition of objects), while simultaneously taking it into account, but as it were preemptively, within its own frame, as "an indicating operation that observes, as if from the corner of its eye, what happens on the other side of form" (*Art*, 147-8). And in doing so, "it employs constraints for the sake of increasing the work's freedom in disposing over other constraints" (*Art*, 148), and this includes, of course, those contingencies that, rather than threatening the work with obsolescence, now increase the resonance of the work with its environment.

Of course, this raises the question of what, exactly, art is, if the formlessness of the object is equated with the strength of its formal statement—if the strongest form of "something" turns out to be "nothing." Here, however, we need only remind ourselves of the point we made a moment ago: that questions of form are not questions of objects (and indeed, if we follow Whitehead, Mead, and systems theory, even objects are not questions of objects). Or to put it another way, it is a question not of the being of the artwork but rather of its meaning. And if that's the case, then we would do well, Luhmann rightly suggests, to remember the lessons of Duchamp, Cage, and conceptual art in general.[25] "One can ask how an art object distinguishes itself from other natural or artificial objects, for example, from a urinal or a snow shovel," Luhmann writes (*Art*, 34). "Marcel Duchamp used the form of a work of art to impress this question on his audience and, in a laudable effort, eliminated all sensuously recognizable differences between the two. But can a work of art at once pose and answer this question?" (*Art*, 34). The answer, as it turns out, is no, because the meaning of Duchamp's snow shovel—the significance of its first-order formal decisions—depends upon (and indeed ingeniously anticipates and manipulates) a second-order discourse of "art" criticism and theory in terms of which those first-order decisions are received. The first-order observer need only "identify a work of art as an object in contradistinction to all other objects or processes" (*Art*, 71). But for those who experience the work and want to understand its significance, the situation is quite different. Here, the project of Cage and Duchamp is "to confront the observer with the question of how he goes about identifying a work of art as a work of art. The only possible answer is: by observing observations" (*Art*, 71):

25. In this connection, we should remember, as Roselee Goldberg reminds us, just how influential conceptual art was for the early, formative stages of Diller+Scofidio's career. Roselee Goldberg, "Dancing About Architecture," in *Scanning: The Aberrant Architectures of Diller+Scofidio* (New York: Whitney Museum of Art, 2003), 44–60.

The observer uses a distinction to indicate what he observes. This happens when it happens. But if one wants to observe whether and how this happens, employing a distinction is not enough—one must also indicate the distinction. The concept of form serves this purpose . . . . Whoever observes forms observes other observers in the rigorous sense that he is not interested in the materiality, expectations, or utterances of these observers, but strictly and exclusively in their use of distinctions (*Art*, 66-7).

Luhmann argues, in fact, that this is the issue that art and art criticism have been struggling with at least since the early modern period. The convention of the still life, for example, which assumes great importance in Italian and Dutch painting, presents us with "unworthy" objects that "could acquire meaning only by presenting the art of presentation itself," focusing our attention on "the blatant discrepancy between the banality of the subject matter and its artful presentation" (*Art*, 69)—a process that is only further distilled (more abstractly and formally, as it were) in Duchamp's snow shovel. Indeed, part of the genius of Duchamp's work is that it reveals how the formula of "disinterested pleasure" fails to clarify what can be meant by artful presentation as "an end in itself," which only begs the question of whether "there is perhaps a special interest in being disinterested, and can we assume that such an interest also motivates the artist who produces the work, and who can neither preclude nor deny an interest in the interests of others?" (*Art*, 69). For Luhmann, such questions index the situation of art as a social system under functionally differentiated modernity, of art struggling to come to terms with its raison d'être—in systems theory terms, to achieve and justify its operational closure, its newly-won "autonomy." "To create a work of art under these sociohistorical conditions," then, "amounts to creating specific forms for an observation of observations. This is the sole purpose for which the work is 'produced.' From this perspective, the artwork accomplishes the structural coupling between first- and second-order observations in the realm of art . . . . The artist accomplishes this by clarifying—via his own observations of the emerging work—how he and others will observe the work" (*Art*, 69–70).

Now such an understanding is well and good, but it would seem to leave wholly to the side the question of the experience of art as a perceptual and phenomenological event—something that would appear to be rather spectacularly foregrounded in Blur, as Mark Hansen has recently argued, moreover, quite self-consciously in terms of the function of spectacle in the tradition of the international Expo as a genre (a matter emphasized in Diller's lectures about the project at Princeton and elsewhere).[26] Indeed,

26. Mark Hansen, "Wearable Space," *Configurations* 10:2 (2002): 325-30. Diller + Scofidio, *Blur,* 92–4.

one might well argue that this, and not the coupling of first- and second-order observations by means of form, is what motivates contemporary art, its experimentation with different media, and so on—a rule that is only proved, so the argument would unfold, by the exception of conceptual art. Yet here, it seems to me, we find one of the more original and innovative aspects of Luhmann's theory of art as a social system. Luhmann's point is not to deny the phenomenological aspect of the artwork, but rather to point out the fact—which seems rather obvious, upon reflection—that the meaning of the artwork cannot be referenced to, much less reduced to, this material and perceptual aspect. Rather, the work of art co-presents perception and communication—and does so in a way that turns out to be decisive for what another theoretical vocabulary might call art's "critical" function in relation to society.

To understand how this happens, we need to remember that for Luhmann, perception and communication operate in mutually exclusive, operationally closed, autopoietic systems, though they are structurally coupled through media such as language. As Luhmann puts it in a formulation surely calculated to provoke: "Humans cannot communicate; not even their brains can communicate; not even their conscious minds can communicate. Only communication can communicate."[27] "Communication operates with an unspecific reference to the participating state of mind," he continues; "it is especially unspecific as to perception. It cannot copy states of mind, cannot imitate them, cannot represent them."[28] At first, this contention seems almost ridiculously counter-intuitive, but upon reflection it is rather commonsensical. As Luhmann explains—and there is ample evidence for this in contemporary neurobiology and cognitive science—"what we perceive as our own mind operates as an isolated autopoietic system. There is no conscious link between one mind and another. There is no operational unity of more than one mind as a system, and whatever appears as a consensus is the construct of an observer, that is, his own achievement."[29] At the same time, however, consciousness and perception are a medium for communication. On the one hand, unperceived communications do not exist (if they did, how would we know?); communication "can hardly come into being without the participation of the mind," Luhmann points out, and in this sense "the relationship is asymmetrical."[30]

On the other hand, "communication uses the mind as a medium precisely because communication does not thematize the mind in question. Metaphorically speaking, the mind in question remains invisible to communication."[31] The mind is its own operationally

27. Niklas Luhmann, "How Can the Mind Participate in Communication?" in *Materialities of Communication,* ed. Hans Ulrich Gumbrecht and K. Ludwig Pfeiffer (Stanford: Stanford University Press, 1994), 371.

28. Ibid., 381.

29. Ibid., 372.

30. Ibid., 374.

31. Ibid., 378.

closed (biological) system, but because it is also a necessary medium for communication, "we can then say that the mind has the privileged position of being able to disturb, stimulate, and irritate communication."[32] It cannot instruct or direct communications— "reports of perceptions are not perceptions themselves"—but it can "stimulate communication without ever becoming communication."[33]

This "irreducibility" of perception to communication (and vice versa) and their asymmetrical relationship are important to art for several reasons. First, as Dietrich Schwanitz notes, perception and communication operate at different speeds—and this is something art puts to use. "Compared to communication," he writes,

> the dimension of perception displays a considerably higher rate of information processing. The impression of immediacy in perception produces the notion that the things we perceive are directly present. Naturally, this is an illusion, for recent brain research has proven that sensory input is minimal compared with the complexity of neuronal self-perception . . . . Together, cultural and neuronal construction thus constitute a form of mediation that belies the impression of immediacy in perception. That does not, however, alter the fact that perception takes place immediately as compared to communication, the selective process of which is a sequential one.[34]

To put it another way, although both perception and communication are autopoietic systems that operate on the basis of difference and distinction, their very different processing speeds make it appear that perception confirms, stabilizes, and makes immediate, while communication (to put it in Derridean terms) differs, defers, and temporalizes. In the work of art, the difference between perception and communication is "reentered" on the side of communication, but (because of this asymmetry in speeds) in a way that calls attention to the contingency of communication— not of the first-order communication of the artwork, which appears incapable of emendation (it is what it is), but of the second-order observation of the work's meaning vis à vis the system of art. This can be accomplished, as in Blur, by making perception "outrun" communication, as it were (a process well described by Hansen), the better to provoke a question that the work itself is made to answer; or, conversely, in a work like On Kawara's *Date Paintings*, by using the calculated deficit of perceptual cues and information in the "paintings" themselves to call attention to the difference between the work's immediate perceptual surface and its meaning.

Thus, the artwork co-presents the difference between perception and communication and it uses perception to "irritate" and stimulate communication to respond to the question, "what does this

32. Luhmann, "How Can the Mind," 379.

33. Ibid., 379-80.

34. Dietrich Schwanitz, "Systems Theory and the Difference between Communication and Consciousness: An Introduction to a Problem and Its Context," *MLN* 111.3 (1996): 494.

perceptual event mean?" And it is this difference—and how art uses it—that allows art to have something like a privileged relationship to what is commonly invoked as the "ineffable" or the "incommunicable."

> The function of art would then consist in integrating what is in principle incommunicable—namely, perception—into the communication network of society . . . . The art system concedes to the perceiving consciousness its own unique adventure in observing artworks—and yet makes available as communication the formal selection that triggered the adventure. Unlike verbal communication, which all too quickly moves toward a yes/no bifurcation, communication guided by perception relaxes the structural coupling of consciousness and communication (without destroying it, of course) . . . . In a manner that is matched neither by thought nor by communication, perception presents astonishment and recognition in a single instant. Art uses, enhances, and in a sense exploits the possibilities of perception in such a way that it can present the unity of this distinction . . . . [T]he pleasure of astonishment, already described in antiquity, refers to the unity of the difference between astonishment and recognition, to the paradox that both intensify one another (*Art*, 141).

And, Luhmann adds—in an observation directly relevant to Blur's audacious formal solution to the "problem" of architecture—"Extravagant forms play an increasingly important role in this process."

This is not, however, simply a matter of "pleasure." In fact, it is what gives art something like a privileged critical relationship to society, because art "establishes a reality of its own that differs from ordinary reality"; "despite the work's perceptibility, despite its undeniable reality," Luhmann writes, "it simultaneously constitutes another reality . . . . Art splits the world into a real world and an imaginary world," and "the function of art concerns the meaning of this split" (*Art*, 142). By virtue of its unique relationship to the difference between perception and communication, art can raise this question in an especially powerful way not available to other social systems. If we think of objects as "eigen-behaviors" (to seize once again on Heinz von Foerster's term), as stabilizations made possible by the repeated, recursive application of particular distinctions, then we might observe that "the objects that emerge from the recursive self-application of communication"—versus, say, rocks or trees—"contribute more than any other kinds of norms and sanctions to supplying the social system with necessary redundancies." They literally fix social space. This is probably even more true, Luhmann observes, of such "quasi-objects" (to use Michel Serres's phrase) "that have been invented for the sake of this specific function, such as kings or soccer balls. Such 'quasi-objects' can be comprehended only in relation to this function"—indeed it is their sole reason for being. Luhmann continues:

> Works of art are quasi-objects in this sense. They individualize themselves by excluding the sum total of everything else; not because they are construed as given but because their significance as objects implies a realm of social regulation. One must scrutinize works of art as intensely and with as close attention to the object as one does when watching kings and soccer balls; in this way—and in the more complex case where one observes other observers by focusing on the same object— the socially regulative reveals itself.[35]

When we remember that for Luhmann this "more complex" case is represented nowhere more clearly than in our experience of the mass media, the relationship between Blur's formal decisions as a work of art and its critical agenda of shedding light on "the socially regulative"—on the terrain of an international media Expo, no less— comes even more forcefully into view. In these terms, works of art, in calling our attention to the realm of "the socially regulative," cast light on precisely those contingencies, constructions, and norms that the mass media, in its own specific mode of communication, occludes. In the first instance (the artwork), we seem to be dealing with completely ad hoc, constructed objects whose realm of reference is not "the real world" but rather that of the imagination; in the latter, we appear to be dealing with the opposite, in which the representations of the mass media are supposedly motivated by the objects and facts of "the real world." In fact, however, this thematization in terms of "imaginative" and "real" only obscures the need to be rearticulate the relationship in terms of the dynamics of first- and second-order observation of different social systems. As Luhmann points out, "the mass media create the illusion that we are first-order observers whereas in fact this is already second-order observing";[36] or, more baldly still, "put in Kantian terms: the mass media generate a transcendental illusion."[37] The mass media's rendering of reality, however—and this is a point that the "post-ethical" character of Diller+Scofidio's work insists on as well—is not to be taken as, "as most people would be inclined to think, a distortion of reality. It is a construction of reality. For from the point of view of a post-ontological theory of observing systems, there is no distinct reality out there (who, then, would make these distinctions?) There is no transcendental subject . . . We have to rely on the system of the mass media that construct our reality . . . If there is no choice in accepting these observations, because there is no equally powerful alternative available, we have at least the possibility to deconstruct the presentations of the mass media, their presentations of the present."[38]

35. Luhmann, *Art as a Social System,* 47. Author's emphasis.

36. Luhmann, "Deconstruction as Second-Order Observing," 775.

37. Niklas Luhmann, *The Reality of the Mass Media* (Stanford: Stanford University Press, 2000), 4.

38. Luhmann, "Deconstruction as Second-Order Observing," 776.

That deconstruction of the mass media in Blur proceeds by means of the artwork's second-order observation of the first-order system of the mass media, but it can carry out that observation only as art, only by "doing what it does" within the codes of the social system of art. The formal symmetry between those two observing systems, however—the fact that the dynamics of communication in autopoietic social systems operate in the same ways in each system (on the basis of the "blind spot" of paradoxical self-reference, and so on)—only throws into critical relief the important difference in the relationship of communication and perception (and in the case at hand, specifically visual perception) that is quite specific to each system: a difference that Blur will put to critical use under the thematics, as Diller suggests, of "spectacle." We can gain a sharper sense of just how this is the case when we remember that for Luhmann, electronic mass media is just the latest in a series of powerful developments in the history of what he calls "media of dissemination," beginning with language and then, crucially, the invention of writing and printing, whose power lies in their ability to make communication independent from a specific perceptual substrate or set of coordinates. "Alphabetized writing made it possible to carry communication beyond the temporally and spatially limited circle of those who were present at any particular time," he writes, and language per se—and even more so writing and printing—"increases the understandability of communication beyond the sphere of perception."[39] Unlike oral speech, which "can compensate for lack of information with persuasion, and can synchronize speaking, hearing, and accepting in a rhythmic and rhapsodic way, leaving literally no time for doubt," writing and printing "enforce an experience of the difference that constitutes communication," and "they are, in this precise sense, more communicative forms of communication."[40]

For Luhmann, the electronic mass media represent the culmination of this general line of historical development. Indeed, "for the differentiation of a system of the mass media, the decisive achievement can be said to have been the invention of technologies of dissemination which not only circumvent interaction among those co-present, but effectively render such interaction impossible for the mass media's own communications"[41] —a process begun with the advent of the printing press, when "the volume of written material multiplied to the extent that oral interaction among all participants in communication is effectively and visibly rendered impossible."[42]

in the wake of the so-called democratization of politics and its dependence on the media of public opinion . . . those participating in politics—politicians and voters alike—observe one another in

39. Luhmann, *Social Systems*, 160.

40. Ibid. 162–3.

41. Luhmann, *The Reality of the Mass Media*, 15–6.

42. Ibid., 16.

the mirror of public opinion . . .The level of first-order observation is guaranteed by the continuous reports of the mass media. Second-order observation occurs via the inferences one can draw about oneself or others, if one assumes that those who wish to participate politically encounter one another in the mirror of public opinion, and that this is sufficient (*Art*, 65).

It is just this situation that Blur attempts to address, if we believe Diller+Scofidio—namely, by subjecting communication in its mass mediated mode (as immediately legible and consumable) to a perceptual Blur, so that spectacle here operates not in the services of an immediately meaningful, pre-fab content (as in the electronic mass media) but rather as the quite unavoidable "irritation" or "perturbation" for another communication—one whose meaning is far from immediately clear and, in being so, operates directly in the services of art's own communication and autopoiesis about itself ("what does this mean?; is this art?"), and its second-order observation of the all-too-tight coupling of perception and communication in the mass media.

In this way, Diller+Scofidio's Blur might be understood as bringing into focus 1) how the contingency of communication is managed and manipulated (quite improbably, as Luhmann reminds us) by the "socially regulative" in the electronic mass media and 2) how that dynamic, in turn, is coupled to a certain "consumerist" schematization of visuality, in which the difference between perception and communication is always already "re-entered" in mass-mediated communication to produce a "pre-digested," iconographic visual space readily incorporated by a subject whose (un)ethical relation to the visual might best be summed up as: "CLICK HERE." We could say, then, that Blur uses the difference between perception and communication in a way diametrically opposed to what we find it in the electronic mass media, and then routes that difference between art and the mass media through the work's formal choices to render them specifically meaningful as art, and not just as well-meaning critical platitude. What is remarkable here, of course, is not that Blur makes this (somewhat unremarkable) observation about the relationship of perception and communication in electronic mass media, a relationship particularly evident in the realm of visuality; what is remarkable is that Blur does so without saying so, by insisting only on itself. This is simply to say that Blur communicates this difference as Art. And if it didn't, we wouldn't pay any attention to it.

Pragmatic Ecologies
Simon Guy

Introduction: Models And Practices

> Uncertainty, ambiguity, and a constantly evolving vision of just what nature is will guide architecture as long as there are buildings.[1]

Debates about sustainable architecture and cities are shaped by different social interests and diverse agendas, based on different interpretations of the environmental challenge and characterized by different pathways, each pointing towards a range of sustainable futures.[2] These competing environmental debates are the result, not of uncertainty, but of the existence of "contradictory certainties: severely divergent and mutually irreconcilable sets of convictions both about the environmental problems we face and the solutions that are available to us."[3] The related analytical framework of sociotechnical theory developed here responds to the contingent and contextual nature of technological innovation and building design. It is further argued that the most fundamental issue, understandably marginalized in the policy debate about industry standards and replicable building codes, is that the environment is a contested terrain, and that implicit within alternative technological strategies are distinct philosophies of environmental place-making and futures.[4] Individual models of the sustainable city, even the boundaries of the city-region, are prefigured by the particular environmental problem presented. Seen this way, environmental concerns are both time and space specific and are framed by the identification of specific and dynamic models of nature, which delimits the selection of design and development responses.

This same logic of selectivity can be applied to technology and to sustainable cities more generally, that is, they are characterized by an "interpretative flexibility." This perspective points towards the need for research and policy to acknowledge how certain development pathways fade away, while others are "economically reinforced as members of a society come to share a set of meanings or benefits" attached to it.[5] Adopting a sociotechnical perspective then has critical implications for sustainable architectural practice, education and research. Rather than searching for a singular optimal

1. Philip Jodidio, *Architecture: Nature* (London, Prestel, 2006), 28.

2. Simon Guy and Graham Farmer, "Re-interpreting Sustainable architecture: the Place of Technology," *Journal of Architectural Education*, 54.3, (2001): 140–8. Simon Guy and S. Marvin, "Constructing Sustainable Urban Futures: From Models to Competing Pathways," *Impact Assessment and Project Appraisal: Journal of the International Association for Impact Assessment* 19.2 (2001), 131–9.

3. John Hannigan, *Environmental Sociology: A Social Constructivist Perspective* (London: Routledge, 1995), 30.

4. Guy and Marvin, "Constructing Sustainable Urban Futures," 131–9.

5. Steven Moore, "Models, Lists, and the Evolution of Sustainable Architecture," in Kim Tanzer and Rafael Longoria, eds., *The Green Braid: Towards an Architecture of Ecology, Economy, and Equity* (London: Routledge, 2007), 25.

technological pathway, this perspective encourages us to recognize and listen to the number of voices striving to frame the debate, and the visions they express of alternative environmental place-making. The search for consensus that has hitherto characterized (and often still does characterize) sustainable design and policy-making must be translated into the search for an enlarged context in which a more heterogeneous coalition of practices can be developed. In this sense, rather than viewing sustainable design practice as the "implementation of a plan for action, it should be viewed as an on-going transformational process in which different actor interests and struggles are located."[6] In an educational context, there is an opportunity to encourage greater reflectivity in the teaching of environmental studies by challenging the search for a true or incontestable, consensual definition of, for instance, green infrastructures and spaces.

If the future direction and success of sustainable city strategies rely on the abilities of urban professionals to act as moral citizens, by engaging in an open process of negotiation, criticism, and debate, then it is vital that students are encouraged to become more sensitive to the range of possible logics of innovation that may surface in design practice. This requires critical methods for understanding technological innovation which transcend both instrumental and deterministic interpretations and which can begin to open "the discourse of technology to future designers in the hopes of engendering a more humane and multi-vocal world."[7] Here, multiple opinions and perspectives are not only valid, but highly desirable. Further, once a diversity of possible approaches has been exposed "they might lead to a more reflective attitude towards certain environmental constructs and perhaps even the formulation of alternative scenarios."[8] But before turning to the development of this perspective it is instructive to explore some of the paradoxes of the debate about sustainable building.

The Paradox of Sustainable Building

> There is no compelling, immediately identifiable formal language on which to pin the cause of environmentalism.[9]

The idea that there is contestation over the meaning or practice of sustainable design is not novel. Neither is the suggestion that context is important or that a geographically comparative perspective may be important and productive. There have been numerous projects

6. Norman Long and Ann Long, *Battlefields of Knowledge: The Interlocking of Theory and Practice in Social Research and Development* (London: Routledge, 1992), 9.

7. Barbara Allen, "Rethinking Architectural Technology: History, Theory, and Practice," *Journal of Architectural Education* 51.1 (1997): 2.

8. Marteen Hajer, *The Politics of Environmental Discourse: Ecological Modernization and the Policy Process* (London: Oxford University Press, 1995), 298.

9. Susannah Hagen, *Digitalia, Architecture and the Digital, the Environment and the Avant-garde* (London: Routledge, 2008), 25.

and initiatives to explore the variability of sustainable ideas, practices and standards. Typical was a series of regional conferences to promote sustainable building held in 2004–2005 promoted by the International Council for Research and Innovation in Building and Construction.[10] A major debate running through all the events was the contested nature of sustainability and the search for some sort of stable knowledge base upon which to act. Of course, variability is not a surprise when we are facing such diverse contexts of development as can be found across Asia, South America, Africa and Europe. Marteen Hajer has pertinently argued that, if examined closely, environmental discourse is fragmented and contradictory.[11] That is, environmental discourse is an astonishing collection of claims and concerns brought together by a great variety of actors. Debate about what the priorities of sustainability are have become very politically charged with some economists even urging us to forget climate change as the least of our worries, and to instead focus on AIDS, water, and hunger.[12] Although the authors were united in opposing this view and urging strategies to engage with sustainability, they were uncertain about what such an agenda may mean. In particular, many authors called for the development of common assessment methods and models and advocated the use of environmental tools and assessment methods, that communication and training should be intensified and sustainable building construction concepts be spread to improve performance and demystify incorrect perceptions.

Of course, there is a key role to be played by such approaches and models but as Cole points out, perhaps we should ask whether "too great an expectation is now placed on their ability to create the desired change at the expense of their relationship with other potential change mechanisms."[13] The critical concern here is that we start to avoid the contingent complexities of sustainability by focusing our attention on apparently universalized systems of measurement as a guide through cultural diversity. "Until a consensus is attained, the ability of the architectural community to adopt a coherent environmental strategy, across all building types and styles of development, will remain elusive."[14] As has been suggested elsewhere, such "environmental realism" is founded on the notion that "rational science can and will provide the understanding of the environment and the assessment of those measures which are necessary to rectify environmental bads."[15]

Further implicit in this model of consensus is a "process of standardization," which means that "particular local conditions" and

10. http://cibworld.xs4all.nl/dllib/0302/SBO I.pdf.

11. Hajer, The Politics of Environmental Discourse.

12. John Vidal, "Forget Climate Change, That Is the Least of Our Worries, Say Nobel Winners," The Guardian, Thursday, 21 October 2004, 3.

13. Raymond Cole, "Building Environmental Assessment Methods: Redefining Intentions and Roles," Building Research & Information, 33.5 (2005): 455–67.

14. John Brennan, "Green Architecture: Style Over Content," Architectural Design 67, no.1–2 (1997): 23–5.

15. Phil Macnaghton and John Urry, Contested Natures (London: Sage, 1998), 1.

competing "forms of local knowledge" tend to be ignored.[16] While some of the researchers also warn against this tendency and call for a recalibration of assessment methods to account for local cultures, there is an inherent danger that the science of assessment may encourage a convergence of priorities that precludes the diversity explored through these conferences.

Searching for Pluralism: Beyond Standardization

> There may well be as many types of relationship between nature and architecture as there are architects and buildings.[17]

There is a growing body of literature now that rejects both these calls for standardization. Brian Edwards, for example, celebrates the fact that the agenda of sustainability is not "leading to a single universal style but to a rich and complex architectural order around the world," arguing that this diversity of interpretation can be too easily "overwhelmed by the internationalization of sustainability as evidenced by scientific literature."[18] Here we find clear recognition that there is "no class or style of design which is unequivocally sustainable architecture, and no fixed set of rules which will guarantee success if followed"[19] Unfortunately, Edwards appears to look for a form of cultural essentialism to explain the alternative formation of sustainability between "west" and "east," suggesting that:

> The West tends to "measure" sustainability whilst the South and East simply "feel" it. Asia and Africa act out good green practices by instinct, and their point of reference is not Newton or Einstein but the local shaman or wisdom keeper ... As a general statement, the spiritual approach to green design is found in the underdeveloped world and the low-energy, high-material approach in the developed.[20]

This analysis usefully recognizes both the contested nature of the sustainability concept and the need to encompass the differing contextual values of the design process across cultures when understanding buildings. However, the result is a relatively limited dualistic categorization of values in which the dilemma of environmentalism is often portrayed as an expression of two distinct and unbridgeable worldviews. Taking another stance, Williamson et al. ask, "How, then, should we look at a building, at architecture as a cultural product that needs to be judged as an integrated entity

16. Ibid., 19.

17. Jodidio, *Architecture: Nature*, 7.

18. Brian Edwards, "Green Architecture," *Architectural Design* 2001, 1–6.

19. Eds. Terence Williamson, Antony Radford, and Helen Bennetts, *Understanding Sustainable Architecture* (Oxford: Spon, 2003), 127.

20. Edwards, "Green Architecture."

while recognizing that it is simultaneously 'coming from' multiple origins and objectives?"[21] They point to the importance of integrating social, economic and environmental sustainability in what is often termed the "triple bottom line." They draw upon the planner Scott Campbell's triangular model of sustainable development,[22] with its tripartite structure of equity, economy, and ecology, and conflicts between these goals over property, development, and resources. The aim of the model is then to mediate these competing priorities and conflicts in the search for a resolution represented by the centre of the triangle. Williamson et al. reinterpret Campbell's model with their own emphasis on the coexistence, parity, and optimization of nature, culture, and technology.

This theme is developed in a collection of essays appropriately titled *The Green Braid*, which seek to flesh out this new paradigm in relation to the three key stands of the "green braid": ecology, equity, and economy.[23] David Orr starts by arguing for design to look beyond the art and science of building design towards a more expansive, three-fold role.[24] First, the "aesthetic standards for design" have to be broadened beyond appearance towards the goal of reducing human or ecological "ugliness" both now and in the future. Second, design should "instruct us" in relation to our "mindfulness" about nature, or as Orr puts it, the "ultimate object of design is not artefacts, buildings, or landscapes, but human minds." Third, design should encompass health, healing, and spirituality. Rejecting the "default setting" of faith in science and technology to meet the environmental challenge, Orr calls for an "ecological design revolution" to convert our "pre-ecological" mind, to "calibrate human behavior," and to "educate people." Strangely, this is a revolution that looks not forwards but backwards, in a "rediscovery of old and forgotten things." Orr strongly equates this design revolution not with any particular approach or strategy, but with a break from the "addictive quality" of modernity and reconnection with a more "sensuous" relationship to nature. Design here is a romantic gesture that locates the "beginning of design" with a "generosity of spirit."

Thomas Fischer develops this theme by invoking Native American practices of living sustainably with each other and with nature.[25] By contrast he argues that architects have become complicit with a system dedicated to providing material surrogates for happiness. Fischer argues that we need a new social contract between architects, communities and nature to produce a "modern-day version of how Native Americans lived before Europeans arrived." Illustrating by reference to the disaster relief work of

21. Williamson, Radford and Bennetts, *Understanding Sustainable Architecture*, 127.

22. Scott Campbell, "Green Cities, Growing Cities, Just Cities? Urban planning and the contradictions of sustainable development," *Journal of the American Planning Association* 62.3 (2006): 296.

23. Kim Tanzer and Rafael Longoria, *The Green Braid: Towards an Architecture of Ecology, Economy, and Equity*, London: Routledge, 2007).

24. David Orr, "Architecture, Ecological Design, and Human Ecology," in Kim Tanzer and Rafael Longoria, *The Green Braid: Towards an Architecture of Ecology, Economy, and Equity*, London: Routledge, 2007),15–33.

25. Thomas Fischer, "A New Social Contract: Equity and Sustainable Development" in Kim Tanzer and Rafael Longoria, T*he Green Braid: Towards an Architecture of Ecology, Economy, and Equity*, London: Routledge, 2007), 34–43.

Architects for Humanity, Fischer suggests that this would mean a new kind of practice for architects based on "advocacy, activism, and attention to what the rest of the world wastes." Again, what is key here is an ethical frame for design that involves commitment to a socially progressive agenda focused on community and spiritual development.

Turning to the third element of the green braid, the economic, Ellen Dunham-Jones further reinforces this critique of modernization, through a critical exploration of architecture's role in treating buildings and places as disposable assets and the concomitant "sprawlscapes" that result. Singling out the work of Frank Gehry, Dunham-Jones equates the representational obsessions of contemporary architectural production with the branding of commodities.[26] Given this complicity, she asks how architecture can promote "even" rather than "uneven" development? The answer, it seems, is in looking beyond the building unit and in embracing the values of a "new urbanism," which again looks backwards, although not as far as Native American society, and echoes a slower, smaller scale, pre-industrial model of development. While working within existing market structures, the objective is to revalue and reconfigure the sprawl of suburbia through design-led place-making. Less radical in its intent than chapters by Orr and Fischer, the aim here is not to transform the system but to stretch its boundaries and possibilities.

Taken together, these three authors attempt to articulate the green braid as a coherent systemic framework for articulating a new contract between architecture, nature and society that is co-constitutive and dynamic. However the tensions are glaring. To work with the market or against it? To look backwards or forwards historically and if so how far? To centralize, decentralize, or suburbanize? To pursue technological complexity or to simplify? And so on. Perhaps the key problem is, as Steven Moore puts it in his chapter, the idea of the "green braid" as an abstract model that balances and optimizes what are actually often competing conceptualizations of sustainability.[27] For Moore, any attempt to model sustainability in this way is bound to fail to represent "the nuance or contingency of history, past, or future." That is, such abstract models tend to obscure local, place-based histories of sustainability that serve to reinterpret the environmental challenge and in doing so add to or develop our understanding of a more pluralistic vision of sustainability. For Moore, the danger in such models is in the premature fixing of definitions resulting in the closing down of debate, or rather the squeezing out of alternative stories of sustainability.

26. Ellen Dunham-Jones, "Economic Sustainability in the Post-industrial Landscape," in Kim Tanzer and Rafael Longoria, *The Green Braid: Towards an Architecture of Ecology, Economy, and Equity*, London: Routledge, 2007), 44–59.

27. Steven Moore, "Models, Lists, and the Evolution of Sustainable Architecture," in Kim Tanzer and Rafael Longoria, eds., *The Green Braid: Towards an Architecture of Ecology, Economy, and Equity* (London: Routledge, 2007): 60–76.

Paradoxically, this metaphor of stories or "environmental talk" provides a rather better frame for what follows in the collection than the "green braid":

> We can look at this as the construction of a reasoned argument that weaves together the ethical, human, scientific, aesthetic and other aspects of these three contexts. If an architect can do this, taking into account all the stakeholders, she or he is performing a beautiful act.[28]

This emphasis on the participation of stakeholders in the rebalancing of priorities points the way towards an alternative conception of sustainable design. Rather than seek the certainties of standardized solutions and universal objectives, Cole describes an approach that emphasizes "process over product" in which "assessment methods . . . facilitate dialogue between stakeholders in formulating and pursuing a design project."[29] Kaatz et al. write similarly of a participative process that considers "biophysical, social and economic issues" and "reflects the different value sets that are at play in a given project context."[30] This emphasis on "conversation" may help to open up a debate about sustainable architecture, to ask "what alternative ways of seeing we can envisage?; how do we analyze environmental problems?; how do we want to live both in and with nature?" and to "appreciate the ways in which we culturally interpret rather than objectively reflect the relationship of society to nature."[31]

Building Hybridity

> What is clear is that there is no still point of the turning world as far as green is concerned. Variations are thrown up by social, political, cultural and economic factors as well as by individual preferences.[32]

Exploring debates and mapping practices of sustainable architecture involves tracing the interplay of competing environmental values and practices through the enactment of alternative design logics as they shape the technonatural profiles of green building development.[33] As Noel Castree has put it, and as practices of sustainable architecture make clear, "ideas about nature" do not:

> somehow touch down uniformly across time and space. Rather they are produced by myriad knowledge communities who possess similar (and sometimes different) outlooks on nature.[34]

28. Williamson, Radford and Bennetts, *Understanding Sustainable Architecture*, 130.

29. Raymond Cole, "Building Environmental Assessment Methods: Redefining Intentions and Roles," *Building Research & Information,* 33.5 (2005): 455–67.

30. Kaatz, E., Root, D. and Bowen, P, "Broadening Project Participation Through a Modified Building Sustainability Assessment," *Building Research and Information* 33.5 (2005), 441–54.

31. Frank Fischer and Maarten Hajer, *Living with Nature: Environmental Politics as Cultural Discourse* (Oxford: Oxford University Press, 1999).

32. Helen Castle, "Editorial-Green Architecture," *Architectural Design* 71.4, (May 2001): 5.

33. Simon Guy and Graham Farmer, "Re-interpreting Sustainable Architecture: the Place of Technology," *Journal of Architectural Education,* 54.3, (2001): 140-148; *Sustainable Architectures: Cultures and Natures in Europe and North America,* Eds., Simon Guy and Steven Moore, (Oxford: Spon Press, 2005).

34. Noel Castree, *Nature* (London: Routledge, 2005), xiv.

Seen this way, alternative design strategies are the result not simply of contestation over technological optimization or expression of the environmental sublime, but of distinct philosophies and practices rooted in differing accounts of the nature–culture relationship. In order to fully understand the heterogeneity of sustainable architecture, we therefore have to account for the multiple ways environmental problems are identified, defined, translated, valued, and then embodied in built forms through diverse design and development pathways. The current "society–nature dualism," which we have shown to structure the debate about sustainable architecture, is, as Castree again suggests, blinding us to the "need for a new vocabulary to describe the world we inhabit."[35] For Castree, this would not be a "vocabulary of pure forms"—in architectural terms, the performative or the iconic—but one that "captures the hybrid, chimeric, mixed-up world in which we are embedded."[36] From this perspective, it is clear that we need to open up and explore the language we use to talk about sustainable architecture. As Andrew Jamison has suggested, "More fluid terms are needed: dialectical, open-ended terms to characterize the ebbs and flows, nuances and subtleties and the ambiguities of environmental politics."[37]

Similarly, David Schlosberg has called for "statements that are open rather than doctrinaire" that "conscript" rather than alienate, and that encourage a debate in which "discourse is never-ending, and solidarity is forever creating new networks and mosaics."[38] Seen this way, we need more "fluid' interpretations of sustainable architecture. This does not mean to suggest that buildings are infinitely flexible, subject only to the whims of designers. The obduracy of certain materials and contingencies of particular technologies are part of the story of building design and development as Annique Hommels has shown.[39] Rather, fluidity here suggests an interpretative flexibility and plasticity of design and technology, or as Steven Moore puts it, "it could have been designed in a different way."[40] Following the fluidity of design, we would ask: How and why are designers pursuing environmentalism in very particular ways, with very different notions of nature and culture, and with highly variable technological strategies? Critically, our use of the term "technology here is an expansive one. We mean by it not only the artefacts associated with sustainable architecture—solar collectors, wind generators, biomass boilers and the like—but the knowledge required to construct and use these artefacts, as well as the practices that engage them. This stance echoes that of Andrew Feenberg who has similarly explored these

35. Castree, *Nature,* 224.

36. Ibid.

37. Andrew Jamison, *The Making of Green Knowledge: Environmental Politics and Cultural Transformation* (Cambridge: Cambridge University Press), 178.

38. David Schlosberg, *Environmental Justice and the New Pluralism: the Challenge of Difference for Environmentalism* (Oxford: Oxford University Press, 1999).

39. Anique Hommels, *Unbuilding Cities: Obduracy in Urban Sociotechnical Change* (Cambridge, MA: MIT Press, 2005).

40. Steven Moore, *Technology and Place: Sustainable Architecture and the Blueprint Farm* (Austin: The University of Texas Press, 2001).

approaches and emphasized the need to avoid the essentialist fallacy of splitting technology and meaning, and to focus instead on the "struggle between different types of actors differently engaged with technology and meaning."[41] Seen this way, the contexts of technology include such diverse factors as "relation to vocations, to responsibility, initiative, and authority, to ethics and aesthetics, in sum, to the realm of meaning." Wrapped up in each technological artefact, or in the case of our architectural interests, each building, is a set of ideologies, calculations, dreams, political compromises, and so on. Eric Swyngedouw has similarly pointed to the "combined metabolic transformations of socio-natures" in the construction of a skyscraper which testifies:

> to the particular associational power relations through which socio-natural metabolisms are organized (in terms of property ownership regimes, production or assemblaging activities, distributional arrangements and consumption patterns).[42]

Tracing these networks would mean looking beyond the polemical debates about architectural visions and sustainable futures to the often messy ways in which architectural artefacts are assembled on local sites, funded by particular financial regimes, utilize specific expertise (or lack of), connect to technical networks, are argued over by a restricted or enlarged community of users are placed within a planning framework (or not). Again, looking beyond the ideological choice between employing the technical disciplines of energy management to produce new forms of "smart buildings," or simply mimicking of organic nature in architectural form, dialogue about sustainability may come to inhabit what Amerigo Marras has termed an "architecture of the inbetween."[43] For Marras, design involves a weaving of ecology and technology in a "transformative flux... a catalytic fusion... intentionally generating some hybrid transgendering paradigms."[44] Rejecting the "extreme positions of being either-or," Marras urges the "fluid process of in-between." Adopting this way of seeing and describing building design as "fluid," we may better recognize both the hybrid nature of the green building and competing pathways towards sustainable futures.

Tracing Fluid Architectures

Tracing these fluid hybrids means looking beyond fixed definitions and dualistic typologies, while at the same time resisting the temptation to either abandon the environmental project or simply swimming along in an ocean of free flowing design options with no

41. Andrew Feenberg, *Questioning Technology,* London, Routledge, 1999.

42. Erik Swyngedouw, "Circulations and Metabolisms: (Hybrid) Natures and (Cyborg) Cities," *Science as Culture* 15.2 (2006), 105–22.

43. Amerigo Marras, Ed. *ECO-TEC: Architecture of the Inbetween,* (New York: Princeton Architectural Press, 1999), 2–9.

44. Marras, *ECO-TEC,* 3.

Guy

fixed reference points. It also means neither accepting the status quo—familiar buildings symbolically retrofitted with wind turbines and solar collectors—nor exclusively searching for radically new typologies. Looking back across the competing definitions of sustainability offered by leading architects reviewed above, we may be unable to identify any semantic solutions to what sustainability really means in architectural terms, but we can find a convincing and workable toolbox of design innovations, technological options, and creative practices. The question is less whether any combination of these might provide a universal blueprint (they won't), but more importantly how may they contribute to meeting specific environmental challenges? Seen this way, we may begin to sketch out some general principles of "fluidity" in order to frame diverse sustainable design approaches which may aspire to be: flexible, situated, pragmatic, and participative. We can very briefly (and tentatively) explore what we may call these design frames and illustrate them with examples of architecture beyond the fold of what is conventionally thought of as sustainable architecture.

First, we should develop "flexibility" to a range of technological options—whether high-tech or low-tech—and an appetite to mix these where it makes sense. Second, we need to look beyond contested league tables of environmental performance in terms of materials (wood vs. concrete), height (skyscrapers vs. ground-scrapers vs. underground architecture), location (cities vs. suburbs vs. rural villages) and be willing to be open to heterogeneous combinations of purpose and program, from "mixed" to "mixed-up" uses. Echoing the emphasis on "interpretative flexibility" found in science and technology studies,[45] the point here is not to abandon judgment but to avoid closing down the evaluative process prematurely, to always be open to other design possibilities.

One exemplar here is the work of Atelier Bow-Wow in Japan who focus their work on the narrow, inbetween spaces of Tokyo where uses are continually shifting. Bow-Wow have made a study of what they term Tokyo's "Pet Architecture," buildings that appear monstrous in their rejection of standardized design and purpose and which instead celebrate wild juxtapositions ·of use: temples and shops, laundries and saunas, shrines and restaurants, pachinko parlours and banks, taxi company with golf driving range.[46] Bow-Wow use these pet architectures as an inspiration for their own design practice, which is characterized by strategic interventions into the existing fabric, responding to new demands through creative conversion and adaptation of the built fabric of Tokyo. While

45. Weibe Bijker, *Of Bicycles, Bakelites and Bulbs. Toward a Theory of Socio-technical Change* (Cambridge, MA: MIT Press, 1995).

46. M. Kaijima, J. Kuroda, and Y. Tsukamoto, *Made in Tokyo* (Tokyo: Kajima-Publishing Co., 2001).

not overtly a "green practice," the work of Bow-Wow is dedicated to satisfying changing human needs, intensifying the use of urban space with great economy and efficiency and focusing on recycling and reusing space.

Second, a frame is necessary to give shape to this fluidity, to enable a design to be "situated." This is a familiar theme in architecture, often promoted in terms of "regionalism" and familiar to environmentalists in discourses of "bio-regionalism."[47] But here the emphasis is away from fixed spatial containers defined in concepts like local, city, region, characterized by their cultural and/or physical attributes, and more on creating unique solutions to local challenges defined according to a specific attribute. These local attributes may vary hugely, from comfort to community and from energy security to emergency shelter to flood prevention. To take this latter example, with climatologists predicting that precipitation in The Netherlands could increase as much as twenty-five percent in the next few years, Dutch architects are now designing built environments that can float and which could grow in the future into "waterproof" towns. In a recent example, the Dutch architecture practice company Dura Vermeer has built twenty-six amphibious homes in Massbommel in The Netherlands, each built on a hollow concrete cube base that is anchored to the land by a single vertical pile. All utilities, including electricity and water, are brought into the house through flexible pipes that allows each house to adapt to a thirteen-foot rise in the water table. While this is a response to a perennial challenge for Dutch urbanism, it is not difficult to think or further applications of this "situated" response to environmental change across the world from New Orleans to Bangladesh.

Third, although environmental change may affect and be effected by us all, our strategies for ameliorating and coping with its causes and symptoms could vary dramatically. And this brings us to "pragmatism." Here we may follow Richard Rorty, in the footsteps of John Dewey, when he calls on us to abandon "the attempt to find a (single) theoretical frame or reference within which to evaluate proposals for the human future."[48] Instead, the pragmatic imperative is to deal with the particular challenge at hand. This is well illustrated in the work of Architects for Humanity, a charity-based practice with its head quarters in California but operating as a worldwide volunteer network. A declared principle for this work is "pragmatism," providing shelter after disaster and to communities in need.[49] A typical project was the provision of global village shelters in Grenada after Hurricane Ivan in 2004. Made from recycled corrugated cardboard

47. Kenneth Frampton, "Technoscience and Environmental Culture: a Provisional Critique," *Journal of Architectural Education* 54.3 (2001): 123–9.

48. Richard Rorty, *Achieving Our Country: Leftist Thought in Twentieth Century America* (Cambridge, MA: Harvard University Press,1998).

49. Architecture for Humanity, Eds., *Design Like you Give a Damn: Architectural Responses to Humanitarian Crises* (London: Thames and Hudson, 2006).

Guy

impregnated with fire retardant and laminated for water resistance, the structures provided speedy transitional shelter that could be distributed and erected easily and quickly. Refinements made from evaluation of the Grenada project led to implementation of almost 500 shelters in Pakistan following the Kashmir earthquake of 2005.

The pragmatic perspective would emphasize, finally, a "participative" approach to design in which voices beyond the architect/developer/investor nexus are heard and make a difference. This frame takes in notions of participatory politics,[50] but also takes inspiration from Bruno Latour's concern in his *Politics of Nature* to multiply the number of representations of any specific issue.[51] More specifically in design terms, it means building with the participation of the community you are building for. Sam Mockbee's Rural Studio practice personifies this approach. They talk about "sharing the sweat" with the community, preferring to see themselves as "citizens" rather than experts.[52] Refusing to abstract architect from their context of work, they aim for low-cost, sustainable "workable solutions," in one scheme made of discarded carpet tiles, for their economically disadvantaged local community in Alabama in the heart of Tornado Alley. The approach of Rural Studio brings together the flexible, situated, pragmatic and participative principles of fluid architecture into an adaptive assembly fit for a purpose and a community, both low in cost and impact.

A "fluid" perspective on sustainable architecture does not mean rejecting one particular typology (skyscrapers) and celebrating another (vernacular). It may mean valuing different aspects of the design. While the examples above are deliberately chosen to stretch our conception of what green architecture may represent, we can equally well re-read some of our current icons of eco-design within this different interpretative frame. Take the celebrated Commerzbank, an ecological skyscraper by Norman Foster in Frankfurt. The designers were able, through a process of public dialogue, to mediate a dispute between images of American (high-rise) and European (low-rise) style urbanism that encouraged both business groups and environmental campaigners to collectively embrace a more sustainable development pathway for Frankfurt.[53]

Our search for flexible, situated and pragmatic solutions requires us to revise our ideas of what constitutes progress. Returning to Rorty we may argue that "instead of seeing progress as a matter of getting closer to something specifiable in advance, we see it as a manner of solving more [local] problems."[54] For

50. Benjamin Barber, *Strong Democracy: Participatory Politics for a New Age* (Berkeley: University of California Press, 1984).

51. Bruno Latour, *Politics of Nature: How to Bring the Sciences into Democracy* (Cambridge, MA: Harvard University Press, 2004).

52. http://cadc.aubum.edu/soalrurai %2Dstudio.

53. Simon Guy and Steven Moore, "Sustainable Architecture and the Pluralist Imagination', *Journal of Architectural Education,* 60.4 (2007), 15–23.

54. Richard Rorty, *Achieving Our Country: Leftist Thought in Twentieth Century America* (Cambridge, MA: Harvard University Press,1998).

designers, this may mean reducing dependency on pre-packaged, universalized design solutions and beginning each project with a process of identifying and prioritizing the key challenges to be tackled for the specific time and place.[55]

Conclusions: Towards Pragmatic Ecologies

> A fundamental feature of the new environmental Politics is that there is no one true, or trusted, form of expertise, no single path to the truth.[56]

To conclude, while acknowledging how a technical performance-based approach to understanding environmental design has brought undoubted benefits in terms of highlighting the issues of energy efficiency in buildings, we must fundamentally revise the focus and scope the debate about sustainable architecture and to reconnect issues of appropriate technological change to the social and cultural processes and practices within which a specific design is situated. Drawing upon more critical, interpretative, participative approaches to sustainable design would involve researchers both in defining the nature of the environmental challenge while encouraging a wider range of context-specific responses. While both checklists and philosophical speculation can be helpful and even necessary to achieve certain objectives, they rarely provoke the wider "public talk" necessary to engage community participation in sustainable design[57]—that is, the "work" of choosing how we want to live, with and in nature, in order to sustain life into the future.

This is not an idle debate. Exploration of diversity in design and development would encourage a deeper engagement with sustainable architecture—one that does not shy away from broader sociological or philosophical questions or merely indulge in the narrowly instrumental debates that characterize so much of the green architecture literature.[58] By exploring sustainable architectures, in the plural, as competing interpretations of our environmental futures, we can begin to ask new questions, introduce some fresh thinking, and find new "socially viable" solutions to the mounting challenges associated with climate change.

55. Simon Guy and Steven Moore, "Sustainable Architecture and the Pluralist Imagination', *Journal of Architectural Education*, 60.4 (2007), 15–3.

56. Andrew Jamison, *The Making of Green Knowledge: Environmental Politics and Cultural Transformation* (Cambridge: Cambridge University Press), 27.

57. Benjamin Barber, *Strong Democracy: Participatory Politics for a New Age* (Berkeley: University of California Press, 1984).

58. Simon Guy and Elizabeth Shove, *A Sociology of Energy, Buildings and the Environment* (London: Routledge, 2000).

Future, Cities, Architecture
Elizabeth Grosz

In consideration of architecture, cities, and the future, I present a series of very brief postulates, or working hypotheses, to help think the connection between them: postulates that bear less on architecture than perhaps they do on the notion of futurity and the new. I do not want to engage particularly in predicting or making projections onto possible futures, but rather to explore how the very concept of the new and futurity (at least as they are presently embodied) impact on and may help reconfigure the way that bodies, cities, and their relations are thought.

1. Fantasies about the future are always, at least in part, projections, images, hopes, and horrors extrapolated from the present, though not simply from the present situation but from its cultural imaginary, its self-representation, its own latencies or virtualities. Whether self-fulfilling and thus prophetic, or wildly fictionalized, these fantasies represent neuralgic points of present investment and anxiety, loci of intense vulnerability, anxiety, or optimism. In this sense, they are more revealing of the status and permeability of the present than they are indices of transformation or guarantees of a present-to-be.

2. Cities have always represented and projected images and fantasies of bodies, whether individual, collective, or political. In this sense, the city can be seen as a (collective) body-prosthesis or boundary that enframes, protects, and houses while at the same time taking its own forms and functions from the (imaginary) bodies it constitutes. Simultaneously, cities are loci that produce, regulate, and structure bodies. This relation is not a simple one of mutual determination nor a singular, abstract diagram of interaction: it depends on the types of bodies (racial, ethnic, class, sexual) and the types of cities (economic, geographic, political), and it is immensely complicated through various relations of intrication, specification, interpolation, and inscription that produce "identities" for both cities in their particularity and populations in their heterogeneity. This relation is not one of "multiple determinations," with the axes of class, race, and sex all systematically interlocked on the one plane, while the types of city—industrialized, commercial, based on one or several industries, a port, located in urban or rural

spaces—can be mapped on one another. Rather, it is a relation of both productive constraint and inherent unpredictability: neither relation is able to take place on the one plane or in a regulated form. While the relations between bodies and cities are highly complex and thoroughly saturated with behavioral, regulative, psychical, legal, and communitarian components, nonetheless the corporeality of cities and the materiality of bodies—the relations of exchange and production, habit, conformity, breakdown, and upheaval—have yet to be adequately thought as corporeal. The corporeality, or materiality, of the city is of the same order of complexity as that of bodies. What that corporeality might consist of, what counts as corporeal or material, is not so readily decidable, but it is clear that unless language, representations, structures, patterns, and habits are considered constitutive ingredients of corporeality, then the complexities of neither bodies nor cities are capable of being understood.

3. In the West, bodies and cities in their broad generality—and those discourses aimed at understanding them (cultural studies, urban studies, geography, as well as philosophy, psychology, and feminism)—are (as is always the case) undergoing major structural and pragmatic changes, changes necessitated and brought about by the complex linkage between global corporatism, the technological revolution in information storage and retrieval, and the transformation of global communications thereby effected. Since the introduction of the personal computer, since the computerization of economic transactions, since the advent of the Internet and instantaneous global communication through cellular phones, satellite networks, and the World Wide Web, transformations in how we understand ourselves, our bodies, our place in cities and communities, and our relation to the future have all been effected, transformations that are in the process of perhaps reconfiguring how we are in the world. Our simultaneous anxiety and joy reside in the extrapolated hopes and fears that an exponentially growing technology promises: its "gift" to us is an increasing edginess about what the future holds in store— whether it promotes our every fantasy to the status of the attainable or the real, or whether we and our hopes are transformed beyond recognition into something other than what we are now.

4. This transformation in technology—let us call it computerization for short—is not simply the creation of a new tool or device more sophisticated than the rest but fundamentally the same in nature. Rather, global computerization is a mode of transformation

of the very notion of tool or technology itself. The space, time, logic, and materiality of computerization threaten to disrupt and refigure the very nature of information and communication, as well as the nature of space, time, community, and identity. These technologies make possible knowledges/sciences, modes of art and representation, forms of communication and interaction, that not only are reconfiguring social and personal life but are also, in a fundamental sense, beyond the knowledge and the control of individuals and communities. These technologies, whose limits are unknown by their designers and foremost researchers, have become subject to historical, perhaps even evolutionary processes or laws that we do not, and perhaps even cannot, know in advance. Computerization transcends the tool or mere cultural innovation, insofar as it has begun an inherently unforeseeable trajectory in global life. Such unforeseen trajectories are not new; they are the forces that shape global transformation, whether dictated by shifts in polar ice caps or the production of nuclear weapons. Technological transformation is not inherently different in its global effect. This is why it may be understood more in the long-term horizon of evolution rather than in the short-term horizon of development or historical change.

5. These technologies have served not to transform bodies in any significant way—at least not yet—but to fundamentally transform the way that bodies are conceived, their sphere of imaginary and lived representation. They promise (and for some they achieve) the fantasy of action, communication, and connectedness at-a-distance, the fantasy of an alternative or virtual existence that may bypass the gravity and weightiness of the body itself: they have mediated spatial relations through the compression of temporal relations, they have transformed interaction and communication through screen and virtual mediation, they have transformed the notion of community through selective global expansion. Bodies clearly are, and always have been, the objects of prosthetic transformation and supplementation, of virtual enhancement and technical mediation. Computerization does not transform this prosthetic hankering; rather, it transforms its degrees of intimacy with the body, the size and nature of prosthetic intervention: micromachines cleaning out veins and arteries, microcomputers pulsating as heart or lung enhancements. It transforms an imaginary anatomy well beyond its technological capacities, yielding the fantasy of the interchangeability, even transcendence, of the body and its corporeal configuration.

As continuous fields of presence are overlaid on architectural and urban space, the ancient distinction between settlers and nomads—long the bedrock of our thinking about cities—is eroding in subtle but important ways. In the emerging wireless era, our buildings and urban environments need fewer specialized spaces built around sites of accumulation and resource availability and more versatile, hospitable, accommodating spaces that simply attract occupation and can serve diverse purposes as required. A café table can serve as a library reading room. A quiet place under a tree can become a design studio. A subway car can become a place for watching movies.

Electronomadic Spatial Practices

The relationships of mobile bodies to sedentary structures have loosened and destabilized; inhabitation is less about doing what some designer or manager explicitly intended in a space and more about imaginative, ad hoc appropriation for unanticipated purposes. We are becoming less like Saint Jerome, immobilized in his study among his accumulated possessions, less like Dilbert stuck at his computer in his cubicle, and more like cyborg foragers navigating through electronically mediated resource fields. We are relying less upon things (or people) being at fixed locations, or available on regular schedules, and more upon electronic tracking and navigation to locate what we want and take us to it. Our mental maps of buildings and cities are becoming less static records of fixed features and more dynamic representations of current conditions.

This condition, understood in the most optimistic way, offers liberation from the rigidities and interdictions of the predefined program and the zone—a release from ways of using spaces produced and enforced by dominant social orders.[1] It opens up the possibility of new, as yet unimagined spatial practices, and the opportunity (in the words of Michel de Certeau) "to rediscover, within an electronicized and computerized megalopolis, the 'art' of the hunters and rural folk of earlier days."[2] Or, if you don't like the pseudo-primitivism of this formulation, you might imagine rediscovering Baudelaire's *flânerie*,[3] situationist "drift,"[4] or whatever it was that Deleuze and Guattari were recommending in *A Thousand Plateaus*.[5] Conversely, for those who would exert state or

1. Michel de Certeau, *The Practice of Everyday Life* (Berkeley: University of California Press, 1984).

2. de Certeau, *The Practice of Everyday Life*, xxiv.

3. Walter Benjamin, "On Some Motifs in Baudelaire," in *Illuminations*, trans. Harry Zohn (New York: Schocken, 1969), 155–200. See also Chris Jenks, "Watching Your Step: The History and Practice of the Flaneur," in Chris Jenks, ed., *Visual Culture* (London: Routledge, 1995), 142-60.

4. This idea was given architectural expression in the "New Babylon" project by the Dutch artist Constant Nieuwenhuys, 1956–74. See Catherine de Zegher and Mark Wigley, eds., *The Activist Drawing: Retracing Situationist Architectures from Constant's New Babylon to Beyond* (Cambridge, MA: MIT Press, 2001).

5. Gilles Deleuze and Felix Guattari, "Treatise on Nomadology:—The War Machine," in *A Thousand Plateaus*, trans. Brian Massumi (Minneapolis: University of Minnesota Press, 1987), 351–423.

corporate power, it offers anonymity and the possibility of avoiding resistance. Today, such power may flow as easily from a fluidly and ambiguously located constellation of cellphones as it traditionally has from a throne room in a palace, a boardroom in a corporate headquarters, or a courtroom in a national capital. As resistance movements have quickly realized, sites for effective confrontation of power are becoming harder to identify.[6] How do you determine a time and locate a place for resistance? Where do you demonstrate? What do you occupy?

The evolution of taxi fleets has dramatized these transformations in the use and control of space. In the past, where urban densities were too low for drivers to rely upon customers hailing them in the street, centralized wireless dispatchers fielded telephone calls and assigned jobs. Now cabbies carry cellphones as well, and rely upon their mobile, distributed, peer-to-peer networks for intelligence about traffic conditions and tips about concentrations of potential customers. In more advanced systems, customers make location-coded cellphone calls, cabs have GPS navigation systems, and software assigns jobs based upon proximity. There is a shift from centralized coordination and control to electronically mediated swarming.

While their elders were trying to figure all this out, kids—employing the short text messaging capabilities of cellphones—imaginatively pioneered the new spatial tactics of ad hoc occupation and electronic appropriation. They quickly learned to fan out through city streets in fluid packs, electronically negotiating and specifying sites for assignations, raves, and street demonstrations. Those who wanted to repress these practices soon came up with the countermeasure (at least for the moment)—have the cops confiscate the phones. And the kids, in response, are discovering how to immobilize opponents by unleashing worms and viruses that clog channels of communication. Control of space—particularly in real time—now requires control of the airwaves.

In many ways, the dynamic ebbs and flows of the basketball court and the soccer field provide compelling models for these new spatial practices. The players are mobile, autonomous actors, but they are in constant visual and auditory communication with one another, and they adjust their actions in response to evolving situations. Over larger chunks of terrain, the wirelessly communicating units of a military operation act in similarly coordinated fashion. Now, spatially dispersed yet coordinated, fluid collections of wirelessly interconnecting individuals—perhaps

6. See, for example, Critical Art Ensemble, "Nomadic Power and Cultural Resistance," in *The Electronic Disturbance* (Brooklyn, NY: Autonomedia, 1994), 11–34.

assembled, from the beginning, in cyberspace rather than at any physical location—are becoming a crucial fact of urban life. They constitute a new category of human assemblage—one to add to our traditional conceptions of the gathering, the throng, the crowd, the masses, the mob, the cadre, the cell, the ensemble, the battalion, and the team.[7]

The connected masses also create problems of differential mobility. Traditional nomads understood these problems well and often dealt with them brutally; they left behind the aged, infirm, and otherwise immobilized. In the context of electronomadics, it is often a matter of relative reliance on bits and atoms, and the consequences tend to be economic. Scholars who can rely upon online resources are highly mobile and can work effectively on the road, but their colleagues who need access to undigitized print material or precious original manuscripts are still tied to traditional scholarly sites and practices. Telephone call centers can readily relocate and may want the flexibility to do so when it becomes economically advantageous, so they may be reluctant to invest in surrounding communities. Financial firms that had their premises destroyed in the World Trade Center attacks could instantly activate backup sites and send their employees into telecommuter mode, but restaurants and other small establishments that serviced those firms in Lower Manhattan were stuck at their sites, lost clientele, and suffered disproportionately badly. The new mobility divide may turn out to be more important than the digital divide.

The Decline and Fall of the Architectural Program
For architects, continuous fields of presence and the destabilization of person-to-place relationships demand some radical rethinking of the fundamentals. The standard procedure of twentieth-century modernism was to start by distinguishing and separating functions—the better to optimize spaces for particular functions and to announce those functions visually. (Communication engineers might think of it as space-division multiplexing of activities.) At an urban scale, housing areas were to be distinguished from industrial and commercial zones. At building scale, there were to be specialized spaces, with associated equipment, for the activities that were to be accommodated. And the physical fabric of a building was to be articulated functionally—for example, by separating the supporting and enclosing functions of a wall by substituting columns for support and a non-bearing curtain wall for enclosure. But this strategy makes little sense when wireless electronic devices can support many

7. One might extend Canetti's well known analysis to the digital wireless era. See Elias Canetti, *Crowds and Power* (New York: Seabury Press, 1982).

Mitchell

different activities at a single location or the same activity at many different locations, and when running different software can radically alter the functions provided by a device without changing its form at all. Time division multiplexing of activities is starting to look smarter than space division.

The key instrument of the traditional spatial organization strategy was the written *architectural program*—a detailed list of required spaces, specifying floor areas, technical requirements, and adjacency needs.[8] Built space made the provisions of the program concrete, and construction bureaucrats compared plans to checklists just to make sure. But the architecture of the twenty-first century can (if we choose to take the opportunity) be far less about responding to such rigid programs and much more about creating flexible, diverse, humane habitats for electronically supported nomadic occupation. It can be an architecture not of stable routines and spatial patterns, but, as Michael Batty has suggested, of continually reconfiguring clusters of spatial events characterized by their duration, intensity, volatility, and location.[9]

This architecture will pursue the benefits of loose binding. Consider these in the context of office space. When office workers have cubicles filled with files and bookshelves, it is relatively difficult and expensive to move them around; churn takes time and costs money, so managers have traditionally tried to minimize it—with the result that organizations are slow to adapt to change, and workers are often left in locations that no longer serve them well. But if the personal information environments of office workers automatically and instantaneously follow them around, they can sit down and work anywhere. The cost of regrouping to meet new needs drops almost to zero. You can also look at this from a long-term space management perspective. When organizations move into new buildings, they usually have carefully worked out space plans. Then, over time, they make incremental changes in response to emerging demands, with the result that the space becomes fragmented and inefficient, much as the disk space does on your computer. Defragmentation is difficult and expensive when move costs are high, but it is easy when move costs become negligible. It is just like running Norton Utilities to clean up your disk.

Furthermore, physical enclosure for information security purposes now matters less, while electronic security matters more. It was once essential to ring cities with defensive walls, but that is irrelevant now. And it was once crucial to lock office doors, so that the papers and files inside could be protected against dispersal or

8. John Summerson, "The Case for a Theory of Modern Architecture," *RIBA* Journal 64 (1957): 307–10, reprinted in John Summerson, *The Unromantic Castle and Other Essays* (London: Thames and Hudson, 1990), 257–66. Summerson's definition runs as follows: "A program is a description of the spatial dimensions, spatial relationships and other physical conditions required for the convenient performance of specific functions ... It is difficult to imagine any program in which there is nor some rhythmically repetitive pattern-whether it is a manufacturing process, the curriculum of a school, the domestic routine of a house, or simply the sense of repeated movement in a circulation pattern."

9. Michael Batty, "Editorial: Thinking about Cities as Spatial Events," *Environment and Planning B*, 29 (2002): 1–2.

destruction, and so that their confidentiality could be preserved. (In fact that was one of the main reasons for the very existence of private offices.) Espionage was a matter of clandestinely breaking in and stealing papers or making illicit copies. If your files are online, though, and accessible to you anywhere you log in, you do not have to work in a physically secure space. You *do* want to be sure that those files are regularly backed up and electronically protected against unauthorized access, and you probably want to sit so that your laptop screen is protected from prying eyes.[10] In other words, information security has been deterritorialized and shifted to a domain of abstract symbol manipulation.

Selectively (though not universally), space-to-space relationships are loosening. For convenience and security, old-fashioned library reading rooms had to be adjacent to book stacks, but that constraint disappears when stacks become servers and carrels become wireless reception points. To make most efficient use of an expensive resource, office staff once needed convenient access to a central copying machine, but that imperative evaporates when making a copy becomes a matter of sending a file through a network rather than carrying an original to a machine, and when inexpensive, networked laser printers are widely distributed. As connectivity matters more, in many contexts, adjacency matters less, and architectural form is less tightly determined by the need to satisfy adjacency requirements.

Even established ideas of flexibility and adaptability require reconsideration. In the past, architects provided these qualities by introducing modular, demountable partitions and furniture, movable components, plug-in devices, and the like. Now the focus is shifting to self-configuring electronic environments—enabled by electronic devices that can immediately begin to communicate wirelessly with one another when they are brought into proximity and that can work together to support whatever activities are taking place.[11] Laptops are beginning to talk wirelessly to video projectors, projectors and cameras to printers, telephones to speaker systems, video cameras to monitors, PDAs to other PDAs, automobiles to gas pumps, and so on.

In some ways, then, we are returning to strategies and practices of preliterate, precapitalist times. Ancient Greek philosophers, for example, did not have offices and classrooms; they strolled with their students through the groves of academe. Then the Hellenistic Library of Alexandria became a site of immobile accumulation, the fixed focus of a unique community,

10. In the period of transition from physical security of paper to electronic security of online files, the question of when and where you could download, and where you could keep electronic copies, suddenly became critical in high security settings. The cases of Wen Ho Lee and John Deutch turned on this point.

11. For an overview of the technical issues involved in this see "Self-configuration and Adaptive Coordination," in National Research Council, *Embedded Everywhere: A Research Agenda for Networked Systems of Embedded Computers* (Washington, D.C.: National Academy Press, 2001), 76–118.

Mitchell

and a place where scholars had to be. Today, the Web is our Library of Alexandria, and mobile wireless connection allows scholars to stroll once more—but without losing access to the resources they need. This does sit uneasily, of course, with some large, petrified chunks of the Western philosophical tradition. If you are a Heideggerian, you will probably fret about "wandering" versus "dwelling." And, if you take the Hegelian position that surrounding oneself with tangible property is a way of imprinting your presence on the world (Jerome's books did not just serve his needs, they defined him), then you will be dispirited by digital dematerialization and networked server access. Perhaps, though, this just means that giants of thought are still creatures of their time—and maybe, in these cases, too prone to generalize from the stability and clutter of the bourgeois drawing room.[12]

Electronic Non-Plan

At a larger scale, the instrument for distinguishing and separating functions has long been land-use *zoning*. This sometimes has a commonsense and unobjectionable function, as for example in mandating the separation of residential areas from noxious industry. But it has frequently been used to enforce far less benign forms of segregation. And there are far fewer good reasons to separate activities—such as working, being entertained, and pursuing your social life—when they are all supported by the same wireless, portable devices, and when, unobtrusively handled in this way, they do not interfere with the activities of others. There is, then, a new kind of opportunity to recoup the "right to the city," which Henri Lefebvre powerfully characterized in terms of heterogeneity rather than monoculture, encounter rather than separation, and simultaneity instead of sequence, and which he saw as threatened by "discriminatory and segregative organization."[13] Land use planners might move toward Lefebvre's "diversification of space," in which "the (relative) importance attached to functional distinctions would disappear."

The sixties Anglo-American counterpart to Lefebvre's insistence on the right to the city was a provocative call for "non-plan," set forth in a notorious *New Society* article by Reyner Banham, Paul Barker, Peter Hall, and Cedric Price.[14] In it, the authors bluntly claimed that "the most rigorously planned cities—like Haussmann's and Napoleon III's Paris—have nearly always been the least democratic," and asked "What would happen if there were no plan? What would people prefer to do, if their choice were

12. The nineteenth-century bourgeois were the inverse of the twenty-first century's emerging electro-nomads. In *History of Bourgeois Perception* (Chicago: University of Chicago Press, 1982), 71, Donald M. Lowe noted that "the bourgeoisie had a compulsion to fill up the visible space of the home with excessive furniture and intricate decoration. They cluttered every room in the house with objects. The eye seemed to abhor any visible, empty space."

13. Henri Lefebvre, *Writings on Cities,* ed. Eleonore Kofman and Elizabeth Lebas (London: Blackwell, 1996), 195. See also Henri Lefebvre, "The Monument" and "The Space of Architects," in *The Production of Space*, trans. Donald Nicholson-Smith (London: Blackwell, 1991).

14. Reyner Banham, Paul Barker, Peter Hall, and Cedric Price, "Non Plan: An Experiment in Freedom," *New Society* 13, no. 338 (20 March, 1969): 435–43. For a reprint and commentaries, see Jonathan Hughes and Simon Sadler, eds., *Non-Plan: Essays on Freedom Participation and Change in Modern Architecture and Urbanism* (Oxford: Architectural Press, 2000).

untrammeled?" This comported with contemporary architectural interest in combining serviced megastructures with plug-in and disposable architectural elements that could be configured by inhabitants themselves—theoretical propositions such as John Habraken's "supports,"[15] Yona Friedman's *architecture mobile*,[16] and Peter Cook's Plug-in City. It also resonated with more pragmatic architectural experimentation focused on flexible "mat" buildings,[17] extensible structures, and "long life, loose fit"[18] design strategies.

These proposals vividly expressed the possibility of flexibility and freedom of choice, but they mostly didn't deliver. Large-scale physical reconfiguration of architectural space in response to changing needs has remained a slow, cumbersome, and expensive process. Furthermore, occupiable space is still a scarce resource, and physical reconfigurability does little to diminish problems of space allocation and coordination. But the proponents of non-plan had glimpsed another possibility in what was then known as the "cybernetic revolution." They wrote: "The essence of the new situation is that we can master vastly greater amounts of information than was hitherto thought possible—information essentially about the effect of certain defined actions upon the operation of a system." Planning had depended upon "simple, rule-of-thumb value judgments" that were held to have "perpetual validity, like tablets of the law." Today, they concluded: "Physical planning, like anything else, should consist *at most* of setting up frameworks for decision, within which as much objective information as possible can be fitted." In other words, information infrastructure that provides a framework for dynamic decision making is more powerful than physical megastructure. If you want adaptability, responsive software beats reconfigurable hardware.

Several decades later, of course, the non-plan group's faith in "objective information" and "scientific management" seems uncritically naive. (The remaining members would, no doubt, be the first to say so.) But mobile connectivity, combined with reduced reliance upon immobile resources, has heightened the need, which they so presciently identified, to replace predetermined space programs and rigid plans with swiftly and sensitively responsive, electronically implemented space management strategies. By the early 2000s, we could see the beginnings of this in the combination of electronic road pricing and electronic navigation systems for managing road real estate, the combination of electronic tracking of parking space occupancy and automatic direction to vacant

15. N.J. Habraken, *Supports* (1961; Urban International Press, 1999).

16. Yona Friedman, *Toward a Scientific Architecture* (Cambridge, MA: MIT Press, 1975).

17. Hashim Sarkis, ed., *Le Corbusier's Venice Hospital and the Mat Building Revival* (New York: Prestel, 2001).

18. Alex Gordon, "Architects and Resource Conservation," *RIBA* Journal (January 1974): 9–12.

spaces, and flexible assignment of office cubicles to mobile, laptop-equipped workers. It is no longer the architectural programmer who controls space use, and thereby expresses power; it is now the software programmer.

Extreme Electronomadics

What if we could go all the way with shaking ourselves loose, shuck the last few atoms from our souls, and simply live on server farms somewhere? The gonzo endpoint of these trajectories of dematerialization and hypermobilization is the suggestion that mental life is just an affair of bits in the brain; you might strip them from this squishy substrate (much as one rips a CD) and download yourself onto disk. You are, on this view, just software—and as device-independent as a Java applet. You don't have to run on a high-maintenance meat machine. You no longer have to be, as Yeats so famously lamented, "fastened to a dying animal." Like saints and shamans in ecstasis, you loosen, to the ultimate, the binding of your persona to materiality and place. Hans Moravec has described the necessary operation:

> Layer after layer, the brain is simulated, then excavated. Eventually your skull is empty, and the surgeon's hand rests deep in your brainstem. Though you have not lost consciousness, or even your train of thought, your mind has been removed from the brain and transferred to a machine. [19]

I'm not too sure about the brain science of all this; no doubt the inscription of information into organic neural networks is rather more complex than that of magnetic bits onto thinly spread iron oxide. [20] And I would be surprised (to say the least) if the continuity of personal identity turned out to be such a straightforward matter, or if the mind/body distinction reduced so neatly to software/hardware. [21] (Belief in this possibility is, of course, the extreme form of the digitalist dogma that "content" can always be cleanly separated from its current material embodiment.) But let us assume we can successfully read, decode, and copy all our brain files—the equivalents of WORD files of memorized text, JPG files of visual memory, MP3 files of unforgettable tunes, EXE files that specify how to get things done, and so on. Let us imagine a "postbiological future" in which "we will think of ourselves as software, not hardware." [22] What then?

It would put land use and transportation planners out of work; real estate requirements would now be measured in megabytes rather than square feet, mobility in terms of bits per second rather

19. Hans Moravec, *Mind Children: The Future of Robot and Human Intelligence* (Cambridge, MA: Harvard University Press, 1988). For a return to the theme, see Hans Moravec, *Robot: Mere Machine to Transcendent Mind* (New York: Oxford University Press, 1999).

20. For a stab at the brain science, see Joseph LeDoux, *Synaptic Self How Our Brains Become Who We Are* (New York: Viking, 2002).

21. As Mark C. Taylor has pointed out, such self-as-software speculations "revise ancient philosophical and theological visions for the twenty-first century." Proponents of this view are "contemporary Gnostics, Platonists, and Cartesians" who espouse "a thoroughgoing dualism between mind and body, form and matter, immateriality and materiality, pattern and substance, etc." *The Moment of Complexity: Emerging Network Culture* (Chicago: University of Chicago Press, 2002), 223.

22. The phrases are Ray Kurzweil's, from *The Age of Spiritual Machines: When Computers Exceed Human Intelligence* (New York: Viking, 1999).

than miles per hour, and accessibility in terms of wireless network coverage. But the result is not disembodiment, in the sense of complete erasure of materiality. Nor is it reincarnation in humanoid avatar form. It is a more complex, spatially distributed, fluid, hybrid form of embodiment enacted with new hardware—one in which silicon, copper, and magnetic subsystems play a vastly increased role, while carbon-based subsystems play a diminished and no longer so privileged one.[23] Mortality reappears as a server crash. (There are some work-arounds, perhaps; you could implement reincarnation as restoration from backup, and transmigration of the soul as a hardware replacement strategy).[24] So, why bother with the messy and problematic brain operation? By other means, anyway, we are already asymptotically approaching that networked cyborg state. Why insist on taking the carbon completely to zero?[25]

We are at the endgame of a process that began when our distant ancestors started to clothe themselves with second skins stripped from other creatures, to extend and harden their hands with simple tools and weapons, and to record information by scratching marks on surfaces. It picked up speed when our more recent forebears began to wire up telegraph, telephone, and packet-switching networks, to place calls, to log in, and to download dematerialized information to wireless portable devices. It is repeated whenever a child learns to do these things; for the cyborg, ontogeny recapitulates phylogeny. It is not that we have become posthuman in the wireless network era; since Neanderthal early-adopters first picked up sticks and stones, we have never been human.[26]

23. There is an extensive literature of shedding flesh and virtual bodies. The fictional locus, in the 1980s and 1990s, was established by Vernor Vinge's novella *True Names* (1981) and the novels of William Gibson, particularly *Neuromancer* (New York: Ace Books, 1984). N. Katherine Hayles provides a critical introduction in *How We Became Posthuman: Virtual Bodies in Cybernetics, Literature, and Informatics* (Chicago: University of Chicago Press, 1999).

24. Ray Kurzweil has pursued this point: "There won't be mortality by the end of the twenty-first century. Not in the sense that we have known it. Not if you take advantage of the twenty-first century's brain-porting technology. Up until now, our mortality was tied to the longevity of our hardware. When the hardware crashed, that was it." *Age of Spiritual Machines*, 128–9.

25. Freudians will be quick to point our one potentially good reason; you may not like your nature-and-nurture-given body very much, and Moravec's brain operation may belong in some murky category with cross-dressing, anorexia, body-piercing, and teenage suicide. But I shall not pursue this fascinating diversion here.

26. Here I paraphrase Bruno Latour. His short and provocative text, *We Have Never Been Modern* (Cambridge: Harvard University Press, 1993), was a witty riposte to the afflatus of postmodernism in French intellectual life.

Mitchell

Metabolic Urbanization:
The Making of Cyborg Cities
Erik Swyngedouw

> A cyborg is a cybernetic organism, a hybrid of machine and organism, a creature of social reality as well as a creature of fiction.[1]
>
> Haraway (1990)

Cities are constituted through dense networks of interwoven socio-ecological processes that are simultaneously human, physical, discursive, cultural, material, and organic. Circulatory conduits of water, foodstuffs, cars, fumes, money, labour, etc., move in and out of the city, transform the city, and produce the urban as a continuously changing socio-ecological landscape. Imagine, for example, standing on the corner of Piccadilly Circus in London, and consider the socio-environmental metabolic relations that come together in this global-local place: smells, tastes, and bodies from all nooks and crannies of the world are floating by, consumed, displayed, narrated, visualized and transformed. The "Rainforest" shop and restaurant play to the tune of eco-sensitive shopping and the multi-billion pound eco-industry while competing with McDonalds' burgers and Dunkin' Donuts, whose products—like burgers, coffee, orange juice, or cream cheese—are equally the result of processes that fuse together and interconnect social and biochemical relations from many places, near and far away. Consider how human bodies—of migrants, prostitutes, workers, capitalists—spices, clothes, foodstuffs, and materials from all over the world whirl by. The neon lights are fed by energy coming from nuclear power plants and from coal-, oil-, or gas-burning electricity generators. Cars, taxis, and buses move on fuels from oil-deposits (now again from Iraq) and pump CO_2 into the air, affecting peoples, forests and climates in places around the globe. All these flows complete the global geographic mappings and traces that flow through the urban and "produce" London (or any other city) as a palimpsest of densely layered bodily, local, national and global—but depressingly geographically uneven—metabolic socio-ecological processes. This intermingling of material and symbolic things produces the vortexes of modern life, combines to produce a particular socio-environmental milieu that welds nature, society, and the city together in a deeply heterogeneous, conflicting and often disturbing whole.[2]

1. Donna Haraway, Simians, Cyborgs and Women: the Reinvention of Nature (New York: Routledge, 1990), 149.

2. Erik Swyngedouw, "The City as a Hybrid—On Nature, Society and Cyborg Urbanization," Capitalism, Nature, Socialism, 7, no.1 (1996): 65–80.

The view that a city is a particular process of environmental production, sustained by particular sets of socio-metabolic processes that shape the urban in distinct, historically contingent ways, a socio-environmental process that is deeply caught up with socio-metabolic processes operating elsewhere, rarely grabs the headlines. Of course, the "Hygienic City" of the nineteenth century already celebrated the making of the city as a system of circulatory conduits that would render the metabolism of the city rhyme in concert with the bio-chemical metabolisms associated with a sanitized urban life.[3] Haussmann's opening up of Paris, King Leopold's sanitation of Brussels, the visionary construction of Vienna's Ringstrasse, and London's slum clearance also point to these combined processes of political-ecological transformation and socio-cultural reconstruction. The ecological anarchism of radical thinkers like Kropotkin or Elisee Reclus, and the various attempts at creating socially or ecologically harmonious "utopian" cities pursued with equal fervour by anarchists, socialists, liberals, and fascists, also illustrate nineteenth- and early-twentieth-century concerns with producing socially just and sustainable urban environments.

Urbanization can indeed be viewed as a process of contiguous de-territorialization and re-territorialization through metabolic circulatory flows, organized through social and physical conduits or networks of "metabolic vehicles." In this article, we consider how nature becomes urbanized through proliferating socio-metabolic processes. "Metabolism" and "circulation" will be the central metaphors that will guide us in this endeavour. They are not randomly selected. Both concepts have a long conceptual, cultural, social, material, and artefactual history. They emerged as coherent concepts and materially mobilized principles in the mid-nineteenth century and both were deeply connected with projects, visions, and practices of modernization, and with the associated "modern" transformation of the city. Most importantly, in contrast to other fashionable metaphors that attempt to fuse together heterogeneous entities—like networks, assemblages, rhizomes, imbroglios, collectives—the former convey a sense of flow, process, change, transformation, and dynamism in addition to the "inner-connectedness" suggested by the other tropes. They embody what modernity has been, and will always be about: change, trans-formation, flux, movement, creative destruction. With its emphasis on movement, change, and process and its insistence on the socially mobilized "materiality" of life, historical materialism has been among the first social theories to embrace and mobilize "metabolism" and

3. Matthew Gandy, "Urban Na-ture and the Ecological Imagi-nary," in *In the Nature of Cities,* ed. Nik Heynen, Maria Kaika and Erik Swyngedouw (New York: Routledge, 2006), 62–72.

Swyngedouw

"circulation" as entry points in undertaking "ontologies of the present that demand archaeologies of the future."[4] These ontologies and archaeologies are what we shall turn to next.

Historical materialism and the remaking of environments

> Certainly we continue to have crickets and thunderstorms . . . and we continue to understand our psyches as driven by natural instincts and passions; but we have no nature in the sense that these forces and phenomena are no longer understood as outside, that is, they are not seen as original and independent from the civil order.[5]
>
> Hardt and Negri (2000)

Both "metabolism" and "circulation" have long conceptual and material histories. "Circulation" gained wide currency after William Harvey's postulation of the double circulation of blood in the body. Movement, flux and conduits rapidly thereafter became formative metaphors that would shape radically new visions of and practices for acting in the world. The concept of "metabolism" arose in the early nineteenth century, particularly in relationship to the material exchanges in the body with respect to respiration. It became extended later to include material exchanges between organisms and the environment as well as the bio-physical processes within living (and non-living or decaying) entities. For example, in the writings of Jacob Moleschott and Justus von Liebig,[6] metabolism denoted not only the exchange of energy and substances between organisms and the environment, but the totality of biochemical reactions in a living thing. In fact, von Liebig's analysis turned organisms into living processes, gave them a history-as-process. Interestingly enough, von Liebig, like Edwin Chadwick, had taken the temporal/spatial separation of spaces of production and spaces of consumption through the emergence of long-distance trade and the process of urbanization (what von Liebig called the "metabolic rift") as the pivotal causes of the decline in the productivity of agricultural land on the one hand, and the problematic accumulation of excrement, sewage and garbage in the city on the other. For them, the "unsustainability" of nineteenth-century forms of urbanization was, as it is today, directly related to the spatio-temporal organization of metabolic flows and circuits. With this view of metabolism as ecological-historical process, and combined with Darwin's equally historical-metabolic views of the biological world, and Lyell's theories of the world's geological reconstruction, historical-geographical materialism could mobilize the concept of metabolism, neither as just

4. Fredric Jameson Jameson, *A Singular Modernity* (London: Verso, 2002), 215.

5. Michael Hardt and Antonio Negri, *Empire* (Cambridge, MA: Harvard University Press, 2000),187.

6. Jacob Moleschott, *Der kreislauf des lebens* (Mainz: Von Zabern, 1857). Justus von Liebig (1840) *Principles of Agricultural Chemistry, with Special Reference to the Late Researches Made in England*. English Edition. London: Walton & Maberly, 1855) and Justus von Liebig, *Animal Chemistry: or, Organic Chemistry in its Application to Physiology and Pathology,* ed. William Gregory (New York: Johnson Reprint, 1842).

7. Dario Padovan, "The Concept of Social Metabolism in Classical Sociology," *THEOMAI*, 2 (2000). Ernst Haeckel, who coined the term ecology (1866), mobilized organic metaphors to describe social conditions, and started a long lineage of human ecological analysis, one that would ultimately drive a wedge between the natural sciences and the social sciences as the legitimacy of such unmediated transformulations was increasingly questioned. Human ecology would subsequently bifurcate into a dematerialized social ecology, primarily through the Chicago School, on the one hand, and industrial ecology on the other. The latter, moving increasingly in the direction of a variety of types of commodity chain or goods-flow analysis, would increasingly distance itself from relational social theory. See Marina Fischer-Kowalski, "Society's Metabolism: the Intellectual History of Material Flow Analysis, Part I, 1860–1970", *Journal of Industrial Ecology*, 2, no. 1 (1998): 61–78; Marina Fischer-Kowalski, "On the History of Industrial Metabolism," in *Perspectives on Industrial Ecology*, ed. D. Bourg and S. Erkman (Sheffield: Greenleaf Publishing, 2003); Marina Fischer-Kowalski and Walter Hüttler, "Society's Metabolism, the State of the Art: the Intellectual History of Material Flow Analysis, Part II, 1970–1998", *Journal of Industrial Ecology*, no. 4 (1999): 107–37; K. Newcombe, "Nutrient Flow in Major Urban Settlements: Hong Kong," *Human Ecology*, 5, no. 3 (1977): 179–208.

8. J.B. Foster, *Marx's Ecology: Materialism and Nature* (New York: Monthly Review Press, 2000).

9. Roy Bhaskar, *The Possibility of Naturalism* (Atlantic Highlands, NJ: Humanities Press, 1979), 100. This statement, of course, does not mean that thought or languages are simply the epiphenomenon of "material" relations. On the contrary, very complex dialectical arrangements infuse the articulation of the real, the symbolic, and the imaginary (for different ways of exploring these articulations. See, for example, Slavoj Žižek and Glyn Daly, *Conversations with Žižek* (Oxford: Polity Press,

an organic analogy to the social order nor as a mere metaphor to be transposed onto society, but as the very foundation of and lasting condition for the social.[7]

In social theory, the concept of metabolism was introduced in an ontological and epistemological framework in the early Marxist formulations of historical materialism. In its most general sense, materialism asserts that both origin and development of what exists is dependent on nature and "matter." Or, in other words, a certain physical Reality exists that is prior to thought, and to which thought must be related or interlinked (although it can never be identical to the Real).[8] As Roy Bhaskar argued, "neither thought nor language form a realm of their own, they are only manifestations of actual life."[9] Karl Marx's historical materialism was arguably the first coherent attempt to theorise the internal metabolic relationships that shape the transformations of the earth's surface and make and remake the social and physical world. In *Grundrisse, Capital* and, in particular, *The German Ideology*, Marx insisted on the "natural" foundations of social development:[10]

> The first promise if all human history is, of course, the existence of living human individuals. Thus the first fact to be established is the physical organization of these individuals and their consequent relationship to the rest of nature . . . The writing of history must always set out from these natural bases and their modification in the course of history through the action of men . . . [M]en must be in a position to live in order to be able to "make history". . . The first historical act is thus the production of the means to satisfy these needs, the production of material life itself.[11]

This environmental "production" process is conceived in the broadest possible sense. It refers to the metabolic process that is energized through the fusion of the physical properties and creative capacities of humans with those of non-humans. For Marx, this is what defines the act of "labouring," i.e. the purposeful metabolic process intended to produce and reproduce (human) life. Production is an organic process in the first instance, similar (but not reducible or identical) to the act of producing things new by other organic and non-organic "actants." What differentiates human actants from others is their organic capacity to wish differentially, to imagine different possible futures, to act differentially in ways driven and shaped by human drives, desires, and imaginations (as distinct from those of rivers, viruses, cows, or tulips). This form of acting differentiates human acting from other active "moments" or "agents" in the production and transformation of "environments." As Marx puts it:

A spider conducts operations that resemble those of a weaver, and a bee in the construction of her cells puts to shame many an architect. But what distinguishes the worst architects from the best of bees is this, that the architect arises his structure in imagination before he erects it in reality.[12]

Labouring is therefore nothing other than engaging the "natural" physical and mental forces and capabilities of humans in a metabolic physical-material process with other human and non-human actants and conditions. It is through the process of "transposition of labour power into human organism"[13] that this metabolic process is mobilized:

Nature builds no machines, no locomotives, railways, electric telegraphs, self-acting mules, etc. These are products of human industry; natural material transformed into organs of the human will over nature, or of human participation in nature. They are organs of the human brain, created by the human hand.[14]

These products of transformed nature and embodied "dead" labour take on a thing-like character, which, like any other actant, is enrolled again in subsequent assemblages. In fact, "[A]ny product can take on a 'life' of its own, and may come to dominate the living labour that makes it. The 'nature of things' is indeed to become non-human actors."[15] If the act of labouring, broadly conceived, constitutes a socio-ecological process, then the particular relational frame through which this labour is socially organized has to become an integral part of understanding the continuous (re-)making of what we can now discern as socio-natural entities.[16] The circulation of goods, or of entities, is evidently directly associated with the notion of metabolism, which involves precisely such a process of transformation-in-movement. In other words, metabolic circulation fuses together physical dynamics with the social regulatory and framing conditions set by the historically specific arrangement of the social relations of appropriation, production, and exchange—in other words, the mode of production. The things, the products used by labour in production always enter the metabolic processes as already configured assemblages, collectives, networks that, in turn, through socio-metabolic circulatory processes, mobilize new human and non-human "actants" and produce new assemblages or collectives. As Timothy Luke notes:

Marx can be seen as an extended critique of Latour's sense of collectivization, inasmuch as he uses the notion of the commodity to describe the association of humans and nonhumans. Since Marx's examination of the commodity form under capitalism looks at ways in which human labor is mixed with nonhuman

2003) or Henri Lefebvre, *The Production of Space* (Oxford: Blackwell 1991) in the construction of the real.

10. Jonathan Hughes, *Ecology and Historical Materialism* (Cambridge: Cambridge University Press, 2000).

11. Karl Marx, *The German Ideology*, ed. C.J. Arthur (London: Lawrence and Wishart, 1974 (first published 1846)), 42, 48.

12. Karl Marx, *Capital,* Volume I (New York: Penguin, 1971 (first published 1867)), Ch. 5.

13. Marx, *Capital,* Volume I, 323.

14. Karl Marx, *Grundrisse* (New York: Vintage Books, 1973 (first published 1858)), 706.

15. Scott Kirsch and Don Mitchell ,"The Nature of Things: Dead Labor, Nonhuman Actors, and the Persistence of Marxism," *Antipode*, 36, n. 4 (2004): 23.

16. Noel Castree, "Marxism and the Production of Nature," *Capital and Class*, 72 (2000): 5–37.Noel Castree, "False Antitheses? Marxism, Nature and Actor-Networks," *Antipode*, 34 (2002): 111–46.

things to create value, much of his analysis is a careful study of who dominates whom in the process of such collectivization, with commodification leading to the endless "co-modification" of human and nonhuman beings in both nature and culture. These ties now define co-evolution.[17]

These "collectives" are those proliferating objects that Donna Haraway calls "cyborgs" or that Bruno Latour refers to as "quasi-objects;"[18] these hybrid, part–social, part–natural—yet deeply historical and thus produced—objects/subjects are intermediaries that embody and express nature and society and weave networks of infinite liminal spaces. These assemblages, like commodities, are simultaneously real, like nature; narrated, like discourse; and collective, like society.[19] They take on cultural, social, and physical forms and enter social and ecological processes in new and transformed manners. The city, in its parts and as a whole, is a kaleidoscopic socio-physical accumulation of human/non-human imbroglios. In the production of these assemblages and entanglements, the figures of "metabolism" and of "circulation" take centre stage in a historical materialist and dialectical account. In the next section, we shall delve deeper into the origin and mobilization of "metabolism" and "circulation" within historical materialism.

Metabolism as metaphor and practice

Marx and Engels were among the first to engage the term "metabolism" to grapple with the dynamics of socio-environmental change and evolution.[20] In fact, "metabolism" is the central metaphor for Marx's definition of labour and for analyzing the relationship between human and nature:

> Labour is, first of all, a process between man and nature, a process by which man, through his own actions, mediates, regulates, and controls the metabolism between himself and nature. He confronts the materials of nature as a force of nature. He sets in motion the natural forces which belong to his own body, his arms, legs, head, and hands, in order to appropriate the materials of nature in a form adapted to his own needs. Through this movement he acts upon external nature and changes it, and in this way he simultaneously changes his own nature. . . . [labouring] is the purposeful activity aimed at the production of use-values. It is an appropriation of what exists in nature for the requirements of man. It is the universal condition for the metabolic interaction between man and nature, the ever-lasting nature-imposed condition of human existence, and it is therefore independent of every form of that existence, or rather it is common to all forms of society in which human beings live.[21]

For Marx, this socio-natural metabolism is the foundation of history, a socio-environmental history through which the natures of humans

17. Timothy Luke, *Capitalism, Democracy, and Ecology* (Urbana-Champaign, IL: University of Illinois Press, 1999), 39.

18. Bruno Latour, *We Have Never Been Modern* (London: Harvester Wheatsheaf, 1993), 51–5.

19. Latour, *We Have Never Been Modern,* 122.

20. Marina Fischer-Kowalski, "Society's Metabolism: The Intellectual History of Material Flow Analysis, Part I, 1860–1970," *Journal of Industrial Ecology*, 2, no. 1 (1998): 61–78; Marina Fischer-Kowalski, "On the History of Industrial Metabolism," in *Perspectives on Industrial Ecology*, ed. D. Bourg and S. Erkman (Sheffield: Greenleaf Publishing, 2003).

21. Marx, *Capital, Volume* I, 283 and 290.

and non-humans alike are transformed.[22] To the extent that labour constitutes the universal premise for human metabolic interaction with nature, the particular social relations through whom this metabolism of nature is enacted shape its very form. Clearly, any materialist approach insists that "nature" is an integral part of the "metabolism" of social life. Social relations operate in and through metabolizing the "natural" environment, and transform both society and nature. For historical materialism, then, ecology is not so much a question of values, morals, or ethics, but rather a mode of "understanding the evolving material interrelations (what Marx called 'metabolic relations') between human beings and nature . . . From a consistent materialist standpoint, the question is . . . one of coevolution."[23] Foster continues to argue that:

> [A] thoroughgoing ecological analysis requires a standpoint that is both materialist and dialectical . . . [A] materialist sees evolution as an open-ended process of natural history, governed by contingency, but open to rational explanation. A materialist viewpoint that is also dialectical in nature (that is, a non mechanistic materialism) sees this as a process of transmutation of forms in a context of interrelatedness that excludes all absolute distinctions . . . A dialectical approach forces us to recognize that organisms in general do not simply adapt to their environment; they also affect that environment in various ways by affecting change in it.[24]

In other words, non-human entities act in their metabolic exchange—in their "enrolment" as Latour would call it—with other human and non-human actants.[25] This materialist view is decidedly "constructionist" in the sense that it considers socio-natural processes as historically specific, produced, and contingent. However, it does not foreground a notion of "social construction," as the non-human plays a pivotal and foundational role in the process; it merely evocates the view of nature as "produced."

Marx undoubtedly borrowed the notion of "metabolic interaction" from Justus von Liebig,[26] the founding theoretician of modern agricultural chemistry. In contrast to other sociologists avant-la-lettre, like Comte and Spencer, who used the concept of metabolism as an analogy to grapple with social metabolism and for whom "nature offered the gnoseological structures to survey the workings of society,"[27] Marx, Engels, or Adam Schäffle, mobilized "metabolism" in an ontological manner in which human beings, like society, were an integral, yet particular and distinct, part of nature.

22. See Maurice Godelier, *The Mental and the Material* (London: Verso, 1986).

23. Foster, *Marx's Ecology*, 10–11. See also Richard Norgaard, *Development Betrayed: the end of progress and a coevolutionary revisioning of the future* (New York: Routledge, 1994). Richard Levins and Richard Lewontin, *The Dialectical Biologist* (Cambridge, MA: Harvard University Press, 1985).

24. Foster, *Marx's Ecology,* 15–6.

25. Latour, *We Have Never Been Modern,* 139.

26. Although Schmidt (1971) and Fisher-Kowalski (1998) maintain that Moleschott (1857) provided the influential insights, this is convincingly rebuked by Foster (2000), who maintained that von Liebig (1840) was of central importance. In any case, the use of "metabolism" was widespread in the emerging social sciences at the time and both Marx and Engels were familiar with the ongoing scientific debates in biology.

27. Padovan, "The Concept of Social Metabolism in Classical Sociology," 7.

The original German word for metabolism is *Stoffwechsel*, which translates literally as "change of matter." This simultaneously implies circulation, exchange and transformation of material elements. As matter moves, it becomes "enrolled" in associational networks that produce qualitative changes and qualitatively new assemblages. While the newly produced "things" embody and reflect the processes of their making (though a process of internalization of dialectical relations),[28] they simultaneously differ radically from their constituent relational parts. For von Liebig, chemical metabolism was a process of "creative destruction" in which the new irrevocably transformed the old. Metabolism as a biochemical process is a contradictory one, predicated upon fusion, tension, conflict, and ultimately transconfiguration, which, in turn, produces a series of new "entities", often radically different from the constituting components, yet equally re-active. Metabolism (with a few rare exceptions), consequently, is a historical process, it has a time arrow. Labour (itself an organic metabolic procedure), then, becomes the organic activity through which this metabolic process is mobilized in a purposeful, human manner by enrolling heterogeneous things into specific metabolic interactions:

> Actual labour is the appropriation of nature for the satisfaction of human needs, the activity through which the metabolism between man and nature is mediated.[29]

While every metabolized thing embodies the complex processes and heterogeneous relations of its making at some point in the past, it enters (or becomes enrolled), in its turn and its own specific manner, into new assemblages of metabolic transformation. These dynamic heterogeneous assemblages form a circulatory (although not necessarily closed) process. Under conditions of generalized commodity production, the process takes on the form of circulation of commodities and the circulatory reverse flow of capital (as embodied dead labour, that is past metabolic transformations). This processual metabolism is, according to Foster, central to Marx's political economy and is directly implicated in the circulation of commodities and, consequently, of money: "[t]he economic circular flow then was closely bound up, in Marx's analysis, with the material exchange (ecological circular flow) associated with the metabolic interaction between human beings and nature."[30] Indeed, under capitalist social relations, the metabolic production of use values operates in and through specific control and ownership relations, and in the context of the mobilization of both nature and labour to produce commodities (as forms of metabolized socio-natures) with

28. David Harvey, *Justice, Nature and the Geography of Difference* (Oxford: Blackwell, 1996).

29. Karl Marx, *Economic Manuscripts, 1861–1863*, http:www.marxists.org/archivejmarx/works/1861/economic/ch13.htm (accessed 30 March 2005)

30. Foster, *Marx's Ecology*, 157–8.

an eye towards the realization of the embodied exchange value. The circulation of capital as value in motion is, therefore, the combined metabolic transformations of socio-natures in and through the reverse circulation of money as capital under social relations that combine the mobilization of capital, nature or dead labour, and labour power. New socio-natural forms, including the transformation of labour power as living labour, are continuously produced as moments and things in this metabolic process.[31] Whether we consider the production of dams, the re-engineering of rivers, the management of biodiversity hotspots, the transfiguration of DNA codes, the cultivation of tomatoes (genetically modified or not) or the construction of houses, they all testify to the particular associational relations through which socio-natural metabolisms are organized (in terms of property and ownership regimes, production or assembly activities, distributional arrangements, and consumption patterns).

Of course, the ambition of classical Marxism was broader than reconstructing the dialectics of historical socio-natural transformations and their contradictions. Historical materialism also questioned and critiqued the process of discursive (or ideological in Marxist terms) purification, of separation and binarization of the world into things "social" and things "natural" that, in Latour's vocabulary, produced the modern "constitution" and derailed the project of becoming "modern" (while, in the process, filling this symbolic void with all manner of socio-natural imbroglios). Historical-geographical materialism as a dialectical (that is, non-teleological) evolutionary (that is, actively produced history) organicism (that is, the unity of the heterogeneous social and the heterogeneous natural) not only addresses the cultural, discursive, "ideological," moral/ethical constructions of nature that were as prevalent in the nineteenth century as they are today, but offered a view of the world that unified the natural and the social while critiquing radically the "modern" separation of "society" from "nature."[32] In fact Marx had already prefigured Bruno Latour's clarion call to "re-modernise," to re-connect the two poles that have been severed by modernity, in Grundrisse:

> It is not the unity of living and active humanity, the natural, inorganic conditions of their metabolic exchange with nature, and hence their appropriation of nature, which requires explanation, or is the result of a historic process, but rather the separation between these inorganic conditions of human existence and his active existence.[33]

However, by concentrating on the labour process as mere social process (as was and is the case for most of modern sociology, Marxist sociology included), some Marxist analysis—particularly

31. Reiner Grundman, *Marxism and Ecology* (Oxford: Clarendon Press,1991); T. Benton, "Marxism and Natural Limits: an Ecological Critique and Reconstruction," *New Left Review,* 178 (1989): 51–86; *The Greening of Marxism,* ed. T. Benton, (New York: Guilford Press,1996); Paul Burkett, *Marx and Nature—A Red and Green Perspective.* New York: St Martin's Press, 1999); Foster, *Marx's Ecology.*

32. This has become engrained in social theory since its founding fathers Durkheim, Weber, and a "socialized" Marx.

33. Marx, *Grundrisse*, 489.

during the twentieth century—tended to replicate the very problem it meant to criticize. The "void" referred to above was silenced rather than problematized, ignored rather than taken as the "space" for politics, for struggle, for pre-figuring radical socio-ecological transformation, and realizing alternative socio-natural relations. In other words, while mainstream economics forgot the natural foundations of economic life (only to rediscover them recently, under the guise of environmental economics),[34] much of Marxist theory equally became an exclusively "social" theory, rather than a socio-ecological one. Put simply, the over-emphasis on the social relations under capitalism that characterized much of Marxist (and other) social analysis tended to abstract away from or ignore the material and socio-physical metabolic relationships, their phantasmagorical representations and symbolic ordering. This resulted in a partial blindness in the social sciences of the twentieth century to questions of political ecology and socio-ecological metabolisms.

Some recent approaches to the society–nature problematic, such as Actor-Network-Theory or (political-) ecological theories of a variety of kinds, have provided a new grammatical apparatus that has "profoundly revitalized empirical studies of human–nature–technology relations . . . But . . . it remains important that we incessantly raise the question . . . why are 'things as such' produced in the way they are—and to whose potential benefit."[35] While a historical-materialist mobilization of metabolism might begin to shed light on the production of socio-natural entities, this has to be fused together with another equally central metaphor and material condition, one that is closely related to metabolism, namely, circulation.

The invention of circulation

> Enlightened planners wanted the city in its very design to function like a healthy body, freely flowing as well as possessed of clear skin. Since the beginnings of the Baroque era, urban planners had thought about making cities in terms of efficient circulation of the people on the city's main streets. The medical imagery of life-giving circulation gave a new meaning to the Baroque emphasis of motion. Instead of planning streets for the sake of ceremonies of movement toward an object, as did the Baroque planner, the Enlightenment planner made motion an end in itself.[36]

Alongside the emergence of the notion of "metabolism" in the natural and social sciences (an emergence not wholly disassociated with the rising "metabolic rift" caused by industrialization and

34. While the Physiocrats were radically and correctly critiqued, the rational kernel of their myth-ical theorization was equally dismissed radically.

35. Kirsch and Mitchell, "The Nature of Things," 687–706.

36. Richard Sennett, *Flesh and Stone* (London: Faber and Faber, 1994), 263–4.

Swyngedouw

urbanization), the notion of "circulation" began to gain greater and wider currency. For example, the idea of "water circulation," that water piped into the city must leave the city by its sewers is not older than the nineteenth century (in the west). Circulating water, following a given path and finally returning to its source, remained foreign to western urban imaginations, spatial representations and engineering systems until then. Modern urbanization, highly dependent on the mastery of circulating flows, was linked with the representation of cities as consisting of and functioning through complex networks of circulatory systems.[37]

Before the "discovery" of circulatory systems, the movement of water was seen merely as evaporation: the separation of the "spirit" from the "water."[38] This view that things happen, appear, or disappear through "extraction" was widely held before circulatory views began to replace them. In chemistry, for example, phlogiston theory of the seventeenth century, formulated by Johann Becher and still defended by Priestley, rested on the basis of extractionist views. Such theories prevailed until Antoine Lavoisier's eighteenth-century discovery, which postulated chemical reactions as (metabolic) transfigurations or re-arrangements of components that in the process produced qualitatively new assemblages, but in which nothing was lost or disappeared. Together with phlogiston theory, the representation of the respiratory system, plant growth, the Physiocrats' view of the production of material wealth from the given natural conditions of the soil, even the Malthusian unidirectional flow of food, all indicate the incapacity of early post-renaissance people to conceive of "circulation" as an infinite cyclical process.

When William Harvey promulgated his ideas of the double circulation of blood in the vascular system of the human body in 1628, a revolutionary insight came into being which would begin to permeate and dominate everyday life, engineering, and intellectual thought for centuries to come, both metaphorically and materially.[39] By the end of the century, medical practice had accepted the idea of the circulatory (metabolic) system, leading to a profound re-definition of the body. In the nineteenth century, the metabolic circulation of chemical substances and organic matter (see von Liebig's contribution above) became increasingly accepted, and would form the basis of modern ecology. The "circulation" and the "metabolism" of matter became fused together as the two central metaphors through which to capture processes of socio-natural change, and of modernity itself.

37. Maria Kaika, and Erik Swyngedouw, "Fetishizing the Modern City: the Phantasmagoria of Urban Technological Networks," *International Journal of Urban and Regional Research*, 24, no.1, (1999): 120–38.

38. J-P. Goubert, *The Conquest of Water: The Advent of Health in the Industrial Age* (Cambridge: Polity Press, 1989).

39. The first person apparently to suggest the circulation of blood in the arterial system was Ibn-al-Nnafiz (physician, born in Baghdad and died in Cairo in 1288). See Ivan Illich, *H20 and the Waters of Forgetfulness*, (London: Marion Boyars, 1986), 40. The idea of circulation remained alien to the imagination of sixteenth-century Europeans. Two sixteenth-century scientists suspected what Harvey would later discover: Servetus (a Spanish genius and heretic burnt by Calvin, he also edited Ptolemy's geography in Lyon—and student of Vesalius in Paris) and Realdus Colombus of Padua (also student of Vesalius). Harvey was a student of Vesalius in 1603.

Indeed, the use of the word "circulation" to refer to the movement of money within a national economy established itself within a generation of William Harvey's claim.[40] Thomas Hobbes, in *Leviathan* (1651), for example, had already compared the problems of a government that was unable to raise sufficient tax revenue to "an ague; wherein, the fleshy parts being congealed, or by venomous matter obstructed, the veins which by their natural course empty themselves into the heart, are not, as they ought to be, supplied from the arterie, whereby there succeedeth at first a cold contraction, and trembling of the limbs; and afterwards a hot, and strong endeavour of the heart, to force the passage of the blood."[41] Francis Bacon, in his essay *Of Empire*, wrote that merchants "are vena porta; and if they flourish not, a kingdom may have good limbs, but will have empty veins, and nourish little."[42]

At the beginning of the eighteenth century, the term "circulation" had become established in many sciences, referring to the flow of sap in plants and the circulation of matter in chemical reactions.[43] "Circulation" becomes a dominant metaphor after the French Revolution: ideas, newspapers, gossip and—after 1880—traffic, air, and power "circulate." From about 1750, wealth and money begin to "circulate" and are spoken of as though they were liquids, flowing incessantly to become a process of accumulation and growth. Society begins to be imagined as a system of conduits.[44] Montesquieu in *Lettres Persanes* speaks of "[T]he more 'circulation' the more wealth" and in *L'Esprit des Lois* of "[M]ultiplying wealth by increasing circulation."[45] Rousseau refers to "[T]his useful and fecund circulation that enlivens all society's labour" and to "a circulation of labour as one speaks of the circulation of the money."[46] Of course, by the mid-nineteenth century, the *flâneur*—dandy, artist, detective, and stroller, the favourite literary characters of Baudelaire and, later, with Walter Benjamin, of the passages—has been well represented and theorized as an object of circulation within this urban space. Of course, in the process, "circulation" became less and less identified with closed circular movement, and more with change, growth, and accumulation. Similar to the way von Liebig discovered the mechanisms of metabolism through considering the "metabolic rift," "circulation" gained greater socio-ecological currency exactly when it became seen as an integral part of a process of change and transformation.

Adam Smith and Karl Marx conceived of a capitalist economy as a metabolic system of circulating money and commodities, carried by and structured through social interactions and relations.

40. A.D. Harvey, "The Body Politic: Anatomy of a Metaphor", *Contemporary Review*, August (1999): 1628. http://articles.findarticles.com/p/articles/mi_m2242/ is_1603_275/ai_55683940 (accessed 12 June 2004).

41. Cited in A.D. Harvey, 1628.

42. Ibid.

43. Mikulá Teich, "Circulation, Transformation, Conservation of Matter and the Balancing of the Biological World in the Eighteenth Century," *Ambix*, 29 (1982): 17–28.

44. Sennett, *Flesh and Stone*.

45. C. de Secondat, Baron de Montesquieu, *Lettres Persane*, Edition établie et présentée par Jean Starobinski, Collection Folio 475 (Paris: Gallimard, 1973), 117.

46. Cited in Illich, *H2O and the Waters of Forgetfulness*.

Accumulation is dependent on the swiftness by which money circulates through society. Each hiccup, stagnation or interruption of circulation may unleash the infernal forces of devaluation, crisis and chaos. Society's wealth and the relationships of power on which wealth is constructed are seen as intrinsically bound up with and expressed by the "circulation speed" of money in all its forms (capital, labour, commodities). Later, David Harvey would analyze the circulation of capital and its urbanization as a perpetual mobile channelled through a myriad of ever-changing production, communication and consumption networks. The development and consolidation of circulating money as the basis of material life, and the relations of domination and exclusion through which the circulation of money is organized and maintained shapes this "urbanization of capital."

By the mid-nineteenth century some British architects also begin to speak of the inner city mobilizing the metaphor of circulation. Sir Edwin Chadwick formulated the ideology of circulating waters effectively for the first time in his 1842 *Report into the Sanitary Conditions of the Labouring Population of Great Britain*. In his report, Chadwick imagined the new city as "a social body through which water must incessantly circulate, leaving it again as dirty sewage." Water ought to "circulate" through the city without interruption to wash it of sweats and excrements and wastes. The brisker this flow, the fewer stagnant pockets that breed congenital pestilence there are and the healthier the city will be. Unless water constantly circulates through the city, pumped in and channelled out, the interior space imagined by Chadwick can only stagnate and rot. This representation of urban space as constructed in and through perpetually circulating flows of water is conspicuously similar to imagining the city as a vast reservoir of perpetually circulating money. Viollet-le-Duc introduced circulation as a bodily metaphor for the organization of the urban villa. In fact, Chadwick's papers were published under the title *The Health of Nations* during the centenary commemoration for Adam Smith.[47] Like the individual body and bourgeois society, the city was now also described as a network of pipes and conduits. The brisker the flow, the greater the wealth, the health and hygiene of the city would be. Just as William Harvey redefined the body by postulating the circulation of the blood, so Chadwick redefined the city by "discovering" its needs to be constantly washed.[48] New principles of city planning and policing were emerging based upon the medical metaphors of "circulation" and "flow." The health of the body became the comparison against

47. Edwin Chadwick, *The Health of Nations,* ed. R.W. Richardson (London: Longmans Green & Co., 1887).

48. Illich, *H2O and the Waters of Forgetfulness*, 45.

which the greatness of cities and states was to be measured. The "veins" and "arteries" of the new urban design were to be freed from all possible sources of blockage.[49]

With circulation as a metabolic process firmly established as practice and as solid representation of the process of socio-ecological change, attention quickly moved from metabolism and circulation to "speed" or, in other words, to the "movement of movement." Metabolic circulation of the kind analyzed by Marx, and now firmly rooted in generalized commodity production, exchange, and consumption, is increasingly subject to the socially constituted dynamics of a capitalist market economy in which the alpha and omega of the metabolic circulation of socio-ecological assemblages is the desire to circulate money as capital. As Douglas notes:

> Not only now would political rationality understand the motion of matter, and of bodies, it would seek above all to perfect the mechanisms of producing it. The "movement-of-movement," or "speed," as a technical achievement, emerges at this time (the early nineteenth century) as a societal principle, reordering the whole of the modern world. In the most radical way possible Virilio begins to answer the question of how efficiency was established in the modern urban landscape . . . The power of movement was subject to a spatial codification (in the city, in the workhouse, in the hospital, in the manufactory). By the beginnings of the nineteenth century this "codification" had been achieved, and a second "reordering" could now be effected. This reordering, rather than charting the middle ground between rapidity and stasis, aimed to "release" the full productive, dynamic efficiency of the (national) population in and through time. Motion had emerged as the destiny and law of a new politics of order. The full equivalence of Virilio's "metabolic vehicles" to Foucault's "bearers of order" becomes clear. Dromological power—or in the words of Foucault, "capillary power"—had emerged as the practical basis and first principle of the "free society" and "coded individual" established simultaneously with the apparatus of modern "governmentality." Mobility, in other words, had become simultaneously the means to liberation and the means to domination; the "accumulation of men" running simultaneously with "the accumulation of movement," and—one might add—the "accumulation of capital.[50]

49. Sennett, *Flesh and Stone:* 262–5. See also A. Corbin, *The Foul and the Fragrant* (London: Picador, 1994).

50. Ian R. Douglas, "The Calm Before the Storm: Virilio's Debt to Foucault, and Some Notes on Contemporary Global Capital." (2004) http://proxy.arts.uci.edu/~nideffer/_SPEED_/1.4/articles/douglas.html (accessed 15 May 2004).

For Paul Virilio, the freedom for people to come and go was replaced by an obligation to move. The creation of urban space as space of movement of people, commodities, and information radically altered the choreography of the city. Places and spaces became less and less shared, motion devalues or threatens to devalue place; connections are lost, identities reconfigured, and attachments broken down. While the urbanization of nature led to a spiralling accumulation of unstable socio-natural assemblages, the

Swyngedouw

components of these assemblages became radically disassociated from their geographical origin as speed, movement and mobility ironically rendered the fields of vision and connections more opaque, transient, and partial. Although the city turned into a metabolic vehicle, the rift between the social and the natural became engrained deeper than ever in the modern urban imagination.

(Hybrid) natures and (cyborg) cities

> The metabolic requirements of a city can be defined as the materials and commodities needed to sustain the city's inhabitants at home, at work and at play. . . The metabolic cycle is not completed until wastes and residues of daily life have been removed and disposed of with a minimum of nuisance and hazard.[51]

> A barrel of crude oil sold for about $13 in 1998. The same quantity of whole blood, in its "crude" state, would sell for more than $20,000 [in Manhattan, NY].[52]

When mobilizing the twin vehicles of "metabolism" and "circulation" from a historical-materialist epistemological perspective, the modernist tropes of "nature" and "society" transform radically. Modernity's bifurcation, separation, and binarization is recognized by historical materialism as exactly what it is: an image, a metaphor, a trope; one that can be and is mobilized for all manner of cultural, social, or political projects.[53] A dialectical approach recognizes both the radical non-identity of actants (human and non-human) enrolled in socio-metabolic processes within an assemblage, while recognizing the social, cultural, and political power relations embodied relationally in these socio-natural imbroglios. The production of (entangled) things through metabolic circulation is necessarily a process of fusion, of the making of "heterogeneous assemblages," of constructing longer or shorter networks. In fact, both "hybridity" and "cyborg" are misleading as tropes, and may even be implicated in radically reproducing the underlying binary representation of the world. Hence, the bracketing of "hybrid" and "cyborg" in the title of this section refers exactly to the "excess of meaning" inscribed in coding the city as either "hybrid" or "cyborg."

Metabolic circulation, then, is the socially mediated process of environmental, including technological, transformation and trans-configuration, through which all manner of "agents" are mobilized, attached, collectivized, and networked. The heterogeneous assemblages that emerge, as moments in the accelerating and intensifying circuitry of metabolic vehicles, are central to a historical-geographical materialist ontology:

51. Abel Wolman, "The Metabolism of Cities", *Scientific American*, 213, no. 3 (1965): 179.

52. Douglas Starr, *Blood: an Epic History of Medicine and Commerce* (New York: Alfred A. Knopf, 1998).

53. Maria Kaika, *City of Flows* (London and New York: Routledge, 2005).

[C]onsciousness, partly as objects of natural science, partly as objects of art . . . so they also form in practice a part of human life and human activity. Man lives physically only by those products of nature; they may appear in the form of food, heat, clothing, housing, etc. The universality of man appears in practice as the universality which makes the whole of nature his inorganic body: (1) as a direct means of life, and (2) as the matter, object, and instrument of his life activity. Nature is the inorganic body of man, that is nature insofar it is not the human body. Man lives by nature. This means that nature is his body with which he must remain in perpetual process in order not to die.[54]

As Luke argues, "the conditions of associating humans and nonhumans in ancient, Asiatic, feudal, or capitalist relations of collectivization can thus be used to understand how power, knowledge, and conflict co-modified people and their things in any given society."[55] These assemblages of humans and non-humans, of dead labor and inert materials, are reminiscent of the "hybrids" and the "cyborgs" of Latour and Haraway, respectively. However, while Haraway asks penetrating questions as to why "cyborgs" are produced the way they are and the relations of power inscribed in these imbroglios, this question remains silent in Latour's work. For him, the key issue centres on transforming the "constitutional" arrangements through which human and non-human actants become mobilized or enrolled.[56] In sum, while Latour defends a democratic republic of heterogeneous associations, Haraway maintains a perspective that emerges from a radically different ontological position. A deep ontological divide opens here. As Benedikte Zitouni convincingly argues:

Haraway views any entity as an embodiment of relations, an implosion, the threads of which should be teased apart in order to understand it. Whereas Latour views any entity as a piece of matter that is continuously affected and that contracts links with a larger networks that allows it to live, to be. On the one hand, the entity crystallizes the network; on the other hand the entity is supported by the network. Haraway studies the network in order to define the entity; Latour studies that same network in order to define the entity's consistency and persistence . . . Dialectics, congealment, crystals, prisms, representations are not possible tools any longer for urban studies but instead we view pieces of matter, of any kind, that act, react and interact with one another, that gain their consistency, persistence and existence or lose them through the affects and links to other agents. Power differences and inequality can no longer be stated as such, as a departure point into the city but have to be explained through the many actions and relations between objects, humans and non humans. There is nothing behind any space or agent, only attachments aside of it that make it stronger or weaker, allow it to exist or lead it to perish.[57]

54. Karl Marx, *Economic and Philosophic Manuscripts, Selected Writings* (London: Lawrence & Wishart, 1982), 63.

55. Timothy Luke, *Capitalism, Democracy, and Ecology* (Urbana-Champaign, IL: University of Illinois Press, 1999), 43.

56. Bruno Latour, *Politics of Nature: How to bring the sciences into democracy* (Cambridge, MA: Harvard University Press, 2004).

57. Benedikte Zitouni, "Donna Haraway and Bruno Latour: an Ontological Divide," Paper presented at the "Technonatures II" conference, School of Geography and the Environment, Oxford University, 24 June 2004.

Swyngedouw

It is in this latter sense that we wish to see the city as a metabolic circulatory process that materializes as an implosion of socio-natural relations, a process which is organized through socially articulated networks and conduits whose origin, movement, and position is articulated through complex political, social, economic, and cultural relations. These relations are invariably infused with myriad configurations of power that saturate material, symbolic, and imaginary (or imagined) practices.

Studies on urban metabolism have often uncritically pursued the standard industrial ecology perspective based on some input–output model of the flow of "things" (see Table 2.1 on London's metabolism). Such analysis merely poses the issue, and fails to theorize the making of the urban as a socio-environmental metabolism.[58] While insightful in terms of quantifying the urbanization of nature, it fails to theorize the process of urbanization as a social process of transforming and reconfiguring nature. It would not be too much of an exaggeration to state that most processes of transformation of nature are intimately linked to the process of urbanization and to the urbanization of nature. From this perspective, it is surely strange to note that relatively little empirical or theoretical work has been undertaken that explicitly attempts to theorise environmental change and urban change as fundamentally interconnected processes.

Modern urbanization or the city can be articulated as a process of geographically arranged socio-environmental metabolisms. These are mobilized through relations that combine the accumulation of socio-natural use and exchange-values, which shape, produce, maintain, and transform the metabolic vehicles that permit the expanded reproduction of the urban as a historically determined but contingent form of life. Such socially driven material processes produce extended and continuously reconfigured intended and non-intended spatial (networked and scalar) arrangements and are saturated with heterogeneous symbolic (representational) and imaginary (wish images) orders, albeit "overdetermined" by the generalized commodity form that underpins the capitalist "nature" of urbanization.[59] The phantasmagorical (spectacular) commodity-form that most socio-natural assemblages take not only permits and facilitates a certain discourse and practice of metabolism, but also, perhaps more importantly, "naturalize" the production of particular socio-environmental conditions and relations. For example, it seems much easier to imagine an apocalyptic environmental future of humankind (of the kind perpetuated by global climate change pundits, bio-diversity preservation activists, or GM-warriors) than to

58. See H. Weisz, M. Fisher-Kowalski, M. Grünbühel, H. Haberl, F. Krausman, F. and V. Winiwarter, "Global Environmental Change and Historical Transitions", *Innovation*, 14/2 (2001):117–42.

59. Louis Althusser, *For Marx* (London: Verso, 1969).

imagine a political change in the actually existing social ordering of the metabolic process, one that would imply a reconstruction of the produced environments.

Table 2.1 The metabolism of Greater London (7,000,000 inhabitants)

Inputs	Tonnes per year
Fuel (oil equivalents	20,000,000
Oxygen	40,000,000
Water	1,002,000,000
Food	2,400,000
Timber	1,200,000
Paper	2,200,000
Glass	360,000
Plastics	2,100,000
Cement	1,940,000
Bricks, blocks, sand, tarmac	6,000,000
Metals	1,200,000

Wastes	Tonnes per year
Industry and demolition	11,400,000
Household, civic and commercial	3,900,000
Wet digested sewage sludge	7,500,000
Carbon dioxide gas	60,000,000
Sulfur dioxide gas	400,000
Nitrogen oxide gas	280,000

Source: www.global-vision.org/city/metabolism.html (H. Girardet).

The urbanization of nature is largely predicated upon a commodification of parts of nature while, in the process, producing new metabolic interactions and shaping both symbolic and material socio-natural interactions. The urbanization of nature necessitates both ecological transformation and social transformation. Urbanized nature propels the diverse physical, chemical, and biological "natural" flows and characteristics of nature into the realm of commodity and money circulation with its abstract qualities and concrete social power relations. Produced nature becomes legally defined and standardized, according to "scientific" politically and socio-culturally defined norms that are enshrined in binding legislation. Homogenization, standardization, and legal codification are essential to the commodification process. The urbanization process makes nature enter squarely into the sphere of money and cultural capital and its associated power relations, and redraws socio-natural power relations in important new ways. Indeed, the political-ecological

Swyngedouw

history of many cities can be written from the perspective of the need to urbanize and domesticate nature and the parallel necessity to push the ecological frontier outward as the city expanded.[60] As such the political-ecological process produces both a new urban and rural socio-nature. The city's growth, and the process of nature's urbanization are closely associated with successive waves of ecological conquest and the extension of urban socio-ecological frontiers. Local, regional, and national socio-natures are combined with engineering narratives, economic discourses and practices, land speculation, geo-political tensions, and global money flows. This metabolic circulation process is deeply entrenched in the political ecology of the local and national state, the international divisions of labour and power, and in local, regional, and global socio-natural networks and processes.

Conclusions

"Metabolism" and "circulation" permit excavating the socio-environmental basis of the city's existence and its change over time. The socio-naturally "networked" city can be understood as a giant socio-environmental process, perpetually transforming the socio-physical metabolism of nature. Nature and society are in this way combined to form an urban political ecology, a hybrid, an urban cyborg that combines the powers of nature with those of class, gender, and ethnic relations. In the process, a socio-spatial fabric is produced that privileges some and excludes many, that produces significant socio-environmental injustices. Nature, therefore, is an integral element of the political ecology of the city and needs to be addressed in those terms. Urbanizing nature, though generally portrayed as a technological-engineering problem is, in fact, as much part of the politics of life as any other social process. The recognition of this political meaning of nature is essential if sustainability is to be combined with a just and empowering urban development; an urban development that returns the city and the city's environment to its citizens. Being modern, as the poet Arthur Rimbaud (1873) captured it in the nineteenth century, is exactly about the active creation of situations and events, and participating in the production of our natures in so doing. Urban modernity as a particular set of processes of socio-metabolic transformations promises exactly the possibility of the active, democratic, and empowering creation of those socio-physical environments we wish to inhabit. In this sense, modernity is not over; it has not yet begun.

60. Erik Swyngedouw, *Social Power and the Urbanization of Water: Flows of Power* (Oxford: Oxford University Press, 2004).

Acknowledgements
I would like to thank the British Academy Research Grant Los Pantanos o la Muerte! Contested modernization, the production of nature and the hydraulic imperative in Fascist Spain, 1938–74. This chapter is adapted and extended from a paper published in *Science as Culture* (2006).

Fig. 16.1 Entrance, view from southwest (courtesy of Minifie van Schaik © Peter Bennetts).

Australian Wildlife Health Center
Minifie Nixon (now Minifie van Schaik Architects)

Architect:
Minifie Nixon (now Minifie van Schaik Architects)

Project Team:
Paul Minifie, Fiona Nixon, Brandon Heng, Matthew Herbert, Nicholas Hubicki, Barend Meyer, Sam Rice, Ellen Yap

Location:
Healesville, VIC Australia

Completion: December 2006

Client:
Zoos Victoria and Healesville Wildlife Sanctuary

Interpretive consultant:
Cunningham Martyn Design

Landscape architect:
Rush Wright & Associates

Awards:
RAIA (Vic) Chapter William Wardell Award for Institutional Architecture, 2006

Premier's Design Award for Cultural Archtecture 2008

Royal Australian Institiute of Architects WIlliam Wardell Institutional Architecture, 2006

From Boullée to Speer, from Pierre-Charles L'Enfant to the new Scottish Parliament, from John Soane to Norman Foster, it seemed possible for architects to provide a literal rendition of what it means to assemble in order to produce the common will. Individuals might be corrupted, feeble or deficient, but above their weak heads there was a heaven, a sphere, a globe under which they all sat.[1]

In his introduction to *Making Things Public*, Bruno Latour describes the symbolic and social ordering power attributed to the dome in the architecture of classically inspired public buildings. The Platonic form "above their weak heads" organizes a transcendent harmony that is inscribed in the body of the building and transmitted into the body politic. Parliaments also imprint an organizing form on the public: via amphitheatre-like array of tiered seating, each voice is rendered visible; every member of the parliament must stand and speak and be seen to make his or her view known. The half-sphere of the dome and the parliamentary amphitheater make visible the public as a social ideal; *vox populi* is given material presence and a symbolic form, which simultaneously reinforces that social ideal in practice.

Yet the politics inscribed therein do not model themselves solely on the Platonic ideal. The political reading of the animal world—its models of governance, territorial negotiations and social dynamics— are, as many have argued, a primary pattern from which politics is derived.[2] "From the time the term 'politics' was invented, every

Lourie Harrison

Fig. 16.2 Entrance, view from west
(courtesy of Minifie van Schaik ©
Peter Bennetts).

Fig. 16.3 Ground floor / site plan
(courtesy of Minifie van Schaik).

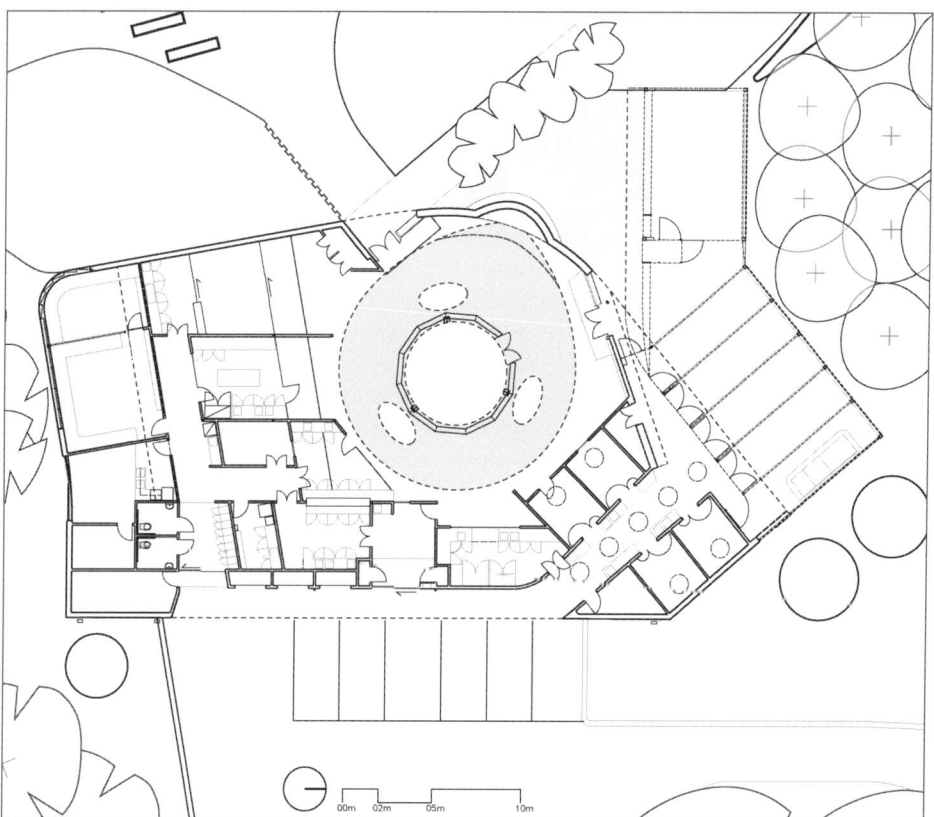

Fig. 16.4 "Apse" on west facade housing reception desk area (courtesy of Minifie van Schaik © Peter Bennetts).

type of politics has been defined by its relation to nature, whose every feature, property, and function depends on the political will to limit, reform, establish, short-circuit or enlightened public life,"[3] notes Latour as he challenges the dichotomy between nature and society, asserting in its place a collective that incorporates humans and nonhumans.

The above precedents and their posthuman implications apply to the 2006 Australian Wildlife Health Center (AWHC), the work of Melbourne-based architectural firm, Minifie Nixon (now Minifie van Schaik). The AWHC pioneers a program that combines wildlife education center, veterinary emergency ward, hospital operating theatres, laboratory, rehabilitation and safe areas for the release of recovered wildlife. Founded in 1921, the Healesville Wildlife Sanctuary outside Melbourne was established as a medical research center focused on native fauna. Currently its seventy-five acres shelter over 200 species and it has become a major tourist destination in the Yarra Valley with over 300,000 visitors annually.[4] This project was sponsored by Zoos Victoria as a response to the increasingly precarious existence of Australia's indigenous fauna, as wildlife habitat gives way to urban development. The AWHC serves as the hospital for the Sanctuary's wildlife but also as a clinic for injured wildlife brought in by members of the public. Healesville Sanctuary's senior veterinarian David Middleton developed the program for the AWHC, proposing to highlight medical procedures for wildlife in a radical departure from the more tourist-friendly deployment

Lourie Harrison

of animals as entertainment. Such a program acknowledges that even "wildlife" exists in an environment that is not wild but rather thoroughly conditioned by human technology. The AWHC therefore manifests one important aspect of what it means to be post-human: the establishment of human/non-human collectives. As Latour writes:

> It will still be necessary to represent the association of humans and non-humans through an explicit procedure, in order to decide what collects them and what unifies them in one future common world.[5]

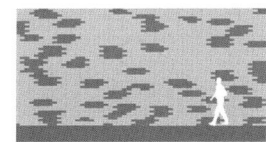

From early forays into complex surfaces with projects such as Batwing (2001) to the realization of computation-driven design at the Edithvale-Seaford Wetlands Discovery Centre (2011), Minifie van Schaik finds in geometrically-complex forms a way to manifest a more complex idea of the "public."[6] In the AWHC, the architectural ambition to grapple with the heterogeneous networks and publics described by Latour succeeds similarly by fusing program and form. The architects evert the traditional dome, turning it inside-out to produce a dramatic figure in gold tensile fabric: continuous compound curves, funneled orifices and helicoid surfaces formalize the mathematical concept known as a "Costa surface," a topologically complex minimal surface discovered by Brazilian mathematician Celso Costa in 1982. In refashioning the classical dome according to a contemporary topology, the architects play on the historical relationship between mathematics and architecture to disrupt the static order of parliamentary architecture. The Costa surface contributes a new form to those already inscribed in architectural theory (the plane, the helicoid and the catenoid), yet its complex geometry accomplishes environmental and programmatic functions as well. The form opens the dome with three sky-lit apertures, contributing to the blurring of interior and exterior atmospheres in the central gathering space of the building.[7] In addition to providing a symbolic opening to the exterior, these apertures serve as solar chimneys: allowing passive heat to vent from the interior.[8] The Costa surface programs an intertwining of humans, animals, and technology to create a form of "public" that we might term a posthuman collective. What some critics view as the perplexing and incongruous aesthetic of the Costa surface may also be interpreted as a visualization of new collective for human-animal relations.[9]

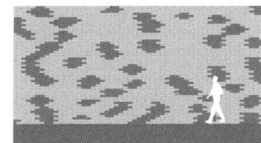

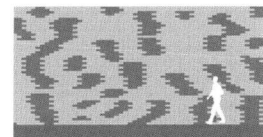

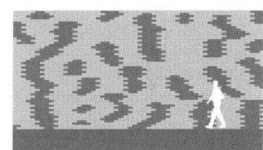

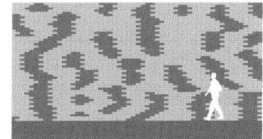

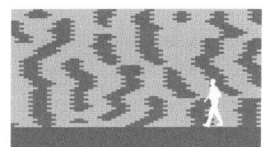

Approaching the building from the west, the visitor's first impression is one of heterogeneous elements: the gold Costa surface floats above the building's single-story enclosure; an open-air cage-like room (a wildlife rehabilitation area) protrudes from one side of the building while a singular bulge appears in the otherwise orthogonal wall. The mottled surface of the wall defining the building's envelope does not aim to unify these elements, rather it references the organic patterning of animal skin that is derived from a cellular-automata algorithm. As Naomi Stead points out in her review of the project, the architects regard the use of computation in design "not as a cold mathematical or experimental exercise."[10] In fact, in the AWHC

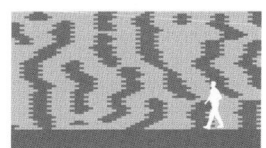

Fig. 16.5 "Cellular automata" algorithm for facade pattern (courtesy of Minifie van Schaik).

they integrate computational design techniques in two independent yet intertwining ways: first, creating a complex geometry (the Costa surface) that symbolically upends the hierarchies of the Classical dome; second, using cellular automata to pattern the façade along the same organic principles that govern the development of animal skin. These two different uses of computational design reiterate the programmatic integration of human technology and animal bodies.

The spaces organized under the Costa surface challenge the programmatic conventions of the traditional zoo and veterinary hospital. "We planned a standard veterinary, peeled back part of it and put glass ends on all the rooms," architect Paul Minifie describes the firm's bringing new perspectives to such traditional programs.[11] Framed within a glass-enclosed courtyard, the Costa surface extends through the section of the building to reach the ground, creating the main information hub of the single-storey building. This central atrium or "brain" of the AWHC in this sense is a grounded rather than transcendent architectural figure.

This circular space is animated by flashing, real-time updates for emergency and operating room procedures and schedules, underscoring, as veterinarian David Middleton describes, "the fact that they [visitors] are in a real, working wildlife hospital with real patients."[12] The wildlife hospital facilities are organized around this centripetally and are divided into eight programmatic zones—Operating Theatre, Laboratory, Emergency, Rescue, Post Mortem, Research, Reintroduction, Care and Rescue— each with glazed viewing spaces that provide an "in the moment" experience of each respective activity or procedure.[13] Transparency of process and directness of observation become the core programmatic

Fig. 16.6 View from main gallery of central atrium "Impact Experience" space and Costa surface (courtesy of Minifie van Schaik © Peter Bennetts).

Lourie Harrison

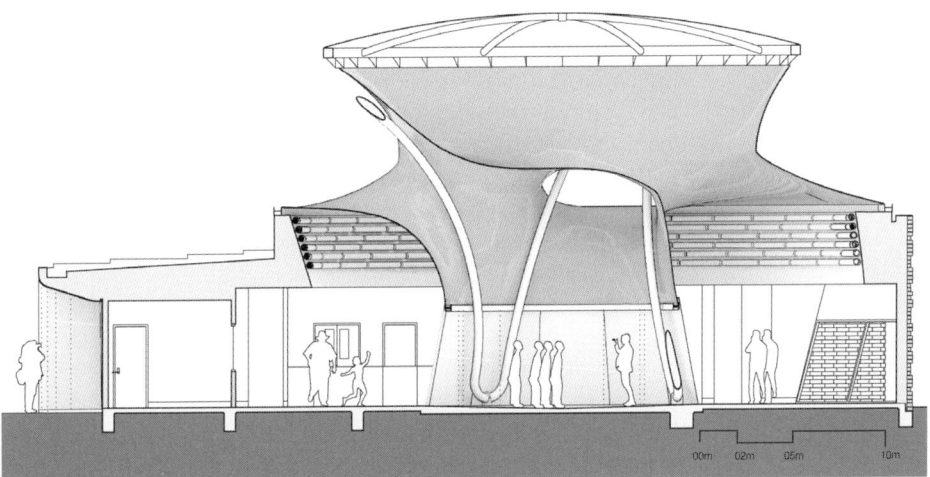

Fig. 16.7 Section highlighting Costa surface (courtesy of Minifie van Schaik).

values of these spaces: for example, at the Operating Theatre, the visitor witnesses the preparation of the animal-patient through the glass, while viewing its health history, which is displayed on plasma screens. Operating Theatre video cameras are linked to the screens, relaying footage of surgical procedures that are narrated by AWHC staff. "With the aid of microphone headsets, staff can communicate directly with visitors as they introduce themselves and briefly describe the procedure to be undertaken," says Middleton, "the procedure staff interprets the action, providing a rare insight into many aspects of wildlife surgery, including demonstration of specialized equipment and surgical techniques."[14] A similar communicative logic enables the observation of emergency procedures: a red "emergency light" flashes on the main menu board in the atrium to indicate that a critical operation is in progress. "Visitors are challenged emotionally as they are faced with the delicacy of life and the pressure of making an accurate diagnosis and formulating a treatment plan without delay!"[15] Likewise, the AWHC program contains a "Post Mortem" viewing area for autopsies. The importance of this programmatic zone relates an unsentimentalized, objective regard for the life/death continuum, often missing from the human view alone, which we might call the essential or remnant "wildness" that separates animals from humans, despite all integration.

In the current Anthropocene period, a new geological age marking man (*anthropos*) as the primary evolutionary force on the globe, we face the need to extend the technological network of care (disease and injury treatment) to wild animals. The visible program of AWHC staff caring for animals becomes a performance in and of itself, one that reinforces this Anthropocene priority, imparting the stakes involved in posthuman human–animal relationships. This programmatic engagement with non-human subjects signals the philosophical inversion that centers the building: man as idealized creature atop a "natural" hierarchy is recast so that man becomes an ordinary member of creature classes that are integrated into complex adaptive formations.

Fig. 16.8 Development of helicoid surfaces (courtesy of Minifie van Schaik).

Rethinking the human–animal relationship within a posthuman approach challenges architects to design spaces in which human–animal programs can unfold. Building on eco-feminist texts included in this anthology, we have seen how critical race, and postcolonial theory become figured in the human–animal relationship. Jennifer Wolch, Sarah Whatmore and Kay Anderson write that human regard for and involvement with animals can be a metaphor for or a model of political practices connected to power, identity, and social control; likewise, these authors argue that certain animal practices naturalize racial oppression in urban settings, while some animals have become encoded with pejorative meanings associated with identity politics. Anderson has studied Australian zoos in particular, noting the manner in which the construction of the relationship between human, nature and animals by zoos "consolidated and legitimated Australian colonial identity, naturalized colonial rule and oppression of indigenous peoples, and reinforced gendered and racialized bases of human–animal boundaries."[16] She analyzes how the zoo served as an exhibition complex with the project of making living things instruments of knowledge. Yet Foucault reminds us that man created the disciplines, or bodies of expert knowledge that differentiate and refine, and that the ultimate purpose of these intellectual scaffolds is to attempt to articulate what the human is by distinguishing what the human is not. Therefore alternative modes of knowledge practices, such as the AWHC's program for exchange with and understanding of wild animal bodies, are essential in constituting spaces that do not cage nonhuman species in the same logic as conventional zoos. The AWHC's formal organization similarly takes on architectural conventions such as the dome or the facade, yet demonstrates, through a thoughtful integration of computation, that more complex geometries and patternings powerfully manifest wildlife's entanglement in today's technology-infused environment.

The posthuman approach to architecture uses disciplinary (formal and programmatic) understanding to identify similarities rather than instituting differences among species, an idea aligned with Wolch's goals for a trans-species urbanism:

> A major consideration here is animal subjectivity; once we abandon a strict human–animal boundary with human subjects on one side and animal objects on the other, we seem to be obligated to figure them into our ethical consideration and everyday practice.[17]

Making visible the extension of the human envelope of consideration over the animal body is but one aspect to this mandate, to which we could add the recent reinvention of zoo as new types of wildlife preserves; yet both approaches require a complementary "un-fixing" of animals into human spatial orders.[18]

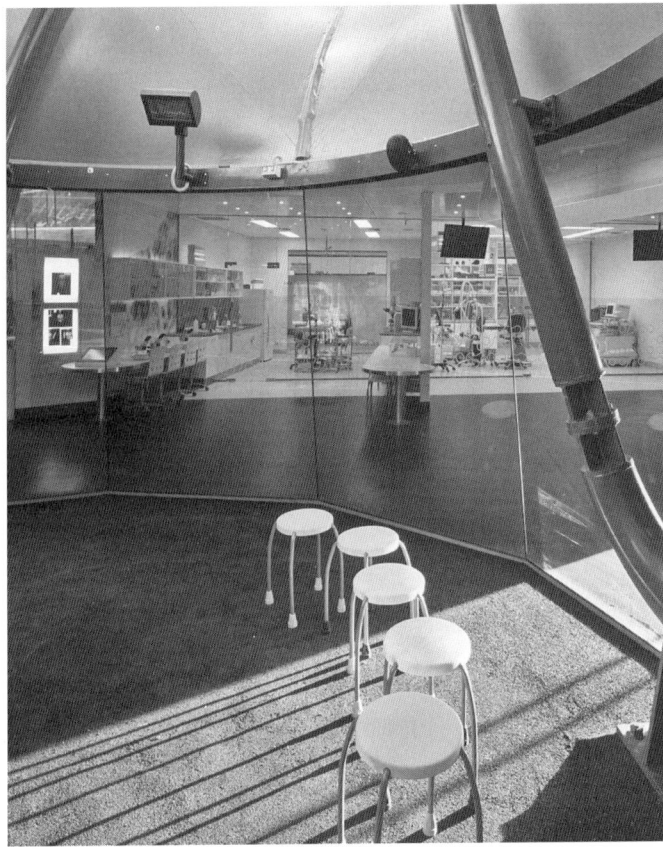

Fig. 16.9 View of medical procedure rooms from inside central atrium "Impact Experience" space (courtesy of Minifie van Schaik © Peter Bennetts).

NOTES:

1. Bruno Latour, "From Realpolitik to Dingpolitik or How to Make Things Public," *Making Things Public: Atmospheres of Democracy*, eds. Bruno Latour and Peter Weibel (Cambridge, MA: MIT Press, 2005), 30.

2. Jennifer Wolch, "Anima Urbis," see Section III of this anthology; Sarah Whatmore, *Hybrid Geographies* (London: Sage, 2002) and see Section I of this anthology.

3. Bruno Latour, *Politics of Nature* (Cambridge, MA: Harvard University Press, 2004), 1.

4. Lorraine Grout, "The Australian Wildlife Center: a working vision," *Award Magazine* (April 2008): 18.

5. Latour, *Politics of Nature*, 41.

6. Leon van Schaik, *Design City Melbourne* (London: Wiley, 2008), 207.

7. Leon van Schaik, "Australian Wildlife Health Center, Healesville Sanctuary, Melbourne," *Architectural Design* 76, no. 2 (March/April 2006): 125.

8. During cold periods of the year, the low level outlets are closed to minimize drafts and the gallery space is heated by an energy efficient radiant floor heating system. Grout, "Australian Wildlife Center,"19.

9. Naomi Stead, "Australian Wildlife Health Center," *Architecture Australia* 95, no. 2 (March–April 2006): 86.

10. Stead, "Australian Wildlife Health Center," 83.

11. Grout, "Australian Wildlife Center,"18.

12. Dr David Middleton, "Healesville Sanctuary: Wildlife Health in the Round," paper presented by Dr Philipa Mason, National Wildlife Rehabilitation Conference 2005, 6.

13. Middleton, "Healesville Sanctuary Wildlife Health in the Round," 3.

14. Ibid., 7.

15. Ibid., 9.

16. Kay Anderson, "Animal, Science, and Spectacle in the City," in *Animal Geographies: Place, Politics, and Identity in the Nature-Culture*, Eds. Jennifer Wolch and Jody Emel (London: Verso, 1998), 27–30.

17. Jennifer Wolch, "Anima Urbis," see Section III of this anthology, 243.

18. Chris Philo and Chris Wilbert, "Animal Spaces, Beastly Places," in *Animal Spaces, Beastly Places: New Geographies of Human-Animal Relations*, ed. C. Philo and C. Wilbert (London: Routledge, 2000), 24–5.

Fig. 17.1 Living Light and World Cup Stadium (courtesy of The Living).

Living Light Pavilion
The Living

Architect:
The Living, David Benjamin and Soo-in Yang

Location:
Peace Park, Seoul, South Korea

Construction: 2009

Client:
City Gallery and the Municipal Government of the City of Seoul

Air Quality Data:
Air Korea of the Korean Ministry of Environment

Optimization programming: Buro Happold New York, Ian Keough, John Locke, Daniel Kidd

Frame Construction: Suam RnC

Lighting Consultation: LED Korea

Fabrication sponsorship: Avery Digital Fabrication Lab at Columbia University

Designed by the New York architecture firm The Living (David Benjamin and Soo-in Yang) for Seoul's Peace Park in 2009, the Living Light pavilion engages both the global reach of wireless communication and specific urbanity of Seoul, South Korea, from an environmental perspective. While the canopied structure communicates real-time information about Seoul's air quality, the installation also establishes a novel dialogue with the city's residents. "People text message the building and it will text them back," explain The Living of their vision for integrating a wireless communication system within the surfaces of the Living Light pavilion.[1] The Living's implementation of a "responsive architecture" poses a broader question about the role of environmental politics in shaping contemporary urbanity.

"What if architecture responded to you?" asked The Living early in 2006 in the first section of their workbook, *Life Size*.[2] Initial efforts toward answering this question found no solutions in conventional architectural materials. Instead, the Living explored shape-memory alloys cast in silicon and "hacked" solar garden lights. *Life Size* offers a step-by-step documentation of the architects' laborious and patient invention of architectural assemblages capable of producing a response. "Is the carbon dioxide level above a given threshold?" was the first question that the architects were able to have a building answer. In the Living Glass installation, a predecessor to the Living Light pavilion, a "yes" involved a gill-like assembly of panels, made of silicon and shape-memory alloy, that undulated while registering increased carbon dioxide levels from human exhalation. The surface

Lourie Harrison

Fig. 17.2 Living Light pavilion (courtesy of The Living).

Fig. 17.3 Seoul World Cup Park, location of Living Light (not to scale).

Fig. 17.4 Underside of Living Light pavilion (courtesy of The Living).

of Living Glass visibly dilated in response to human presence. If Living Glass signaled an invisible atmospheric change to its immediate audience, then Living Light's ambition is to extend environmental information to an urban population.

The Living makes architecture into responsive human infrastructure using "hand made" and heterogeneous materials that incorporate information networks. Living Light envisions a building envelope as an experiential medium for conveying environmental information. This approach reflects the architects' profiting from the city's "indigenous" materials: abundant smog, which fluctuates dramatically during the day; the Korean Ministry of Environment's city-wide air-monitoring systems, which while extensive, has limited visibility; and "a growing number of facades with dynamic patterns of lighting," which do not display environmental information.[3] When an air quality monitoring system and facade display technology are linked together, they can be "optimized" (a term often used by The Living) by their integration into a shared assemblage: building envelope as an experiential medium for environmental information. Form and surface reiterate communicative function.

Living Light's canopy takes the form of an abstracted map of Seoul divided into the twenty-seven zones, or *gu*, in which the Korean Ministry of Environment operates air monitoring stations in the city. The transparent acrylic panels panels are etched with the city streets of their respective zones and bounded by fiber optics that blink and brighten in response to fluctuating data. Urbanity is literally inscribed in the panel surface; the underlying steel frame and "branching" column structure further emphasize the constructed quality of urban environments. The Living stresses the material efficiency of this steel structure:

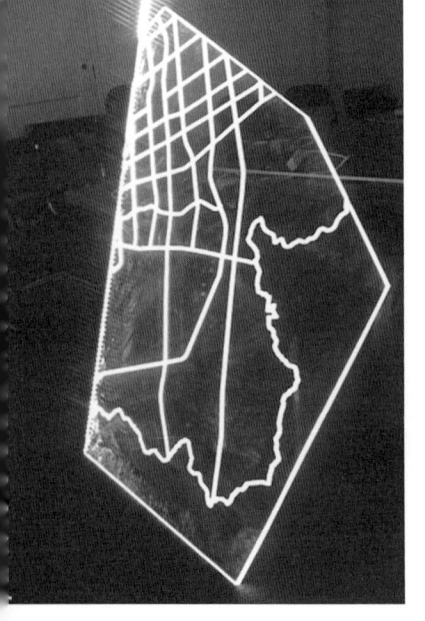

Fig. 17.5 Etched acrylic panel test for Living Light pavilion (courtesy of The Living).

> We set up an automated test with a search algorithm and a fitness function combining two objectives: best structural performance and least amount of material. We then used a workflow of multi-objective optimization to generate and evaluate 25,000 possible designs . . The experiment involved looking for high-performing design permutations but also ones that were unexpected. We were interested in exploration more than exploitation.[4]

The exploration resulted in unexpected column distributions, clusters of structure and asymmetrical branching supports: logics that depart from the premise of a rational grid yet respond to structural and material efficiency more effectively. According to The Living:

> Performance in terms of metals and material limits quickly overlapped with performance in terms of atmospheric effect, civic engagement, and communication through architectural envelopes. The result was not merely an unlikely solution to a technical design problem. The more essential result was a canopy that seemed to float on a sparse scattering of trees.[5]

Lourie Harrison

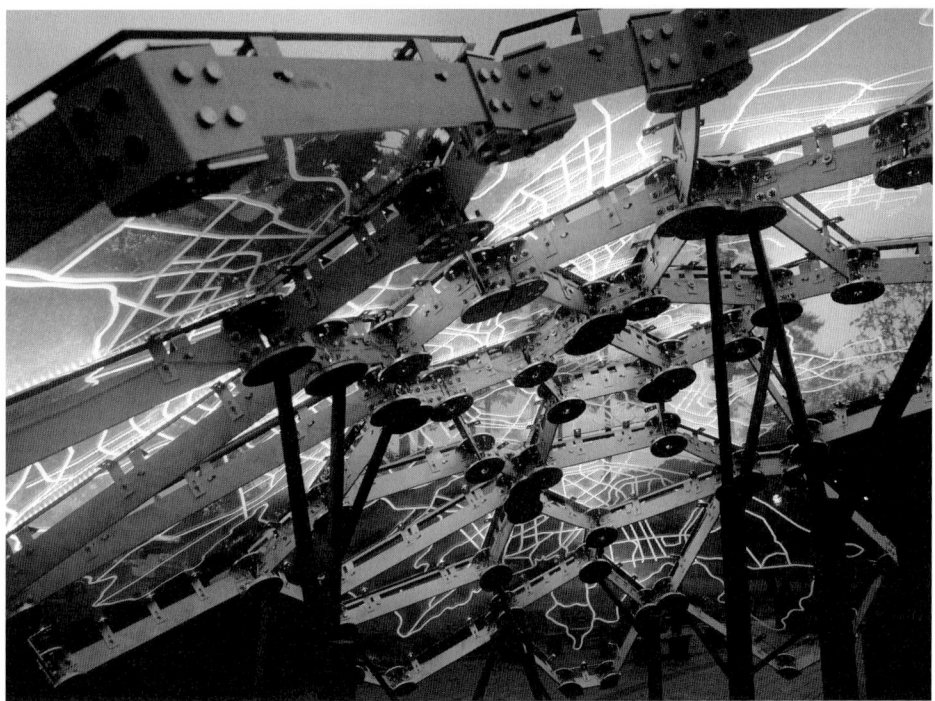

Fig. 17.6 Detail of lit panels in the Living Light pavilion (courtesy of The Living).

Living Light's curved canopy, perched on slender steel columns, serves as shelter, meeting point, and informational network, yet it is important also to distinguish its multiple modes of address: as a physical encounter with the responsive surfaces of the pavilion; as a dialogue with the building through a cell-phone interface; and as a remote repository of environmental information.

In terms of the physical encounter with Living Light, the pavilion's acrylic panels blink and flicker, giving fifteen-minute air quality updates from each of the twenty-seven municipal environmental stations. Improvements in air quality cause zones to light up, offering a panel-by-panel real-time visualization of the city's "best" to "worst" performing urban zones in terms of air quality. To achieve urban-wide "responsiveness" requires that data be communicated visually and relatively simply to as broad an audience as possible: the panel does not register gradations, rather it registers whether Seoul's air quality is above or below a given threshold. This binary display is what The Living describes as "low resolution" information. Low-resolution information may be comprehended at a glance, and does not require close reading of architectural form nor the study of intricate patterns. Yet the light coursing through the panels reflects the lively pulse of an information exchange between the building and the public. The panels also illuminate in response to text-messaged requests for information on specific urban areas, blinking in response to text messages and lighting the zone in question.

Our work begins with the promise of a dynamic world. Political and cultural conditions change . . . air and water quality fluctuate. . . A dynamic world calls for responsiveness in architecture. This, in turn, calls for new systems."[6]

The integration of an architectural facade system with wireless communication networks further reflects the "new systems" that The Living layer into architecture's simultaneous modes of address. This is not to suggest that the interface of hand-held devices should be considered a "public" interface, nor that the Living Light pavilion presumes a democratic reach based on consumer devices; the pavilion instead overlaps physical and virtual means of communication. "Our project aims to combine real-time data about the environment with dynamic lighting to create an interactive facade of the future."[7] Moreover, the pavilion results from a conjoined effort—supported by the Municipal Government of the City of Seoul and the City Gallery Project—to animate urban space with interactive installations that engage the environment as a theme and as a specific site.

Living Light's prominent location, directly across from the World Cup Soccer Stadium in the sector of the World Cup Park known as Peace Park, nuances the simultaneously physical and mediated experience of the pavilion. The Stadium, completed in 2001 for the 2002 FIFA World Cup with a capacity 66,000, serves as a substantial draw to the western outskirts of the city. The Stadium is a uniquely accessible structure, with its own subway station, a central transportation hub at the Yongsan KTX Terminal, and even a sunken bikeway connecting to the city's network of trails. Directly facing the Stadium is the Pyeonghwa "Peace" Park, the site of the Living Light pavilion and one of the five parks comprising the World Cup Park, which itself emerged from an extensive rehabilitation of the city's garbage dump. The World Cup Park incorporates a heterogeneous array of symbolic features: the expansive UNICEF Plaza; the Himang Forest, resulting from "The Planting of 10 Million Trees of Life"; the "mountain" of Nanjido, marking the site of the city's hundred-meter high garbage landfill; and the nine-hole golf course at Noeul Park, capping another landfill.[8] Living Light is perched on the edge of Pyeonghwa Park, which incorporates a children's playground, parking

Fig. 17.7 Diagram of Seoul's 27 zones as the formal basis of the pavilion (courtesy of The Living).

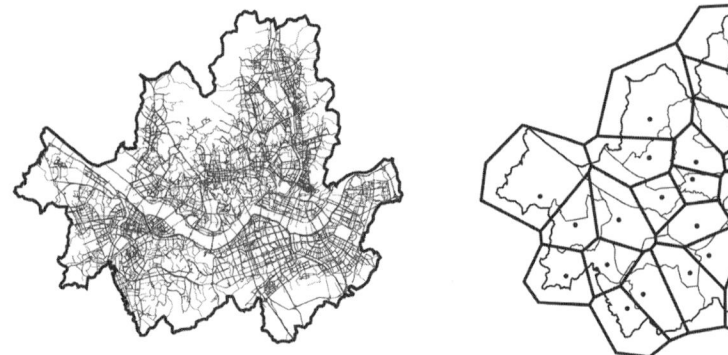

Lourie Harrison

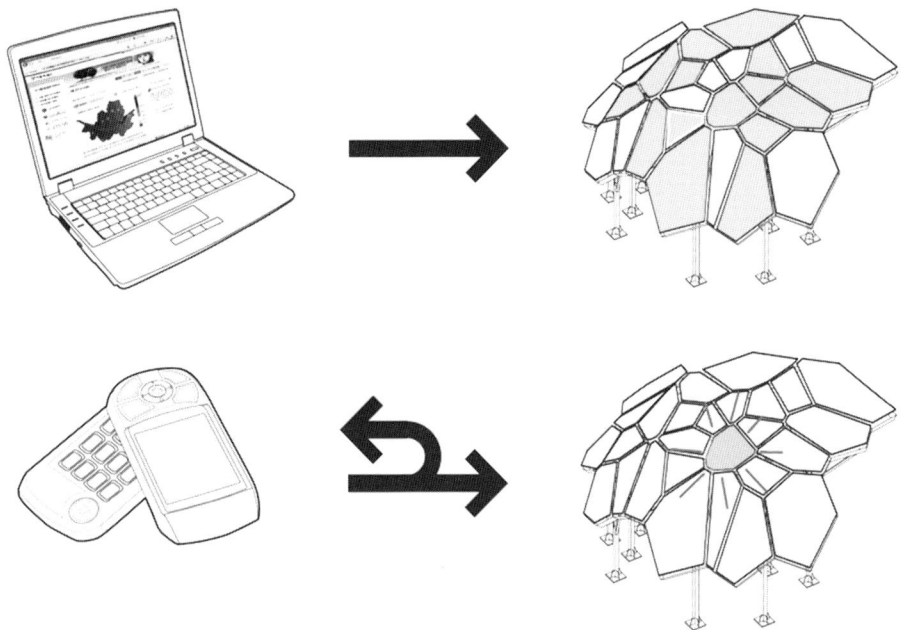

Fig. 17.8 Diagram of Living Light communication interface (courtesy of The Living).

and picnic areas. This site is a thoroughly produced "nature," the result of extensive public lobbying against the landfill and a remediation effort that dovetailed with the nationalistic goal of hosting a world sporting event. Thus the site manifests the confluence of multiple levels of interest, the lines of which we can trace in the interconnected parkways and water networks, subway lines, and bus stations, sporting centers and cultural installations. This network exemplifies the cyborg urbanization described by urban geographer Erik Swyngedouw:

> The urban world is a cyborg world, part natural part social, part technical part cultural, but with no clear boundaries, centres, or margins. All socio-spatial processes are invariably also predicated upon the circulation and metabolism of physical, chemical, or biological components. Non-human "actants" play an active role in mobilizing socio-natural circulatory and metabolic processes. It is these circulatory conduits that link often distant places and ecosystems together and permit relating local processes with wider socio-metabolic flows, networks, configurations, and dynamics.[9]

Swyngedouw has described the urban environment as a circulatory exchange, the metabolic processes of which are dynamic and ever-changing: "Metabolic circulation, then, is the socially mediated process of environmental, including technological, transformation and trans-configuration, through which all manner of 'agents' are mobilized, attached, collectivized, and networked."[10] Building on this idea, urban political ecologist Matthew Gandy invokes the cyborg as a more precise means to interrelate the social and physical networks of metabolic urbanization with information networks:

The cyborg metaphor allows for the simultaneity of concrete and imaginary perceptions of urban infrastructure so that the categories of the "real" and the "virtual" become interconnected facets of urban experience. The cyborg metaphor is, in other words, peculiarly suited to an understanding of the contemporary metropolis not only as a morphological entity entwined with various technical and aesthetic discourses, but also as an abstract and inter-subjective realm through which political and cultural ideas become constituted or "fleshed out" in parallel with the concrete development of the city. [11]

The cyborg model allows us to consider Living Light as an architectural means of establishing connections between the body, technology and urban space. Such connections suggest that what has been criticized as a "deterritorialized" urbanity leading to fractured identity—characterized by Gandy as consisting of ubiquitous computing networks, capital and labor mobility—may be countered by the new collective space founded on increasing environmental consciousness, a sensibility that Ursula Heise demonstrates to be simultaneously place-specific and global.[12] This is not to suggest that the public space fostered by environmental consciousness is always one of harmony and consensus, as is implied by the heavy-handed symbolism of World Cup Park. Rather, the Living Light Pavilion, in its simultaneously personal and distributed address of its public highlights the uneven distribution of negative environmental conditions in the city. Urban dwellers are thus encouraged to remain mindful of the global implications of local pollution. Thus by embedding sensing and actuating technologies in its surfaces, The Living's form of responsive architecture fosters an urbanity that becomes a public space of active debate.

Proper urban politics fosters dissent, creates disagreement, and triggers the debating of and experimentation with more egalitarian and inclusive urban futures: this process is wrought with all kinds of tensions and contradictions, but also opens up spaces of possibilities. [13]

Lourie Harrison

NOTES

1. David Benjamin and Soo-in Yang, "Living Architecture Lab," Graduate School of Architecture, Planning and Preservation, Columbia University, www.arch.columbia.edu/labs/living-architecture-lab (accessed 3/7/2012).

2. David Benjamin and Soo-in Yang, *Life Size* (New York: Graduate School of Architecture, Planning and Preservation, Columbia University, 2006), 33.

3. The Living, http://www.livinglightseoul.net/04.htm (accessed 3/15/2012).

4. David Benjamin, "Testing Material Limits, Testing Material Territories," in *Post-Ductility: Metals in Architecture and Engineering*, ed. Michael Bell and Craig Buckley (New York: Princeton Architectural Press, Forthcoming), page 3 of 7, manuscript courtesy of David Benjamin.

5. Benjamin, "Testing Material Limits," page 4 of 7, manuscript courtesy of David Benjamin.

6. Benjamin and Yang, *Life Size,* 115.

7. David Benjamin and Soo-in Yang, "Living Light, Seoul," http://www.livinglightseoul.net/05.htm (accessed 3/7/2012).

8. Seoul Metropolitan Government, "World Cup Park," 2002, http://worldcuppark.seoul.go.kr/worldcup_eng/index.html (accessed 3/12/2012).

9. Erik Swyngedouw, "Circulations and Metabolisms: (Hybrid) Natures and (Cyborg) Cities, *Science as Culture*, Vol. 15, No. 2 (June 2006): 118.

10. Erik Swyngedouw, "Metabolic Urbanization: the Making of Cyborg Cities," in *In the Nature of Cities* ed. Nik Heynen, Maria Kaika and Erik Swyngedouw (New York: Routledge, 2006), 33.

11. Matthew Gandy, "Cyborg Urbanization: Complexity and Monstrosity in the Contemporary City," *International Journal of Urban and Regional Research*, Volume 29.1 (March 2005): 39.

12. Ursula Heise, *Sense of Place, Sense of Planet: the Environmental Imagination of the Global* (New York: Oxford University Press, 2008).

13. Erik Swyngedouw, "The Zero-Ground of Politics: Musings on the Post-Political City," *New Geographies* 1 (2009): 53.

Fig. 17.9 Living Light in use (courtesy of The Living).

Fig. 18.1 Section through auditorium space (courtesy of and copyright Studio Gang Architects).

Ford Calumet Environmental Center
Studio Gang Architects

Architect:
Studio Gang Architects

Landscape Architects:
SCAPE

Location:
Hegewisch Marsh, Calumet, Chicago, IL.

Competition: 2004

Construction documents:
2008. Integration into Millenium Reserve Initiative, 2011.

Size: 28,000 sq. ft.

Client:
City of Chicago Department of Environment, Public Building Commission of Chicago, Millennium Reserve Initiative.

Awards:
2011 North American Holcim Awards Acknowledgement Prize.

Can architecture accommodate multiple species with conflicting needs? On one level, this is a philosophical question challenging architecture's anthropocentric bias and its privilege of the human subject. On another, the question takes on immediate and pragmatic ecological concerns, such as those raised by Studio Gang Architects about the possible cohabitation of two landscapes—post-industrial wasteland and wildlife preserve—that would seem mutually exclusive for the Calumet wetland area in Chicago. Studio Gang demonstrates that the architecture of their Ford Calumet Environmental Center can anchor a site as a wildlife habitat while opening a window onto the unique residual landscapes that form in the wake of modernization.

Calumet's Hegewisch Marsh bears many of the attributes of what the landscape architect Gilles Clément identifies in his *Manifeste du Tiers paysage* (*Manifesto on the Third Landscape*) as a type of abandoned space or *third landscape*, widely characterized as wasteland resulting from past agricultural or industrial use but taking several different forms.[1] The abandoned or *délaissé* space, with its implication of fallow ground, is a residue of human development, unlike other types of third landscapes: the overlooked *réserve*, an inaccessible and therefore non-exploited territory, and the nature preserve or *ensemble primaire*, which is protected by state governance. The *délaissé*, Clément suggests, is further distinguished by its almost symbiotic relationship with the city: while representing the abandoned land, isolated plots and roadside medians that dot urban fabric, the *délaissé* embodies ecological rather than real-estate value. As a typology, "third landscapes are not perceived as places for the regeneration of diversity but they are. They are important spaces, not for economic reasons, but because they engender

Lourie Harrison

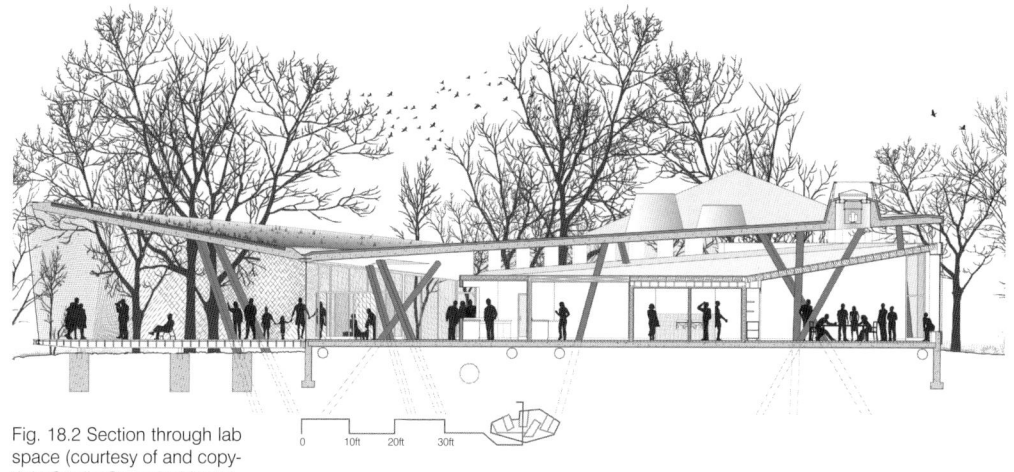

Fig. 18.2 Section through lab space (courtesy of and copyright Studio Gang Architects).

0   10ft   20ft   30ft

Fig. 18.3 Ground plan and slag grass gardens (courtesy of and copyright Studio Gang Architects).

auditorium

lab & classrooms

entry

screen porch

slag grass gardens

0 10ft   30ft   90ft

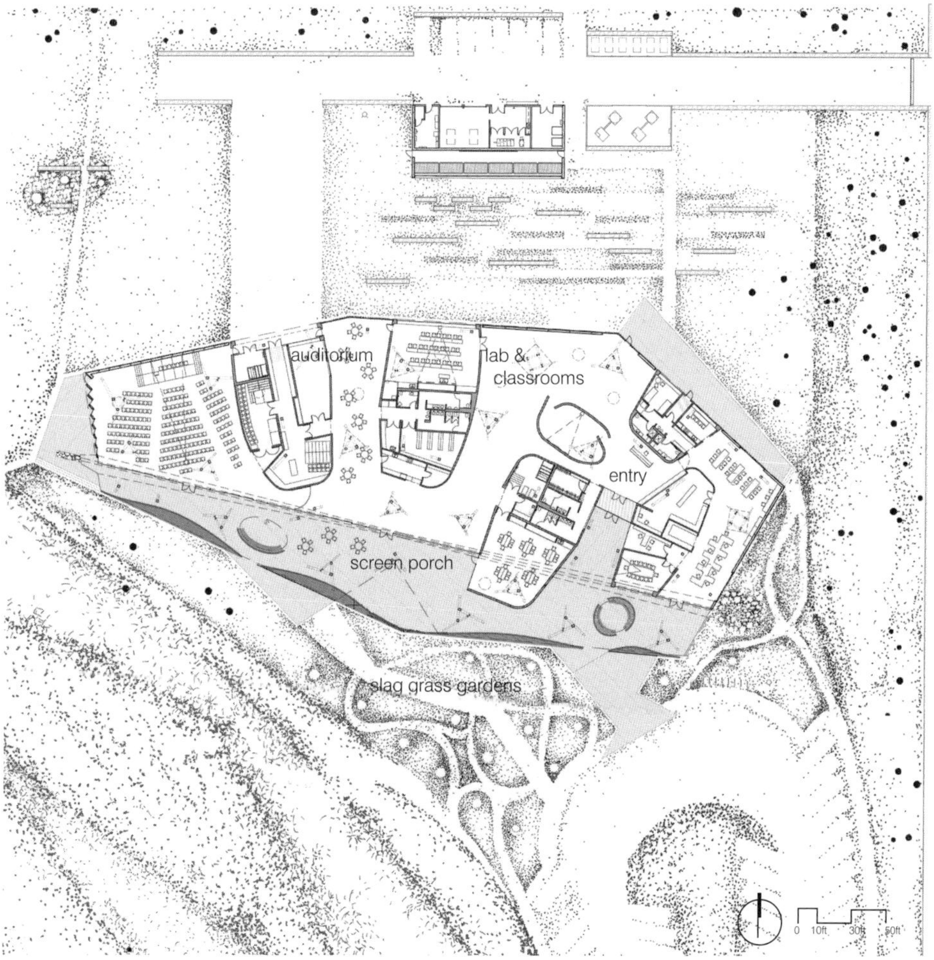

Fig. 18.4 Calumet's post-industrial wetland (courtesy of and copyright Studio Gang Architects).

biodiversity."[2] Clément describes a diversity that pertains not only of plant and animal species, but also to modes of human life: "The third landscape can be regarded as a natural preserve (when the third landscape is protected); a space of leisure, a non-productive space."[3] Clément's theoretical writings on the third landscape highlight the ecological and cultural potential of post-industrial spaces, especially in proximity to or within the city.

Occupying a defunct industrial site south of Chicago's Loop, the 117-acre Hegewisch Marsh is flanked by existing manufacturing companies, such as Baldwin Steel Re-bar Corp. and Calumet Harbor Lumber Co. It also neighbors Wolf Lake with its surrounding wildlife conservation areas. Decaying steel mills, rusting cooling equipment, parking lots and mounds of black slag—a byproduct of steel production—punctuate the wetland area, which occupies a strategic position at the intersection of two major drainage basins. The waters of the Hegewisch Marsh, however, retain the hallmarks of industrial activity and contain residual contaminants (lead, chromium, benzene and arsenic), which in turn have stripped the wetland's vegetation to a few species of cottonwood and phragmites. The site's location along the Mississippi Flyway (a migratory bird route), its marshland patches, and mix of defunct and working factories nevertheless provide the habitat for twenty-six rare and endangered bird species, reiterating Clément's observation that third landscapes can become harbors for biodiversity. The ecological interest of such post-industrial waste spaces, once understood as third landscapes, raises wider questions about how these zones of biodiversity can serve an exemplary role, and how ecological and industrial usages in the Calumet region can overlap while fostering education about the environment.

Fig. 18.5 Calumet's post-industrial landscape at Hegewisch Marsh: wetland habitats are embedded between decaying steel mills, the railway and the area's plentiful waterways (courtesy of and copyright Studio Gang Architects).

Lourie Harrison

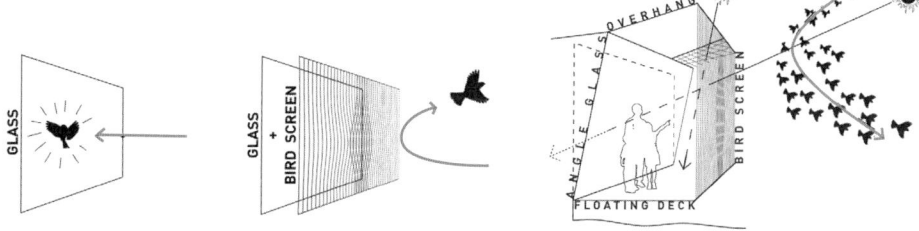

The Ford Calumet Environmental Center frames its site as a third landscape, revealing its entangled industrial and ecological usage. Striving "to expose something that is not normally seen, is under-represented, or is frequently overlooked, whether it's a quality of a physical material, an unusual building type, a pattern in an ecological system, or a social mechanism," Studio Gang's monograph *Reveal* reiterates what is a clear objective of the Ford Calumet Environmental Center:[4] to embody an ecological approach to materials while making visible the hidden properties of this area as a harbor for biodiversity. The clarity with which this agenda was legible in architectural terms may account for the symbolism of announcing Studio Gang's winning design on Earth Day 2004 as a building distinguished by its intelligent weave of sustainable materials and local history, its accommodating space for environmental education and its deference to the wildlife on its proposed site.

Studio Gang developed the bird's nest as a motif to intertwine the narratives of species preservation and post-industrial waste treatment. As a symbol, it recalls the large numbers of bird deaths (between .5 and 5 percent of the bird population per year in the US) resulting from birds' colliding with glass buildings, which from a birds' perspective are not understood as solid; glazed skyscrapers posing the largest threat, among other buildings, to migrating birds.[5] As a process, the nest is an exemplar of how to fashion a seasonally durable shelter from materials scavenged from the nearby area. Studio Gang suggests that the didactic value of "making architecture from nearby scrap, [which] seems both elementary and urgent in a world that is overflowing with waste,"[6] may be especially appropriate for an environmental center that seeks to manifest the interwoven histories of a site that is both industrial site and wildlife preserve. Intended to serve as a centralized naturalist resource for the region, this project anticipates hosting and housing visiting researchers and welcoming over 100,000 visitors annually in a 27,000 square foot learning facility. Frequent bird watchers campaigned for the new environmental center, despite the fact that such a construction could disturb the habitat. Yet humans, and human needs and preferences—including the preference to observe birds in their "natural" habitat—contribute to the ecology of the site.

Fig. 18.6 A basket-like mesh protects against bird strikes, (courtesy of and copyright Studio Gang Architects).

Fig. 18.7 Map with overlay of the ecological and industrial networks in the Calumet region; bird migratory pathways are indicated (courtesy of and copyright Studio Gang Architects).

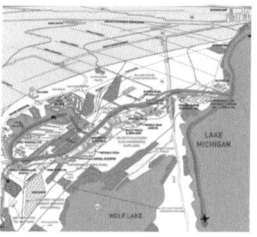

Fig. 18.8 Rendering of south porth during winter (courtesy of and copyright Studio Gang Architects).

Sensitive to the Hegewisch Marsh's migratory bird routes, the design team introduced a finely woven "bird-visible" screen in front of windows; the screen enables visitors to see outside yet signals to birds the presence of an obstruction to flight, thereby avoiding fatal collisions. A mesh of salvaged metal wraps the south porch of the Ford Calumet Environmental Center, creating a metal screen that both protects birds from collision with glass and reflects the industrial history of the site back to itself. The mesh of salvaged local steel and rebar also hews to principles of sustainability, emphasizing Anthropocene era obligations to conserve material while remediating the local ecology for visitors, birdwatchers and researchers. The metal elements also bear the history of their own industrial manufacture in the Calumet region as individuated welding marks. Studio Gang highlights this industrial history in their design for the building's structure: rather than the conventional grid of regular columns, the design proposes bundles of salvaged steel, each revealing markings indicating the metal's origins. The screening and structure thus materializes the metaphor of human responsibility for the post-industrial environment in deploying reclaimed metals directly applicable to historical usage of the site: an emblematic and utilitarian re-deployment of local waste into raw material. In another example, the cement floor finds utility in slag, an industrial waste product from steel manufacture, which when added to cement improves durability and therefore reduces maintenance costs. Locally salvaged materials redeploy derelict remnants of Calumet's industrial heritage in a new format, reintegrating the evidence of local human industrial activity into a built structure intended as an icon of the Anthropocene future.

The single-story building is oriented to shade southern sun with its long metal-screened porch. Its plan offers a gradient of semi-enclosed and enclosed spaces in its amoeboid groupings of classrooms and educational programs. Administrative functions, the cafe, and classrooms form bubbles in the accommodating plan, which is also dotted with tables to emphasize that the learning process need not solely be contained to classrooms. The section further reiterates the porosity between the rooms.

The gardens designed by SCAPE form the outermost southern band of the design, with meandering paths flanked by "slag gardens" and cisterns, as if reiterating in smaller and more ecologically sensitive form the broader context of the post-industrial site. SCAPE's landscape design addresses the site as a third landscape rather than as a remediation project. SCAPE found, in researching the history of the site, that the original course of the Calumet River had been altered to accommodate barge traffic. Recognizing that the earthworks and infrastructural intervention required to reroute the river back to its original course would represent, even if financeable, a treatment worse than the disease, SCAPE proposed instead to "reset" the forest succession process from the Calumet site's current and post-industrial incarnation. A gradual introduction of new plant species provides the conditions for restored biodiversity with minimized disruption over a multi-year timeframe. This is a theme operating throughout the Ford Calumet Environmental Center: there is no return to an original or pristine landscape but rather a current ecology that incorporates man's interventions and history. Only by adding to can one remediate, and even then, the return is not to an original nature, though the principles that governed the original ecosystem may be incorporated.

The Ford Calumet Environmental Center's energy systems, also on display, ally the site's industrial past with an anticipation of new industries in renewable energy. Passive systems include building orientation and roof pitch, natural displacement ventilation to exhaust air through the roof, passive solar panels, and geothermal heating systems to minimize electric use. The leaf-like shape of the roof funnels water to cisterns, which collect rainwater for reuse in wastewater treatment, systems which include a living machine using plant and bacteria as biological filters to process wastewater. A biomass boiler, integrated into the Center's environmental education program, produces heat in the colder seasons and cools air in the summer. Such energy systems, in addition to the use of recycled materials, contribute to the Center's anticipation of a LEED Platinum status. While such sustainable design strategies address the building's energy consumption and aim to reduce its carbon footprint, a posthuman approach encourages new sustainability metrics such as LEED's pilot credit for bird collision deterrence, integrating bird-friendly facade treatment as well as light-pollution containment. Yet should further metrics be developed to assess the impact of visitors on this emergent industrial marshland? Gilles Clément proposes something of a decoy strategy: a proposal at Vassivieres in which he "mapped the terrain and the third landscape spaces and planned paths and recreation areas with the intent of drawing visitors away from the lake . . . basically to protect the water."[7] Perhaps LEED credits should include similar deterrence strategy. Yet the Ford Calumet Environmental Center offers a way forward through a third landscape, suggesting a hybrid, in which the envelope of ecological thinking is extended to incorporate man's activities and those of the species indigenous to the environments in which man builds.

Fig. 18.9 Rendering of night view of south porch and view across slag garden (courtesy of and copyright Studio Gang Architects).

Its status as an Earth Day marker and wildlife reserve has not sheltered the project from the vagaries of urban politics. After a delay on its 2011 ground-breaking, the Ford Calumet Environmental Center is now being positioned as a future anchor of the Millennium Reserve Initiative, a new 140,000 acre open space reserve system that will connect green spaces throughout northeast Illinois, with the Calumet region at its core.[8] In December 2011, Chicago Governor Pat Quinn announced the start of the Millennium Reserve Calumet Core phase, which involves restoration of 15,000 acres of open space. The Calumet Core Reserve is proposed as a catalyst to promote economic growth by framing partnerships between the forty-four government agencies, community groups, and advocacy organizations.[9] If we understood the Ford Calumet Environmental Center as a project invested in integrating seemingly disparate usages, we should not be surprised to find the building as a central motif of the Millennium Reserve Initiative: an exemplar of building for multiple species and, as a new locus for developing job training and skills in environmental remediation, restoration, and conservation.

Lourie Harrison

NOTES

1. Gilles Clément, *Manifeste du Tiers paysage* (Paris: Editions Sujet/Objet, 2004).

2. Denise Bratton, "An Interview with Gilles Clément," *Log* 12 (Summer 2008), 89.

3. Clément, *Manifeste du Tiers paysage*, 55.

4. Jeanne Gang, *Reveal: Studio Gang Architects* (New York: Princeton Architectural Press, 2011), 11.

5. Because birds behave as if clear reflective glass is invisible to them, sheet glass poses a significant risk for birds. The annual toll of bird deaths lies between 100 million to 1 billion birds in the US alone, which has a bird population estimated at 20 billion. Daniel Klem, "Sheet Glass: invisible and lethal hazard for birds: making our homes and workplaces safe for birds," in Gang, *Reveal*, 50.

6. Gang, *Reveal*, 35.

7. Bratton, "An Interview with Gilles Clément," 84.

8. Information courtesy of Studio Gang (email 3/21/2012).

9. http://www.illinois.gov/PressReleases/ShowPressRelease.cfm?SubjectID=2&RecNum=9909 (accessed 3/20/2012).

Section III

Posthuman Territory

Zones of Indistinction:
Bio-political Contestations in the Urban Arena
Matthew Gandy

The relationship between the body and the city might appear to be a natural focus for urban analysis and debate, yet the "body/city" nexus has tended to be refracted through a series of theoretical discourses within which the body itself plays only a tangential role. Even within Foucauldian-inspired readings of the "bio-political" impulse behind modernity, the physicality of the body retains a somewhat ambiguous position within the disciplinary apparatus of the modern state: the emphasis on the discursive production of the body has tended to occlude any clear engagement with the lived experience of space.[1] There is, therefore, a tension running through Foucault's writings between materialist and idealist interpretations of urban change in which the analysis of discursive responses to material developments has tended to take precedence over the physical realm of the body itself. Yet if we are to make sense of the modern city—and its post-industrial, late-modern and post-modern permutations—we need to engage with the body both as a site of corporeal interaction with the physical spaces of the city and as a symbolic field within which different aspects to the legitimation of modern societies are played out.

Recent changes in the structure and characteristics of the modern city demand a rethinking of the spatial conceptualization of power developed by Foucault in his institutional critique of modernity. The influential notion of "governmentality," for example, needs to be reconsidered in the light of the radical dispersal of power emerging from new modes of urban governance and the declining role and legitimacy of many institutions associated with the state.[2] The modern state—that somewhat diffuse arrangement of practices and institutions—has long been a pivotal focus of Foucault's thought, yet "the State" in all its various manifestations is now undergoing such a far reaching transformation that we need to reassess some of the core elements behind his analysis of power. The historical contrast that Foucault draws between liberal and more authoritarian forms of governmentality, for example, has become less clear in recent years, with a proliferation of spaces that reside "outside the law" and a growing geographical dislocation between spaces of production and consumption that characterize the post-industrial city. Whilst Foucault identifies a disciplinary apparatus that gradually

1. On the relative absence of the physical body as opposed to the discursively constructed body in Foucault's writings, see for example C. Shilling, *The Body and Social Theory* (London: Sage, 2003). On the body-city interface, see also Elizabeth Grosz, "Bodiescities," in *Sexuality and Space*, B. Colomina, ed., (New York: Princeton Architectural Press, 1992), and Grosz, *Architecture From the Outside: Essays on Virtual and Real Space* (Cambridge, MA: MIT Press, 2001).

2. On debates surrounding "governmentality" see for example C. Gordon, "Governmental rationality: an introduction," in *The Foucault Effect: Studies In Governmentality*, G. Burchell, C. Gordon and P. Miller, eds., (Hemel Hempstead: Harvester Wheatsheaf, 1991), 1–52. On some of the anomalies see for example M. Walzer, 'The politics of Michel Foucault', in D. Couzens Hoy, ed., *Foucault: a Critical Reader* (Oxford: Blackwell, 1986), 51–68.

engulfs the body in the modern era, more recent scholars in this tradition, such as Giorgio Agamben and Zygmunt Bauman, have identified anomalies and contradictions in this conceptualization of power that highlight systematic forms of bodily and spatial exclusion. A focus on the material inscriptions of power in the everyday spaces of the city, for example, involves a consideration of how power can be sustained through architectonic forms that are independent of discursive practices. Similarly, the identification of different spatial manifestations of power—and, crucially, the relationships between these spaces—enables us to explore power relations extending beyond a narrowly European frame of analysis.

This essay explores connections between the body/city nexus and the idea of the "bio-political" as a characteristic feature of modernity. We begin by sketching an outline of the emergence of bio-political power and its relations with processes of social and spatial exclusion. The idea of the bio-political is extended to include those "spaces of exception" and conditions of "bare life" that play a critical role in the ideological and material sustenance of modern societies. We then examine the complexities of power in relation to the development of the physical infrastructure of the modern city with emphasis on discourses surrounding hygiene, public health, and different conceptions of urban order. The development of the disciplinary apparatus of the modern state is located within the context of the material exigencies of the industrial city and the bio-political impetus behind new forms of "governmentality." In the final section we consider some of the implications for power, urban governance and the bio-political realm engendered by current processes of urban change. It is suggested that a tendency towards the "bacteriological city"—focused around a distinctive arrangement between bio-political power and the institutions of modern governance—has been partially displaced by a new urban constellation marked by a different kind of interaction between cultural, economic, juridical and other sources of power.

From bio-politics to bare life

The rise of the industrial city necessitated a transformation in relations between the human body and emerging institutions of modern governance. The body became a focal point for a plethora of different concerns ranging from the need for productive labour to anxieties over the control of human behaviour. The body developed into an increasingly politicized terrain around which the defining aspects of modernity could derive a sense of symbolic unity. The gradual incorporation of the body within an extending web of rules, mechanisms, structures and behavioural codes was not only an inevitable outcome of the practical exigencies of an increasingly urbanized modernity but also reflected a strategic intervention on the part of the state into almost every aspect of everyday life. In the writings of Michel Foucault and of a succession of scholars since the 1970s, this emerging calculus of state power can be characterized as a distinctively "bio-political" dynamic, so that the field of political strategy and state activity becomes radically extended into areas of life which were previously largely perceived as lying outside the political realm. In the first volume of *The History of Sexuality*, for example, Foucault traces the origins of modern bio-politics to two different yet interlinked developments:

> One of these poles—the first to be formed, it seems—centered on the body as a machine: its disciplining, the optimization of capabilities, the extortion of its forces, the parallel increase in its usefulness and its docility, its integration into systems of efficient and economic controls, all this was ensured by the procedures of power that characterized the *disciplines*: an *anatomo–politics of the human body*. The second, formed somewhat later, focused on the species body, the body imbued with the mechanics of life and serving as the basis of the biological processes: propagation, births and mortality, the level of health, life expectancy and longevity, with all the conditions that can cause these to vary. Their supervision was effected through an entire series of interventions and regulatory controls: a bio-politics of the population. The disciplines of the body and the regulations of the population constituted the two poles around which the organization of power over life was deployed.[3]

The emerging focus of bio-political power is thus centered on individual bodies and populations, so that the regulation of the modern subject becomes connected with the strategic needs of the nation state. We encounter, therefore, a complex interplay between the health of the "body politic" and the associated discourses of nationalism, militarism and colonialism, which became reflected in a nexus of ethological formulations culminating in the socio-biological justification of geo-political power. What remains less certain, however, is how this emerging dynamic between bio-political power and the development of the nation-state originally evolved. It is not clear, in other words, how political manifestations of power first began to gain control over the human body and thereby evolve into the institutional and juridical structures of the modern state. Whereas Foucault's conceptualization of the "bio-political" focuses on the professional discourses which developed around

3. Michel Foucault, *The History of Sexuality,* vol. 1, trans. R. Hurley (New York: Random House, 1978 [1976]), 139, (emphasis in the original). See also *Michel Foucault: Beyond Structuralism and Hermeneutics,* H. Dreyfus and P. Rabinow, eds, (Chicago: University of Chicago Press, 1992).

the body during the modern era, the influential recent writings of the Italian philosopher Giorgio Agamben pay closer attention to the historical origins of emergent forms of "sovereign power" over the body. In *Homo Sacer* Agamben traces the bio-political dynamic of modernity to the Greek distinction between *zöe*, meaning "bare life" or "natural life," and *bios*, denoting a way of living, incorporating social, political and cultural aspects to human existence:

> The Foucauldian thesis will then have to be corrected or, at least, completed, in the sense that what characterizes modern politics is not so much the inclusion of *zöe* in the *polis*—which is, in itself, absolutely ancient—nor simply the fact that life as such becomes a principal object of the projections and calculations of State power. Instead the decisive fact is that, together with the process by which the exception becomes everywhere the rule, the realm of bare life—which is originally situated at the margins of the political order—gradually begins to coincide with the political realm, and exclusion and inclusion, outside and inside, *bios* and *zöe*, right and fact, enter into a zone of irreducible indistinction.[4]

The bio-political can thus be characterized as the gradual colonization or "politicization" of "bare life" by an increasingly elaborate skein of institutional structures and relationships which find their axiomatic expression in "law" and various manifestations of "sovereign power." Power is in its very essence a question of control over the body, within which the differentiation between different bodies to create a politically defined community forms the originary basis for social exclusion through the operation of the "ban." In this way, the "state of exception" takes on the form of a distinctive "space of exception," whether reflected in the huddled communities beyond the walls of a medieval city or the marginalized belts of deprivation in the contemporary metropolis.

This emphasis on the spatialization of the political exception in the writings of Agamben moves beyond the "interior landscapes" of Foucault to build a conceptual schema that can connect between the peculiarities of urban planning and architectural design to encompass broader processes of metropolitan growth and development. By focusing our analysis on the politics of the body we can explore the shifting relationship between the city as a distinctive *polis* or political space and the emerging material characteristics of urban form through successive historical periods. We can observe a subtle movement between the Renaissance ideal of the "city-state" as a space of relative freedom to the closely administered "state-city" of the modern era in which human freedoms are subject to a panoply of different forms of direct or indirect control ranging across

4. Giorgio Agamben, *Homo Sacer: Sovereign Power And Bare Life*, trans. D. Heller-Roazen (Stanford: CA, Stanford University Press, 1998 [1995]), 8–9. Agamben is careful to point out that the Nazi concentration camp had its juridical origins in the detention of political prisoners in the Weimar era. The use of the camp also finds earlier precedents in the control of colonial insurrections in Cuba and South Africa by Spanish and British authorities respectively. Agamben, *Homo Sacer*, 166–9.

Gandy

different modes of liberal and authoritarian governmentality.[5] The city emerges, then, as the primary locus for these new strategies of disciplinary control and the development of new interactions between different bodies of professional knowledge and expertise. For both Foucault and Agamben the term "bio-politics" denotes not merely a blurring of the epistemological strategies of the life sciences and the human sciences but a cumulative process by which human life itself becomes incorporated within the aegis of the state. The direct bio-political manipulation of the body finds its ultimate manifestation, however, in eugenic attempts to improve human societies, and its most complex medico-scientific challenges in the shifting definition of death enabled by the cyborgian enhancement of the human body in conditions of severe mental or physical impairment.[6]

Agamben takes Foucault's argument further by positing the "fundamental biopolitical structure of modernity," so that the increasing control of the body becomes the defining criterion of modernity and in this sense takes precedence over other developments such as the secularization of science, the spread of capitalist labour relations or the growth of the nation state. He argues that Nazi Germany represents the first "radically biopolitical state" through its eugenic programme to merge the biological with the political, whereby "the physician and the scientist move in the no-man's land into which at one point the sovereign alone could penetrate."[7] The disciplining of the body becomes "the decisive event of modernity," and reveals the underlying similarity between the "modern ideologies seemingly most distant from one another," so that fascism, for example, is seen as the culmination of a series of incipient trends within twentieth-century modernity.[8] Agamben identifies a radical similarity between, for instance, the bio-political impulse behind both "modern totalitarianism" and contemporary societies "of mass hedonism and consumerism" that is leading towards a merging of different political systems around a globalized bio-political constellation in response to the "dissolution" of the nation-state and established forms of sovereign power.[9] This emphasis on the contemporary emergence of a global bio-political dynamic marks an extension to Foucault's arguments, and takes the intersection between biology and politics to a new level of intensity, whether reflected in genocidal conflict over access to resources or systematic processes of exclusion from medical care for the world's poor.[10] These "wasted lives," to use Zygmunt Bauman's phrase, represent a literal as well as metaphorical process of permanent and deadly exclusion for the poor, the marginalized and others who have no value within the global economy.[11]

5. Mitchell Dean, for example, who, following Foucault, traces the origins of modern governmentality to sixteenth-century Europe, distinguishes authoritarian governmentality "from liberalism in that it regards its subjects' capacity for action as subordinate to the expectations of obedience." M. Dean, *Governmentality* (London: Sage, 1999), 9. Hence the particular significance of this distinction in a colonial context where versions of modernity have been imposed in the absence of modern citizenship rights. See for example P. Joyce, *The Rule of Freedom: Liberalism and the Modern City* (London: Verso, 2003).

6. See for example M. Lock, "Death in Technological Time: Locating the End of 'Meaningful Life'," *Medical Anthropology Quarterly* 10 (1996): 575–600.

7. Agamben, *Homo Sacer*, 143, 159.

8. Ibid., 4.

9. Ibid., 11.

10. On the global politics of death and disease see for example P. Farmer, "Social Scientists and the New Tuberculosis," *Social Science and Medicine* 44 (1997): 347–58; M. Gandy, "Deadly Alliances: Death, Disease and the Global Politics of Public Health," *Public Library of Science: Medicine* 2 (2005): 9–11; L. Garrett, *Betrayal of Trust: The Collapse of Global Public Health* (New York, Hyperion, 2000); S. Szreter, "Economic growth, disruption, deprivation, disease and death: on the importance of the politics of public health for development," *Population and Development Review* 23 (1997): 693–728.

11. Zygmunt Bauman, *Wasted Lives: Modernity and Its Outcasts* (Cambridge: Polity Press, 2004). Agamben describes the systematic division of the world along bio-political lines as a form of "thanatopolitics" in which the production of death is functional to the system as a whole: *Homo Sacer*, 142. He also warns that the "bio-political machine" is pushing towards a "global civil war"—a term he borrows from Hannah Arendt and Carl Schmidt—rooted in new

The merging of different modes of political and ideological incorporation of the body within ostensibly disparate structures of power illuminates a fundamental uncertainty over the origin of sovereign power itself. How, in other words, has "bare life" become integrated into the governmental apparatus of late modernity although the sources of this bio-power remain unclear? By extending our conception of power from the traditional emphasis on "juridico-institutional models" to its diffusion into the constitution of the modern self and the micro-geographies of everyday life, we find that power is radically dispersed both in its practical operations and in its disparate sources of legitimacy.[12] These observations reveal not just conflicting forms of individual identity but also tensions between different legacies of both direct and indirect forms of governmentality in an intellectual manoeuvre that renders conventional political science largely redundant. This shift of emphasis also has wide-ranging implications for both the scope and methodology of historical research, not least by a move away from a conception of history as an accretion of legislative change towards an engagement with the everyday spaces of modernity through which power is radically dispersed rather than concentrated in formal agencies and structures.

Through the bio-political impulse to control "bare life," Agamben posits a radical if largely concealed continuity "between modern power and the most immemorial of the arcana imperii," and in so doing extends the implications of Foucault's insights both historically with his investigations into the pre-modern origins of power and also spatially through his emphasis on the "camp" as the logical end point of bio-political rationality.[13] Sovereign power involves a complex set of spatial relations between "outside and inside, the normal situation and chaos," so that "chaos" is incorporated into "the juridical order through the creation of a zone of indistinction between outside and inside." The intersections between power and space in which "ordering" and "localization" (or spatialization) become intertwined are driven by the role of the "sovereign exception" by which law and power is itself instituted from an abstract "outside."[14] In addition to an abstract "outside" we must also contend with the presence of a tangible "outside" which manifests as the "absolute space of exception."[15] For Agamben this "absolute space of exception" is exemplified by the "camp" in which citizens are deprived of their rights and reduced to a state of bare life at the whim of a sovereign power:

> The political system no longer orders forms of life and juridical rules in a determinate space, but instead contains at its very center a *dislocating localization* that exceeds it and into which every

forms of sovereign intervention and the ideological legitimation of unending conflict. Giorgio Agamben, *State of Exception*, trans. K. Attell (Chicago: University of Chicago Press, 2005 [2003]), 3.

12. Agamben, *Homo Sacer*, 5.

13. Ibid., 6.

14. Ibid., 19.

15. Ibid., 20.

form of life and every rule can be virtually taken. The camp as dislocating localization is the hidden matrix of the politics in which we are still living, and it is the structure of the camp that we must learn to recognize in all its metamorphoses into the *zones d'attentes* of our airports and certain outskirts of our cities. The camp is the fourth, inseparable element that has now added itself to—and so broken—the old trinity composed of the state, the nation (birth), and land.[16]

The "camp" is for Agamben not only a concrete artefact exemplified by the Nazi death camp but also a zone of radical indistinction in which human communities find themselves cut adrift from the institutional and legal frameworks underpinning modernity—a distinction that allows an explicit connection to be drawn between his philosophical explorations of the origins of bio-political sovereignty and the abandoned or marginal spaces of the contemporary city.[17] These insights also shed light on the seemingly anomalous characteristics of those deprived spaces that are only partially integrated into the global economy. From this perspective, for instance, the stark forms of social stratification associated with the colonial state, which have been so vividly described by Mahmood Mamdani and other scholars, appear not so much as an exception but as an integral dimension to modernity itself, in the sense that the "exception" or the state of exception is actually fundamental to the operation of the system as a whole. By invoking this coherence of apparent opposites, a radical critique of modernity is instituted in which a shadowy other is revealed that exposes the basis of its own legitimacy in processes of violence, exclusion and elimination. This dual dynamic of space and power is founded on a repeated differentiation between "citizens" and "subjects": whilst citizens have the right to participate directly in the political affairs of the state, the rest of the population are relegated to the status of "subjects," "guests" or mere "inhabitants" at the margins of society.[18] The apparent order manifested within modern societies rests on its antinomy, whether located in the run-down banlieues of northern Paris or the polluted oil fields of West Africa. In what is popularly referred to as the "Third World," for example, we find a proliferation of zones of exception in which conditions of "bare life" are produced by a combination of economic marginalization, resource expropriation and military subjugation. "At once excluding bare life from and capturing it within the political order," writes Agamben, "the state of exception actually constituted, in its very separateness, the hidden foundation on which the entire political system rested."[19]

16. Agamben, *Homo Sacer*, 175–6, (emphasis in the original).

17. "The camp," writes Agamben, "which is now securely lodged within the city's interior, is the new biopolitical nomos of the planet." *Homo Sacer*, 176. See also Giorgio Agamben, *Remnants of Auschwitz: the witness and the Archive*, trans. D. Heller-Roazen (New York: Zone Books, 2002 [1999]), and C. Minca, "The return of the camp," *Progress in Human Geography* 29 (2005): 405–12.

18. M. Mamdani, *Citizen and subject: contemporary Africa and the legacy of late colonialism* (Princeton: Princeton University Press, 1996). See also E. Balibar, "Outlines of a Topography of Cruelty: Citizenship and Civility in the Era of Global Violence," *Constellations* 8 (2001): 15–29; M. Mamdani, "Making Sense of Political Violence in Postcolonial Africa," in *Documenta 11_Platform* 2. Experiments with truth Ed. O. Enwezor, C. Basualdo, U. Meta Bauer, S. Ghez, S. Maharaj, M. Nash and O. Zaya (Ostfildern-Ruit: Hatje Cantz, 2002), 21–42; A. Mbembe, *On the Postcolony* (Berkeley: University of California Press, 2001); and A. Norris, "Giorgio Agamben and the Politics of the Living Dead," *Diacritics* 30 (2000): 38–58.

19. Agamben, *Homo Sacer*, 19.

Power, space and the bacteriological city

How have these spatialities and genealogies of power impacted on the development of the modern city? The modern city is structured around a series of demarcations between "inside" and "outside," exemplified by the delineation between "public space" and "private space," yet these crude distinctions actually tell us relatively little about the emergence of those "power geometries" that structure everyday life. We need to consider, for example, how the public realm extends to those "zones of indistinction" which reside within the fabric of the city so that disparate elements are bound together in order to produce a functional combination of different spaces. It is immediately clear that the city is a concentration of social and economic activity, yet this is not to argue that the city is little more than a nodal point within a wider system of flows. The city, above all, retains its political salience as a material space because the development of new forms of modern consciousness is inextricably related to the emergence of bio-political forms of governmentality.[20]

The bio-political dynamic behind the development of the modern city can be illustrated by the example of public health. The origins of modern perspectives on public health are conceived by Foucault as an outcome of new approaches to the control of "privileged breeding grounds of disease" such as harbours, prisons, *hôpitaux généraux,* and other spaces of confinement.[21] Since the eighteenth century the human body has become progressively incorporated into a nexus of architectural and regulatory structures to produce a new spatial order in the modern city. The politics of public health involved a shift from a preoccupation with death to a focus on life in which "the health and physical well-being of the population in general" emerges "as one of the essential objectives in political power."[22] The development of what Foucault terms the "disciplinary society" involved both the construction of new institutional forms of control and the systematic collection of information about modern societies. The gathering of data on urban populations became gradually incorporated into a complex analytical schema that effectively combined the circulatory insights of the medical sciences with an organicist conception of the modern city.[23]

If we take Foucault's term "medicine" in a more general sense to mean the regulation of the body and its relation to the urban environment then we can trace a link between the development of "medico-administrative" knowledge and the hygienist preoccupation with the control of urban space.[24] The spread of new attitudes towards hygiene and cleanliness involved a transformation in the cultural meaning and "stigmatization" of the human body as

20. The tension between conceiving the city as an outcome of generalized processes or as an autonomous catalyst for political change is captured in the intellectual antinomy between the interventions of Manuel Castells and Henri Lefebvre in the 1970s. See for example D. Cunningham, "The Concept of Metropolis: Philosophy and Urban Form," *Radical Philosophy* 133 (2005): 13–25. More recently, however, there has been a renewed engagement with the less determinist neo-Marxian legacies of Lefebvre along with Siegfried Kracauer, Georg Simmel and other classic accounts that recognize the role of the city as a symbolic focus for political action with concrete implications for society as a whole.

21. M. Foucault, "The Politics of Health in the Eighteenth Century," in *The Foucault Reader*, ed. P. Rabinow, trans. C. Hubert (Harmondsworth:Penguin, 1984), 283. Originally published in *Power/Knowledge: Selected Interviews and Other Writings, 1972–1977*, ed. C. Gordon (New York: Pantheon, 1980). See also M. Foucault, "The Birth of Bio-politics," in *Michel Foucault: Ethics. Essential works 1954–1984*, vol. 1, ed. P. Rabinow (Harmondsworth: Penguin, 2000), 73–4.

22. Foucault, "The Politics of Health in the Eighteenth Century," 277.

23. T. Osborne, "Security and Vitality: Drains, Liberalism and Power in the Nineteenth Century," in A. Barry, T. Osborne and N. Rose, eds, *Foucault and Political Reason: Liberalism, Neoliberalism and the Rationalities of Government* (London: UCL Press, 1996), 99–121.

24. Foucault, "The Politics of Health in the Eighteenth Century," 283.

Gandy

new forms of social distinction emerged. The development of new social formations in the industrial city coincided with the spread of intensified forms of spatial differentiation as transport improvements enabled the middle classes to escape the poverty and congestion of the inner city. In tandem with the newly emerging socio-spatial disparities of the industrial city, we encounter an emphasis on increasingly individualized forms of identity and a growing aversion to the communal sensory realm of the past.[25] The handling of human faeces, for example, which had for centuries been an everyday aspect of urban life as night soil collectors delivered human waste to regional agricultural hinterlands, suddenly became caught up in a new set of behavioural, olfactory, and scientific discourses.[26] Human waste, which had previously enjoyed a sacred role within organic conceptions of urban order, was transformed into an object of disgust. This "ambiguity of the sacred," to use Èmile Durkheim's expression, reveals the way in which the significance of the same object can oscillate between auspicious or inauspicious meanings without changing.[27] The body is thus intertwined with shifting topographies of dirt and defilement that reflect wider processes of social and cultural change within the modern city as the mixed, compact and cyclical characteristics of the pre-modern city were superseded by an increasingly differentiated and sprawling urban form underpinned by the cyclical perturbations of capital rather than the organic demands of a bio-regional economy.

The gradual shift from a cyclical pre-modern city towards the modern "bacteriological city" reveals that, rather than a clear sequence of changes, there is in fact a phased, overlapping and frequently contradictory set of developments. The term "bacteriological" in this instance denotes the replacement of the organic city—with its emphasis on cyclical and more narrowly utilitarian conceptions of nature—by a far greater penetration of capital and scientific expertise into the governance of urban space. The plethora of governmental and techno-scientific discourses associated with the first half of the nineteenth century gradually coalesced around the bacteriological city with its emphasis on the technical rationalization of space to counter the public health threats of the past.[28] Yet this characteristic urban form emerging out of the governmental dilemmas of the industrial city masks a diversity of different elements, some of which are derived from the persistence of past forms, structures and ideologies, and others that are revealed through the political contestation of social and spatial inequalities emerging within urban space. In a colonial or post-colonial context we find that these "multiple modernities" are even more

25. A. Corbin, *The Foul and the Fragrant: Odor and the French Social Imagination* (Cambridge, MA: Harvard University Press, 1986 [1982]).

26. M. Gandy, "Rethinking Urban Metabolism: Water, Space and the Modern City," *City* 8 (2004): 371–87.

27. Agamben, *Homo Sacer*, 78.

28. See for example E. Heidenreich, Fliessräume. *Die Vernetzung von Natur, Raum und Gesellschaft seit dem 19. Jahrhundert* (Frankfurt: Campus, 2004); J. Vögele, *Sozialgeschichte städtischer Gesundheitsverhältnisse während der Urbanisierung* (Berlin: Duncker & Humblot, 2001), and J. von Simson, *Kanalisation und Städtehygiene im 19. Jahrhundert* (Düsseldorf: Verein deutscher Ingenieure, 1983).

29. See for example S. Kaviraj, "Filth and the Public Sphere: Concepts and Practices About Space in Calcutta," *Public Culture* 101 (1997): 113.

30. See for example M. Gandy, "Cyborg Urbanization: Complexity and Monstrosity in the Contemporary City," *International Journal of Urban and Regional Research* 29 (2005): 26–49; A. Picon, *La Ville Territoire des Cyborgs* (Paris: Les Editions de L'imprimeur, 1998), and Erik Swyngedouw, "The City as a Hybrid: on Nature, Society and Cyborg Urbanization," *Capitalism, Nature, Socialism* 7 (1996): 65–80.

31. The Metropolitan Working Classes' Association for Improving Public Health, *On Household Cleanliness* (London, John Churchill & B. Wertheim, 1847), 4. During the first half of the nineteenth century we find a proliferation of tracts and pamphlets giving advice on the correct use of water for washing and bathing, yet the per capita usage of water remained very limited in comparison with the second half of the nineteenth century. Very few dwellings had private bathrooms, and only limited quantities of water were used for washing. Most of the existing sewer networks were primarily intended for storm water, and were rarely connected into the plumbing systems of individual dwellings, which continued to rely mainly on cesspools, cesspits and other private means of disposing of human waste. On the cultural complexities of water infrastructure; see for example A. Guillerme, "Sottosuolo e Construzione della Citta: Underground and Construction of the City," *Casabella* 542/543 (1988): 118; M. Kaıka and E. Swyngedouw, "Fetishising the Modern City: the Phantasmagoria of Urban Technological Networks," *International Journal of Urban and Regional Research* 24 (2000): 120–38; N. Lahiji and D.S. Friedman, eds. *Plumbing: Sounding Modern Architecture* (New York: Princeton Architectural Press, 1997); and D. Laporte, *History of Shit*, trans. N. Benabid and R. el-Khoury (Cambridge, MA: MIT Press, 2000 [1978]).

apparent through the interweaving of different geometries of power, belief and social stratification in urban space. In modern India, for instance, we can observe the close intersection between conceptions of holiness and uncleanness through the role of scheduled or Dalit castes in the handling of refuse and human wastes (the word *dalit* is derived from the Sanskrit word *dalita* meaning "oppressed"). The handling of wastes and the complex relationship between "dirt" and the public sphere reveals the limitations of Habermasian conceptions of a unitary public sphere and the coexistence of multiple and oscillating modernities.[29] The shifting contours of dirt and defilement operate at both a symbolic and a structural level, so that everyday practices or encounters provide ritualized contestations of the use and meaning of modern space. The transformation of the meaning of "dirt" tells us much about fluid interrelationship between modernity, the modern city and the way in which stigma and oppression combine to produce 'marked' or contaminated bodies.

The bio-political dynamics of the modern city originate within an extending nexus of hybridized relations between the body, nature and urban space, so that the structure of the city tends towards a cyborgian synthesis between the physiological needs of the human body and the physical infrastructure of the city.[30] The idea of the "cyborg city" can be invoked in this sense as a technological enhancement of urban life that involves an increasingly elaborate intersection between nature and culture in the urban arena. The provision of basic necessities such as food, water, and warmth rests on a web of technological and organizational structures that have facilitated the interaction between the cyclical dynamics of capital and the transformation of nature into exchangeable commodities. In the case of water the rationalization of the modern city involved not just a transformation in the physical structure of the city—often extending far beyond the city boundaries—but also changes in the use and meaning of private and public space. The incorporation of the human body into the physical fabric of the modern city via the circulatory dynamics of water infrastructure illustrates the extent to which new forms of government or "governmentality" have impinged on everyday life as communal spaces for washing or bathing became associated with "sensuality and individual debasement."[31] At first these changes were instituted simply by improved access to water, but through time the hydrological dynamics of the modern city were embellished by a plethora of new technologies and advertising campaigns, so that hygienist ideologies became intertwined with popular culture. The modern home became an axiomatic space of liberal governmentality where new codes of behaviour evolved in tandem with a panoply of architectural and technical innovations. The role of women, for example, was transformed into that of "environmental managers" for the domestic interior, whilst the modern bathroom instilled new standards of bodily hygiene.[32] Although the spread of these new technological and architectural interactions with the human body was largely restricted to middle-class homes until the wider diffusion of prosperity in the second half of the twentieth century, the emphasis on water and health extended beyond the private bathroom to include the construction of municipal baths, lidos, and other elements in an emerging modernist intersection between water, architectural design and urban culture.[33] By the early decades of the twentieth century the "domesticated" human body had become fully woven into the social and institutional nexus of modernity, even if the technological transformation of the home had only been partially completed.

The miasmic conceptions of disease epidemiology in the pre-bacteriological era informed the circulatory dynamics of urban design and provided a powerful focus for institutional architecture. Yet as the spatial problematic of disease became more explicitly an issue of urban governance, the focus began to shift from architectural innovation to institutional reform.[34] Advances in epidemiological science provided the basis for a new form of bio-political rationality in which moral discourses could be partially displaced by a technical emphasis on the mechanisms of public health improvement. This rationalizing impetus reaches its acme in the "bacteriological city" as a distinctive and enduring set of social, cultural, technological and institutional developments, ranging from the development of new financial innovations such as municipal bonds for the "fixing" of capital in space to the marginalization of landed elites and other political obstacles to urban reform. Yet this emerging synthesis between liberal governmentality and "scientific management" rested on a fragile set of foundations most strikingly revealed in the chaotic public health situation facing many colonial and post-colonial cities.[35] Behind an apparent uniformity of developments—at least within much of Europe, North America, and parts of Asia—lies a complex set of debates concerning the precise role and limitations of government.[36] A Foucauldian reading of the history of public health not only risks a historical elision between different phases in the emergence of the bacteriological city and different forms of "scientific urbanism" but also overlooks the tensions between different combinations of scientific expertise and

32. See for example S. Frank, *Stadtplanung im Geschlechter-kampf: Stadt und Geschlecht in der Großstadtentwicklung des 19. und 20. Jahrhunderts* (Opladen: Leske & Budrich, 2003); K. Ross, "Starting Afresh: Hygiene and Modernization in Postwar France," *October* 67 (1994): 23–57; G. Vigarello, "Higiene e Intimidad del Bano: las Formas de la Limpieza Corporal," *A & V Monografias* 14 (1988): 25–32; G. Wright, "Sweet and Clean: the Domestic Land-scape in the Progressive Era," *Landscape* 20 (1975): 38–43; G. Wright, *Moralism and the Model Home* (Chicago: University of Chicago Press, 1980).

33. See for example D. Glassberg, "The Public Bath Movement in America," *American Studies* 20 (1979): 5–21; J.-P. Goubert, "Wasser und Intimhygiene am Beispiels Frankreichs," in B. Busch and L. Förster, eds, *Wasser,* trans. S. Barmann (Cologne: Wienand, 2000), 168–76; C. Trupat, "'Bade zu Hause—" *Zur Geschichte des Badezimmers in Deutschland seit der Mitte des 19. Jahrhunderts'*, *Technikgeschichte* 63 (1996): 219–36; and T. van Leeuwen, *The Springboard in the Pond: An Intimate History of the Swimming Pool* (Cambridge, MA: MIT Press, 1998).

34. Osborne, "Security and Vitality."

35. M. Gandy, "The Bacterio-logical City and its Discontents," *Historical Geography* 34 (2006): 14–25.

36. Consider the contrast between narrowly Chadwickian attempts to rationalize the technological struc-ture of the modern city and the wider political reforms demanded by public health advocates such as Robert Koch and William Put-ney Alison. See for example C. Hamlin, *Public Health and Social Justice in the Age of Chadwick* (Cambridge: Cambridge Univer-sity Press, 1998).

rival political ideologies. We should be careful, in other words, not to read the technical and institutional transformation of the modern city in functionalist terms, since the precise outcome of these complex deliberations varied significantly in different local contexts.

An emphasis on the bio-political regulation of urban space tells us much about the institutional context for the modern politics of the body, yet Foucault's theoretical legacy reveals less about the dynamics of urban change as a political struggle to create a functional public realm in the place of multitudinous private interests. There is, for example, an ambiguity surrounding the institutional and legislative legacy of the nineteenth century for the development of modern infrastructure: an empirical lacuna which is perhaps underpinned by Foucault's neglect of civil engineering in his analysis of professional discourses relating to the health of the human body.[37] Foucault also has little to say about the reconstruction of the public realm or the "physical city" as a political as well as an architectural project. There is, in other words, an uncertainty surrounding the architectonic expression of a rational "public interest" in urban space, whether this relates to sanitary discourses or nascent forms of urban planning. And his theoretical legacy remains detached from any workable system of universal norms which might facilitate a more general critique of modernity as evidenced by the intellectual tensions between Foucault and Habermas in their rival interpretations of the meaning and significance of the practical and philosophical legacy of the Enlightenment.[38] Yet the Habermasian response to these questions is in turn hampered by its somewhat naive attachment to the prospects for political consensus, and a failure to register the intersection between multiple and often contradictory modernities whose legitimation often rests not on the basis of some form of rational deliberation but on a panoply of competing claims, desires and justifications.

Dispersed geometries

These theoretical tensions become even more apparent when we explore the bio-political dynamics of the contemporary city. The partial demise of the bacteriological city posits a new kind of relationship between the body and evolving forms of municipal politics in which the historical associations between public health and urban reform have been extensively severed. People are now connected to each other in different ways so that the cholera-driven "corporeal unity" of the nineteenth-century city has given way to a radical dissimulation and fragmentation of bodily interconnections. In the shift towards what we might term "anti-biotic urbanism," an increasingly individualized

37. In his 1984 interview, "Space, Knowledge, and Power," however, Foucault does concede the critical significance of the *Ecole des Ponts et Chaussees* and the role of engineers in "thinking space" through "the three great variables—territory, communication, and speed" which "escape the domain of architects" (Rabinow, *The Foucault Reader*, 244).

38. On tensions between Foucault and Habermas, see for example J. Habermas, *The Philosophical Discourse of Modernity: Twelve Lectures,* trans. F. Lawrence (Cambridge: Polity Press, 1987 [1985]), and D. Ingram, "Foucault and Habermas on the Subject of Reason," in G. Gutting, ed., *The Cambridge Companion to Foucault* (Cambridge: Cambridge University Press, 1994), 215–61. On the limitations of the Habermasian approach see for example C. Mouffe, "For an Agonistic Public Sphere," in *Documenta 11_Platform 1. Democracy unrealized* (Ostfildern-Ruit, Hatje Cantz, 2002): 87–96.

health regime has displaced the earlier interconnections between urban governance, social reform and medical advocacy. Yet this earlier corporeal unity engendered by the threat of disease has not entirely dissipated, as evidenced by the potential impact of viral mutations or the resurgence of infectious diseases such as tuberculosis that had until recently been in long-term decline. The locus of power in the contemporary city has increasingly shifted from concentrated and visible manifestations of state power (governmental bureaucracies, police services and so on) to a diffuse set of networks dominated by capital (corporate lobbies, financial derivatives and other dispersed and ultra-mobile elements). In positing a distinction between concentrated and dispersed sources of power we should be careful, however, not to set up a misleading duality within which the role of centralized state apparatuses is exaggerated in relation to other forms of power in modern societies.[39] The current emphasis on "governance," for example, can be read as an adjunct to the neo-liberalization of public policy where the power of the state is increasingly circumscribed by a mesh of organizational structures that originates from outside the democratic arena. The legitimacy of the state and existing forms of urban governance has also been challenged by processes such as the "de-secularization" of modern societies and the rise of new forms of ethnic chauvinism and religious zealotry.[40] What is critically significant in the case of cities such as Mumbai and Jakarta, which have recently seen widespread violence and sectarian unrest, is the interconnection between economic instability and community breakdown so that the "public realm"—however we wish to define this term—is placed under severe strain. These neo-liberalized and politically unstable cities are increasingly characterized by "marked bodies" rather than citizens—in a reprise of twentieth-century fascism—so that landscapes of paranoia become interwoven with longstanding structural inequalities to produce volatile topographies of hatred and mistrust. The interplay between formal and informal networks of power, and between the visible and invisible manifestations of authority, has significantly altered the relationships between different sources of power engendered by the Foucauldian notion of "governmentality." Modes of governmentality have diversified, to encompass at one end of the spectrum a highly sophisticated technological fusion under the aegis of "digital citizenship" and at the other end various forms of "authoritarian governmentality" involving the co-opting of a vast reserve army of human bodies to protect interests, lives and property, ranging from security personnel patrolling individual premises, streets or neighbourhoods to the co-opting of

39. See J. Allen, "The Where-Abouts of Power: Politics, Government and Space," *Geografiska Annaler* 86 B (1) (2004): 19–32.

40. On ethnic and religious violence in Mumbai, for example, see A. Appadurai, "Burning Questions: Arson and Other Public Works in Bombay," *ANY: Architecture New York* 18 (1997): 44–7; J. Masselos, "Postmodern Bombay: Fractured Discourses," in S. Watson and K. Gibson, eds, *Postmodern Cities and Spaces* (Cambridge, MA: Blackwell, 1995), 199–215; and D. Padgaonkar, ed., *When Bombay Burned* (New Delhi: UBS Publishers' Distributors, 1993).

militias to undertake operations such as the guarding of pipelines or industrial installations.[41] In the wealthier and more strategically significant urban centres of the global North, the bio-politics of the body has entered a new phase marked by an intensification of the disciplinary modes of intersection between the human body and dispersed or hidden sources of power. The enhanced panopticism of contemporary cities, enabled by new data-gathering and biometric measuring devices, has introduced an anticipatory governmentality where even facial expressions can produce visual algorithms capable of triggering new forms of preemptive security interventions.[42] In the poorer cities of the global South, however, the tendency is towards an array of physical barriers to restrict entry into communities in combination with a human shield of poorly paid security personnel. In the contemporary city the disciplinary techniques and strategies of the past have acquired new spatial forms. The placing of social deviants within institutions so that they might be "improved" or re-educated in preparation to rejoin society has been displaced by the logic of permanent exclusion exemplified by the carceral archipelagos developing around many US cities.[43] Though the public rhetoric of social control is now primarily focused on terrorism or violent crime, the principal concern of these new disciplinary structures and practices is aimed at the control of those forms of social deviance which threaten economic activity such as the presence of "undesirable" people in public or quasi-public spaces.[44] There is a proliferation of private security services, for example, whose uniformed visibility presents a form of "state ventriloquism" so that their authority appears to derive from state institutions rather than private interests. The classic notion of one entity or sovereign power with control over society as a whole has fundamentally changed, so that society is increasingly controlling itself through innumerable surveillance networks. The radical dispersal of power poses new dilemmas for the relationship between the body and the city, in which the rationale for urban order is no longer linked to the cohesive demands of the industrial city but to the role of cities as competitive nodes within the global economy.

The body has become a critical terrain for new processes of differentiation and exclusion within urban space, whether in terms of the commodification of individual bodies or the pervasive use of body images as part of the visual culture of late modernity. The trafficking and exploitation of bodies, for example, is an increasingly significant component of the "flesh economy" of the contemporary city. The postindustrial city is also marked by a libidinous and hyper-sexualized interaction between economy and society, rooted

41. For contrasting perspectives on oil, imperialism and "authoritarian governmentality," see A. Barry, "Technological Zones," paper presented to the London Group of Historical Geographers, Senate House, University of London, 24 May 2005, and Michael Watts, "Development and Governmentality," *Singapore Journal of Tropical Geography* 24 (2003), 6–34. On topographies of fear and social difference in the cities of the global South, see for example T. Caldeira, *City of Walls: Crime, Segregation and Citizenship in Sao Paulo* (Berkeley: University of California Press, 2000), 334–5. "Cities of walls," notes Caldeira, "do not strengthen citizenship but rather contribute to its corrosion." See also J. Holston and A. Appadurai, "Cities and citizenship," in J. Holston, ed., *Cities and Citizenship* (Durham: Duke University Press, 1999), 1–18.

42. See for example M. Gray, "Urban Surveillance and Panopticism: will We Recognize the Facial Recognition Society?" *Surveillance and Society* 1 (2003): 314–30.

43. See Mike Davis's diagrammatic representation of the "gulag rim" in *Ecology of Fear: Los Angeles and the Imagination of Disaster* (New York: Metropolitan Books, 1998).

44. See for example S. Thabe, ed., *Raum and Sicherheit* (University of Dortmund: Institüt für Raumplanung, IRPUD, 2001); K. Ronneberger, S. Lanz and W. Jahn, *Die Stadt als Beute* (Bonn: J.H.W. Dietz Nachfolger, 1999); and R. Rorty, 'Feind im Visier', trans. K. Wördemann, *Die Zeit* (18 Mar. 2004).

Gandy

in intensified modes of consumption whereby social control is effected not by repression but by ever greater degrees of sensory stimulation.[45] No longer the focus of the disciplinary and health campaigns associated with the "productive body" of the industrial city, the post-industrial body has instead become the visual icon of an aesthetic feeding frenzy. The contemporary city has taken on a quality of bodily excess in which an idealized body aesthetic has become an increasingly ubiquitous if not iconic dimension to urban culture. The depiction of the fascist body exemplified by Leni Riefenstahl's *Olympia* (1938), for example, bears striking similarities to the idealized figures that gaze from illuminated billboards in the contemporary city, in an illustration of the ideological proximity of ostensibly diverse visual cultures (and arguably a corollary of Agamben's observations on the bio-political continuities between liberal and authoritarian states).[46] The pervasive blurring of aesthetic and ethical discourse also provides ideological legitimation for new and widening forms of social and economic inequality. Product branding, generalized ennui and a vast extension in oligopolistic power structures have reduced the democratic arena to little more than a digitized chimera: a consultative forum within which every alternative has already been ruthlessly circumscribed.[47] Where opposition fleetingly appears it is often an expression of negation, whereby a refusal to engage or the rejection of "choice" marks a sudden rupture or striation across the verisimilitude of consensus.

The intensified cycles of investment and disinvestment in the post-industrial metropolis lend a "bulimic" quality to the contemporary city. The bulimic metaphor is especially apposite for many of the vast mega-cities of the global South, where waves of investment in the built environment are subject to violent perturbations in response to factors such as political instability, the vicissitudes of state finances and the effects of drastic currency devaluations: cities such as Lagos, for example, are characterized by dilapidated networks of oil-financed urban infrastructures from the 1970s engulfed within the pyroclastic expansion of the informal city.[48] In these and other "postproductive" cities, only partially or tangentially connected with the global economy, the bio-politics of urban space takes on new and uncertain dimensions.

When Georg Simmel described the blasé attitude as an inevitable response to the sensory overload of the modern city, he cannot have anticipated the degree to which the consumption-driven political dynamic of the post-industrial city would work assiduously to eliminate any real sense of "shock" from those critical social strata that

45. M. Foucault, "Power/Knowledge," 57.

46. For a classic account of fascist aesthetics in relation to the body, see S. Sontag, "Fascinating Fascism," in *Under the Sign of Saturn* (New York: Farrar, Straus & Giroux, 1974).

47. Günther Grass, for example, makes a trenchant defense of democratic institutions and warns that the German parliament is "degenerating into a subsidiary of the stock exchange." G. Grass, "The High Price of Freedom," *The Guardian* (7 May 2005).

48. On urban "bulimia" see for example N. Tadiar, "Manila's New Metropolitan Form," in V.L. Rafael, ed., *Discrepant Histories* (Philadelphia: Temple University Press, 1995), 285–313. On crisis-driven patterns of urban development in Lagos, see M. Gandy, "Learning from Lagos," *New Left Review* 33 (2005): 37–53.

underpin the new global economy. The people who generate profits either as workers or shoppers are no longer blasé but fearful and powerful groups who live in an increasingly isolated sphere whether outside the city itself or confined to chic enclaves within it. The new strategies of bodily exclusion form part of a globalized bio-political dynamic in which the earlier differentiation and stigmatization of the body has been radically extended. The body remains a crucial locus for strategic intervention within which the disciplinary approaches of the past have been extensively supplanted by a new set of relations between the body, space and power.

With the fracturing of the contemporary city the relationship between a sovereign power and a clearly defined, territorially demarcated population has become increasingly porous. The body has become subject to multiple and often conflicting jurisdictions, so that the urban polity or "social body" from which power seeks its legitimacy and raison d'être has become ever more opaque. A characteristic feature of modern political discourse has been its emphasis on the "people" as a political abstraction in contrast with the recognition of the people as a "fragmentary multiplicity of needy and excluded bodies."[49] An emphasis on what Deleuze, following Spinoza, terms the "multitude" holds very different implications for how we might conceptualize processes of governance and legitimation in modern societies. The idea of the "public" or the "public realm" needs to be reconsidered in the light of the impossibility of achieving an imaginary social or political unity. Drawing on Elias Canetti's *Crowds and Power,* for example, Deleuze distinguishes between, on the one hand, "mass multiplicities" associated with classic conceptions of "the crowd," identified by their size, the similarity of their constituents and the dominance of one-way hierarchies of power, and, on the other hand, "pack multiplicities" marked by dispersion, variability and the "impossibility of a fixed totalization or hierarchization."[50] These explorations of the political manifestations of social complexity have important implications for any attempt to reformulate Foucauldian conceptions of "governmentality" in a context of radical dispersal of power and greater fluidity in the institutional basis for modernity. Yet the contemporary emphasis on the multitude as a new locus for political agency advanced by Michael Hardt, Antonio Negri, Paolo Virno and others does not satisfactorily resolve the tension between individual and collective will: the role of reason in distinguishing between private or common benefits remains obscure in an intellectual swerve that leads from Hobbes via Spinoza to a position not radically dissimilar from the "polycentric order" espoused by Friedrich von Hayek.[51]

49. Agamben, *Homo Sacer,* 177.

50. G. Deleuze and F. Guattari, *A Thousand Plateaus: Capitalism and Schizophrenia,* trans. B. Massumi (London: Athlone Press, 1987 [1980]), 33.

51. M. Bull, "The Limits of Multitude," *New Left Review* 35 (2005): 19–39. See also M. Hardt and A. Negri, *Multitude: War and Democracy in the Age of Empire* (London: Hamish Hamilton, 2005); P. Virno, *A Grammar of the Multitude,* trans. I. Bertoletti, James Cascaito and Andrea Casson (New York: Semiotext(e), 2004).

Gandy

Under what the anthropologist Marc Augé terms a drift towards "supermodernity" and the production of "non-place," it appears that the Baudelairean modernity of the historical palimpsest is being displaced by a hybridized uniformity of architectural expression whereby design, consumption and spatial form have become fully integrated in the service of a faux authenticity.[52] The suppression of "class" as an analytical category, in combination with the erasure and repackaging of historical memory, lends the contemporary city a sense of cultural and political disorientation. Or, to express this scenario in slightly different terms, modernity appears to be "transparent to itself," in Claude Lefort's apt phrase, but the possibilities for critical or independent thought have actually diminished.[53] This is not to argue that urban space can no longer be interpreted in any systematic way but rather to underline the degree to which the contemporary city has evoked a cognitive hiatus that necessitates an extensive rethinking of both the objects and the methods of urban enquiry. What Deleuze brings to this discussion is a radically extended phenomenology of human experience that presents opportunities for connecting urban design with intensified spaces of human imagination and creative potential: through his blurring of the boundaries between art, philosophy, and everyday life, Deleuze complements the emancipatory currents in Foucault's biopolitical schema to engage with a range of novel forms of architectural practice.[54] Yet the theoretical implications of both Foucault and Deleuze remain vague in relation to the practical dilemmas of urban *Realpolitik* at the scale of an entire city or metropolitan region. It is here that we can detect an emerging field of philosophical engagement between the limits of the public realm associated with the industrial city (and its bacteriological counterpart) and attempts to delineate different forms of social and political complexity in the post-industrial metropolis.[55]

Conclusions

If we trace the intellectual lineage from Foucault to more recent explorations of power in modern societies, we can detect an emphasis on the radical indeterminacy of power and its contradictory implications for the maintenance of social order. The Foucauldian notion of "governmentality" needs to be complemented by a fuller recognition of the materiality of the body, the diversity of spatial manifestations of bio-political power and the political implications of social and spatial complexity. The work of Agamben and other scholars is suggestive of a renewed engagement between political economy, material histories of the body and Deleuzian-inspired

52. M. Augé, *Non-Places: Introduction to an Anthropology of Supermodernity,* trans. J. Howe (London: Verso, 1995 [1992]), 78. See also H. Foster, *Design and Crime (and Other Diatribes)* (London: Verso, 2002).

53. C. Lefort, cited in P. Fitzpatrick, "Bare Sovereignty: *Homo Sacer* and the insistence of law," *Theory and Event* 5 (2001): 11.

54. The philosopher John Rajchman, for example, writes of "an exuberant detachment of form" associated with what he terms "postindustrial electronic architecture," and calls for a fundamental rethinking of current architectural practice. John Rajchman, *Constructions* (Cambridge, MA: MIT Press, 1998), 30.

55. See for example O. Enwezor et al ., *Documenta 11_Platform 1.*

reflections on complexity. But can this somewhat inchoate analytical framework actually work in practice? At times, for example, Agamben appears to elide "bare life" and "sacred life" in his conception of the bio-political, and in so doing tends towards a meta-historical interpretation of social change. Equally, his account of processes of exclusion from sovereign power appears at times to blur markedly different phenomena under an overarching analytical framework: it is questionable, for example, whether the anomie experienced in airports is comparable with the experience of inmates in a concentration camp. We need to engage with those marginal, invisible or "indistinct" spaces that reveal tensions or anomalies in the structures of power underpinning the modern city. There is, therefore, a clear spatialization or "localization" to the manifestation of power which runs counter to the flattening morphologies encountered in some "rhizomatic" and neostructuralist conceptions of space which eschew any directionality or hierarchy in the distribution of power.

By bringing together the critical insights of Foucault and Deleuze we might begin to move our focus from abstract, discursively constructed generalities to a set of more concrete and specific manifestations of the bio-political realm. Current Deleuzian-inflected discussions of ideas surrounding urban complexity have, however, tended to be restricted to design-related issues, and have yet to be systematically linked to either Foucauldian insights into power or wider historiographic recognition of the multiple modalities of urban history in relation to the cultural politics of the body. The Deleuzian emphasis on multiplicities as autonomous rather than dialectical entities, for example, is seemingly at odds with the adoption of a realist ontology that can include cultural and historical analysis.[56] The role of bio-political power in urban space—whether expressed explicitly or implicitly—is rooted in shifting strategies for determining modes of inclusion and exclusion. These power geometries are linked by a web of different mechanisms and belief systems ranging from the diffusion of capitalist labour relations to the persistence of patriarchal cultures of male domination. Like capitalism itself, therefore, the impetus behind bio-political power has displayed a chameleon-like ability to augment or incorporate pre-existing structures of control as part of a wider dynamic behind the development of modern cities and the formation of a fully networked global economy. A critical reflection on the bio-political dynamics of urban space not only exposes the limitations and dangers lurking behind unitary conceptions of modernity but also underpins the centrality of the body to contemporary developments in social theory.

56. Hence the influence of the bio-physical sciences and a resurgent "naturalism" within a variety of Deleuzian-inflected architectural writing and design. See for example M. DeLanda, "Deleuze and the Use of the Genetic Algorithm in Architecture," in N. Leach ed., *Designing for a Digital World* (Chichester: Wiley-Academy, 2002), 117–20, and M. DeLanda, "Space: Extensive and Intensive, Actual and Virtual," in I. Buchanan and G. Lambert, eds, *Deleuze and Space* (Edinburgh: Edinburgh University Press, 2005), 80–8, 516.

Acknowledgements
Many thanks to the referees for their detailed and helpful comments. Earlier versions of the paper were presented to audiences in Berlin, Denver and London, and the research was supported by the Economic and Social Research Council and the Alexander von Humboldt Foundation.

Gandy

Anima Urbis
Jennifer Wolch

In the spring of 2002 the Huntington Library in Los Angeles held a conference the theme of which was "Los Angeles: nightmare or paradise?" The day of the conference dawned so blue, balmy, and glorious that there could hardly have been much uncertainty about the answer to this question, especially among the affluent urban scholars in attendance. By the middle of the meeting, however, the conversation had become less complacent and had turned to the question of "whose urban nature?" Discussion focused on how access to urban parks varied by race and class. Despite this outbreak of intersubjective sensitivity, only Lewis MacAdams—not an urban scholar, but rather a poet fighting to restore the Los Angeles River—had mustered up the courage to mention that maybe the four-leggeds, no-leggeds and wingeds needed space in the city too. The notion of the city as solely human habitat had, once again, trumped a more inclusive vision for the metropolis.

As McAdams suggested, cities are replete with animate, sentient beings with legs, wings, antennae, and tails—namely, animals. Yet, despite the fact that explaining relations between nature and human society is ostensibly a primary goal for geographical research, animals rarely figure in urban geographical studies. We see them as parts of urban ecosystems, raw materials powering the growth of great industrial cities, or symbols of urban popular culture. Mirroring larger trends in human geography, particularly over the last twenty-five years, urban geography has largely ignored animals as a topic for serious scholarly attention.

Recently, however, some geographers have begun to consider animals, and in ways that emphasize their subjectivity and agency as well as their utilitarian or symbolic value. The reasons for this new direction are varied, but they stem in part from the increasing public awareness of the plight of animals, especially so-called "food" animals raised in intensive settings, animals endangered by habitat loss and environmental pollution, and recent developments in biotechnology that raise the specter of widespread use of animals as spare body parts. In addition, new approaches to ethics and social theory have blurred the human–animal divide, revealed how human–animal bonds and conflicts shape health and everyday cultural practices, and contextualized the larger role of animals under modernity—as mimetic of capitalist culture–nature relations, and as industrial capital itself.[1]

In this article, I want to focus attention on the issue of animals in the city. My purpose is to encourage geographers to include animals in their studies of urbanization, and suggest why it might be important, not only for intellectual reasons but also for ecological and moral reasons, to re-imagine the anima urbis—the breath, life, soul, and spirit of the city—as being embodied in its animal life. First, I briefly chart the intellectual history of geographic investigations, emphasizing the rise of a culturally orientated animal geography, out of which a consideration of animals in the city arises. Then I explore the ways in which human geographers are investigating urban human–animal relations. Finally, I outline the research that needs to be done in order to better understand how people interact, and perhaps could in future interact, with non-human others.

Trends in twentieth-century animal geography

Animal geography as a subfield has gone in and out of fashion within the discipline over the course of the twentieth century, and only at the very end of the millennium did interest in, and scholarship about, animals re-emerge. For the first half of the twentieth century, geographers focused on animals, either from a scientifically orientated zoögeographic perspective focused on space, spatial patterns, and spatial relations, or from the vantage of cultural animal geography, emphasizing places, regions, and landscapes, motivated in part by environmental concerns. Both had fallen out of fashion and receded from view by mid-century, as zoögeographic research was taken over by branches of biology, and traditional cultural ecology came under attack, to be supplanted by more social theoretically orientated approaches. By the 1970s, the term "animal geography" was no longer to be found in the geographical literature. Stimulated by social movements around animals and the environment, however, as well as by new intellectual currents that turned many scholars toward a consideration of marginalized groups—including animals—by the century's end animals had once again become a focus of geographical inquiry.

A field of geography known as "animal geography" was clearly recognized in the early twentieth century, as laid out in Marion Newbigin's 1913 book *Animal Geography*.[2] Newbigin pointed to the need for distributional studies of animal populations, examining floral and faunal regions and their relations. Animal geography

1. See J. Emel and J. Wolch, "Witnessing the animal moment" in *Animal geographies: Place, Politics and Identity in the Nature-Culture Borderlands* ed. Wolch, J. and J. Emel (London: Verso, 1998), 1–26, and M. Watts, "Enclosure," in *Animal Spaces, Beastly Places: New Geographies Of Human-Animal Relations*, ed. C. Philo and C. Wilbert (London: Routledge, 2000), 292–304.

2. See also M. Newbigin, *Plant and Animal Geography* (London: Methuen, 1936) and A.M.C. Maddrell, "Scientific Discourse and the Geographical Work of Marion Newbigin," *Scottish Geographical Magazine* 113 (1997): 33–41.

also appeared in Hartshorne's (1939) book, *The Nature of Geography*. Hartshorne's well-known version of regional geography was accomplished through integrating results from the various systematic subfields to create portraits of specific geographical areas; for Hartshorne, animal geography was one such systematic subfield, linked to zoology.

Thus, through the first half of the twentieth century, animal geography was an active if small portion of the discipline. Two approaches were clearly articulated, reflecting the widening divide between physical and human geography: zoögeography, focused mainly on animal distributions, and rooted in physical geography, zoology, and ecology; and a culturally orientated geography of animals, focused on animal domestications, rooted in human geography and the social sciences.

Zoögeography

Zoögeographers focused on geographic distributions of animals, and determinants of distributional patterns at various scales, incorporating notions of space, spatial patterns and spatial relations into their work. Where did different animals live and play out their life histories, and what aspects of climate, topography, hydrology, soils and vegetation, other fauna, and species-specific habitat preferences determined their geographies?

Such basic questions were addressed through application of scientific, empirical methods, in order to formulate general zoögeographical laws.[3] Zoögeographers rarely considered animal-society relations, but they did worry about human impacts on animals, and in some instances what animals meant to people. Cansdale explored the relations between animals and humans in terms of "competition, conflict, domestication and biological control." Even earlier, at the turn of the nineteenth century, Eagle Clarke had noted human influences on bird migration, including the frequent deaths of migrating birds crashing into the lanterns of light stations in foggy weather, while Moebius despaired about human violence against whales. Moreover, the pioneering early work of Fitter on *London's Natural History* (1946) noted that human–animal interactions often intensified around the city, and that many animals were adapting to life in this settlement type. Nonetheless, attention to society–animal interactions was minimal and not theorized within larger frameworks for understanding cities or nature–society relations. Animals, like plants, were regarded as natural entities whose distributions could be mapped and modeled.

3. G. Cansdale, "Some Problems in Animal Geography," *Geographical Magazine* 22 (1949), 108–9; G. Cansdale, *Animals and Man* (London: Hutchison, 1952). Thanks to Chris Philo for bringing this early zoögeographical work to my attention; see C. Philo and J. Wolch, "Through the Geographical Looking Glass: Space, Place and Human-animal Relations," *Society and Animals* 6 (1998): 103–18. See D. Matless, *Landscape and Englishness* (London: Reaktion Books, 1998).

Cultural animal geography

This second approach to animals arose in the mid-twentieth century, out of earlier work in cultural geography and its dominant subfield, cultural ecology, where topics of interest included the prehistory of animal domestication, and the role of animals in evolution of place, region and landscape. At the University of California, Berkeley, Carl Sauer was cultural ecology's key figure in North America, studying domestication and diffusion of animal husbandry, cultural, and economic roles of animals in agrarian societies, and environmental changes attendant upon agriculture- and livestock-based lifeways.[4] This work revealed the centrality of certain animals to cultural practices and environmental conditions.

Although not his primary concern, animals, according to Sauer, were implicated in the conversion of "natural landscapes" into "cultural landscapes."[5] Notably, he resisted economism in understanding society–animal relations. Other geographers in the Sauer tradition, both in the USA and the UK, similarly argued that economic benefits of domestication were secondary to religious motivations for taking animals into the human fold, and even that pet-keeping practices depended at least in part on the character of the prospective pets themselves.[6]

Such work prompted Charles Bennett to propose a cultural animal geography that could reinsert animals into geographical research and discourse.[7] He called for research on human–animal interactions, involving studies of how humans shape animal distributions, echoing zoögeography's emphasis on space and spatial distributions. However, Bennett also considered animal behavior, and suggested that geographers study how animals reacted to domestication efforts, subsistence hunting and fishing, and more indirect anthropogenic changes to their habitats. He also called for studies of how animals influenced human life chances, and their potential dangers to human life and livelihoods in rural settings.

Yet, rather than emphasizing animal subjectivity or agency, traditional cultural geography treated domestic animals primarily simply as cultural artifacts, an evolutionary technological development or a medium of environmental transformation. McKnight, for example, suggested that Australia's feral livestock "represents an immense amount of wandering protein on the hoof" constituting a "biomass approaching 800,000,000 pounds" but with deleterious ecological and economic impacts on their host regions.[8] While appropriately emphasizing human agency and ecological dynamics, possible roles of non-human animals were

4. M. Price and M. Lewis, "The Reinvention of Cultural Geography," *Annals, Association of American Geographers* 83 (1993): 1–17.

5. C.O. Sauer, *Seeds, Spades, Hearths and Herds* (Cambridge, MA: MIT Press, 1969).

6. R.A. Donkin, "The Peccary," *Transactions of the American Philosophy Society* 75 (1985): 1–145. R.A. Donkin, *Meleagrides* (London: Ethnographica, 1991).

7. C.F. Bennett, "Cultural Animal Geography," *The Professional Geographer* 12, no. 5 (1960): 12–14, and C.F. Bennett, "Animal Geography in Geography Textbooks," *The Professional Geographer* 13 (1961): 13–6.

8. T.L. McKnight, *Friendly Vermin* (Berkeley: University of California Press, 1976).

seen as limited. They were either there to be dominated and used, or symbols of human culture and meaning.

Mid-century animal geography, threatened and endangered

By the mid-twentieth century, zoögeographers had practically become an endangered species, although they were still accorded a chapter in James's and Jones's catalogue of the discipline.[9] Zoologists, ecologists and population biologists had turned their attention to animal distributions and species–habitat interactions, stimulated by advances in island biogeography theory, technologies for monitoring animal movements, and mathematical modeling approaches to population biology. Increasingly, as their work became facilitated by the advent of remote sensing, availability of satellite imagery and the use of geographic information systems, biogeographers turned away from animals, and focused on plant distributions instead.

For very different reasons, traditional cultural geography, represented by Sauer and the Berkeley School, had also receded from view by around mid-century. Heavily criticized for its simplistic approach to culture–economy relations, lack of attention to political power, and super-organic approach to culture, as well as on the basis of conflicting archeological evidence, Sauerian cultural geography was overtaken by both the "new" cultural geography and political ecology.[10] While the new cultural geography emphasized the social construction of urban landscapes, political ecology focused on the connections between political-economic structures, poverty and marginalization, and environmental degradation in rural third-world settings. Ironically, just as the environmental movement emerged during the 1970s, and concern about endangered species was rising, culminating in the passage of the US Endangered Species Act in 1973, "animal geography" had vanished from the geographical lexicon.

Recovering animal geography

In the 1990s, however, interest revived. Inspired by new developments in GIS and remote sensing, as well as geomorphology, new work in zoögeography began to emerge.[11] Moreover, and of primary interest here, new studies in cultural animal geography arose out of encounters between human geography and social theory, cultural studies, selected natural sciences and environmental ethics. Tuan's book *Dominance and Affection* (1984), which highlighted the power relations entailed in pet-keeping and its similarities with other forms of

9. J.L. Davies, "Aim and Method in Zoogeography." *Geographical Review* 51 (1961), 412–7, and L.C. Stuart, "Animal Geography," in *American Geography*, ed. P.E. James and C.F. Jones (New York: Syracuse University Press, 1954), 442–51.

10. J. Duncan, "The Super-organic in American Cultural Geography," *Association of American Geographers* 70 (1980): 181–98; D. Cosgrove and P. Jackson, "New Directions in Cultural Geography," *Area* 19 (1987): 95–101; and C.M. Rodrigue, "Can Religion Account for Early Animal Domestications?" *The Professional Geographer* 44 (1992): 417–30.

11. D. Butler, *Zoogeomorphology* (Cambridge: Cambridge University Press, 1995); B.A. Bryant, "A Generic Method for Identifying Regional Koala Habitat Using GIS," *Australian Geographical Studies* 35 (1997): 125–39; L.D. Baer and D. R. Butler, "Space-Time Modeling of Grizzly Bears," *The Geographical Review* 90 (2000): 206–21; T.W. Gillespie, "Remote sensing of animals," *Progress in Physical Geography* 23 (2001): 355–62.

domination, also inspired some attention to animals within geography. By the end of the twentieth century, theme journal issues and edited collections had appeared.[12] Such efforts instigated a wave of research that once again has become known as animal geography.

What stimulated this resurrection of this culturally orientated animal geography? One factor was the larger social context: the rise of powerful environmental movements during the 1970s and 1980s, generated scores of new organizations working on behalf of animals, such as People for the Ethical Treatment of Animals, the Animal Liberation Front, the Fund for Animals, and Greenpeace. The most radical of these groups rejected human domination of the planet and animals, and drew explicit linkages between racism, sexism, and "speciesism"; slavery, postcolonial oppression, and animal captivity; and the Holocaust, factory farms and research labs.

As well as this social context of activism around animals and the environment, social theorists expressed interest in animals during the 1980s, spurred by new ideas from feminism, postmoderism and poststructuralism, postcolonial theory, and critical race theory. One result was a reconsideration of culture and its importance (the "cultural turn"). Suddenly, movies like *Babe* or *Chicken Run* were no longer merely Hollywood flotsam but potent representations—and cultural critiques—of human–animal relations. Another outcome was a broadening conception of personal subjectivity. As critical social theorists drew attention to a wider range of subjects and multiple, mixed and dynamic subjectivities, the notion of the classical universal subject was rejected, opening up space to consider the possibility of animal subjectivity.[13]

This possibility was furthered by scientific research in cognitive psychology, ethology, landscape ecology, and conservation biology which revealed the complexity of animal thinking and behavior; suddenly humans were not the only animals with sophisticated cognitive abilities or even culture, and not just primates.[14] Simultaneously, genetic engineering, cloning, and xenotransplantation called into question boundaries between machines, animals and humans, making the notion of a "cyborg" world startlingly realistic.[15] Both sorts of work undermined long-standing stereotypes of "dumb animals" that served to maintain human identity and position at the top of a perceived hierarchy of beings. Along with the "new" environmental history as practised by Worster and Cronon, who argued persuasively for an inclusion of nature in efforts to understand urbanization and economic change, these currents led to new ideas about nature as agent.[16]

12. J. Wolch and J. Emel, "Bringing the Animals Back In," *Environment and Planning D*, 13 (1995): 631–760; C. Philo and J. Wolch, "Through the Geographical Looking Glass: Space, Place and Human-animal Relations," *Society and Animals* 6 (1998), 103–18.

13. S. Baker, *Picturing the Beast* (Manchester: Manchester University Press, 1993), 26.

14. M. Bekoff and J.A. Byers, *Animal Play* (Cambridge: Cambridge University Press, 1998); Diane Fossey, *Gorillas in the Mist* (Boston: Houghton-Mifflin. 1983); B. Galdikas, *Reflections of Eden* (Boston: Little, Brown. 1995); D.R. Griffin, *Animal Minds* (Chicago: University of Chicago Press, 1992); J. Goodall, *The Chimpanzees of Gombe* (Cambridge, MA: Harvard University Press, 1986); C. Moss, *Elephant Memories* (New York: Fawcett Columbine Books, 1988);. E.S. Morton and J. Page, *Animal Talk* (New York: Random House,1992); F. De Waal, *Chimpanzee Politics* (New York: Harper and Row, 1982).

15. D. Haraway, *Simians, Cyborgs and Women* (New York: Routledge, 1991); ed. J. Sheehan and M. Sosna, *The Boundaries of Humanity* (Berkeley: University of California Press, 1991); *Changing Life*, ed. P. Taylor, and S.E. Halfon and P. Edwards, (Minneapolis: University of Minnesota Press, 1997).

16. D. Worster, *Nature's Economy* (Cambridge: Cambridge University Press, 1994); W. Cronon, *Changes in the Land* (New York: Hill, 1983); W. Cronon, *Nature's Metropolis* (Chicago: University of Chicago Press, 1991).

Along with many activists, social theorists, scientists, and environmental historians, by the end of the twentieth century geographers from various intellectual traditions had began arguing for animal subjectivity and the need to get beyond the generalities of the nature–society relations paradigm, and look more closely at human–animal interactions in order to revivify geographical understandings of the world.

Animals in the city

The idea that cities are the exclusive domain of humans is widespread, especially within the academy. While there is a strong tradition of urban economic, social, and political geography, there is barely any urban cultural ecology, political ecology, or biogeography from which to launch studies of human-animal relations in the city. The Chicago School, for example, ignored animals (and plants for that matter), despite their appropriation of an overtly ecological lexicon.

Yet the importance of recognizing nature and animals in the city is indisputable. As Botkin argues: "Without the recognition that the city is of and within the environment, the wilderness of the wolf and the moose, the nature that most of us think of as natural cannot survive, and our own survival on the planet will come into question."[17] This recognition has stimulated some recent work on animal geographies focused on the city per se. Efforts to reanimate urban scholarship over the last decade have considered issues of how animals shape identity and subjectivity, the role of animals and urban place formation, and the evolution and dilemmas that arise when animals are allowed to figure in our urban moral reckoning.

Urban identity and subjectivity

The 2000 movie *Best in Show* offered a witty parody of the famous Westminster Dog Show in New York's Madison Square Gardens. Anyone who has seen either the movie or the dog show itself can hardly deny that certain sorts of animals are intimately tied up with stereotypical urban identities (suburban white trash; urban gay couples; preppy, neurotic DINKS (double income no kids)) as well as rural good ol' boys steeped in the wisdom of coon dogs. Moreover, the dogs in question clearly took things into their own paws (so to speak), ingratiating themselves with their handlers as well as "resisting" human domination by, in one case, biting the judge!

Drawing on new ideas about culture, nature and subjectivity, animal geographers have explored questions of animals' role in the social construction of culture, individual as well as collective identity,

17. D. Botkin, *Discordant Harmonies* (New York: Oxford University Press, 1990) 167.

the human–animal divide and its shiftiness, and the nature of animal subjectivity and agency itself.[18] Only a few have taken up questions of identity and subjectivity in an explicitly urban context, yet their work suggests the rich terrain that such questions elicit. Building on critical race and postcolonial theory that highlighted connections between race, gender, and representations of "animality," animal geographers have sought to understand the role of animals in the development of heterogeneous identities that urban residents adopt or have ascribed to them. Such identities may have ties to temporal periods, geographic places or imagined communities such as nations, as well as to racial/ethnic, cultural, or gendered identities. While concepts of human and animal are universally understood, the boundary shifts over time and space. The result is a dynamic but place-specific assemblage of animals, valued and used according to particular, legitimized codes—codes that are increasingly contested under conditions of globalization and world city formation.

Within the urban realm, Kay Anderson, for example, developed a cultural critique of Adelaide's urban zoo as an institution that inscribes various human strategies for domesticating, mythologizing and aestheticizing the animal universe, while at the same time helping to construct a national identity among Adelaide residents.[19] Through its constructions of nature and animals, zoo practices consolidated and legitimated Australian colonial identity, naturalized colonial rule and oppression of indigenous peoples, and reinforced gendered and racialized bases of human-animal boundaries. Investigating the emergence of an explicitly urban identity in Victorian England, Chris Philo argued that animals played a notable role in setting apart rural from urban standards of civility, public decency and sexual license, and norms of compassion.[20] Constructing the new urban order—and standing apart from rural stereotypes—necessitated the removal of live urban meat markets and in-town slaughterhouses, such as Smithfield in London, that forced civilized city-dwellers to witness sexual intercourse among animals on their way to market, exposing their delicate senses to the violence of auction and slaughterhouse, and risking their moral decay by forcing them to mingle with drovers perceived by bourgeois reformers as inclined to drink and sexual excess. As a result, meat markets and slaughterhouses were excised from the city, reinforcing urban identities defined in opposition to a countryside populated by beastly people and animals.

Howell's study of dog-stealing in Victorian London shows both dogs and bourgeois women as victims of a patriarchal society, confined to domestic captivity but vulnerable to the actions of

18. K. Anderson, "A Walk on the Wild Side: a Critical Geography of Domestication," *Progress in Human Geography* 21 (1997): 463–85; Kay Anderson, "The Beast Within," *Environment and Planning D* 18, (2000): 301–20; J.R. Ryan, "Hunting with the camera," in *Animal Spaces*, 203–21. J. Emel, "Are you Man Enough, Big and Bad Enough?" *Environment and Planning D*, 13 (1995): 707–34; C. Wilbert, "Anti-this—against-that: Resistances Along a Human–nonhuman Axis," in *Entanglements of Power*, ed. J. Sharp, P. Routledge, C. Philo, and R. Paddison (London: Routledge, 2000): 238–55.

19. K. Anderson, "Culture and Nature at the Adelaide Zoo," *Transactions of the Institute of British Geographers* 20 NS (1995): 275–94.

20. C. Philo, "Animals, Geography and the City," *Environment and Planning D* 13 (1995): 655–81.

Wolch

lower-class men, the venal public world of commerce, and dangers lurking in the city's poorest districts.[21] Borrowing from Virginia Woolf's satirical tale of the theft of Elizabeth Barrett's dog, written from the dog's point of view, he articulates a political geography of dog-stealing characterized by class antagonisms and exploitation of rich by poor, and deeply ingrained practices of "domestication" itself—both of dogs and women confined by Victorian ideals of femininity, obedience to male authority and middle-class domesticity. Gender relations and animals are also at the forefront of Van Stipriaan's and Kearn's study of billboards as an influential aspect of Auckland's built environment that shapes ideas about gender and local urban culture.[22] They consider the case of a notorious Royal New Zealand Society for the Prevention of Cruelty to Animals spay-neuter campaign, showing a dog "dressed" in a woman's wig, sexy glasses, a frilly skirt and high heels, wearing lipstick and smoking a cigarette, and urging Auckland residents to "de-sex your bitch." Van Stipriaan and Kearns argue that the campaign and the controversy it generated destabilized human–animal relations and highlighted the gendered nature of animal representations in popular culture—thus indicating that animals not only have a bodily presence in the city but also play important representational roles in local cultural formations.

Building on postcolonial and critical race theory, others have considered animals to help understand the dynamics of racialization in culturally diverse world cities under conditions of globalization.[23] Today, as international migration brings together heterogeneous people, "out-of-place" animal practices risk being interpreted as transgressions of species boundaries. Exploring attitudes toward animals among women of diverse racial/ethnic and cultural background living in a major US world city, Griffith discovered a willingness to tolerate dog-eating among Filipinas that seemed to reflect their own experience as a marginalized group in American society, and their sensitivity to racialization based on color and culture.[24] Filipina respondents hesitated to condemn other groups whose animal practices, while alien or distasteful, were rooted in their particular culture, instead adopting a position of cultural relativism.

Animal-based practices that vary by race/ethnicity may reflect or reproduce urban racial formations. Central-city African American women queried about their attitudes towards animals tended to segment the animal world into three categories: "food," "pet," and "wildlife." "Food" animals were simply necessary for survival; people had to distance themselves from their unfortunate fate. Pets and wild

21. P. Howell, "Flush and the banditti," in *Animal Spaces*, 35–55.

22. B. Van Stipriaan and R.A. Kearns, "Bitching about a Billboard: Advertising, Gender and Canine (Re)presentations," (2002), Unpublished manuscript, Department of Geography, University of Auckland (available from authors).

23. G. Elder, J. Wolch, and J. Emel, "La Practique Sauvage: Race, Place, and the Human-Animal Divide," In *Animal Geographies*, 72–90.

24. M. Griffith, J. Wolch, and U. Lassiter, "Animal practices and the racialization of Filipinas in Los Angeles," *Society and Animals*, (2002), 221–48.

animals, in contrast, demanded compassion—people should help wildlife in distress, just as people should help each other regardless of color, hinting at their solidarity with animals as brethren due to their outsider status.[25]

Animals can also become links to a past identity and so cushion the shock of the new urban environment, just as they also play a role in assimilation. For Latina immigrants, keeping animals like chickens in the backyard is one way to retain connection to the rural landscapes they left behind, but over time the culture of pet-keeping, and the assimilation that it implies, seems to take over.[26] When animals once relegated to the barnyard or backyard are welcomed into the house, traditional human–animal boundaries become destabilized.

What about the animals and their subjectivity? Whatmore and Thorne, stimulated in part by actor-network theory, have argued for consideration of animal agency.[27] Following Ingold, they suggest that animals are "strange persons" similar to outsider human groups. In like manner, Philo sought to view animals as akin to marginalized, socially excluded persons; he speculated on the terror of cattle at the hands of drovers and the possibility of their transgression of human-set limits, as they jump through shop windows and engage in "beastly" sexual conduct.[28] Yet neither Whatmore and Thorne nor Philo, nor most other animal geographers, have considered animal thinking and behavior per se to better understand their subjectivity and ideas about people. One exception is the "thought experiment" performed by Gullo, who excavated scientific literature on cougar ecology and behavior to explicitly assess lion attitudes toward people—do they, as one cougar expert claimed, see a child as a little fat pig to eat?[29] How, if at all, have cougar ideas changed with the encroachment of urbanization into their habitats?

This strategy—of trying to figure out what animals are thinking or feeling—is fraught with difficulties (to which I return later in this article) that include lack of sufficient scientific knowledge, and the temptation to indulge in excessive anthropomorphism. But such work attempts to go beyond speculation and engage animals on their own terms to try to better understand their interactions with people, especially as they shift under pressures of urbanization.

Animals and the making of urban places

Animals are critical to the making of places and landscapes. This point was driven home during the Clinton Administration when virtually the entire metropolitan region of Seattle was declared critical

25. J. Wolch, A. Brownlow, U. Lassiter, "Constructing the Animal Worlds of Inner-city Los Angeles," in Animal Spaces, Beastly Places, 71–97.

26. J. Wolch and U. Lassiter, "From Barnyard to Backyard to Bed: Attitudes toward Animals among Latinas in Los Angeles," in Land of Sunshine: The Environmental History of Greater Los Angeles, ed. G. Hise and W. Deverell (Pittsburgh: University of Pittsburgh Press, 2005), 267–87.

27. S. Whatmore and L.B. Thorne, "Wild(er)ness: Reconfiguring the Geographies of Wildlife," Transactions of the Institute of British Geographers NS 23 (1998): 435–54; T. Ingold, "Culture and the Perception of the Environment," in Bush Base, Forest Farm: Culture, Environment and Development (London: Routledge, 1992), 39–56.

28. C. Philo, "Animals, Geography and the City: Notes on Inclusions and Exclusions," Environment and Planning D 13 (1995): 655–81.

29. A. Gullo, J. Wolch and U. Lassiter, "The Cougar's Tale," in Animal Geographies, 139–61.

habitat for salmon. This stirred much controversy, but it was also clear that salmon are central to the identity of the Northwest as a place, and to the city of Seattle in particular. Part of this is economic—the fish is a powerful image that attracts tourists far and wide to come and spend their dollars. Some of them even fish. But in many neighborhoods and individual homes in the city, residents devote themselves to bringing back streams, restoring spawning areas and trying to make the city—even if only their small share—safe for salmon. Thus, not surprisingly, in the wake of the Clinton Administration's ruling, Seattle's political leadership asserted that "economic growth and saving the salmon were not incompatible" while residents turned out to rally in defense of the fish, holding placards that proclaimed: "What's good for salmon is good for people."[30]

Such episodes, along with academic debates about the social construction of landscapes and places, led animal geographers to explore animals and the networks in which they are enmeshed, leaving imprints on particular places, regions and landscapes over time. Within the academic realm, the idea that animals might play a role in place-making was stimulated by a larger rethinking of how nature, culture and subjectivity are embodied in landscape, led by "new" cultural geographers.[31] This vanguard used poststructuralism, discourse theory, and deconstruction to identify landscape not as the product of a realist "nature" or an enigmatic "culture group" but as a "text" composed of signs and symbols whose hegemonic reading both represented and reproduced power relations, knowledge claims and discourses that initially inscribed them. Simultaneously, they promoted alternative readings of landscape by those marginalized and/or exploited by virtue of their gender, race, class, and sexual orientation (categories themselves often "naturalized" or "animalized" by patriarchal or colonial powers.[32]

Such approaches were in the contradictory position of making discursive space for animals while criticizing any notion of an extra-discursive or external nature of which animals might be a part or from which they might act. For many political ecologists, animal rights theorists, eco-feminists and activists, such views also seemed to deny the very liveliness of the world.[33] Moreover, denaturalizing nature and treating geographic places as cultural productions denied the agency of nature and especially animals. This "writing out" of nature catalyzed an energetic debate with "new" environmental historians such as Worster and Cronon, trying to demonstrate nature's agency.[34] This debate, in turn, stimulated a reconsideration of the role of animals in the making of places, regions, and landscapes.[35]

30. S.H. Verhovek, "An Expensive Fish," New York Times 16 March (1999), section A, 14.

31. D. Cosgrove and S. Daniels, Iconography of Landscape (Cambridge: Cambridge University Press, 1988); P. Jackson, Maps of Meaning (London: Unwin Hyman, 1989); ed. T.J. Barnes and J.S. Duncan, Writing Worlds: Discourse, Text and Metaphor in the Representation of Landscape (New York: Routledge, 1992), 1–17; M. Price and M. Lewis, "The Reinvention of Cultural Geography," Annals, Association of American Geographers 83 (1993): 1–17.

32. K. Anderson, "The Racialization of Difference," The Professional Geographer 54, (2002): 25–30; M. Davis, Ecology of Fear (New York: Metropolitan Books, 1998).

33. Ecofeminism, ed. G. Gaard, (Philadelphia: Temple University Press, 1993).

34. D. Demeritt, "The Nature of Metaphors in Cultural Geography," Progress in Human Geography 12 (1994), 163–85.

35. F. Ufkes, "Lean and Mean: US Meatpacking in an Era of Agro-industrial Restructuring," Environment and Planning D 13 (1995), 683–706; R. Yarwood and N. Evans, "New places of 'Old Spots'" Society and Animals 6 (1998), 137–66; R. Yarwood and N. Evans, "Taking Stock of Farm Animals and Rurality," in Animal Spaces, 98–114; J. Proctor, "The Spotted Owl and the Contested Moral Landscape of the Pacific Northwest," in Animal Geographies, 191–217; D. Matless, "Versions of animal-human," in Animal Spaces, 115–40; and A. Brownlow, "A Wolf in the Garden," in Animal Spaces, 141–58.

Within the urban context, work has primarily focused on the meanings associated with areas for the public viewing of animals (namely zoos); how the presence/absence of animals leads to distinctive perceptions of neighborhoods in the city; the creation of urban animal-centered spaces, through community activism or restoration efforts; and the dynamics of urban borderlands where people and animals share space. For example, stating that "[i]f the zoo is a 'space,' Adelaide Zoo is a 'place'," Anderson advanced general claims about urban zoos as pivotal sites in the cultural construction of nature, and how particular colonial and national identities were promoted through the constructed landscapes of the nineteenth-century Adelaide Zoo.[36] Similarly, Philo and Howell explored nineteenth-century London, focusing on places characterized by the presence/absence of animals, and how human–animal interactions can create distinctive urban landscapes and landscape imagery.[37]

More contemporary examples show the complexity of human-animal spatial orderings in the city and the ambiguity of resident attitudes toward nature and civilization as manifest in place. Gaynor, for example, reviewed attempts by urban managers in Perth to exclude productive animals such as chickens, goats, and pigs (once common in Australia's urban backyards) from residential areas.[38] Using zoning and other planning tools, local officials worked to sanitize the city, attract the more affluent classes and change the city's sense of place. This process of spatial reordering served to privilege animals as part of middle-class lifestyles of consumption—in this case, promoting animals as household pets—rather than working-class relations with animals focused on production (for cash as well as direct sustenance). In so doing, local managers generated conflict and inflicted a loss of identity for many of the city's working-class residents by changing the character of their neighborhoods.

In another investigation of why some animals are deemed out of place in urban areas, Griffiths cast the city of Hull's feral cats as a marginalized social grouping existing within the urban realm, and explored human responses to feral cats in relation to ideas about the proper order of urban places.[39] Their analysis revealed how some human residents saw wild places associated with feral cats as sites of anxiety and aversion, while others viewed them as refuges for an otherwise lost wild nature. Responses to feral cat colonies among local residents were affected by their social constructions of the built environment. They rendered cat spaces either discrepant or acceptable urban features, and promoted ideas of feral cats as

36. K. Anderson, "Culture and Nature at the Adelaide Zoo," 275–94.

37. C. Philo, "Animals, Geography and the City," 655–81, and Howell, "Flush and the Banditti," 35–55.

38. A. Gaynor, "Regulation, Resistance and the Residential Area: the Keeping of Productive Animals in Twentieth-Century Perth, Western Australia," Urban Policy and Research 17 (1999), 7–16.

39. H. Griffiths, I. Poulter, and D. Sibley, "Feral Cats in the City," in Animal Spaces, 56–70.

either legitimately wild or domestic "convicts on the loose," ultimately engendering urban social conflict.

Grassroots activism can also lead to the creation of new, more formal urban spaces orientated toward animals and the human-animal bond. The urban dog park movement in the USA is an example. Initially controversial, these are now standard urban park system elements, but were initially created through intense activism. Wolch and Rowe, for instance, documented how a degraded public park was "taken back" from drug-users and prostitutes by an informal group of dog-owners who invested in improvements and security, and used the presence of large off-leash dogs—illegally—to discourage less desirable uses.[40] Paradoxically, just as the park became more attractive, other local residents signaled their desire to use the park but objected to off-leash dogs, framing the issue as "dogs versus kids." Dog-owners prevailed in part by normalizing dogs as legitimate members of the American family and urban community. Like other urban dog parks, this park is now a distinctive place for both people and animals, and remains a locus for grassroots participation in the governance of urban park and recreation facilities.

Urban ecological restoration efforts to bring wild animals back into the city also reveal conflicting ideas about animals and wildness in the city, and what restoration implies for human dominance. Waley, for instance, showed how riparian restoration plans in urban and suburban Japan, based on new ecological thinking, often prioritized animals linked to threatened ways of life, such as rice farming, and harnessed the rich symbolism of fireflies, dragonflies and fish.[41] Yet such ecological landscaping was feared as privileging animals over people, and faced opposition from powerful construction interests unwilling to relinquish space in the city. The result is apt to be humanized urban streamscapes unable to support riparian wildlife.

Nowhere is the complexity of human–animal spatial orderings more evident than in the urban–wildlands border zones of metropolitan regions. Here, zoning ordinances and land use plans have often been used to allocate animals and people to designated areas, but such crisp divisions are rarely so straightforward on the ground. As Davis indicates: "On land use and planning maps . . . the division between 'developed' and 'undeveloped' areas is drawn as a straight-edged border. Spuriously precise boundaries likewise define parks, wildlife refuges national forests, and official wilderness areas. In reality, there is an infinitely more intricate interpenetration of the wild and the urban."[42] Even the idea that fringe urbanization is inversely related to

40. J. Wolch, and S. Rowe, "Companions in the Park," *Landscape* 31 (1992), 16–33.

41. P. Waley, "What's a River Without Fish? Symbol, Space and Ecosystem in the Waterways of Japan," in *Animal Spaces*, 159–81.

42. Davis, *Ecology of Fear*, 204.

biodiversity is often erroneous, since urban-edge environments often display remarkable ranges of both native and exotic animals and plants, and some species flourish under the patchwork habitats of the metropolitan borderlands, at least for a time, with some becoming so numerous as to fall into the "pest" category.

Davis traces the history of human interaction with wildlife in southern California, characterizing it as a "relentless chain of slaughter and extinction,"[43] in which brutal nineteenth-century ranching practices, market hunting, and fishing, and relentless predator "control" led to the wholesale eradication of much of the budding urban region's natural bounty and heritage. Animals were particularly integral to the runaway growth economy of the California Gold Rush era, with the enormous numbers of cattle causing environmental disaster—extensive erosion, invasions of exotic plants and crowding-out of native grassland animals. Market hunting to serve urban markets was ultimately curtailed not only because target species dwindled but also as a result of elite demands to protect animals for recreational hunters, leading to the emergence of state-led game-management strategies, that also involved efforts to eliminate predators from a newly defined urban fringe now zoned for humans.

At present, however, wild animals have returned to many metropolitan regions in significant numbers—for example, deer, moose, elk, bears, coyotes, bobcats, beavers, javelina, and cougars, to say nothing of a vast array of smaller creatures and invertebrates. In part such "repopulations" are about sprawl-driven urban encroachment into animal habitat, but they also arise as a result of changing attitudes toward wildlife and associated wildlife-management practices. Gullo, for example, considered the changing relations between people and mountain lions in contemporary California.[44] There, urbanization-driven increases in human–cougar interactions, along with scientific discord over cougar ecology, stimulated a polarized public discourse. This discourse was characterized by renewed advocacy of trophy hunting by gun/hunting lobbyists, and proposals from ecologists for wildlife reserves, movement corridors and urban buffer zoning to protect both people and cougars. Yet, although media coverage during this debate suggested that the public had moved from thinking of cougars as symbols of wilderness heritage to seeing them as cold-blooded suburban serial killers, the voting—and largely urban—public nevertheless refused to reinstate cougar hunting.

Community activists also shape such debates, however, as shown by Michel in her study of golden eagle rehabilitators and

43. Davis, *Ecology of Fear*, 208.

44. Gullo, Lassiter, and Wolch, J. "The Cougar's Tale," 139–61.

Wolch

wildlife educators in San Diego's metro fringe.[45] There, conventional planning around endangered species and habitat conservation relies on scientific discourse and legitimacy and excludes alternative arguments based on the connections people feel with wild animals that have been injured as the result of urbanization. Grounded in struggles to save injured eagles and starving eagle chicks, and to nurture responsibility and consideration for animals among children, eagle rehabilitation and wildlife education for children constitute an eco-feminist, personal politics of both animal and human social reproduction that asserts the agency of wildlife in defining pathways to human-animal coexistence and shared places. This practice allows children, and by extension their parents, into the world of the golden eagle and the birds' fight for survival, helping them voice their views to the larger public through letter-writing campaigns and special events—in this way helping recast the nature of grassroots environmental activism in southern California.

At a larger scale, geographers have also investigated how conflict over human–animal relations—particularly the "taking" of endangered species—is linked to convulsive urban growth and ultimately shapes the landscapes of entire metropolitan regions through the creation of habitat conservation plans and similar zoning efforts. In southern California, where between 1982 and 1997 over 400,000 acres were lost to urban sprawl, Feldman and Jonas, for instance, harnessed urban growth regime theory to understand the evolution of land-use conflict and decision-making among property owners, environmental organizations, local governments and growth coalitions in Riverside County, California.[46]

Driven by the Endangered Species Act (ESA), the result has been a large-scale regional planning exercise designed to zone some areas of the county for urbanization, and others as habitat reserves. Similarly, Ryan details the meaning of new urban growth boundary policies in southern California for endangered species and critical habitats, while Pincetl has detailed the ways in which distinctive sub-regional growth regimes are responding to Endangered Species Act provisions, generating major integrated land-use, transportation and habitat-conservation plans as well as prompting land-owners to surreptitiously kill endangered animals.[47] These studies begin to sketch out how relations with some animals, codified into law, are imbricated into the dynamics of urbanization under capitalism, and shape the overall footprint of the metropolis, patterns of human–wildlife relations, and the life chances of its non-human residents.

45. S. Michel, "Golden Eagles and the Environmental Politics of Care," in *Animal Geographies*, 162–90.

46. J. Wolch, A. Brownlow, and U. Lassiter, "Constructing the Animal Worlds of Inner-city Los Angeles," in *Animal Spaces*, 71–97; T.D. Feldman and A. Jonas, "Sage Scrub Revolution?" *Annals, Association of American Geographers* 90, no. 2 (2001), 256–92.

47. C. Ryan, J.P. Wilson, and W. Fulton, "Living on the Edge: the Region's Endangered Species and Habitats," and S. Pincetl, "The Preservation of Nature at the Urban Fringe" in *Up Against the Sprawl? Public Policy and the Making of Southern California*, ed. Wolch et al. (Minneapolis: University of Minnesota Press, 2002).

Animals and the city's moral compass

A sensational media story cropped up in California during 2002 about a San Francisco apartment dweller on trial for the "murder" of her neighbor, committed by her dog—a Presa Canaria whose moniker was (of all things) "Bane." A classic wacky California story, it was replete with lurid links to criminal dog-fighting rings, the Aryan Brotherhood, and interspecies sex. Of course animals used to be put on trial for various crimes during the Middle Ages, and indeed Bane has already been executed (although he was never made to stand trial); but this is the first time in recent memory that a human has been held so directly responsible for an animal's killing spree.[48] Clearly, the moral compass of human–animal relations in the city is shifting and, like so many other aspects of city life, is subject to constant renegotiation.

Writings on environmental ethics, deep ecology and animal rights during the later part of the twentieth century generated deep polarization on the issue of animal subjectivity and moral status, and how humans should relate to the non-human world.[49] Ultimately, however, what seems to have emerged is a more postmodern environmental ethics that tends to take non-human subjectivity seriously, stresses the situatedness and partialness of knowledge, and emphasizes the interconnectedness of living creatures and environments, as well as between nature and culture. Such an approach offers more contextual pathways to ethical choice.[50]

Evolving in conjunction with these debates, some animal geographers have asked questions about how animals figure into the moral landscape, once claims of human dominion and lack of animal subjectivity or agency are open to question. In addressing such issues, geographers have explored animal rights to sustenance,[51] ethical perspectives toward meat-eating,[52] the ethics of animal protection movements,[53] the role of animals in creating "moral geographies" of particular places and regions,[54] conflicts between animal rights perspectives and an ethics arising from an understanding of the ways in which the very structure of the capitalist economy produces animal suffering,[55] and more general ethical frameworks for thinking about geographically emplaced human-animal interactions.[56]

However, we have just begun to think about the moral choices we make in building and living in cities, and what they mean for animals. This is despite the moral issues that abound in urban places: pet euthanasia, extermination of non-endangered wildlife, sprawl-induced habitat destruction, pollution of urban waterways,

48. E.P. Evans, *The Criminal Prosecution and Capital Punishment of Animals* (London: Heinemann, 1906); S. Berry, "The Importance of Seeming Human," *Los Angeles Times Magazine* (2 June, 2002): 20–1.

49. C. Stone, *Should Trees Have Standing?* (Los Altos: Kaufmann, 1974); R. Nash, *The Rights of Nature* (Madison: University of Wisconsin Press, 1989); J.B. Callicott, *In Defense of the Land Ethic* (Albany: State University Press of NY, 1989); B. Devall and G. Sessions, *Deep Ecology* (Layton: Gibbs Smith, 1985); A. Salleh, "Class, Race, and Gender Discourse in the Ecofeminist/Deep Ecology Debate," *Environmental Ethics* 15 (1993): 225–44; P. Singer, *Animal Liberation* (New York: Avon Books, 1975); T. Regan, *The Case for Animal Rights* (Berkeley: University of California Press,1983).

50. V. Plumwood, *Feminism and the Mastery of Nature* (London: Routledge, 1993); M. Oelschlaeger, *Postmodern Environmental Ethics* (New York: SUNY Press, 1995).

51. J.L. Wescoat, "The 'Right of Thirst' for Animals in Islamic Law," *Environment and Planning D* 13 (1995), 637–54.

52. P. Robbins, "Shrines and Butchers: Animals as Deities, Capital, and Meat in Contemporary North India," in *Animal Geographies*, 218–40.

53. L. Thorne, "Kangaroos: the Non-issue," *Society and Animals* 6 (1998), 167–82.

54. J. Proctor, "The Spotted Owl," 191–217.

55. M. Watts, "Enclosure," in *Animal Spaces*, 292–304.

56. W. S. Lynn, "Animals, Ethics and Geography," in *Animal Geographies*, 280–97.

and ecosystem appropriation to feed consumption-orientated urban lifestyles. If animals are granted subjectivity, agency and maybe even culture, how do we determine their survival opportunities in the city? To what urban arenas should our moral compass direct us— homes, businesses, streets, parks and open spaces, restaurants and supermarkets? The implications of training our moral gaze on such urban places are enormous. For example, federal law mandates water-quality standards for all waterways, but these standards are designed for humans; what is tolerable for humans is not necessarily tolerable for, say, frogs. Does this mean that the US EPA needs amphibian water-quality standards for urban watersheds? The answer is probably yes—and this implies the need for an astonishing range of research and, ultimately, urban regulation.[57]

If urban social and environmental justice is eventually broadened to include animal justice as well, questions also arise about how radical an urban democracy we can visualize, or handle in practice. In a recent survey, respondents living in a large, diverse metropolitan region were asked about their tolerance toward a number of controversial animal practices, such as cock-fighting, dog-eating, rodeo and so on.[58] It turns out that tolerance—one measure of respondents' ethical positions—was fairly low but differed widely across race/ethnic groups, hinting at the difficulties of coming to agreement about ethical norms for human–animal interactions even in a world city with considerable exchange of cultural norms and values.[59] There has been no consideration yet as to if or how animals themselves could be included in any such decisions.

In thinking prospectively about morality, animals and urban places, my own work has sought to reconceptualize the ways in which the human-animal divide plays out in terms of ethical practices for city planning and living. A major consideration here is animal subjectivity; once we abandon a strict human–animal boundary with human subjects on one side and animal objects on the other, we seem to be obligated to figure them into our ethical consideration and everyday practice. As if the challenges of doing so, particularly at the level of the political economy, were not large enough, we also must face a set of tougher questions. What do animals want? Can we ever really know?

A classic argument against the possibility of answering such questions was made by the philosopher Thomas Nagel, who asked: what is it like to be a bat?[60] He answered by saying that it was impossible for humans to know. Is it, in fact, impossible to "think like a bat," however? On the one hand, it is—we are unlikely to ever know a bat's innermost desires! But we also have a very

57. I am grateful to Travis Long-core for making this important point.

58. J. Wolch with M. Griffith, U. Lassiter and J. Zhang, *Attitudes toward Marine Wildlife Among Residents of Southern California's Urban Coastal Zone* (Los Angeles: USC Sea Grant Program, 2001).

59. This is the sort of conflict that boiled over in 2002, as international protests of dog-eating were staged in advance of the World Cup in Seoul, generating much controversy among animal advocates and Korean-Americans in the USA, see J. Feffer, "The Politics of Eating Dog," *Toronto Star* (5 June 2002), DO2.

60. T. Nagel, "What Is It Like To Be a Bat?" *The Philosophical Review* 83 (1974), 435–50.

hard time knowing the innermost desires of people, especially people who are unlike us in fundamental ways, such as gender. Thus humans may not be able to literally "think like a bat," but, rather than nihilistic relativism or denial of human–animal differences, the human response could recognize that both people and animals are embedded in social relations and networks with others (both human and non-human) upon which their social welfare depends.

This realization allows for the recognition of kinship but also difference, since identities are defined by the ways in which we are similar to, as well as different from, related others. People should come to know, however partially, the animals with whom they coexist, thereby sustaining webs of connection and an ethic of respect and mutuality, caring and friendship. The obvious challenge is to figure out ways to transform such sentiments into practice, and actually design cities as if animals mattered; in short, to figure out how to transform the metropolis into a zoöpolis—a place of habitation for both people and animals.

Re-animating the city

Geography is now providing new leadership in explicating the history and cultural construction of human and non-human animal relations, the gendered and racialized character of these relations, and their economic embeddedness. In the case of human–animal relations in the city, however, much work remains if we are really to re-animate the city in both our thinking and practice.

How can we best go about this? One place to start is at the theoretical level, with an eye to rethinking urban theory and unsettling its anthropocentric traditions, to create a new political ecology of people and animals in the city. The goal of this sort of theory is to bring together disparate discourses, ranging from social theory to urban wildlife ecology, and stimulate empirical studies utilizing a broad toolkit. The content of this kit should include not only the sorts of methods already in use by urban geographers but also new approaches to understanding the patterns and behaviors of animals themselves derived from ethnography) and urban history,[61] as well as recent zoögeographical research, noted above, stimulated by new technologies and efforts to integrate human and physical geography (for example, GIS and remote sensing, and time geography).

Such an agenda would seek to achieve four major goals.[62] To understand urbanization from the perspective of its meaning for animal life. Urban geographers (among others) have developed a rich theoretical literature on urbanization, utilizing, for example,

61. E. M. Thomas, *The Hidden Life of Dogs* (Boston: Houghton Mifflin, 1993); T. Vuorisalo, R. Lahtinen, and H. Laaksonen, "Urban Biodiversity in Local Newspapers," *Biodiversity and Conservation* 10 (2002), 1739–56.

62. J. Wolch, "Zoöpolis," *Capitalism Nature Socialism* 7 (1996), 21–48.

political economy, postmodern theory, urban regime analysis, studies of racial, gender, and housing segregation, fiscal disparities, and critical race theory.[63] But urban nature rarely figures in such accounts, and recent research in urban animal geography has yet to bridge the gap between macrostudies of sprawl, habitat conservation planning and endangered species, and microstudies of the role of particular species (livestock, predators, pets, etc.) in urban development. Ideas from the new environmental history, animal commodity chain analysis, evaluations of local state–nature relations and cultural studies of popular movements to save urban space for animals could expand the research agenda on urbanization to encompass the role of animals. In turn, such approaches could help us understand what urbanization means for animals, their habitats and life chances, and their patterns of interaction with people.

To trace how and why attitudes and practices toward animals and patterns of urban human–animal interactions change over time and space. We know very little about the evolution of such interactions, but the field of human–animal interactions is growing rapidly, and, as noted above, animal geographers have contributed with studies of how animals and animal representations shape urban and individual identity, underlie social conflict or contribute to racialization of particular urban populations such as immigrants. Additional work could be much broader, however, tackling larger time-space sweeps, and linking analyses of human–animal interaction to the evolution of nature–cultures in the city, urban actor networks around animal-based products, changing attitudes to the urban environment, and the impacts of globalization.

To explore how urban animal ecology is produced by science, social discourse and political economic forces. The ability of animals to co-exist in the city is strongly shaped by powerful discourses around ecological science, animal welfare and rights, environmentalism and urban property rights. Animal geographers have contributed to our understanding of these dynamics, but much more could be accomplished by scrutinizing underlying precepts of urban biogeography through the lenses of science studies and feminism, for example, investigating the politics of major urban biodiversity studies and plans, and more generally developing a more sophisticated urban political ecology that accounts for the role of discourse in shaping habitat conservation and restoration efforts, wildlife population management decisions and so on.

To grasp how human–animal relations as an urban practice are shaped by managerial plans, grassroots activism and the

63. M. Davis, *City of Quartz* (London: Verso, 1990); M. Dear, *From Chicago to LA* (Thousand Oaks: Sage Dear, 2002); *The Urban Growth Machine*, eds. A. Jonas and D. Wilson, (Albany: State University of NY Press, 1999); S. Hanson and G. Pratt, *Gender, Work, and Space* (New York: Routledge,1995); E. Wyly and D. Hammel, "Capital's Metropolis," *Geografiska Annaler B*, no. 4 (2000), 181–206; P. Joassart-Marcelli, J. Musso, and J. Wolch, "Federal Expenditures, Intra-metropolitan Poverty and Fiscal Disparities in Southern California Cities," in *Up Against the Sprawl?*, 195-224; L. Pulido, "Rethinking Environmental Racism," *Association of American Geographers* 90, no. 1 (2000), 12–40.

agency of animals. Most studies of urban managerialism and planning practice (even those focused on the environment) rarely take animals into account except as exemplars of endangered species. Thus, as Thorne points out, wild animals tend to obtain value through death and extinction. Similarly, urban design and landscape ecology are seldom attuned to the needs or desires of animals living in the city. Increasingly, however, grassroots activism and new social movements around urban animals and nature are shaping up, designed to make discursive as well as material space for animals in the city.[64] Almost no work has attempted to see the city from an animal's viewpoint.[65] This could be remedied through ethnographic and time-space studies of urban animals.

As one exemplar, perhaps an interrogation of the Los Angeles River and its role in shaping the city's economic, political, social and natural environments can illuminate how such a revivified, transspecies approach to understanding cities and urbanization might work in practice. Addressing the questions raised by the role of this one urban river demands that we pay attention to animals, in a variety of ways. Early on, the urbanization of Los Angeles and its economic base relied upon the LA River, on its water and natural bounty. Fish and wildlife flocked there—at times, the numbers of migratory birds that it supported was so huge that they darkened the daytime sky.[66] What role did these animals play in building the economic wealth of the region, and for whom? How was the city's growth machine and the local state involved in successive decisions about the river—were their objectives simply to use it as both a source of accumulation and a convenient sewer?

The river's creatures eventually vanished due to market hunting, and as industrialization and population growth polluted the river transportation infrastructure destroyed its tree-lined banks, and the Army Corps of Engineers channelized, straightened and armored it, altering its features so much that it is the most denaturalized US river today.[67] What attitudes toward nature and wild animals prevailed at the time that decisions to armor the river were made? Why did a "control of nature" ideology become so prevalent in this place?[68] What cultural and political shifts led the image of the LA River to re-emerge so powerfully at the end of twentieth century, so that it is now widely perceived as the city's spiritual heart?[69]

Today, the restoration of the river has become a quest to bring nature back into a city best known for sprawl and pollution, and to bring people of diverse social class and racial background together in a place famous for class conflict and civil unrest. For example,

64. Several US cities have altered their legal codes to remove the terms "pet owner" and "pet" in favor of such terms as "animal guardian" and "companion animal," in order to destablize the legal tradition of considering animals as property.

65. A. Beck, *The Ecology of Stray Dogs* (Baltimore, York Press. 1973).

66. B. Gumprecht, *The Los Angeles River: its Life, Death, and Possible Rebirth* (Baltimore: Johns Hopkins University Press, 1999).

67. W. Graf, "Damage Control: Restoring the Physical Integrity of America's Rivers," *Association of American Geographers* 91 (2002): 1–27.

68. J. McPhee, *The Control of Nature* (New York: Farrar, Straus and Giroux 1989).

69. D. Browne and R. Keil, "Planning Ecology: the Discourse of Environmental Policy Making in Los Angeles," *Organization and Environment* 13 (2000): 158–205.

innovative ways to do urban design—to prevent river pollution and allow the steelhead trout to return—have been developed as a result of scientific discourse, social movements and political economic forces on the urban environment. Created by the hydrologists and ecologists, as well as advocacy groups, some design practices are now mandated; but local governments are contesting them, afraid of their impacts on growth, pushed by developers and builders. What, if any, were the scientific disputes involved in coming to such design solutions, and how did political factors and activist efforts affect the design standards now in effect to regulate total minimum daily pollutant loads going into the river and coastal ocean? How are images of animals—especially charismatic marine wildlife—being mobilized to promote river restoration and coastal ocean water-quality improvements through urban design?

There are major urban managerial plans afoot to restore the river—to build retention basins, spreading grounds, bike paths and trails, and a green ribbon of parks and open spaces. Many plans are not state-led, but rather are being developed by national and regional non-profit organizations and land conservancies with various agendas and divergent views about how animals fit into the urban fabric. What is the emergent structure of conservancies and non-profit organizations, and what is their role in the city's land-use governance? Have they become a shadow state apparatus or third-party government? How are grassroots organizations and community groups involved in attempts to secure places for animals along the river?

As funding for the river materializes, the possibilities of restoration approach, as well as riverside economic revitalization for poor inner-city communities and recreation for a park-starved metropolis. A vibrant network of grassroots action groups has emerged, each with their own ideas about what to plan and representational politics. Will it be soccer fields for Latinos, nature trails for birdwatching Anglos, skateboard parks for kids, boardwalks for macho dudes to show off their Pit Bulls, riverside coffee houses for singles, dog parks for canine family members? What kinds of urban nature and river ecologies, and whose nature, will eventually emerge from such political ecological dynamics?

In an evolving green corridor of this scale, animals are bound to reappear (even big predators) and will exert their agency. What room will be made for animals? Many residents support coexistence in theory and the torrent of people (especially children) already visiting the river (from which no concrete has yet been removed) is impressive. But practice may be another matter. Will people be able or willing to coexist with the river's animals? Will fear of crime, demands for access and pastoral landscape ideals lead to a river of bright lights, traffic, noise, and simplified vegetation—making it unbearable for timid, nocturnal, or solitary creatures or those that need a rich plant biota to survive? If so, will anyone speak out for such animals? Or will those animals returning to the river need to develop new subjectivities, new ways of interacting with people and the built environment, in order to coexist in the heart of the city?

This article began with LA poet Lewis MacAdams, and to him it returns, to tell his lovely story about how the US Army Corps of Engineers recently tried to restore a stretch of the river. Because flood control is still required, the "restored" river does not actually replace the older armored channel but runs right alongside it—it is, in short, fake nature, a purely aesthetic device rather than functional landscape feature. But the willows and rushes are back, as are the dragonflies and at least some of the birds. Will people care if the river is not actually "real" again? Or will they be content to let the presence of diverse four-legged, winged, and no-legged animals—the reassertion of an anima urbis—be the measure of our success in re-animating the city?

Hybrid Cartographies for a Relational Ethics
Sarah Whatmore

> What is inter-subjectivity between radically different kinds of
> subjects? How do we designate radical otherness at the heart of
> ethical relating?[1]

Bringing ideas of difference-in-relation to bear on the question of
political and ethical community has been most extensively explored
in the work of Haraway and Latour in their elaboration of concepts of
hybridity. Haraway's argument is that we "cannot not want" something
called humanity because nobody is self-made, least of all humans.[2]
But in order to recuperate a progressive commitment to humanity as
a moral community the dualisms associated with humanism have to
be jettisoned. This line of argument informs several so-called "posthuman" efforts to reconfigure ethical competence and conduct by
disturbing the consolidation of difference at the borders between
the "human"/"non-human." As Halberstam and Livingston suggest:

> the human functions to domesticate and hierarchize difference
> within the human (whether according to race, class, gender)
> and to absolutize difference between the human and the
> nonhuman. The posthuman does not reduce difference-from-
> others to difference-from-self, but rather emerges in the pattern of
> resonance and interference between the two.[3]

Haraway's cyborg figure (1985), for example, articulates a political
vision which appreciates the unstable and porous borders between
human, animal and machine and the multiple modalities of subjugation
that such an appreciation brings into view. Here, the possibilities of
social agency are constituted through "webs of connection" between
radically different and particularly embodied subjects, connectivities
that are fashioned through what she calls "shared conversations" and
"semiotic-material technologies."[4] Ethical praxis likewise emerges in
the performance of multiple lived worlds, weaving threads of meaning
and matter through the assemblage of mutually constituting subjects
and patterns of association that compromise the distinction between
the "human" and the "nonhuman."

 As with so many of Haraway's provocative ideas, what she
means by "semiotic-material technologies" is hard to fix. Her favorite
examples are the body-technologies of prosthetics, genetics and
organ transplants in which particular codified knowledges become

1. Donna Haraway, "Other-
worldly Conversations; Terrain
Topics; Local Terms," *Science
as Culture* 3, no. 1 (1992): 89.

2. Haraway, "Otherworldly Conversations," 64.

3. Judith Halberstam and Ira
Livingston, eds., *Posthuman
Bodies* (Bloomington: Indiana
University Press, 1995), 10.

4. Donna Haraway, "Situated
Knowledges: the Science
Question in Feminism and the
Privilege of Partial Persective," in
*Simians, Cyborgs and Women:
the Reinvention of Nature* (Lon-
don: Free Association Books,
1991), 192.

stabilized as technological artefacts which, in turn, are grafted into and mobilized by living beings. These examples tend to site the dilemmas of hybrid subjectivity, and the cyborg figure used to signify them, within an individuated body-subject—"a hybrid creature composed of organism and machine."[5] There is a tension then in Haraway's account of the status and configuration of her hybrid subject—the cyborg. It is not clear whether, as Kruks asks, these hybrid subjects stitch their own parts together, in which case they become more cohesive than Haraway wants to admit, or whether this "stitching together" is better understood as an operation taking place from without.[6] If the first, then Haraway's hybrid subject falls back on an account of political and ethical agency which privileges cognitive and discursive faculties in the constitution of "knowing selves" (however partial or unfinished the project of self-fabrication). If the second, then it is not clear from Haraway's account just what it is that connects these diverse knowing selves together other than the capacity for "shared conversations." As Kirkby observes:

> Haraway's "disassembled and reassembled recipe" for cyborg graftings is utterly dependent upon the calculus of one plus one, the logic wherein pre-existent identities are then conjoined and melded. The cyborg's chimerical complications are therefore never so promiscuous that its parts cannot be separated, even if only retrospectively. Put simply, for Haraway, there once was not a cyborg.[7]

I am not so sure that it is (ever) that simple for Haraway. But, while her account of hybridity successfully disrupts the purification of nature and society and the relegation of "non-humans" to a world of objects, I agree that it is less help in trying to "flesh out" the fabric of connectivity that transacts difference and, therein, the promise of a more than human ethical praxis. Such an exercise requires closer scrutiny of the inter-corporeal complications of heterogeneous life practices, or what Deleuze and Guattari characterize as the "overlapping territories of affectivity and becoming,"[8] than Haraway's cyborg figuration of hybridity seems to conjure.

In this context, I find Latour's account of hybridity, figured in terms of a "networking" effect, more suggestive for elaborating a relational understanding of ethical considerability and conduct. This networking ontology, like the rhizomatics of Deleuze and Guattari, emphasizes the affective relationships between heterogeneous actants, distributing their morphological particularity and mutability through all manner of energetic exchanges within and between them.[9] Cast in these terms, hybridity signals not just the inter-connectedness of pre-given

5. Donna Haraway, *Simians, Cyborgs and Women: the Reinvention of Nature* (London: Free Association Books, 1991), 1.

6. Sonia Kruks, "Identity Politics and Dialectical Reason: beyond an Epistemology of Provenance," *Hypatia* 10, no. 2 (1995): 9.

7. Vicki Kirkby, *Telling Flesh: the Substance of the Corporeal* (London: Routledge, 1997), 147.

8. Gilles Deleuze and Felix Guattari, *A Thousand Plateaus* (London: Athlone Press,1988), 267.

9. Ansell-Pearson provides a useful account of Deleuze and Guattari's acknowledged debt to Bergson's philosophical account of creative evolution and the biologist von Uexküll's contrapuntal conception of biological processes and forms, Keith Ansell-Pearson, *Germinal Life: the Difference and Repetition of Deleuze* (London: Routledge, 1999). See also Tim Ingold, "Building, Dwelling, Living: How Animals and People Make Themselves at Home in the World," in *Shifting Contexts: Transformations in Anthropological Knowledge*, ed. M. Strathern (London: Routledge, 1995), 57–80.

entities but the condition of immanent potentiality that harbors the very possibility of their coming into being. Moreover, Latour spells out the difference that this interpretation of hybridity makes for the re-ordering of ethical community beyond the "human." Hybrid networks, he argues, force us to "take into account the objects that are no more the arbitrary stakes of [human] desire alone than they are the simple receptacle of our mental categories."[10] Articulated through the cartography of networks (or rhizomes), hybridity disturbs the habits that reiterate the cumulative fault-lines between human/subjects and non-human/objects prescribed by an ethical reasoning abstracted from the particularity of embodiment and territorialized as the exclusive preserve of a "Society" from which everything but the universal human subject has been expunged. Instead a multitude of affective actants-in-relation take and hold their shape performatively, as precarious achievements whose durability and reach is spun between the potencies and frailties of more than human kinds. It is in assemblages such as these that the "forces, bonds and interactions" of Serres' cryptic "natural contract" can make their presence felt in the vital topology of ethical relations; lived relations which are neither rooted to the spot nor the culmination of some singular chronology, but which stretch and fold multiple space-times through provisional alignments of polyvalent rhythms and passages of bodies and elements, energies and devices, memories and skills.

Latour's account of hybrid networking involves an important shift in tense from relational "being" to relational "becoming" and a more fluid sense of the spatiality and temporality of hybridity than Haraway's cyborg figure. These are important steps for my attempts to chart a topology of ethical relating. Latour's own gestures towards the ethical and political import of his account of hybridity bring us to his image of a "parliament of things" or, as he has put it more recently, "to the point that, today, the whole planet is engaged in the making of politcs, law and, soon I suspect, morality."[11] But this is the point at which I find Latour's extraordinary work most problematic because of its apparent indifference to the witness of those living (and dying) at the sharp end of technoscientific re-orderings.[12] There is an important divergence in analytical stance between ANT's emphasis on the effectivity of (quasi)objects and that of feminist science studies on the affectivity of (body)subjects. But there is something more than this. As Elam has noted, there is something scriptural in the demeanour of Latour's writing that "assumes a position outside of action, only to reappear as science-in-action

10. Bruno Latour, We Have Never Been Modern, trans. Catherine Porter (Hempstead: Harvester Wheatsheaf, 1993), 117.

11. Bruno Latour, Pandora's Hope: Essays on the Reality of Science Studies (Cambridge, MA: Harvard University Press, 1999), 214.

12. Leigh Star, "Power, Technology and the Phenomenology of Convention," in A Sociology of Monsters, ed. J. Law (Oxford: Blackwell, 1991), 25-56.

personified ... [it is as though he] cannot help re-enacting the imperial ambitions that infuse the networks he charts."[13] In contrast, say, to Haraway's sustained commitment to "taking sides" or even the "cosmopolitics" of Isabelle Stengers which he so admires, Latour is too chary of situating his own knowledge practices or risking his intellectual acumen by association beyond the academy to nourish the kinds of connection between analytical adventure and everyday apprehension that are the measure of the "passionate" mode of enquiry that I am after here.[14]

My argument throughout has been that it is both more interesting and more pressing to engage in a politics of hybridity that is not defined as/by academic disputes like the so-called "science wars," important though these are, but in which the stakes are thoroughly and promiscuously distributed through the messy attachments, skills, and intensities of differently embodied lives whose everyday conduct exceeds and perverts the designs of parliaments, corporations and laboratories. For those of us trained to earn our living in such centers of calculation, the epistemological imperative to acknowledge the situatedness (and affectiveness) of our own knowledge practices is at least well rehearsed, particularly in feminist science studies. Of more concern to me in this section of the book is how little onus science and technology studies seem to place on according such close and respectful analytical attention to the practical knowledges and vernaculars of everyday sense-making.[15] But this is no less vital if, as Haraway insists,

> taking responsibility for the social relations of science and technology means refusing an anti-science metaphysics, a demonology of technology, *and so* means embracing the skillful task of reconstructing the boundaries of daily life, in partial connection with others, in communication with all our parts.[16]

So, let me return to that most mundane of worldly transactions, eating, to illustrate the steps I have taken here towards a relational ethics that places corporeality and hybridity at its heart. As I noted in the introduction to this section, food is one of the most potent vectors of the "bodily imperatives" that enmesh us in the material fabric and diverse company of "livingness." The skills and (dis)comforts of growing, provisioning, cooking and eating have long accommodated and intensified the proliferation of hybrids—through the cultivation of plants and animals; the wayward energies of wastes and additives circulating in water, soils and in the flesh; and the bacterial mutations and viral infections that traffic

13. Mark Elam, "Living Dangerously with Bruno Latour in a Hybrid World," *Theory, Culture, and Society* 16, no. 4 (1999): 21.

14. Obviously this is not to suggest that Latour is not passionate about his work. One has only to think of the title and style of his book about the unrealized blueprint for a rapid transport system in Paris, See Bruno Latour, *Aramis or the Love of Technology* (Cambridge, MA: Harvard University Press,1996), or his zealous efforts to ally science and science studies (*Pandora's Hope*,1999) against their caricatured enmity in the so-called "science wars." But rather that his work is not passionate in the sense taken in this book from Game and Metcalf's *Passionate Sociology*, namely that he "masterfully refuse[s] to place [himself] within the social life [he]) studies," Ann Game and Andrew Metcalfe, *Passionate Sociology* (London: Sage,1996), 5. In so far as he positions himself beyond the academy at all it is by dissociation. For example, his aversion to "a conception of left-wing radicalism that has not yet been renewed as forcefully as science has been," (Bruno Latour, "Foreword," in Isabelle Stengers, *Power and Invention* (Minneapolis: University of Minnesota Press, 1997), xvii; or his repudiation of the misguided terms on which "green" parties and movements have sought to put "nature" on the political agenda (Bruno Latour, *Politics of Nature* (Cambridge, MA: Harvard University Press, 2004)).

15. John Shotter, *Cultural Politics of Everyday Life* (Buckingham: Open University Press,1993).

16. Donna Haraway, "Manifesto for Cyborgs: Science, Technology and Socialist Feminism in the 1980s," *Socialist Review* 80 (1985): 100, *author's emphasis*).

between life and death.[17] The rhythms and motions of these inter-corporeal practices configure spaces of connectivity between more-than-human life worlds; topologies of intimacy and affectivity that confound conventional cartographies of distance and proximity, and local and global scales. These are the kinds of performative and immanent geographies of/for relational ethics that I have been working towards in this chapter; "projects of making" more livable worlds made possible by the "ongoing interweaving of our lives" with manifold others.[18]

As I suggested, food scares are events that condense the metabolic intimacies habitual to eating, mapping gut apprehensions into cogitable rationalities that are discordant with those of industrial food production. Perhaps the most archetypal such event in recent times is that known popularly as Mad Cow Disease. An "unintended consequence" of the intensive feeding regime of the industrial cow, this disease took passage through protein meal supplements derived from rendered animal carcasses (including those of cows) and routinely fed to cattle (and other animals) to speed growth and increase bodily productivity. Its manifestation in an epidemic of the degenerative brain disease BSE (Bovine Spongiform Encephalopathy) in Britain's cattle population in the 1980s and 1990s turned out, against scientific and government assurances at the time, not to stop there. Humans too began to exhibit pathologically similar and equally fatal symptoms of infectivity in cases numerous and distinctive enough to be categorized as a new variant of CJD (Creutzfeldt Jakob Disease).[19]

The ethical (and political) import of the BSE-vCJD epidemic in Britain begins by acknowledging the corporeal specificities of cows as herbivorous ruminants, and following the incongruous "rationale" of a feeding regime indifferent to them through to the eating habits and food choices of consumers. The practice provoked revulsion and disbelief in equal measure among an unsuspecting public. What kind of rationality was it that could make sense of such routine cannibalism? The rationalities both exposed and overshadowed by the specter of the disease were those of cost-cutting and profit margins in a corporate animal feed industry careless of the offensive detail of how their products were derived, and of balance sheets and productivity gains for farmers accustomed to gauging their husbandry in terms of the metabolic conversion of inputs into outputs. At once "manmade" and "pathogenous" the hybrid potency of the disease resonated with gut apprehensions of the corporeal kinship and fleshy currency between cows and people.

17. Richard Cone and Emily Martin, "Corporeal Flows: the Immune System, Global Economies of Food and Implications for Health," *The Ecologist* 27, no. 3 (1997): 107–11.

18. Ingold's "weaving"/"making" variant of the Heideggerian distinction between "dwelling" and "building" purposefully rejects its insistence that human rationality and subjectivity mark an absolute break from the animal world. Tim Ingold, "Making Culture and Weaving the World," in *Matter, Materiality and Modern Culture*, ed. P. Graves-Brown (London: Routledge, 2000), 69. See also Simon Glendinning, *On Being With Others* (London: Routledge, 1998), 73–4.

19. These transpecies infectivities were not limited to cattle and humans but have been recorded in increasing numbers in companion animals (notably cats) and zoo animals (notably deer), giving rise to the generic term TSEs (Transpecies Spongiform Encephalopathies). Rosalind Ridley and Harrry Baker, *Fatal Protein: the Story of CJD, BSE and Other Prion Diseases* (Oxford: Oxford University Press, 1998); and Scott Ratzan, *The Mad Cow Crisis* (London: University College London Press, 1998).

Mad Cow Disease became an uncanny familiar in homes and workplaces, conversations and mass media, extending its presence through all manner of intermediaries: the sombre figures and graphs plotting the rising incidence of disease and declining sales of meat (particularly beef); hidden camera journeys into the once alien worlds of abattoirs and rendering plants; and the sickening image that still endures of a cow staggering, collapsing and trembling on a concrete farmyard floor. Scientists, government ministers and industry spokespeople were disconcerted to find their authoritative pronouncements and scripted assurances enmeshed as more or less compelling storylines in this intricate national drama.[20]

The symptoms being so widely witnessed only became officially consolidated around the acronym BSE in 1987. Early government policy towards the disease was informed by the report of the Southwood Report (1989) which broadly accepted the then preferred theory that scrapie, a disease endemic in the sheep population, was the most likely infective agent being transmitted through animal feed to cattle. The Southwood Report concluded that "from the present evidence it is most unlikely that BSE will have any implications for human health."[21] Seven years later in 1996, the British Government finally admitted that the disease could, and had, spread to humans. This about-face followed the unwelcome advice of its Expert Panel on BSE in 1995. The Panel accepted evidential claims supporting another theory, that the infective agents in BSE (like scrapie and other Transmissible Spongiform Encephalopathies–TSEs) were "proteinaceous infectious particles" or "prions."[22] They concluded that it was much more likely that the BSE epidemic had been caused by the recycling of BSE-infected cow carcasses in cattle feed, rather than those of scrapie-infected sheep, and that the disease was capable of transmission to humans through the ingestion of infected tissue and body fluids, blood transfusion and the like.[23]

As the sticky properties of prions gained scientific and policy adherents, so too did they become potent spokesthings for the porosity of the corporeal borders between cows and people, effecting their indifference to species location and slow tempo replication in the spatial and temporal ordering of agri-food networks.[24] As such, they bore credible witness to the metabolic geographies bodying forth in the gut apprehensions of eating. Incarnating connectivities between the sites and practices of food production and consumption, animal and human wellbeing, these "rogue" proteins proved unlikely allies in undermining the prevailing commercial, policy and scientific cartographies of affectivity and responsibility,

20. David Miller, "Risk, Science and Policy: Definitional Struggles, Information Management, the Media, and BSE," *Social Science and Medicine* 49 (1999): 1239–55.

21. Miller, "Risk, Science and Policy," 1255.

22. See Ridley and Baker, *Fatal Protein*.

23. The most exhaustive account of the shifting sands of Government policy and scientific advice towards BSE-CJD in the 1980s to 1990s and assessment of the distribution of responsibility for its devastating failings is provided by the voluminous report of the Lord Phillips' enquiry into BSE (see *The BSE Inquiry* (London: HM Stationary Office,1999) and www.bse.org.uk.

24. See Steve Hinchliffe, "Indeterminacy Indecisions: Science, Policy, and Politics in the BSE Crisis," *Transactions of the Institute of British Geographers* 26, no. 2 (2001): 182–204.

and making space for more relational ethical possibilities. The realignments of inter-corporeal sensibilities to collective modes of sense-making nourished by BSE have been honed through any number of subsequent food scares in Europe, galvanizing changes in shopping and eating habits, producing and retailing practices, and policy architectures and instruments. Red meat, particularly beef, consumption has never recovered. More and more people are choosing organic and/or animal welfare certificated foods. The rationale and practices of product traceability developed in these "alternative" food networks, are increasingly becoming mainstream marketing and policy standards.[25] Such polyvalent mappings into knowledge of the affectivity of embodied difference diagram new modes of connectivity that are the stuff of ethical relating.

Becoming Other-wise

> [I]n the cyborg context, of . . .hybrids of nature/culture, the question is not who will get to be human, but what kinds of couplings across the humanist divide are possible—or unavoidable.[26]

In an effort to articulate a relational understanding of ethical connectivity that does not presume or reinforce the cartographies of humanism, I have identified corporeality and hybridity as key modalities for reconfiguring the spaces and constituencies of ethical practice. Far from abandoning the collective moral claims of humanity, this enterprise is concerned with recuperating them from the grip of a universal ethical subject configured as the autonomous self, and recognizing that their efficacy depends on admitting more than human difference into the compass of considerability. As Hayles argues in her account of *How We Became Posthuman*,

> to think of the subject as an autonomous self ... authorizes the fear that if the boundaries are breached at all, there will be nothing to stop the self's complete dissolution. . . . When the human is seen as part of a distributed system, the full expression of human capability can be seen precisely to depend on the splice rather than being imperiled by it.[27]

But, like the traces of one-plus-one logic that haunt Haraway's cyborg, the "splice" here betrays Hayles's post-human as a cybernetic novelty; an epochal breach in the otherwise settled borders between the human and the non-human, and one expressive of "our" capabilities. The splice merely stitches over the cut. The kind of relational ethics that I have been working towards here casts hybridity in a different tense, defined less by its

25. See Jonathon Murdoch, Terry Marsden, and Jo Banks, "Quality, Nature and Embeddedness," *Economic Geography* 76, no. 2 (2000): 107–25.

26. Cary Wolfe, *Critical Environments: Postmodern Theory and the Pragmatics of the "Outside,"* (Minneapolis: University of Minnesota Press,1998), 84.

27. N. Katherine Hayles, *How We Became Posthuman* (Chicago: University of Chicago Press, 1999), 290.

departure from patterns of being that went before than with how it articulates the fluxes of becoming that complicate the spacings-timings of social life, and expressive of the creative impulse of more than human energies.[28] On this account, hybridity compels us to acknowledge that not only does "humanity" always already "dwell among badly analyzed composites [like nature or the non-human] but that 'we' ourselves [the human-all-too-human) are badly analyzed composites."[29]

Taking feminist and environmentalist critiques of the individualist currency of mainstream ethical discourse as my starting points, I have argued that their various efforts to articulate more relational ethical praxes by either "embodying" or "enlarging" the company of ethical subjects are often thwarted by a residual humanism that condemns them to trafficking between (human)/society and (non-human)/nature as pre-constituted domains of categorically different kinds of being. The radical pluralism of hybridity variously invited by science studies can only do its work by refusing the Cartesian terms of this settlement in which "human identity is wagered entirely on the use of 'words', while the animal body, with all its inarticulate sounds, is relegated to the mechanical universe of automatons and chiming clocks."[30] It is a settlement that both diminishes human conduct, reducing it to the dictates of a disembodied reason, and disqualifies everything else from the company of agential efficacy. In so far as they temper the lingering one-plus-one calculus of "couplings," hybridity and corporeality redirect our attention to the affective relations between heterogeneous bodies in terms of their specific enunciative consistencies within a material-semiotic register of mutual prehensions and sensibilities that exceeds the signal monopoly of the word.[31] Learning (how) to map these affectivities into knowledge, like

> learning to swim or learning a foreign language means composing the singular points of one's own body or one's own language with those of another shape or element which tears us apart but also propels us into a hitherto unknown . . . world of problems.[32]

In the manner of "food scares," hybridity and corporeality trip those habits of thought that hold "the body" apart from other bodies and "the human" apart from other mortals, motioning instead to the shifting fabric of differentiation produced through their lively enfolding and which, as De Landa puts it, "keeps the world from closing."[33] In this they amplify the repertoire of skills and associations enjoined in the praxis of ethical relating and help to open up the "possibility

28. "Couplings," like "cyborgs," betoken a version of hybridity in which difference is prefigured in the alterity of already constituted kinds. By contrast, the emphasis in my account on the indeterminacy of difference draws on Bergson's bio-philosophy, particularly his notion of differentiation as an explosive "internal" life force, subsequently taken up and reworked by Deleuze and Guattari. This distinction is important in understanding the contrast between, say, the approaches of Latour and Haraway to hybridity. For valuable discussion on these points, see Ansell-Pearson, *Germinal Life*, 33–69; and Mark Hansen, "Becoming as Creative Involution? Contextualizing Deleuze and Guattari's Biophilosophy," *PostModern Culture* 11, no. 1 (2000): 1–42.

29. Keith Ansell-Pearson, *Viroid Life: Perspectives on Nietzsche and the Transhuman Condition* (London: Routledge, 1997), 7.

30. Matthew Senior, "'When Beasts Spoke': Animal Speech and Classical Reason in Descartes and La Fontaine," in *Animal Acts*, ed. Jennifer Ham and Matthew Senior (London: Routledge, 1997), 62.

31. Mark Hansen, *Embodying Technesis: Technology Beyond Writing* (Michigan: University of Michigan Press, 2000), 13.

32. Gilles Deleuze, *Difference and Repetition*, trans. P. Patton (London: Athlone Press, 1994), 164.

33. Manuel De Landa, "Deleuze, Diagrams and Open–Ended Becoming," in *Becomings*, ed. Elizabeth Grosz (London: Routledge,1999), 36.

and actuality of connections, arrangements, lineages, machines,"[34] in at least three ways. Firstly, by dispersing ethical considerability beyond the unified (and always) human subject without resorting to its wholesale extension to other living kinds. It is no longer, as Wolfe puts it, a "question of who will get to be human" but rather one of how the "we" of ethical communities is to be renegotiated on account of its heterogeneous, intercorporeal composition. Secondly, by complicating this bodily redistribution of ethical subjectivity in terms of the profusion of intermediaries—instruments, signals, machines, elements—which insinuate their energies and inertias in the intimate assemblages of corporeal becoming. Hybridity and corporeality interfere, in other words, with ethical prescriptions that would disown such familiars, making it possible

> instead of demonizing technologies [to] assess their promise and those of the new bodily configurations [afforded] by them in terms of the extent to which they promote and preserve the space of differentiation that makes our corporeal exchanges possible.[35]

And thirdly, by releasing the spatial imaginaries of ethical community from both the geo-metrics of universalism and the confines of propinquity and geneology, they disturb the territorialization of self, kinship, neighborhood and nation and invite other "languages of attachment."[36]

34. Elizabeth Grosz, *Volatile Bodies: Toward a Corporeal Feminism* (Bloomington: Indiana University Press, 1994), 197.

35. Gail Weiss, *Body Images: Embodiment as Intercorporeality* (London: Routledge, 1999), 6.

36. Michael Ignattieff, *The Needs of Strangers* (London: Chatto and Windus, 1984), 139.

The Emergent Alternative
Gilles Clément

Translated by Ariane Lourie Harrison*
Edited by Denise Bratton

I. The Invention of Ecology

In 1866, the German biologist and naturalist Ernst Haeckel (1834–1919) had "the idea and the privilege to name the body of knowledge regarding the *links* between living organisms and their environment, or in other words, *ecology*."[1]

This field of study—concerned with that which is "between" and not only that which "is"—comes as the logical result of the enlightened observations of Jean-Baptiste Lamarck (1744–1829) and Charles Darwin (1809–1882), which drew the links between living beings in a process of filiation and transformation over the course of time: Evolution.[2] Haeckel spoke of the *direct* link, broaching the question of exchanges between species and their immediate environment and, without naming it as such, reveals the *economy of nature*.

Lamarck, Darwin, and Haeckel together produced a shock that the dominant global civilization, wedded to monotheism and principles of certainty, could not bring itself to absorb. Instead, the specter of *evolution* was forcefully cast into shadow, so contrary was it to official cosmologies, according to which an omnipotent deity designed and governed the universe. With equal force, those humans suffering from a diabolical impulse to come closer to nature were marginalized. The sense of being above nature, inherent to humans since their appearance on Earth, pervades the sacred texts and, by virtue of a series of technological innovations and increasingly fundamentalist convictions, holds humans at a distance from their environment. Belgian philosopher Isabelle Stengers locates the origin of the word "nature" in ancient Greece, where observers of the environment, seeking to remove this realm from the domain of the gods and superstition, attempted to study natural phenomena and to develop an objective science of the environment.[3] French geographer Augustin Berque suggests that "objective analysis" deepened and developed this with the deployment of technology—microscopes, telescopes, tools, and machines—installed between humans and their environment as the means of intervention, but also as barriers.[4]

* Any quotations from texts not published in English elsewhere have also been translated by Ariane Lourie Harrison.

1. Bernard Dussart, "Concepts et unités en écologie," in *Encyclopédie de l'écologie, Le present en question*, ed. J. P. Charbonneau (Paris: Larousse, 1977), 9. See Ernst von Haeckel, *Generelle Morphologie der Organismen: allgemeine Grundzüge der organischen Formen-Wissenschaft, mechanisch begründet durch die von Charles Darwin reformirte Descendenz-Theorie*, 2 vols. (Berlin: Georg Reimer, 1866).

2. The first theory of evolution was Jean-Baptiste Lamarck's *La philosophie zoologique, ou, Esposition des considérations relative à l'histoire naturelle des animaux* (Paris: Dentu et L'Auteur, 1809), published in English as *Zoological Philosophy: An Exposition with Regard to the Natural History of Animals*, trans. Hugh Elliot (London: Macmillan and Co., 1914); the second was Charles Darwin's *On the Origin of Species* (London: John Murray, 1859).

3. See Ilya Prigogine and Isabelle Stengers, *Order Out of Chaos: Man's New Dialogue with Nature* (Toronto and New York: Bantam Books, 1984); based on *La nouvelle alliance: Métamorphose de la science* (Paris: Gallimard, 1979).—Trans.

4. See Augustin Berque, *Être humain sur la Terre. Principes d'éthiques de l'écoumène* (Paris: Gallimard, 1996) and *Écoumène. Introduction a l'étude des milieux humains* (Paris: Berlin, 2000).—Trans.

As the notion of ecology spread and became the object of scientific education toward the middle of the twentieth century, the will to dominate nature—to guarantee agricultural production, to nourish the populace, and to bring an end to misery—reached its apogee. At the end of the Second World War, advertising campaigns for products created by the chemical industry and the industrialization of agriculture reassured a population in thrall to a much better future, because everything, finally, was under control.[5]

Nascent ecology found itself in direct opposition to the dominant trend of viewing the planet as a productive terrain for exploitation, unlimited and inexhaustible. The scientific world, using traditional methods of observation, revealed the fragility of ecosystems and proposed the contrary notion of *ecological finitude*, but the concept was met with total indifference. In fact, this idea, revolutionary and traumatic, confronted humanity with a new responsibility: to protect and ensure life on Earth.[6]

Exploitation of the land modifies the quality of the environment. We know that the environment functions as a closed system, perpetually recycling the biomass, water, and all of its aggregate elements in new or older forms. Despite this knowledge, which simultaneously affirms both the performance and fragility of ecosystems, land management qualitatively transforms environments to the point of rendering them sterile, non-productive, or toxic. The collapse of many species representative of *biological diversity* adds to the general concern. The *planetary garden*, an enclosed sphere, urgently needs new gardeners.[7] There have been those who argued that such a change was necessary. But neither the slogans of 1968 nor the speeches of René Dumont in 1974 succeeded in influencing the course of a mechanism far too deeply entrenched in society.[8] Productivity and consumerism, both founded on religious precepts, deploy an arsenal of techniques of seduction and propaganda to chase ecology out of minds contaminated by rash and sectarian science. The stock market depends on it, and for some, as we know, the stock market signifies life itself. This is also an urgent issue.

In effect, a concept capable of shaking religious faith and undermining the global economy could not be tolerated. Considering the phenomenon of "ecology" with some perspective, one understands how this idea could not be received as a simple product of scientific thought, quasi-logical; instead, it has been a disruptive idea in the history of the rapport between humanity and nature—simply put, in human history. Ecology thus becomes in and of itself an event whose importance and profundity human societies are only just beginning to comprehend.

5. The exhibition *Affiches de campagnes, le rural et ses images 1860–1960* (Advertising the Countryside: The Rural and its Image, 1860–1960), presented by the Conservatoire de l'agriculture (Le Compa) in Chartres, France, October 2006–December 2008, included material in this vein.

6. Rachel Carson's *Silent Spring* (Boston: Houghton-Mifflin, 1962) raised awareness for the first time of the damage caused by the industrial exploitation of planet.

7. The *jardin plánetaire,* or planetary garden, a term I first proposed in *Thomas et le Voyageur, Esquisse du Jardin Planétaire* (Paris: Éditions Albin Michel, 1996), became the subject of an exhibition at the Grand Hall, La Villette, in Paris (1999–2000) to celebrate the millennium. The planet Earth, viewed from the ecological perspective, meets the very definition of the garden (*Garten*: enclosure), a space in which life is limited by the boundaries of the biotic territory (the biosphere).
On Clément's *Planetary Garden* exhibition at La Villette, see: http://www.ina.fr/art-et-culture/litterature/video/I05276528/gilles-clement-sur-l-exposition-le-jardin-planetaire-a-la-villette.fr.html. On the progression of Clément's projects from The Garden in Movement, to the Planetary Garden, to the Third Landscape, and Symbiotic Humanity, see the introduction to an interview with Clément by Denise Bratton in *Log: Observations on Architecture and the Contemporary City* 12 (Spring/Summer 2008): 81–90.—Trans.

8. French agronomic engineer, sociologist, and politician René Dumont ran for president in 1974 as France's first ecological candidate, effectively founding the movement of political ecology in France.—Trans.

II. The Eradication of Ecology

This importance and profundity—fundamental to the creation of a real political project—has not escaped the notice of certain observers, certain detractors. In order to preserve the consumer market, ecological thought must be eradicated. Two lobbying efforts aim to do this without being able to completely banish the sense of ecological crisis. Indeed, a shared sense of impotence remains as humanity contemplates its own impending disaster. The first campaign frames the ecologist as an "*ayatollah*," with a nod to deep ecology (*l'écologie radicale*), which is prone to rigor. French philosopher Luc Ferry traces a purist fascist *dérive*, insisting on the fact that the ecological movement, born in Germany, was not opposed by Hitler—in fact, quite the contrary.[9] The second, more common approach characterizes the ecologist as frivolous, ridiculous, and incapable of addressing social and economic realities.

Only a third campaign—in full swing as I write—wields the means of mastering the project to eradicate ecology, that is, a management strategy for the planet. After having been ridiculed, assimilated to the delirium of infantile poets or that of dangerous fanatics, ecology—imagined to be is emerging at last from a long period of isolation—submits to the ultimate assault by its detractors: appropriation.

How to do away with an inconvenient truth, intrusive and recurrent, antagonistic to all options for growth? How to contradict scientific findings and verified facts—global warming, the loss of biodiversity, or any other phenomena obvious to the naked eye—without discrediting oneself and losing face? How to suppress the discourse of those who oppose the productivist systems that were supposed to solve all of humanity's problems, if not by absorbing it into the system itself in order to make ecology disappear forever?

As the discourse of ecology becomes incontrovertible, this strategy engenders alternatives to anti-globalization propositions, avoiding at all cost any prospect of reduced development. This third campaign adopts the vocabulary of recuperation: everything can be achieved in the name of *sustainable development*, that is to say, of development itself. Economists are hard at work on this issue.[10] The main outcome of the Kyoto Earth Summit, the outcome favored by all parties (and from the perspective of anyone who understands the workings of markets, the greatest folly and the most perverse idea), is the *right to pollute*.[11] Pollution is rendered a non-problem as it is tied to profit-making activity. If corporations engaged in

9. Luc Ferry, *The New Ecological Order*, trans. Carol Volk (Chicago: University of Chicago Press, 1995); originally published as *Le nouvel ordre écologique: L'arbre, l'animal, et l'homme* (Paris: Bernard Grasset, 1992). See esp. Preface, xxii, and Chapter 5, "Nazi Ecology: the November 1933, July 1934, and June 1935 Legislations."—Trans.

10. According to the American economist and Nobel Laureate Joseph E. Stiglitz, to imagine an infinite development in a finite world, one must be either crazy or one must be an economist.

11. Negotiated in Kyoto, Japan, in December 1997, the Kyoto Protocol is an amendment to the United Nations Framework Convention on Climate Change (UNFCCC), an international treaty intended to bring countries together to reduce global warming. Under terms of the agreement, the Kyoto Protocol would not take effect until ninety days after it was ratified by at least fifty-five countries involved in the UNFCCC. Another condition was that ratifying countries had to represent at least fifty-five percent of the world's total carbon dioxide emissions for 1990. The first condition was met on May 23, 2002, when Iceland became the fifty-fifth country to ratify the Kyoto Protocol. When Russia ratified the agreement in November 2004, the second condition was satisfied, and the Kyoto Protocol entered into force on February 16, 2005. While the U.S. signed the Kyoto Protocol in 1997, in 2001, President Bush withdrew U.S. support for the protocol. Grassroots support in the U.S. led 165 U.S. cities to vote to support the treaty. In May 2011, President Barak Obama confirmed that the US would not join an updated protocol. The Kyoto Protocol expires in late 2012, and in May 2011, leaders of Russia, Japan, and Canada confirmed they would not join a new Kyoto agreement.—Trans.

petroleum production, which contributes to the greenhouse effect (to cite but one aspect of environmental pollution), reach a limit (determined by whom?), they can purchase environmental credits from another firm, effectively granting them the right to continue polluting. The traffic in pollution rights, transformed into market value, induces enough transactions to be profitable. During a year in which the consumption of goods linked with petroleum production declines, the value of pollution rights falls. The process demonstrates how a regulation intended to limit pollution in reality perpetuates it.[12]

III. Green Business

At no point has the problem of human suffering in the "planetary garden" been confronted, but many give the impression of doing so. First of all, they communicate. The primary task of the partisans of sustainable development is to establish a communications strategy. Words and images. Images, above all. Make the aestheticized claim of a planet in crisis with photographs that are marvelous and tragic, taken from a bird's eye views, or from afar—make books, speeches, proclaim good intentions—to change the climate, we will find the means. The technology of the twenty-first century is repositioned under the sign of sustainable development. In France, the *Grenelle de l'environnement,* a round table debate on the environment (whose positive aspect consists in raising *official* awareness of environmental problems),[13] contributes to the dissemination of disinformation by highlighting an array of modest environmental interventions: insulating houses, separating waste, and saving water. These are obvious, useful, and responsible civic gestures that all of Earth's passengers must undertake, or they can be considered responsible for the consequences.

It thus becomes possible to develop immense polluting industries, and to destroy landscapes and human societies on the planet in utter tranquility. Much energy is concentrated on the automobile industry, highway development, industrial cultivation of bio-fuels, development of increasingly powerful pesticides and fertilizers, proliferation of genetically-modified organisms (GMOs), recourse to nuclear power, etc. A single principle governs this system: "does it pay or not?" If "it pays," then there is no objection to a particular solution, even if it leads millions of people to misery or death, because "it pays." In the inverse scenario ("it does not pay"), an alternative solution would not even merit consideration, even though it promises to improve or save lives. In this way, finally,

12. On July 4, 2008, on radio France Inter, Jean-Louis Borloo (former French minister of Energy, Ecology and Sustainable Development and an initiator of the *Grenelle de l'environnement,* discussed in the following note.—Trans.) declared that carbon credits (a tradable certificate or permit representing the right to emit one ton of carbon dioxide) will be officially listed on the stock market. He added— and this was before the crisis: "and you will see, it will work!"

13. The *Grenelle de l'environnement* was convened in the summer of 2007 by President Nicolas Sarkozy to define the key points of public policy on ecological and sustainable development issues (biodiversity, climate change, waste management, and environmental governance) over a five-year period.—Trans.

ecology is muzzled, appeased, and enslaved to the market. Thus it re-enters the liberal system by virtue of its own commodification. Ecology is laundered, filtered, and stripped of its cautionary intentions and threatening agendas, so it can be a clean and well-oiled machine for business. Such is the agenda behind the organization of a capitalist cartel pillaging the planet with a violence unequalled in the history of mankind. In *The Coming Insurrection*, an anonymous group of contributors calling themselves the Comité Invisible (Invisible Committee) painted a scathing profile of this new economic engine:[14]

> Ecology isn't simply the logic of a total economy; it's the new morality of capital. The internal state of crisis and the rigorous screening that's underway demand a new criterion in the name of which this screening and selection will be carried out. From one era to the next, the idea of virtue has never been anything but an invention of vice.... Tracking, transparency, certification, eco-taxes, environmental excellence, and the policing of water, all give us an idea of the coming state of ecological emergency. Nothing is permitted to a power structure that bases its authority in Nature, in health and in well-being.... Those who claim that generalized self-control will spare us from an environmental dictatorship are lying: the one will prepare the way for the other, and we'll end up with both.[15]

The environmental dictatorship cited by the Comité Invisible is based on the moralizaion of ecology. With this reversal, the system assumes a unique position according to which everything, effectively, is permitted. But this dictatorship is subject to the fragility of structures or systems that are indifferent to the complexity of materials, living beings, and behaviors: it relies on the singular credo of profitability, on which the dictate depends. It therefore finds itself subject to the same risks of collapse. One should not confuse this with an ideological dictate, but rather understand it as a dictate of money disguised as the remediating engine of humanity. And in any case, as ecology proves through its complexity, no dictate based on a single ideology or singular material value can contend with the unpredictable behaviors of living beings. One must accept the obvious: if the possibility exists for humanity to accommodate ecological complexity in order to secure its own existence on the planet, it will occur in the most empirical realm of experience on the planet with the unfolding of events, and not in response to an arsenal of authoritarian accounts that are contradictory and dangerously reflect the technocratic thinking of government.[16]

14. The Invisible Committee, *The Coming Insurrection, Intervention Series 1* (Los Angeles: Semiotext(e), 2009); originally published as Comité Invisible, *L'insurrection qui vient* (Paris: Éditions La Fabrique, 2007), a popular anticapitalist tract attributed (without evidence) to political activist Julien Coupat, who was accused (also without evidence) of an attack on a TGV train as one of the alleged "Tarnac Nine," and arrested on charges of criminal association for purposes of terrorist activity.

15. Comité Invisible, *The Coming Insurrection*, "Sixth Circle," 78–80.

16. The notion to protect landscapes considered remarkable for their beauty leads, for example, to UNESCO's classification of the Jurisdiction of Saint-Émilion as a World Heritage Site. Yet in environmental terms, these vineyards are generally considered to be among the most degraded landscapes, condemned by the European Landscape Convention (Convention Européenne du Paysage, CEP), which promotes the protection, management, and planning of European landscapes and organizes European cooperation on landscape issues. Thus, the UNESCO landmarking legislation comes to protect practices that are condemned elsewhere.

Green business is nothing other than a logical avatar for the dictate of money. But it forgets that money has no true value, only exchange value. Nothing more. The accumulation of cash, stocks, bonds, and other virtual instruments—susceptible to sudden change and collapse—will be regulated by the sole fact of their becoming worthless; this is the fate of all who pretend to be interested in life by putting a price on it. That which the "green world" abusively calls "value" corresponds to nothing from an ecological perspective. The compatibility between ecology and finance is not only illusory, but proceeds from a pathological operation in which humanity, locked into an infantile pattern, stubbornly resists breaking with a system which, according to its own fantasies, plays the role of its protector and models its beliefs.

IV. Planetary Consciousness

Conflicts of interests have continued to mar the history of the world's peoples, and they are always resolved by the victory of the most able, the strongest, and often the most barbaric. The identifiable enemy consolidates his position at the frontier of a country or region. He is Other. He thinks differently, and because of this single cultural difference, this enemy represents all conceivable dangers. The lack of transparency displayed by the strategists of power keeps the planet divided and therefore under control. Fear and divisiveness facilitate governance. Our leaders use and abuse these techniques to the point of rendering suspect the most justifiable preventative measures.

However, unbeknownst to the grand strategists, a unified movement binds—each day more firmly—Arab and Jew, poet and banker, poor and wealthy, who suddenly find themselves suddenly aboard a singular and unique ship: the planet. A *planetary consciousness*, born of ecological thought, is dramatically overturning relationships among institutions, and between institutions and individuals. A kind of solidarity, necessary and inherent to the conditions of life on Earth, is taking hold of the collective consciousness in parallel with and even transcending traditional conflicts of interest. Each living being takes its place in an ecosystem, and each ecosystem finds itself linked to a neighboring ecosystem, and finally to that of the planet.

Humanity suddenly discovers its common enemy, one that comprehensively threatens all the people on Earth. This enemy does not bear the name of people situated at the border of a given country, or hidden within neighborhoods under the guise of a diffuse terrorism, or positioned at the limits of the stratosphere in some vessel from another galaxy. No, humanity discovers that it is its own enemy: it has the capacity to self-destruct.

Thus, taking stock of itself, humanity becomes morose. The past is inglorious, there is no future. Taking refuge in the present, humanity connects in cyber-space, declaring emotional solidarity via raw and instantaneous information offered with compassion by simultaneous media. But in so doing, humanity fails to act. It remains passively complicit within a system which, it seems, leaves no project opposable. It is struck with fear.

Planetary consciousness has the effect of paralyzing humanity. As living conditions deteriorate and the population increases, humanity remains lost in the fog of its beliefs, in the stagnation of economies, and in the face of clear limits to its territorial resources. It wanders in the garden, not knowing where to begin.

V. Fear Tactics

This paralysis benefits some, while it conditions the others to a "wait and see" scenario. It prevents action, discourages adventurous spirits, and confines enterprise to the pursuit of profits. The systematic erosion of job security confronts each individual with the risks of losing the little that he possesses, and undermines any concerted efforts to fight or resist. This process, an extensive rolling mill, wears down resistance in a sheep-like society, where each is shorn according to the rule of maximum exploitation with no possibility of rebellion. In government institutions, public services, and universities, the market is prioritized regardless of the actual needs of, and risks to, public services, teaching, or research. Preferring quiet conformism to debate, bold minds are encouraged not to share their ideas in a climate of surveillance and evaluation by the official machine. Schools and specialized academies are not immune to this unhealthy timidity on the part of those who should on the contrary protest and change the orientation of a project (certain among them being professional schools), regardless of the risks. Worse still is their tacit compliance with unfair propositions by ministries of higher education to undermine the status of teachers, even if some are independent of those ministries. This proposal, we know, aims to separate teaching from research and introduces the scandalous principle that teaching is the penalty for unsuccessful researchers. Gérard Dessons, professor of French literature at the University of Paris VIII, analyses the situation in terms that could be applied, word for word, to a professional school:

It is a mistake to think that a teacher-researcher—if this person is a researcher who teaches—teaches indiscriminately. He or she teaches on the subject of his and her research. To disassociate the two activities can be equated with the instrumentalization of teaching: assigning to teaching a strictly communicative function. If the University valorizes the researcher and condemns the teacher, what effectively would be taught? What is the object of learning? Is it that which a "real" researcher has already elaborated? This view overlooks the fact that beyond the goal of research, the teacher-researcher is teaching a practice. He or she teaches how to research, that is to say, the method—each time specific to the teacher—of questioning the unknown, or in other words, of inventing the unknown. In this sense, the work of the teacher-researcher has risk. More or less risky, more or less expensive, but a risk nonetheless, since in showing how what he makes is linked to how he makes it, he is in some sense working without a safety net.[17]

A school, university, or laboratory—any place where active thought is prized—renounces risk only at its own peril. The compartmentalization, the general principles of evaluation, the stigmatization of good and bad, and the atmosphere of surveillance all belong to the tactics of fear that have infiltrated every field and all structures of society, from the corporation to the university, from agriculture to the art world.

Fear tactics aptly express society's present lack of confidence. It signals in this sense its weakness, and to pretend otherwise, society reinforces its front lines. The terrain of ecology offers a way forward, ready to exploit all rumors of catastrophe, it yokes its discourse to disaster and makes sustainable development its ideal, without envisioning modification of the institutional bases of the catastrophe. Thus the socioeconomic system is based on a perversion of its own perpetuation in which any deviation invokes repression, and where the space of surveillance extends across the entire territory.

One might think this is a closed circle, and that we are forever condemned to replay the same scenario in which abortive attempts to effect change conclude with a farcical patching of cracks that menace the entire system. But this is not the case. Not only do observers of society—economists, scientists, and philosophers—announce the looming collapse of this dominant structure, but even society itself, aware that change is imminent, modifies its vision of the world, erecting a vocabulary of anticipation, focusing on questions (which may be only be ambient, "in the air," but which are also carefully thoughtfully considered) concerning approaches to life on the planetary level.

17. Gérard Dessons, "Enseigner ce qu'on cherche," *Cassandre/ Hors Champ* 77 (Spring 2009): 38.

VI. The Emergent Alternative

While radical ecology, circumscribed by its rigorous precepts, tends to resist, and while green business is organized to capitalize on its version of the "bio" market, a third way, which has no name, but which I will call the *emergent alternative (l'alternative ambiante)* arises at the interstices of these interrelated rumors, contradictory analyses, catastrophic forecasts, and hazardous predictions, but also from a foundation for empirical observation, experience, and solid research.

There is too much protest on a global scale for minds by now saturated with information and images not to grasp the fact that the discourse of ecologists has a basis in reality. Even if the complex mechanisms of exchange inherent to the ecosystem remain largely unknown, the sense of an intimate connection between the present and the past has infiltrated society's understanding; this sense fosters a network of planetary citizenship, which exists outside of all governmental structures.

The emergent alternative considers the prospect of reduced economic growth without actually being its advocate: it withdraws from the green business perspective, which it considers excessive, and rather than simply wait for elusive solutions to be handed down by elected members of government, the emergent alternative prepares itself by questioning the possible consequences of the "butterfly effect:"[18] what we do in one place will have repercussions around the globe; everything that we send up into the atmosphere eventually falls back down upon us; the wind carries clouds of particles around the world, and the biosphere functions like the drum of a washing machine, in which everything is intermingled: the water in the seas, the moisture in the atmosphere, the water in the rivers, and the water in our bodies. Yes, the garden is planetary, few can doubt this any longer, but those who are alert to the dimensions of such a demanding question, ask themselves "How does one become the gardener of such a garden?" There are no simple answers. A cynical humanity, either lulled to sleep by media or awakened by crisis, tests new ways of life in an unknown terrain. Everything must be invented, everything becomes a challenge. Ecology sets the guidelines with its forty years of leadership, but only in this first decade of the twenty-first century does one begins to reflect on what might be required to address the situation and to formulate new approaches.

On the political plane, the emergent alternative triggers an unanticipated leveling of the social classes. It rejects the proposals of both the right and the left, as if participating in a childish game

18. Clément refers to the meteorological implications of the butterfly effect postulated in Chaos Theory; see his *Nuages: Le Rayon des curiosités* (Paris: Éditions Bayard, 2005), 18f. The term "butterfly effect" itself is often attributed to Edward Lorenz (1917–2008), who used it to describe a sensitive dependence on initial conditions. The phrase refers to the idea that a butterfly's wings could create small atmospheric changes that could ultimately trigger a chain of effects leading to large-scale environmental events.—Trans.

of ping-pong, in which it refuses to serve as arbiter. For what good would it do to advise on the best methods of sustainable development, if the question is not one of development? Where politicians of all stripe adhere to traditional models, continuing to push their strategies of speculation, the emergent alternative looks for immediate, concrete solutions whose substance, and in certain cases value, is obvious. In France, the Association for the Preservation of Rural Agriculture (AMAP) models simple, local, and economically effective responses to the problem of providing healthy products.[19] In its very operations, AMAP illustrates the principle of short networks of production and distribution, which diminish the ecological burden of consumer goods with their inherent global cost. AMAP supplies a diversified network of food production, one that is aligned with the seasons, produced in real-time, of high quality, and affordable to all. These things constitute, in and of themselves, *value* that is inscribed within the ecological discourse but not yet manifest, because they are unquantifiable in the language of management. They can also be regarded as emblematic of a much larger system, for which the grid of *new values*—quality of food, of substrates (air, water, soil), of public services and infrastructure, and of modalities for the distribution of manufactured goods, etc.—constitutes a real *political project*.

French political ecologist Alain Lipietz's assertion that "[t]he global economy produces too much for too few people and produces too inefficiently while creating too much pressure on the Earth" summarizes the situation in pointing out the aberrant character of contemporary systems of production.[20] But he also alerts us to the sometimes undemocratic aspect of solutions to crisis over the course of history, and warns us against increasing the power of the state, which takes advantage of crisis to reinforce its power and its security systems. At the same time, Lipietz denounces the excesses of "planning," the technocratic tendency of authoritarian regimes maintained by a scientific belief that it is possible to master nature.

The emergent alternative weighs the hazards of planning founded on old patterns of stimulus. It observes from a distance the exchange of billions of euros, the launch of government bonds, the infusion of funds into banks and targeted industries (automotive, nuclear, bio-fuels), and the play of the global stock market. The emergent alternative listens, without paying real attention, to radio broadcasts hawking the benefits of insurance, the advantageous returns of investments, the miracle of guaranteed returns. From

19. Association pour le maintien d'une agriculture paysanne.

20. Alain Lipietz, *Face à la crise: L'urgence écologiste* (Paris: Éditions Textuel, 2009), 21.

all of this, the emergent alternative turns away. For this is none of its concern.

Invited to lecture and participate in debates on ecology and landscape by agricultural universities as well as art and architecture schools, I travel around Europe and to other continents. The concerns being raised in these venues center on one issue: How is a growing human population to be sustained on a territory—the planet—that is limited? This question, posed innumerable times over the last half-century without ever finding a satisfactory answer, remains relevant, but elicits the pathos of resignation: there is no solution.

VII. Abandoning the Cartesian Project

At the outset of this new century, the people of Earth gamble on their future. Either they invent an approach capable of dealing with this future, or they only pretend to do so and thus face self-destruction.

One cannot underestimate the effort required, not only to invent a new economy (experts on the matter have delighted in training their focus on this), but also to adopt a different perspective on the world. It is not a question of technical, but rather cultural foundations. To say that the future depends on a new paradigm is not to imply an intellectual game. Ours is an exceptional epoch, a moment in which we are being asked to redefine ourselves within the cosmos, a situation in which humanity has probably never found itself.

It is true that humanity is relatively young. Reflecting on the scale of geological time, humanity appears in history as a recent avatar, or as a nanosecond of the Earth's history. Humanity does not yet understand the terrain it inhabits. Even given the short history of human thought, there nevertheless has been enough time to produce numerous cosmogonies and fantastic visions of the creation of the world, all freighted with poetry and improbability. Considering ecology in light of other conceptions of the world, one finds a convergence between ecological thought and animist civilizations, where respect for nature is based on belief rather than science.

While animistic belief situates humans in a relationship of equivalence with other living beings, "modern" civilization holds these living entities at a distance. This distance—to which Stengers, Berque, and Descola refer—persists even within the vocabulary of ecological thought, born in the West, under the regime of mastering nature. The word "environment," used to describe the world around us, implies that humans do not belong to this *mis-en-scéne*, that the human is situated behind, above, or elsewhere, but not within the environment. Ministries of the environment—ministries of the surroundings—see the creature and its landscape as a complex ensemble to be analyzed in order to quantify it, not as a living space in which humanity, to the same degree as all the other living entities, finds itself *immersed*.

Thus, the ancient Cartesian project of mastering nature persists. Reinforced by scientism and absolute confidence in performative technology, it continues to pit humanity against a wild nature, submissive or hostile. Humanity tests its own power, believing itself to be the master of weather, of carbon dioxide production, and of greenhouse gas emissions; it invents a technical vocabulary that imprints its domination on all things, as if the right to name things equals mastery. The decision of the G8 in July 2009, in Aquila, to halve the carbon footprint by 2050 was accompanied by a ludicrous injunction: We will not tolerate a global warming of more than two degrees. In declaring that the G8 was incapable of judging the state of the planet, President Lula of Brazil might have added that the eight richest countries had already reached this limit.[21]

In order to engage a policy for humanity's survival on the Earth more seriously, one must effectively descend from an artificial observatory positioned above "nature," considered to be the realm of experience, mastery, and the market. One needs to *immerse* oneself, to accept oneself as an entity within nature, to revise one's position in the universe, no longer above or in the center, but rather *within and with*.

"There is no 'environmental catastrophe'," stated the Comité Invisible, and further, "The catastrophe is the *environment itself*.... What makes the crisis desirable is that in the crisis the environment ceases to be the environment. We are forced to reestablish contact, albeit a potentially fatal one, with what's there, to rediscover the rhythms of reality. What surrounds us is no longer a landscape, a panorama, a theatre, but something to inhabit, something we need to come to terms with, something we can learn from."[22]

This condition of *immersion*—perhaps the most difficult to achieve, since it requires from us cultural change and real humility— must be accompanied by the material and technical conditions that will give birth to the political project of humanity's survival on the planet.

The material and technical conditions are at hand, at least virtually. To decide to use them requires a political courage to this day absent in all government directives. With respect to Europe, the storefront of a liberal capitalist West, the only guidelines that seem

21. The thirty-fifth G8 summit took place in the city of L'Aquila in Abruzzo on July 8–10, 2009; in attendance was Luiz Inácio Lula da Silva, president of Brazil 2003–2010, who is popularly referred to as "Lula." The G8 is an unofficial annual forum for the leaders of Canada, the European Commission, France, Germany, Italy, Japan, Russia, the United Kingdom, and the United States.—Trans.

22. Comité Invisible, *The Coming Insurrection,* "Sixth Circle," 74 and 82.

to resemble such a project to manage society are issued by the combined power of lobbies reassembled in Brussels. The lobbyists' aggressiveness stands in for the political project that society, in general, so urgently needs.

On the other hand, green business legitimizes itself only in relation to the mechanisms of the stock markets, which are essentially devoid of ethics and morality. Regardless of regulatory intentions, the market accelerates the process of unequal distribution of wealth and the degradation of the environment, and therefore of the conditions for life on the planet.[23] It ignores the fact that humanity is made a party to the play of the stock market. In the present state of the planet, the stock market is a powerful and soulless machine, insensitive to the destruction for which it is responsible. Contrary to other causes of disaster, like pandemics or war, the market functions openly, with complete peace of mind, regardless of the plight of humanity. By a well-orchestrated deception, sleepwalking humans find nothing to correct in its workings. Do we not receive the stock quotes each hour on the radio together with the weather and advertisements for life insurance? Who could have imagined that the media would regularly, with the rigor of a bombardment, make itself the delivery system for a killing machine?

Silencing the lobbies and the stock market: *Voilà!* the work of a future generation for whom life would not hinge on a game of chance and necessity, but rather on the vast complexity of life. What project could be mounted immediately to oppose this infernal combination of green business and stock quotes?

VIII. Resistance: The Hypothesis of Shifting Interest

Crisis instigates tyranny, fascism, and a hardening of power, which satisfies reactionary spirits: such is the lesson of history. We are there. We must watch the ludicrous escalation of power, whereby the police state allies itself with the increasing conservatism of society, in order to see how an order based on fear falters. Once this occurs, one can finally take up the social project. The only worthwhile goal is to advance humanity's understanding of itself, and of how it functions within its environment, and in doing so, to attempt to improve the conditions.

The project requires a planetary effort, and it requires time. It cannot be initiated in a brutal fashion without provoking violent opposition from those who today possess both power and arms. Hence the need for *resistance*. A new regime, diffuse and fragmented, but pervasive in the world, lays the foundation for a future humanity. Resistance, as I understand it, concerns all efforts to act in the name

23. See Hervé Kempf, *How the Rich are Destroying the Earth*, trans. Leslie Thatcher (White River Junction, VT: Chelsea Green, 2008); originally published as *Comment les riches détruisent la planète* (Paris: Éditions du Seuil, 2007).

of a political project focused on ecological urgency. Or, at least, one can imagine such a political project today, because we can expect that knowledge about behavior and communication among all human beings will evolve and therefore modify the way that biological energy is to be used, transformed, and preserved.

Resistance relies on the *emergent alternative* to experiment with new policies for territorial and social management. Resistance bases its legitimacy on *planetary consciousness* according to which the planetary garden and the role of gardeners can be understood. It rejects fear tactics at the same time that it contravenes green business in order to develop a world of exchange and equal distribution of wealth. Finally, it progressively abandons the *Cartesian project of mastering nature*, instead inventorying the possibilities of *dialogue* with nature in a process where *immersion* in the realm of the living is accompanied by a real knowledge and understanding of all living entities and their inventions. Such is the *hypothesis of the shifting interest* of our society, which, I think, operates in silence in this agitated world. One does not hear it. There is only the need for will and benign intelligence.

Shifting interest coincides with a redefinition of values where there is a reappraisal of materials, goods, and services in response to restricted access and distribution, these being triggered when a minority of the population accumulate a majority of the profits. What some refer to as the Gross National Happiness (GNH) index comes thus to stand in for the Gross Domestic Product (GDP), which orients current politics.[24]

Shifting interest presupposes the slow pace of a progressive process. It is a project that takes time and requires raising the consciousness of the masses. It represents the reasonable outcome of the crisis that threatens human populations. It entails a strategy of substitution rather than one of violence, and thus represents the best imaginable resolution to this crisis.

Shifting interest is not a random hypothesis. It is already functioning at the core of the most environmentally attuned societies. But the principle of a *peaceful* movement emerging out of the profound malaise in which humanity finds itself today constitutes a hypothesis, and at the moment, it is no more than this. The accumulated pressure from government leaders, blind to humanity and its suffering, could lead instead to a more rapid but devastating resolution, a global conflict in which true ecology and green business confront one another to disastrous ends. Whether the resolution to the crisis is achieved peacefully or violently,

24. In French, *Ronheur Intérieur Brut* (BIB). The term "Gross National Happiness (GNH)" was coined in 1972 as an indicator to measure quality of life or social progress in more holistic and psychological terms than the economic indicator Gross Domestic Product (GDP).—Trans.

shifting interest completes its trajectory: human society, slowly and progressively, changes its *model of desire*. Such is evolution.

In his work on the distribution of wealth on the planet, Hervé Kempf returns to the perspective of the nineteenth-century economist Thorstein Veblen,[25] who showed how the model of desire propels the economy, and how on the basis of this dynamic it becomes possible to anticipate production and supply of "consumables." Veblen maintained that a social class, regardless of its level, desires that which is used and consumed by the class that is immediately above it. Despite the leveling of social classes, the division between wealth and poverty, an increasingly large gap, operates according to this same dynamic today.

Changing the model of desire while effecting a shift of interest from material products to those that are less material—for example the acquisition of knowledge, revaluation of the environment, promotion of wellness, etc.—permits us to seriously envisage an ecological form of planetary management. It is also necessary to invent an economy capable of supporting this kind of society and its exchanges on the basis of new interests, which are situated in a realm of unquantifiable profits, removed from the financial regime, but extending to all degrees of subjectivity in the mental space of individuals and communities.

This new economy marks a break with the existing economy, which will, in all likelihood, remain in place until the demise of all of the post-crisis financial regimes currently installed on the planet.

Shifting interest is concerned with the future. However, the displacement of desire has already begun; the growth of the organic market is evidence of this. Green business transforms this evidence into a market reality. However, not everything is marketable: improvements in the quality of life, laughter and friendship, warmth and irony are not quoted on any stock exchange, yet manage to thrive. In a society driven by a political project that is both ecological and humanist, what would constitute its workings and operations?

IX. Demurrage Currency

If Veblen's discourse denounces a comprehensive human logic, he said nothing about the principle of acquisition with respect to the model of desire. Should one borrow, which leads to debt, and by extension, the loan, the investment, and therefore speculation?

The project of the Belgian economist Bernard Lietaer aligns itself with the proposals of ecologists: one can only envisage a conscientious governing of human societies which looks at the *long term*.[26]

25. Kempf references Thorstein Veblen, *The Theory of the Leisure Class: An Economic Study of Institutions* (New York: The Macmillan Company, 1899) and his notion of "conspicuous consumption."—Trans.

26. Bernard A. Lietaer, *Mutation mondiale, crise et innovations monétaires* (Paris: L'Aube, 2008).

As we know, today's entire economy and therefore all policy and all legislative decisions function according to short-term goals: "Let us begin by noting," writes Lietaer, "that corporations today determine what we eat, how we dress, how we travel, how we live, what energy and what technologies we use, etc. Neither governments nor citizens make these decisions. From this I conclude that as long as corporations are fixated on the short term, we will continue to head blindly into a series of disasters."[27]

Lietaer assumes that businesses will not choose to shift into this long-term management mode of their own volition, arguing that regulations will remain ineffectual with respect to long-term investment. According to him, only financial incentive can lead to the desired solution. Lietaer's argument merits being reproduced in its entirety:

> Suppose we live in a world where there are only two types of investments available: short-term and long-term. For example, the first could be an investment in a pine tree plantation, where the value of each tree would be 100 euros after ten years, and the second an investment in a plantation of oak trees worth 1000 euros after a hundred years. We also assume that all these values are adjusted for inflation, so that the figures remain comparable. A rational investor should be indifferent to the differences between these two types of investment: it could indeed cut all the pine trees every ten years and obtain 1,000 euros after 100 years, the same financial return from planting oak trees.

> Now, lets introduce the monetary factor. Suppose we use a conventional currency (the euro, the dollar, etc.) with, for example, an interest rate of 5 percent. The value of a ten-year old pine tree in 10 years is, discounted to the present day, 61.39 euros. Indeed, if I invest 61.39 euros for 10 years with an interest rate of 5%, I obtain exactly 100 euros. However, by the same rational calculation, our oak tree worth 1000 euros in 100 years discounted to the present day would be valued at only 7,60 euros. In any society that uses a conventional monetary systems with positive interest rates, one will eventually cut down the oak trees to plant only pine trees. This metaphor illustrates how the conventional monetary system automatically gears all financial decisions to the short term.[28]

Lietaer proposes instead to use a new currency that he calls "*complementary*," with "*demurrage*," that is to say, with a negative interest rate comparable to a charge for "parking."[29] Assuming this demurrage rate of 5 percent per pine tree per year, discounted to the present day, would bring its value to 167 euros, while the oak tree, following this same principle, would be worth 168,000 euros. Anyone who makes this calculation is investing in the long term.

27. Lietaer, *Mutation mondiale, crise et innovations monétaires*, 19.

28. Lietaer, *Mutation mondiale, crise et innovations monétaires*, 20f.

29. See Bernard A. Lietaer, *The Future of Money: Creating New Wealth, Work and a Wiser World* (London: Century, 2001), 28 (and passim), where he defines "demurrage" as "a form of negative interest which discourages hoarding in the form of currency." These findings are encompassed and elaborated in Bernard A. Lietaer and Stephen Belgin, *New Money for a New World* (Kassel: Qiterra Press, 2011).—Trans.

History offers examples of this phenomenon. The power of ancient Egypt, and of Europe during the epoch of cathedral building coincided with the use of currency with negative interest rates; the concept of demurrage was inaugurated in France with the first railway companies, which were paid for unused railroad cars remaining (parked) on the tracks. But the instrument dates back to the ancient monetary system of the Nile Valley. A farmer who produced more than he could use deposited the surplus at the local temple. A scribe recorded the deposit (ten sacks of wheat, for example). If the farmer wanted to take back his wheat after a year, nine sacks were returned to him; the tenth sack was used to pay the guards. Otherwise, the farmer had the option of using as currency the discounted value of the ten bags based on a note called the "*ostrakon*." Lietaer has proposed the "*terra*" as a complementary planetary currency with a negative interest rate.[30] Such an arrangement encourages discounting instead of savings. It encourages reinvestment and not warehousing, it does not offer an investment advantage (in contrast to the stock markets), but constantly stimulates the economy.

Complementary currencies have been invented and used in numerous countries. Certain of these function on the model of exchange (time, services, and goods) like SEL, SOL, etc.[31] None thus far has succeeded in replacing the existing monetary system. Without a doubt, it is time to think about what will, almost mechanically, best accommodate an ecological regime for the planet. The question of what form tomorrow's currency may take is not a matter of which currency will dominate (the dollar, the euro, the yen, the euro-yen!); rather, it is a matter of what philosophy of exchange and sharing is required for the survival of humanity on the planet. Numerous exchange models, on the order (to some extent) of social security, aptly demonstrate how this type of transaction "places everyone on an equal footing."[32]

Lietaer's proposal is strictly concerned with the process of exchange in which basic commodities (such as wheat) and exchange value (*ostrakon, terra*) lead to long-term management, which according to him shelters the economy from crisis. If the argument works in favor of ecological management in general, which itself relies on the long term, then does it not enable the definition of a political project through which it becomes necessary and useful to resort to *demurrage currency*?

It is worth noting that with respect to the economy and to crisis, Lietaer speaks to us of landscape: a pine forest in the short term, an oak forest over the long term.

30. Lietaer made his case for the terra in *The Future of Money: Creating New Wealth, Work and a Wiser World*, 249–52.—Trans.

31. Clément cites two examples of complementary currencies in use in France today. Acknowledging the "explosive nature of the multiplication process of complementary currencies when the unemployment conditions are serious enough," Lietaer treats the case of the SEL, or *Grain de Sel* (grain of salt), established by an organic farming specialist from Ariège in 1993, noting that, "in French, as in English, [it] has the double meaning of something not taken quite seriously," but adding that SEL is also the acronym for *Systeme d'Echange Locaux* (Local Exchange System)," *The Future of Money: Creating New Wealth, Work and a Wiser World*, 166f. The SOL (in homage to "*solidaire*," or solidarity), established in 2008 as a collective experiment, embraces three systems: time dollars, commercial loyalty currency, and national funds earmarked for particular purposes; the SOL is used by a national network that includes Alsace, Aquitaine, Bretagne, Franche-Compté, Île de France, Midi-Pyrénées, Nord-Pas-de-Callais, Poiteau-Charante, and Rhône-Alpes. Its express purpose is to "add a social and interdependent dimension to the economy." See http://www.sol-reseau.org.—Trans.

32. See the discussion between Paul Ariès and Jean-Louis Sagot Duvauroux published in *Le Sarkophage* 13 (July 2009) and Paul Ariès, "Sauvons l'écologie antiproductiviste," http://www.politique-actu.com/debat/sauvons-ecologie-antiproductiviste-paul-aries-sarkophage/8085 (accessed 3/15/2012).

X. Symbiotic Humanity

A global system therefore must be invented: in the history of the relationship between humanity and nature, the advent of ecology leads to a complete revision of human behavior, of individual gestures in relation to collective action, and of all modes of governance. If printing in the fifteenth century and industry in the nineteenth century fueled social change, these changes relied on technology. We can refer to these as "revolutions," but they did not modify humanity's Cartesian approach toward the domination of nature; on the contrary, they reinforced it. One must look back to an earlier epoch during which nomadic cultures, in becoming sedentary, created a rupture with "tradition," and imagined a relationship with nature that was quite different from hunting and gathering—which are always risky endeavors—in order to engage nature in a rational dialogue: the birth of the garden.

The *first garden*, thus located along the historical trajectory of humanity's relationship with nature, serves as a paradigm: it inscribed a world view.

The *first ecological garden*, while impossible to precisely situate in time, belongs to the millennial shift in which humanity inscribes a new vision of the world; we are there—we are!—and all the opposing forces are not able to contravene those who serve this new paradigm.

Between the first faltering steps toward agriculture in the Upper Paleolithic and the twenty-first century, there are only some thousands of years. How is that period meaningful with respect to the hundreds of millions of years during which the planet arrived at the stage in which we know it today? In the timeline of living organisms, humanity has only just been born. It has made experiments, made mistakes, discovered its brain (of which it uses only one eighth—what does it do with the rest?); it shouts, cries, and complains about every little blemish or wrinkle. At each crisis of growth, a crisis of conscience. We are there, in effect.

Ecological thought not only demonstrates how the economy of management is closely related to species survival and the quality of substrates; it not only proposes rational exploitation calibrated to the biodiversity (the planetary garden) on which our future depends; ecological thought also reveals *the finitude of our territory, and it is from this understanding that an entire political project must be defined.*

Biomass, water, and land: everything is recorded and subjected to gain or loss in such small measurements that we can think about it in *finite* quantities.

Two urgent questions:

How to recycle our waste in a territory that is finite?
How to control population in this same finite territory?

A *symbiotic humanity* would ideally be able to restore to the environment the full measure of energy that it consumes, like a tree whose leaves (produced from solar energy) return to the soil and become its nourishment (humus). What kind of humus could our civilizations obtain by placing industry in the service of life, as opposed to placing life in peril? Between a bed of forest undergrowth and nuclear waste lies nothing less than a matter of life and death.

The symbiotic humanity of which I speak does not exactly resemble that proposed by Joël de Rosnay,[33] but it does take advantage of the same planetary network, the same "backdrop." However, instead of assessing humanity's achievements solely on the basis of the technology of connectivity—leading to De Rosnay's half-human/half-machine "Cybionte," humanity advances by acquiring ever more refined knowledge of the functioning of life on Earth. Knowledge of biological diversity—its benefits and its protection within the general process of evolution—allows symbiotic humanity to imagine the project of biological recycling by acting in the appropriate time and place—therefore sparingly—on the factors that will determine transformation.

Symbiosis refers to the absolute interdependence of two entities or two biologically related systems. Humanity depends entirely on the diversity that it exploits, but over the course of its evolution, it has reached a point where the environment itself—its diversity—has become dependent on humanity. At the height of this interdependence, it takes only one element of the system to disappear for another in turn to disappear. Symbiotic humanity is named after this interdependence. For the first time in its history, the human race discovers that one false move sends everyone—poor and rich—to the same precipice. Symbiotic humanity, without considering the consequences, lays the foundation for an unconscious but very real solidarity on the planetary level.

Never has it been so urgent to teach the principles of biological diversity, which we exploit without understanding. For symbiotic humanity, knowledge about living organisms—plants, animals, the vital substrates of life on Earth—contributes to the understanding of its own operations, their complexity, and their cultural diversity. Within this set of disciplines, one form of knowledge contributes to

33. Joël de Rosnay, *The Symbiotic Man: A New Understanding of the Organization of Life and a Vision of the Future* (New York: McGraw Hill, 2000); originally published as *L'homme symbiotique: Regards sur le troisième millénaire* (Paris: Éditions du Seuil, 1995).

Acknowledgements:
I would like to express my profound gratitude to Denise Bratton for directing me to Clément's "L'Alternative Ambiente" for translation, and for her extraordinary insights regarding this piece.—Trans.

Clément

another, and none can be the exclusive purview of specialists, or science will remain sealed off in a hermetic bubble.

Symbiotic humanity thus establishes a hierarchy of values from which unfolds a political project. The first ministry of an ideal government for symbiotic humanity would certainly be the ministry of *knowledge*. The ministry of knowledge would contribute to the refinement of thought at all levels, reaching all strata of society. It would facilitate understanding of mechanisms that specifically justify the politics of symbiotic humanity, even among the poorest people. Self-regulation of population growth would be one aspect of this. If it seemed "inhuman" and violent to legislate one child per family in Maoist China, an injunction addressed to a largely undereducated or even illiterate populace, it could on the other hand be possible to raise awareness among the same people about how to determine their very mode of survival.

Symbiotic humanity represents one level of reflection on the ecological paradigm and its consequences.

Gilles Clément
La Vallée, August 26, 2009

*

Risk, Globalization, and the Cosmopolitan Imaginary
Ursula K. Heise

The theories of the relation between risk and modernity proposed by Perrow, Hughes, Giddens, and Beck, among others, foreground how experiences of risk are imbricated in far-flung ecological, technological, economic, and social systems that operate across a variety of scales from the local to the planetary.[1] Beck's concept of the "world risk society," indeed, represents one of the most important recent ways of imagining the global from an environmentalist perspective.[2] Lawrence Buell has gone so far as to envision Beck as the latter-day counterpart of James Lovelock, in that Beck turns Lovelock's theory of Planet Earth as a self-sustaining, harmoniously balanced feedback system upside down into a theory of a world thrown permanently off-balance by the unintended and uncontrollable consequences of technological development.[3] Considering the lasting influence of the Gaia hypothesis on environmentalist thought and culture, one would expect such an inversion of global vision to have similar reverberations in the realm of the local and the everyday.

Indeed, in what for a cultural critic may well be one of the most intriguing facets of his theory, Beck examines the awareness of pervasive risk in its impact on modes of everyday reasoning. Some contemporary risk scenarios, unlike those of earlier ages, he claims, challenge conventional modes of perception and experience through their "mediatedness" or "second-handness" (or what other risk theorists would call "social amplification and attenuation"). Most individuals, even many scientists and engineers, cannot identify and analyze such scenarios on their own, in a process he calls "expropriation of the senses": given the complexity and specificity of contemporary technological hazards, only highly specialized experts can examine them, while the majority of scientists are as non-expert as laypersons. In Beck's view, the fact that knowledge about risks comes in such highly mediated form to the overwhelming majority of individuals leads gradually to a transformation in the logic that structures everyday experience:

> In order to perceive risks as risks and to make them a reference point for one's own thought and action, one has to believe in fundamentally invisible causal connections between conditions that are often substantively temporally and geographically far removed from each other, as well as in more or less speculative projections

1. In the prior section of the chapter, "Narrative in the World Risk Society," from which this section is selected, Heise discusses Charles Perrow's analysis of "system accidents;" see Charles Perrow, *Normal Accidents: Living with High-Risk Technologies* (Princeton: Princeton University Press, 1999). She further describes historian of technology Thomas Hughes' broad analysis of the complexity of large scale systems into which technology is embedded: see Thomas Hughes, *American Genesis: A Century of Invention and technological Enthusiasm, 1870–1970* (New York: Viking, 1989); British sociologist Anthony Giddens' analysis of risk in the context of the social transformations that characterize modernization: see Anthony Giddens, *The Consequences of Modernity* (Cambridge: Polity Press, 1990); and the German sociologist Ulrich Beck's concept of risk in relation to theories modernization and globalization. Heise notes Beck's coining the aphorism: "Poverty is hierarchical, smog is democratic;" see Ulrich Beck, *Risikogesellschaft: Auf dem Weg in eine andere Moderne* (Frankfurt: Suhrkamp, 1986), 48.—Ed. note.

2. See Ulrich Beck, *World Risk Society* (Cambridge: Polity Press, 1999).

3. Lawrence Buell, *The Future of Environmental Criticism: Environmental Crisis and Literary Imagination* (Oxford: Blackwell, 2005), 90.

. . . . But that means: the invisible, more than that: that which as a matter of principle cannot be perceived, that which is only theoretically connected and calculated becomes . . . an unproblematic component of personal thought, perception, experience. The "experiential logic" of everyday thought is, so to speak, turned upside down. One no longer only induces general judgments from one's own experiences but instead general knowledge that is not based on any experience becomes the determining center of one's own. Chemical formulae and reactions, invisible toxins, biological circuits and causal chains must dominate vision and thought to lead to active fighting against risks. In this sense, risk awareness is not based on "second-hand experience," but on "second-hand non-experience." Even more pointedly: ultimately no one can know of risks if knowing means having consciously experienced them.[4]

As opposed to, say, epidemics of contagious diseases, with which human societies have been familiar for millennia, modernization, and globalization create risk scenarios with no known precedents in Beck's analysis. No one can forecast with certainty, for example, what the cumulative health effects might be of dozens of different toxic substances in our daily surroundings, each one at a level officially considered acceptable, but never assessed in combination. Neither is it easy, even for experts, to predict the long-term consequences of large-scale risk scenarios such as climate change or loss of biodiversity. Yet all of us, Beck points out, have come to live with a daily awareness and indeed expectation that these types of risks form part of our ordinary environment; toys of the kind I described at the beginning of this chapter, representing people in protective suits and gas masks that have come to form part of childrens' normal inventory of toys, indicate one of the earliest stages of initiation into daily life in the risk society.[5]

Obviously, this logic of "secondhand experience" and "secondhand non-experience" can also be expected fundamentally to transform modes of spatial belonging and inhabitation. Indeed, the change in experiential logic that Beck describes, in which insights and incidents from other places and facets of expert knowledge come to reshape everyday reasoning, can be understood as one form of deterritorialization. Deterritorialization, as I pointed out, involves the detachment of cultural practices from their anchoring in place and their reconfiguration in relation to other places as well as other scales of spatial experience. Some of this transformation brings about alienation, social uprooting, economic displacement, cultural unease, or psychological discomfort, but some of it may also entail welcome new forms of connectivity, new choices, and a general broadening of existential horizons. Risk

4. Beck, *Risikogesellschaft,* 96.

5. It is tempting to relate Ulrich Beck's concept of "secondhand non-experience" to Baudrillard's notion of the hyperreal, the copy without an original. But the context and import of the two concepts is ultimately different: Beck's argument is not so much about imitation as about anticipation, and his aim is to explore the ways new types of risk overturn the modes of commonsense reasoning, rather than to suggest the broader skepticism vis-a-vis the authenticity of contemporary culture that Baudrillard proposes.

scenarios, especially those that do not originate locally but at the national, regional, or global scale, contribute to deterritorialization processes as they prompt individuals and communities to reconfigure their practices of inhabitation in relation to these larger socio-spatial scales.

Such reconfigurations come in a wide variety of changes and adjustments that have been examined across vast portions of the social scientific literature on environmental impacts. Most obviously, risk perceptions can either intensify or break individuals' and communities' bonds to a local place. In the first case, the desire to protect an area from danger may deepen residents' affective attachments to it, or victims of a local hazard may pull together to eliminate it or defend themselves against its consequences by a variety of means (including, of course, the well known tendency of early environmentalism toward NIMBYism that sought to ward off risks from one's own backyard without close attention to the risk scenarios this displacement might generate in other communities). Conversely, the perception of danger can break inhabitants' bonds with a place and prompt them to move away, or stigmatize a site to such a degree that its material as well as aesthetic and cultural value decreases.[6] More indirectly, risk perceptions affect ways of inhabiting, using, or enjoying a place through transformations of daily habits or social customs. Local inhabitation is sometimes consciously and sometimes unconsciously, sometimes subtly and sometimes manifestly shaped by risk perceptions relating to a variety of concerns, including food sources or ways of cultivating land that are chosen with pressures from ecological depletion or market demands in mind; patterns of mobility that are shaped by perceptions of what people and places are dangerous or safe; distinctions that are drawn between activities and products that are "clean" or "dirty," "pure" or "polluted;" and processes and institutions of governance and surveillance that are designed to prevent or manage particular dangers.

Some of these adaptations to risk are short-lived responses to a temporary threat, as when food scares involving bovine spongiform encephalopathy in Britain or avian flu in Germany over the last decade prompted people to change their diets or seek out different food providers, or when news about severe acute respiratory syndrome in 2003 led tens of thousands of travelers to cancel travel plans to East Asia and Canada. Others involve more permanent changes in ways of life, such as the switch from trawling to more sustainable kinds of fishing in some parts of the world due

6. The notion of "stigma" was proposed by Flynn, Slovic, and Kunreuther to characterize such adverse effects of risk perceptions. In the same volume, however, Vern Walker warns that stigma, far from being a neutral term, usually suggests an irrational or objectively unfounded social process by means of which people, places, or objects are singled out for opprobrium. Introducing this term into risk theory, he warns, might well surreptitiously reintroduce old biases against lay perceptions that the field overcame in the 1980s and 1990s (see Vern Walker, "Defining and Indentifying 'Stigma'," in *Risk, Media, and Stigma: Understanding Public Challenges to Modern Science and Technology*, eds. James Flynn, Paul Slovic, and Howard Kunreuther (London: Earthscan, 2001), 354–7. Most likely for this reason, the term has not found wide usage in the field.

to fears of fish stock depletion, or changes in building, heating, or waste disposal practices in view of risks from resource exhaustion or contamination. One would expect the more permanent changes to be associated with more deep-seated cultural transformations; yet temporary crises and disasters of the kind I mentioned earlier, even if they are quickly resolved, sometimes propitiate more long-lasting conceptual and cultural changes.

A similar multivectoral causality characterizes local and translocal risk scenarios in their impact on forms of inhabitation. Strictly local hazards can at times resonate culturally and politically far beyond their limited geographical domain, according to the logic of "secondhand experience," as in the case of Love Canal, which led to community activism against toxic waste disposals in many other regions of the United States and beyond. Regional and global risk scenarios fall into at least two distinct categories that involve local perception and experience in quite different ways. In Turner et al.'s useful distinction, systemic risks such as climate change or the depletion of the ozone layer arise from systems that are global in scale,[7] so that if they undergo change anywhere, the system as a whole is affected. Cumulative risks, by contrast, derive from the planet-wide summation of local changes that end up affecting large portions or even the totality of a global environmental phenomenon or resource. Cumulative risks result either from their global distribution, as in the case of groundwater depletion or biodiversity loss, or from the magnitude of their impact on a global resource, for example in the case of agricultural soil depletion or deforestation. Systemic risks can result from human activities that are not themselves global, while cumulative risks do tend to derive from very widespread processes.[8] For the purposes of my discussion here, this distinction matters because cumulative global risk scenarios tend to be perceptible at the local scale in a way that systemic ones are not, or only with a far longer delay. As a consequence, the perceptual, cognitive, and ultimately cultural mechanisms by means of which such systemic risks are addressed can be expected to differ substantially from those pertaining to cumulative ones.

It might seem intuitively plausible that in the case of cumulative risks, locally perceptible signals of environmental change—shortages of water, erosion of arable soil—would make it easier to conceive of regional and global risks that result from the multiplication of such changes. A form of inhabitation attuned to local changes in nature, in other words, might seem to offer an obvious gateway to the understanding of larger-scale risk

7. B.L. Turner, Roger Kasperson, William Meyer, Kirstin Dow, Dominic Golding, Jeanne Kasperson, Robert Mitchell, and Samual Ratick, "Two Types of Global Environmental Change: Definitional and Spatial-Scale Issues in their Human Dimensions," *Global Environmental Change* I (1990): 14–22.

8. "Two Types," 15–6.

9. Tim Gallagher, *The Grail Bird* (Boston: Houghton Mifflin, 2005), 138.

10. The following paragraph, which refers to the structure of Heise's book *Sense of Place, Sense of Planet,* has been removed from the body of the text and reproduced here: "The texts I will analyze in chapters 5 and 6 negotiate this question of how an awareness of risks at different scales of the local, regional, and global transforms ordinary modes of language, narrative, and thought through their novelistic scenarios. DeLillo's protagonist Jack Gladney provides an example of an individual confronting a perceptible local risk scenario with imperceptible consequences for his health and life expectancy. Powers's Laura Bodey encounters a less tangible local risk that ramifies into a global one in ways that are not quite captured by the distinction between systemic and cumulative risks, as the pesticide that perhaps caused her cancer turns out to be produced by a multinational chemical corporation with branches around the globe. The protagonists of Wolf's and Wohmann's novels, situated in post-Chernobyl East and West Germany, experience the more subtle forms of deterritorialization that a large-scale regional disaster imposes on them. All of these novels are concerned with distinctively modern risk scenarios (though they have not always been interpreted in this way) and explore how cultural practices of inhabitation are transformed through risk scenarios that link the local in various ways to risks and institutions encompassing large regions or the planet as a whole. In the process, they also experiment with the different ways such risk experiences might be translated into narrative form and arrive, as I will show, at quite different conclusions," Ursula Heise, *Sense of Place, Sense of Planet* (Oxford: Oxford University Press, 2008), 154–5.—Ed. Note.

scenarios—and that is indeed, the basis for many environmentalist calls for a return to the local. Yet even in the case of cumulative risks, cultural awareness does not always follow such a direct trajectory. Tim Gallagher, in the description of his long quest for the extinct ivory-billed woodpecker that finally led to the rediscovery of one specimen in 2004, provides an interesting example of local awareness actually blocking the perception of more large-scale risk. Gallagher mentions his repeated visits to old-growth cypress forests resembling those of the southern United States in the nineteenth century, the preferred habitat of the ivory-bill, and dwells on his feelings of mourning and loss over the massive logging that eliminated most of this landscape. One of his sources, an elderly man from Louisiana, remembers asking loggers about the almost inconceivable magnitude of this forest destruction in his youth:

> When Greg was young, he talked to every old logger he could find and asked them about the old days there. Many times they would say, "You should have seen it when the big trees were here." And he would get frustrated and ask them, "Why did you cut them down if you liked them so much?" The answer was complicated. Most of the loggers were isolated, with no connection to any other group. Times were hard, the money was good, and there were thousands and thousands of trees. How could it ever end?

> The loggers seemed to have no idea that dozens, if not hundreds, of other crews were out there cutting away. Many came from other states—Mississippi, Arkansas, Texas—to take part in the harvest. And the logging continued right up till the end of the 1920s. "They were surprised when there were no more trees to cut," said Greg. "So that was that."[9]

This account is an intriguing example of a case in which detailed local knowledge apparently not only failed to lead to any awareness of the cumulative regional risk scenario but in fact prevented such awareness in the absence of more mediated information about the larger context. Beck's claim about the crucial importance of highly mediated information for the understanding of modern risk scenarios here confirms itself in a somewhat unexpected way; in this case, it is not so much that mediated information provides knowledge that cannot be obtained on the evidence of the senses as that it establishes the connection between perfectly perceptible evidence and the more elusive ecological systems to which it points.[10]

The distinction between systemic and cumulative risks not only raises the question what purchase local experience has on global ecological systems but also how such a distinction relates to social networks based on risk. Many of the nonfictional texts on individuals and places exposed to ecological and technological threats, as well as quite a few of the fictional ones, centrally rely on the assumption that the experience of risk is detrimental to social cohesion; at the same time, risk in these texts sometimes brings about a collective social impulse that leads to political action as well as to a more deeply experienced local community. As Lawrence Buell has pointed out, environmental justice discourse in particular tends both to presuppose the existence of tightly knit historical communities with long traditions, and to fashion communities that seem to have coherence only in the face of risk, such as the residents of a certain ZIP code.[11] Especially in the last two decades, the environmental justice movement has also increasingly attempted to forge international alliances between communities at risk, in the hope of creating global coalitions that might be able to resist the power of multinational corporations and, in some cases, institutions of international governance such as the World Bank or the International Monetary Fund.

From a different political perspective, the assumption that risk-sharing can generate new forms of community and political agency has led Beck to postulate the rise of what he calls a new kind of cosmopolitanism:

> Risk-sharing or a "socialization of risk" can . . . become a powerful basis for community, one which has both territorial and non-territorial aspects. . . . Post-national communities could thus be constructed and reconstructed as communities of risk. Cultural definitions of appropriate types or degrees of risk define the community, in effect, as those who share the relevant assumptions. "Risk-sharing" further involves the taking of responsibility, which again implies conventions and boundaries around a "risk community" that shares the burden. And in our high-tech world, many risk communities are potentially political communities in a new sense-because they have to live with the risks that others take. There is a basic power structure within world risk society, dividing those who produce and profit from risks and the many who are afflicted with the same risks.[12]

This argument is not in essence so different from some claims of the environmental justice movement, except that Beck is less interested in the idea of already existing communities and their confrontation with risk than in the possibility of emergent communities and political agents that he envisions as explicitly transnational. In his perspective, such risk collectives hold the promise of transcending NIMBYist tendencies, not just through temporary action coalitions but also by becoming the building blocks of a new cosmopolitan

11. Lawrence Buell, *Writing for an Endangered World: Literature, Culture and Environment n the US and Beyond* (Cambridge, MA: Harvard University Press, 2001), 41.

12. Beck, *World Risk Society*, 16.

culture, quite different from the official institutions of cosmopolitan democracy on which political scientist David Held and others have based their theories of global citizenship.[13] This risk-based cultural solidarity, which Beck takes to be more important than bureaucratic processes and institutions, ultimately harkens back to Marx and Engels's vision of an international working class:

> Without a politically strong cosmopolitan consciousness, and without corresponding institutions of global civil society and public opinion, cosmopolitan democracy remains, for all the institutional fantasy, no more than a necessary utopia. The decisive question is whether and how a consciousness of cosmopolitan solidarity can develop. The Communist Manifesto was published a hundred and fifty years ago. Today, at the beginning of a new millennium, it is time for a Cosmopolitan Manifesto. The Communist Manifesto was about class conflict. The Cosmopolitan Manifesto is about transnational–national conflict and dialogue which has to be opened up and organized .... The key idea for a Cosmopolitan Manifesto is that there is a new dialectic of global and local questions which do not fit into national politics.[14]

In his writings during the 1990s, Beck saw these questions taking shape in what he called a global "subpolitics" that unfolds both above and below the scale of the nation-state, involving actors such as nongovernmental organizations and a variety of institutions and citizens' initiatives whose role he perceives as increasingly important in the coming world risk society. In his more recent work, the idea that interdependencies arising from risks related to ecology, economy, and terrorism enforce the shaping of a cosmopolitan political order moves center stage; rather than "subpolitics," global risks in this perspective reconfigure mainstream politics itself. *Der kosmopolitisclze Blick* (*The Cosmopolitan Perspective*) explores the consequences of this shift both for politics and for sociological methodology.[15]

As my main concern here is with the cultural articulations of cosmopolitanism, I cannot delve deeply into the political models that such an approach to cosmopolitanism might generate. Yet Australian political scientist Robyn Eckersley, in an original and lucid account, has explored in far greater detail than Beck what political structures an ecological democracy that thinks beyond national boundaries might aim to build, and her approach is at least worth mentioning here. Eckersley's concept of "transnationally oriented green states" situates itself in between two models of transnational democracy:[16] Jürgen Habermas's model of supranational communities and institutions modeled on the nation-state, whose democratic structures rely on the "communitarian" principle of belongingness or membership,

13. David Held, *Democracy and the Global Order: From the Modern State to Cosmopolitan Governance* (Stanford: Stanford University Oress, 1995).

14. Beck, *World Risk Society*, 14–5.

15. Ulrich Beck, *Der kosmo-politisclze Blick oder: Krieg ist Frieden* (Frankfurt: Suhrkamp, 1986).

16. Robyn Eckersley, *The Green State: Rethinking Democracy and Sovereignty* (Cambridge, MA: MIT Press, 2004), 202.

and David Held's model of global democratic structures based on the "cosmopolitan" principle of affectedness, according to which individuals should not be ruled by norms to which they have not given their consent.[17] Eckersley pursues a model

> that remain[s] mindful of the insights of communitarians while also moving practically toward the ideals of cosmopolitans. Without knowledge of and attachment to particular persons or particular places and species, it is hard to understand how one might be moved to defend the interests of persons, places, and species in general. Local social and ecological attachments provide the basis for sympathetic solidarity with others; they are ontologically prior to any ethical and political struggle for universal environmental justice. Most environmental activists intuitively understand this and work from the premise of our unavoidable social and ecological embeddedness in particular places and communities. Yet it is impossible to arrest the growing gap between those who generate ecological problems and those who suffer the consequences, along with the increasing disembeddedness brought about by the processes of economic globalization, without developing sympathetic solidarity with environmental victims wherever they may be located. The transnationally oriented green state takes the next step and offers practical democratic procedures for ecological citizenship within and beyond the state.[18]

In her exploration of what political procedures and structures might enable such a transition from an ethic of proximity to an eco-cosmopolitan ethic (in the vocabulary I suggested in chapter 1),[19] Eckersley proposes that instead or projecting comprehensive transnational political institutions and structures,

> it is quite possible and feasible to transnationalize democracy in piecemeal, experimental, consensual, and domain-relative ways. Such an approach would enable the practical negotiation of principles in response to particular transnational problems, rather than a priori. Formal democratic space-time coordinates would still need to come into play for the proper enactment of legal norms and for the substantive enjoyment of ecological citizenship rights in trans boundary environmental domains, but these coordinates would not necessarily be the same for all domains .... Such a project would thus entail building upon, qualifying, and supplementing (rather than replacing) the principle of belongingness with the principle of affectedness.[20]

Eckersley here provides a general outline, filled in with more detail elsewhere in her discussion, of how transnational risk scenarios (as well as other ecological conflicts) might become the points of departure for new forms of democracy.

17. Eckersley, *The Green State*, 173. Eckersley principally explores Habermas's *Die postnationale Konstellation* and Held's *Democracy and the Global Order.* As is obvious from this juxtaposition, Eckersley works with a somewhat different definition of cosmopolitanism than the cultural theories I have mostly relied on in my discussion.

18. Ibid., 190.

19. In view of the argument I made in chapter 1, I would want to qualify Eckersley's insistence on the ontological priority of the local, which she here seems to equate with the specific —even as she also mentions solidarities with people or species that do not of necessity have to be local. But the more important point is Eckersley's own admission that an ethic of proximity will not suffice.

20. Eckersley, *The Green State*, 192–3.

Beck's vision of an international risk-based solidarity, by comparison, hovers on the border between the descriptive and the non-native, between a realistic account of current political conflicts and the projection of an ideal development that is itself based on more than a little utopian thinking. Yet to the extent that one is willing to concede the usefulness of utopian models, this tendency may be less problematic than Beck's simplistic assumptions about the relationship between risk and culture. From much of the risk-theoretical work that I have surveyed in this chapter, Beck takes the important insight that the experience of risk only takes on meaning within particular cultural contexts and assumptions. But from this general insight he seems to infer that shared risk automatically implies enough cultural commonality to serve as the basis for new kinds of communities. The experiences of environmental justice advocates who have actually tried to forge such alliances, however, tell a more complex story that highlights "barriers such as differences in language, culture, education, class, and access to resources."[21] Risk communities in the developing world, as Kiefer and Benjamin show, often retain vivid memories of colonialism and neocolonialism and therefore sometimes react with wariness or suspicion to the overtures of environmental groups in the developed world. At the same time, differences in basic cultural habits such as how to advance a conversation, what kinds of knowledge to rely on, or how to act politically exacerbate the difficulties in creating collective action coalitions, let alone more long-lasting transnational communities of risk.[22] Shared risk, in other words, remains only a first stepping-stone, so long as it is not accompanied by a more comprehensive cultural literacy that allows the members of one community to grasp what sociocultural significance the risk scenario has for the members of another.[23]

Beck's vision of a cosmopolitan consciousness and an alternative global culture that might arise from the politics of shared risk, then, needs to be complemented by the more acute sense of sociocultural differences that emerge in stark relief from the fieldwork of environmental justice activists. Yet it is also true that the environmental justice movement has often focused primarily on the urgencies of political action, mobilization, and coalition-building, with no in-depth attention to the shaping influence of different cultural frameworks of understanding. While the movement has sometimes drawn on the insights of feminist, postcolonial, and critical race theory, it has done so mostly by reconfirming central assumptions of these bodies of theory rather than showing how

21. Chris Kiefer and Medea Benjamin, "Solidarity with the Third World: Building an International Environmental Justice Movement," in *Toxic Struggles: the Theory and Practice of Environmental Justice*, ed. Richard Hifrichter (Philadelphia: New Society, 1993), 233.

22. Kiefer and Benjamin, "Solidarity," 234–5.

23. For empirical studies of cross-cultural risk perceptions, see *Cross-Cultural Risk Perception: A Survey of Empirical Studies* ed. Ortwin Renn and Bernd Rohrmann (Dordrecht, NL: Kluwer, 2000).

Heise

the context of communities exposed to ecological, economic, and technological endangerment might transform some of these foundations. As environmental justice scholar T. V. Reed has argued, "the environmental justice movement, as currently constituted, has often worked with a rather thin sense of culture and has not utilized cultural workers as much as it might."[24]

Rather than a sophisticated theoretical framework for approaching questions of cross-cultural understanding and misunderstanding in an ecological context, the accounts of environmental justice fieldwork offer a rich inventory on which such a theory needs to draw in order to elaborate Beck's approach to the relationship of risk and the emergence of cosmopolitan forms of solidarity. By contrast, the attempts of anthropologists, sociologists, philosophers, and literary critics to re-envision cosmopolitanism as an effort at cross-cultural literacy do offer such a more nuanced account. These recuperations of cosmopolitanism consciously situate themselves in the unequal political and economic playing fields created by various types of globalization, though they do not, for the most part, concern themselves either with the nonhuman world or the global environmental risk scenarios I have been chiefly concerned with here. As I proposed earlier, an environmentally inflected cosmopolitanism needs to combine sustained familiarity and fluency in more than one culture with a systemic understanding of global ecology that goes beyond environmentalist clichés regarding universal connectedness and the pastoral understanding of ecology that informed earlier kinds of modern environmentalist thinking. The merit of environmental justice activism along with Beck's more sweeping vision of new forms of solidarity emerging out of global risk scenarios is their analysis of how such an eco-cosmopolitanism might link experiences of local endangerment to a sense of planet that encompasses both human and nonhuman worlds.

24. T. V. Reed, "Toward an Environmental Justice Ecocriticism," in *The Environmental Justice Reader*, ed. Joni Adamson, Mei Mei Evans and Rachel Stein (Tucson: University of Arizona Press, 2002), 153.

Fig. 24.1 Amphibious Architecture installation on East River (courtesy of The Living).

Amphibious Architecture
The Living and Natalie Jeremijenko

Architect:
The Living (David Benjamin and Soo-in Yang) with xDesign Environmental Health Clinic (Natalie Jeremijenko)

Location: East River, New York

Date: 2009

Client:
The Architecture League of New York

Exhibition:
Toward the Sentient City, The Urban Center, NY, 2009, curated by Mark Shepard.

Sentient City: Ubiquitous Computing, Architecture and the Future of urban space, Ed. Mark Shepard (Cambridge, MA: MIT Press, 2011).

"[W]hen people decide to ask a question about their environment through our SMS system the river becomes a contact on their phone. . . . And when people start talking in a smart way to objects and public places in the city, all kinds of new things become possible."[1]

The goal of Amphibious Architecture, an aquatic installation developed by David Benjamin and Soo-in Yang (The Living) and Natalie Jeremijenko (xDesign Environmental Health Clinic) for the Architectural League of New York's 2009 exhibition, *Toward the Sentient City*, is communication among multiple urban species; the approach combines a DIY approach to creating new networked systems and a playful take on urban performance. This installation introduced floating networks of chemical and motion sensors, each connected to an SMS interface, into New York's East River. The network contains a grid of twenty-five tubular components with a submerged "sensory" assemblage (sonar for detecting fish presence; chemical sensors for assessing levels of dissolved oxygen, nitrates, and the pH of the water; accelerometer for capting hydrodynamic forces). Water data was transmitted to the installation's buoyant LED-clad devices (photovoltaic/battery pack; stack of LED lighting disks) and communicated to the viewer as colored lighting patters and text messages. As submerged sensors monitor aquatic conditions, information was relayed in real-time to LED light displays that glowed in hues ranging from blues and purples to hot pink and reds, adjusting to the changing water data captured by the submerged sensors.

Lourie Harrison

Fig. 24.2 Amphibious Architecture installation on East
River (courtesy of The Living).

Fig. 24.3 Site plan on East
River (courtesy of The Living).

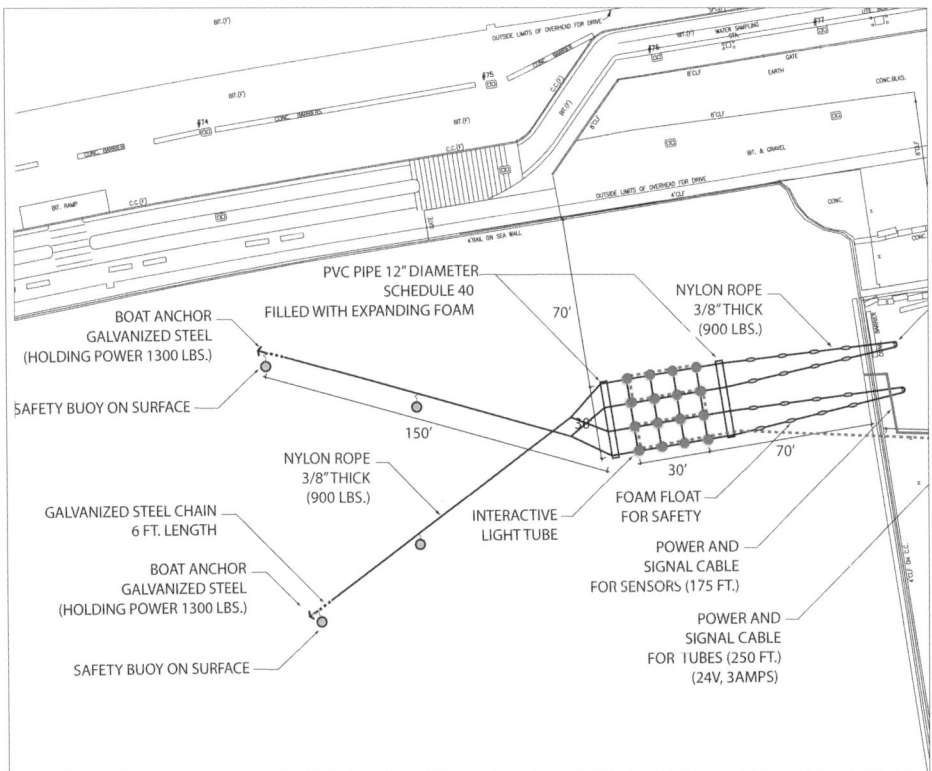

Amphibious Architecture

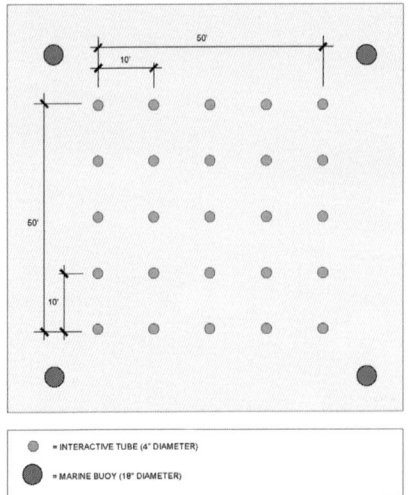

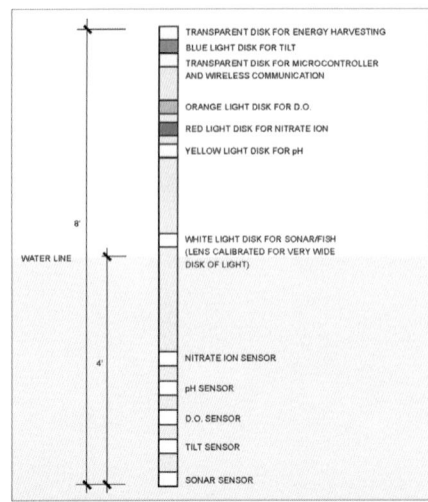

Fig. 24.4 Interactive Tube network (courtesy of The Living).

This information was also transmitted through an SMS interface that allowed visitors to both receive real-time information about the river and "text-message the fish;" wireless communication making a step toward "establishing a two-way interface between environments of land and water."[2] On this rudimentary level, Jeremijenko and The Living seek to democratize environmental information that is normally the precinct of experts regulating urban coasts and waterways. Amphibious Architecture synthesizes DIY experimentation and remote sensing into a form of urban ecological activism, one animated by its inclination towards a trans-species urbanism.

According to the Amphibious Architecture website, "instead of treating the rivers with a 'do-not-disturb' approach, the project encourages curiosity and engagement."[3] Curiosity and engagement are neither scientific nor objectively verifiable, yet these terms reiterate the performative goals of the riverfront installation: "will the public interact with fish?; will the signaling system interact with fish?; and will the public interact with water as an animate urban surface?" Jeremijenko expands the concept of "public" that Amphibious Architecture is intended to address: "Fundamentally, the interaction was intended for a local audience: human, piscine, avian and one or two beavers and turtles": human and nonhumans comprise its "local" publics.[4] This approach responds to Jennifer Wolch's request for more experimental research in the service of trans-species urbanism:

> In thinking prospectively about morality, animals and urban places, my own work has sought to reconceptualize the ways in which the human-animal divide plays out in terms of ethical practices for city planning and living. A major consideration here is animal subjectivity; once we abandon a strict human–animal boundary with human subjects on one side and animal objects on the other, we seem to be obligated to figure them into our ethical consideration and everyday practice.[5]

Lourie Harrison

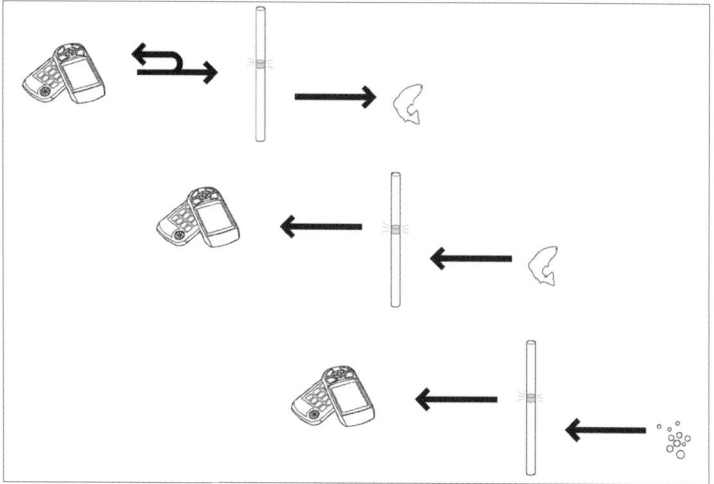

Fig. 24.5 Diagram of fish interaction (courtesy of The Living).

Designing interfaces that explore animal subjectivity within urban space poses a challenge that both Jeremijenko and The Living approach using interactive design, or in Jeremijenko's terms, "an architecture of reciprocity." Sensors linked to computing networks allow animals to register their "responses" to human environments in human terms. For example, the electronic perches of Jeremijenko's 2005 MassMOCA installation, *Becoming Animal*, enabled birds to trigger human sound-tracks thereby opening the possibility that animals might intentionally communicate with humans: "these interfaces resemble the experiments in operant conditioning, a technique that works equally well on humans as it does on animal models."[6] The performative aspect of this interface, like that of Amphibious Architecture, deploys ubiquitous computing to create a communication network between humans and fish, albeit one that relies on human interpretation.

Amphibious Architecture builds on both Jeremijenko's 2006 Glow Fish Interface, a series of buoys in the Hudson River that lit in response to fish movement underwater, and The Living's 2006 River Glow, a floating network of vibrant illuminated water quality sensors. Both of these water-based works deployed low resolution information systems—lights are on or off—to visualize data generated by underwater conditions. The low resolution of information has both a political and practical implication in these works. For The Living, the low resolution environmental display of River Glow reflected its facture from commonly available consumer technologies: fiber optic strands, solar-harvesting cells and a rewired low cost pH sensor to detect changes in water quality. The installation was autonomous in terms of its energetic intake and output: thin film photovoltaics, which had been "hacked" to support the LED display of data from water quality sensors, produced energy locally. "The work from this method is raw. It is quick and rough. It explores unknown territory,"

Amphibious Architecture

Fig. 24.6 SMS interface for Amphibious Architecture: tracking fish presence (courtesy of The Living).

describes Benjamin, "you will find amateurs hunched over the workbench."[7] The Living's workbook *Life Size* offers a step-by-step manual for the DIY-er, specifying steps, materials, costs and system diagram so that anyone can reproduce this installation.[8]

"Everything is an experiment; everyone is an experimenter," Jeremijenko shares the DIY sensibility of The Living.[9] But in her installation Glow Fish, she hoped to widen the number of participants in the work by incorporating a provocative script: the buoy illuminating in response to fish presence prompts human visitors to sprinkle chelating agents into the river, a symbolic act of detoxification of New York City's waters. The specific toxins cited are psychotropic drug residues flushed into city plumbing by millions of anxious or depressed urban dwellers; these have made their way into the river with storm water overflow and aging infrastructure and produce slightly drugged fish.[10] The scientific veracity of the experiment is less important than Glow Fish's capacity to incite imaginative extrapolations regarding the long-term ecological effects of collective habits and behaviors. Recalling the close ties between posthumanism and performance theory established in 1977 by Ihab Hassan,[11] the performative approach of Glow Fish invokes terms we find in posthuman discourse: situated contexts, embodied information, and human–nonhuman interaction. This performative dimension challenges disciplinary boundaries of scientific experimentation, an aspect present in many of Jeremijenko's works:

> What I see and in many senses try to instantiate in particular examples is the capacity to change the structure of participation: who is producing the data, who is interpreting that data, and who can do something with that data. So in a participatory democracy that means restructuring participation from the production of scientific or authoritative data and knowledge to this structured participation.[12]

Lourie Harrison

"Structured participation," like "citizen science," promotes public action in the collection of environmental data by volunteers, many without specific scientific training. Both xDesign and The Living suggest that the gathering and interpretation of environmental data can be productively situated in a public sphere. Amphibious Architecture builds on both the politics of producing information on the environment and the activist DIY stance towards designing human/non-human interfaces. Rather than adopt the given view of water as a decorative but conceptually inert component of the urban landscape, the project animated water as an urban network or a non-human assemblage in Latour's terminology, its actors made visible by simple electronics and low resolution displays. In the Science Technology Studies perspective, the assemblage displaces humans as the sole producers of knowledge, and agency emerges through the performance of the assemblage. Agency is not considered to be a property of things, persons, or networks, but rather is an action; it is performed. "Interpretations do not inform as much as they perform," suggests Latour in his cultural analysis of scientific practice, *Laboratory Life*.[13]

In this sense, Amphibious Architecture is grounded in a posthuman performative approach addressing multiple species. The project's website offers a tutorial on procedures for SMSing the fish as a set of diagrams, which, with a deadpan humor, suggest that communication with fish and with water is just an arrow away. That such communication is entirely mediated by human technology is further underscored by Jeremijenko's suite of Amphibious Architecture "animal business cards." The idea of SMSing fish, or naming fish as collaborators, may be a joke but one which performs in ways that outlasts its punch line—if we appreciate the project's fundamental questioning of architecture's anthropocentism. This approach personalizes environmental data, inscribing its gatherers and

Fig. 24.7 SMS interface (courtesy of The Living).

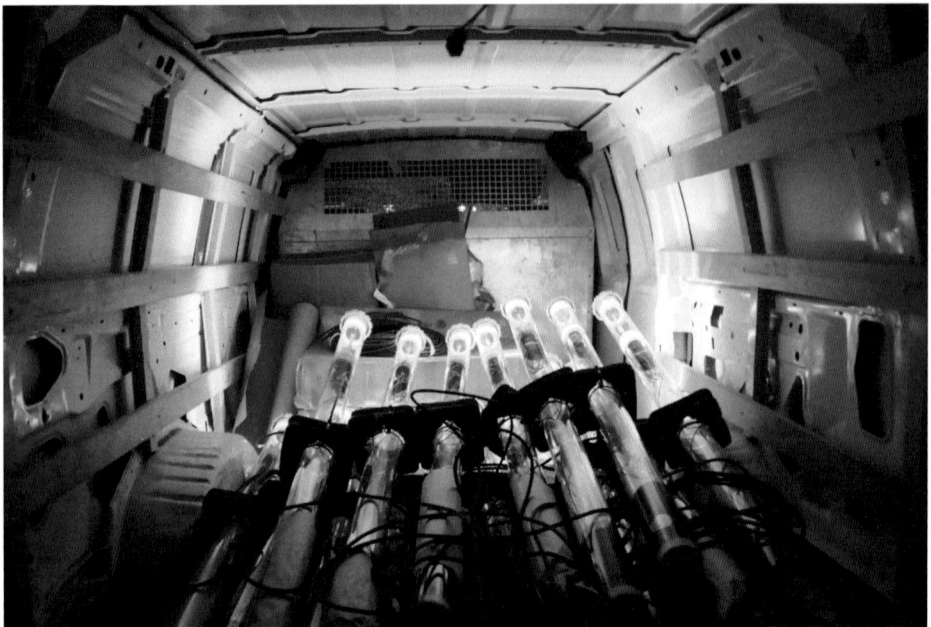

Fig. 24.8 Tubular network in transport to East River (courtesy of The Living).

interpreters into the real-time experience of the site. The meeting of living matter with reasoned hypotheses produces an assemblage that can not be so easily distanced from its object of study. Amphibious Architecture played on the comic potential of humanity having a "balanced" relationship to the environment. The installation offered what might be considered in filmic terms to be an "outtake" of the scientific experiment, an experiment not necessarily gone awry but one that prompts the participation of a broad, non-expert audience, thereby staging the conditions for new approaches to urban ecology.

In contravening the conservationist approach to the environment (that it is best left untouched by humans and remain the exclusive province of scientific experts), Amphibious Architecture integrates piscine, human and media within an urban experiment to visualize a posthuman ecology as a continuum of humans, non-humans, and technology. The hybrid subjects imagined by The Living and Jeremijenko, are animal-technological assemblies; the installation reflecting the ontological and ethical status of animals and plants as hybrid subjects. The political stakes of such a performative approach are worth noting:

> We have just begun to think about the moral choices we make in building and living in cities, and what they mean for animals. . . . For example, federal law mandates water-quality standards for all waterways, but these standards are designed for humans; what is tolerable for humans is not necessarily tolerable for, say, frogs. Does this mean that the US EPA needs amphibian water-quality standards for urban watersheds? The answer is probably yes—and this implies the need for an astonishing range of research and, ultimately, urban regulation.[14]

Lourie Harrison

The installation originally proposed to the Architectural League was somewhat more provocative by virtue of its paired locations: "an East River location in Lower Manhattan that is public and high profile in New York City's role as a global center of tourism and commerce, and a Bronx River location in the South Central Bronx that is much lower profile, perhaps unknown and for the most part certainly ignored, because it falls outside of typical reaches of New York's affluent arts, technology, media and finance communities."[15] This multi-site strategy would begin to provide the scale and scope of environmental data necessary to analyze the river's ecological value, and remains a goal for subsequent iterations of this provocative installations and its environmental activism.

How Amphibious Architecture expanded the category of research capable of revising urban regulation remains a question. There is a distinction between the installation's effectiveness at communicating environmental data, its power as a trans-species performance, and its aesthetization of the river surface. The installation retained its autonomy in some respects due to the limited content conveyed to users, both visually and by SMS. Amphibious Architecture's LED lights glinting off of the night-time river produced a beautiful image, but risked contributing to a "data smog" of environmental information. Instead it sought to demonstrate how rivers participate in a dialogue about information on public space, as described by media theorist Benjamin Bratton:

> Part of the progressive narrative for pervasive computation and ecological governance is of a world in which every square inch is in some way constantly outpouring infinitely communicable information about itself, and that this would overwhelm inherited layers of expert systems—certain people in certain circumstances that collect data from certain instrumental means—enabling the world to declare itself as a functionally open "data continent." From this new basic infrastructure a new kind of political institutionality could emerge.[16]

NOTES:

1. David Benjamin quoted in Alice Vincent, "Ahoy Anchovy," *Wired* (accessed 8/26/2012).

2. The Living, www.thelivingnewyork.com/amphibiousarchitecture.htm (accessed 3/1/2012)

3. Nathalie Jeremijenko and David Benjamin and Soo-in Yang, "Case Study: Amphibious Architecture," *Sentient City* (Cambridge, MA: MIT Press, 2010) and Jordan Gieger, "The Living: surface tensions," *AD Territory* (2010): 60–65.

4. Natalie Jeremijenko and Benjamin Bratton, "Suspicious Images, Latent Interfaces," *Situated Technologies* 3 (New York: The Architectural League of New York, 2008): 21.

5. Jennifer Wolch, "Anima Urbis," *Progress in Human Geography* 26 (2002): 734.

6. Natalie Jeremijenko, www.nyu.edu/projects/xdesign/ooz/ (accessed 3/12/2012).

7. David Benjamin, "Open," *Matter,* ed. Gail Borden and Michael Meredith (New York: Routledge, 2012), 143–53.

8. David Benjamin and Soo-in Yang, *Life Size* (Vol. I), (New York: The Graduate School of Architecture, Planning and Preservation, Columbia University, 2006), 63–76.

9. Natalie Jeremijenko, www.nyu.edu/projects/xdesign/ooz/ (accessed 3/12/2012).

10. Kevin Berger, "The Artist as Mad Scientist," *The Best Technology Writing*, Ed. Steven Levy, (Ann Arbor, MI: University of Michigan Press, 2007),

11. Ihab Hassan, "Prometheus as Performer: Toward a Posthuman Culture?" *Georgia Review* 31 (1977): 830–50.

12. Jeremijenko, "Suspicious Images, Latent Interfaces," 20.

13. Bruno Latour and Steve Wolgar, *Laboratory Life* (Princeton: Princeton University Press, 1986), 285.

14. Wolch, "Anima Urbis," 734.

15. Living Architecture Lab, Amphibious Architecture Proposal for The Architectural League of New York .

16. Bratton, "Suspicious Images, Latent Interfaces," 13.

Oyster-tecture
SCAPE

Fig. 25.1 Rendering of the Oyster-tecture reef park at Bay Ridge Flats (courtesy of SCAPE).

Landscape Architect:
SCAPE, Kate Orff.

Date: 2010–11

Pilot Project date: 2011–present

Pilot location:
Brooklyn Marine Terminal.

Exhibition:
Rising Currents, invited exhibition and workshop at the Museum of Modern Art, New York.

Exhibition Catalogue:
Rising Currents: Projects for New York's Waterfront. ed. Michael Oppenheimer, Barry Bergdoll and Judith Rodin. New York: Museum of Modern Art, 2011

SCAPE's Oyster-tecture is on one level a visionary project responding to the threat posed by rising sea levels to American coastal cities. Developed as part of MoMA's *Rising Currents* exhibition, Oyster-tecture proposes a site-specific implementation of a water filtration system for Brooklyn's notoriously polluted industrial waterfront: an oyster hatchery and ecological park at the Gowanus interior that over time will generate a wave-attenuating reef out in the Gowanus Bay. Yet the context addressed by the project is more expansive than its proposed site (which included the Bay Ridge flats, the Gowanus Canal, and Governor's Island), or even the multiple watersheds that drain into this industrial waterfront. The work is best understood when placed in dialogue with the concept of *cosmopolitan ecologies* that SCAPE's founder, Kate Orff, outlined in her provocative essay on the remediation of Jamaica Bay for the National Park Service's vision for Gateway National Recreation Area.

> Viewing civilization and nature as one system—one that exists at local, global and more significantly now at metropolitan scales of thinking—we have come full circle to a fully cosmopolitan ecology. Crucial within this paradigm is the understanding that all citizens share in the production of urbanity, in its making and remaking.[1]

Orff's reference to cosmopolitan ecologies draws attention to the urban matrix into which ecological strategies could (and should) be introduced. Yet the implications of the term *cosmopolitanism* and its dialogue with Ursula Heise's discussion of *eco-cosmopolitanism* significantly expand the territory engaged by Oyster-tecture.

x

x

Lourie Harrison

Fig. 25.2 Rendering of Oyster-tecture reef living (courtesy of SCAPE).

Fig. 25.3 Oyster-tecture reef map (courtesy of SCAPE).

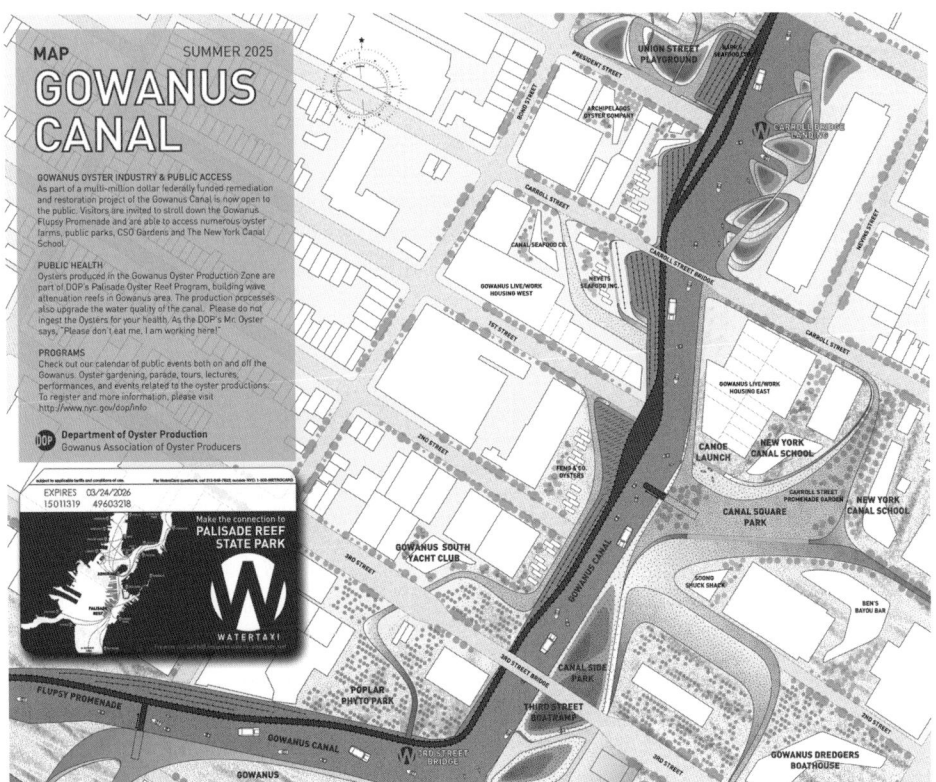

The cosmopolitanism of SCAPE's marine landscape intervention can therefore engage the broader issues of environmental regulation and the politics of urban life framed in this anthology by Matthew Gandy and Jennifer Wolch. *Cosmopolitanism* refers to the making of groups or collectives that extend beyond the binaries of local and national; the term critiques the naturalization of both attachments to nation, which are in reality constructed by complex cultural practices, and to place-based ideals, which have grounded American environmentalist thought. For the sociologist Ulrich Beck, the cosmopolitan emerges as a transnational form of solidarity based on the shared exposure to risk, in particular to that of environmental catastrophe. Heise further qualifies this term:

> While cosmopolitanism has generally been understood as an alternative to nationally based forms of identity, it confronts more local attachments in the case of environmentalism in the United States, which have been articulated by means of such concepts as "dwelling," "rehabilitation," "bioregionalism," and "erotics of place," or a "land ethic." Without denying that under certain circumstances such affirmations of local ties can play an important role in environmentalist struggles, I argue that ecologically oriented thinking has yet to come to terms with one of the central insights of current theories of globalization, that the increasing connectedness of societies around the globe entails the emergence of new forms of culture that are no longer anchored in place.[2]

Heise builds on this idea by introducing the term *eco-cosmopolitanism*, with its implications of environmental world citizenship and its address of the embedded nature of local and ecological systems within global

Lourie Harrison

networks. An eco-cosmopolitan approach addresses a variety of actors within the biosphere, proposing a planetary community—if only imagined today—of humans and nonhumans. The point of an eco-cosmopolitan critical project would be to go beyond the aforementioned "ethics of proximity" to understand by what means individuals and groups in specific cultural contexts act concretely to frame an ecological consciousness of the global biosphere, or by what means they might be enabled to do so.[3] In emphasizing the making concrete of one's relationship to the biosphere, Heise suggests that design is well positioned to further the eco-cosmopolitan project by constructing frameworks that help bridge the concrete individual experience and the abstract idea of the biosphere. Orff's concept of cosmopolitan ecologies is similar, implicating a collective bound by an ecological mandate to address the effects of globalization. The eco-cosmopolitan approach suggests that we remain suspect of the notion of "natural" ties to a place and to the idea that connections are "spontaneously" produced during the course of inhabitation, and instead examine how these ties are produced.

Oyster-tecture creates processes and systems that could generate connectivity by transforming the hard edges of a metropolitan harbor into an aqueous ecological and cultural infrastructure. Orff describes the project as less of a landscape design and more of a process for generating new cultural and environmental narratives. In Oyster-tecture, water—remediated by biological organisms such as the hardy Eastern oyster and the ribbed mussel—becomes the critical element in a massive restoration of the New York coast. This statewide vision is built up from a series of smaller scale, site-specific interventions, starting with the Gowanus Canal, a Superfund site. In what may seem like a perverse proposition by SCAPE—that the extremely polluted waters of the Gowanus Bay have the makings of a productive oyster hatchery—lies a pragmatic and phased proposal that introduces aquatic life to the canal once the ongoing Superfund cleanup of the heavy metals and toxins is complete. Oysters filter excess nutrients, such as nitrogen and phosphorous, that are also present in the canal and harbor waters due to the region's combined sewer outfalls; this is an ongoing infrastructural problem that introduces wastewater into the harbor with every stormwater surge. SCAPE's proposal incorporates this type of systemic environmental problem into Oyster-tecture's appraisal of both the oyster's mighty nutrient filtering capacity—fifty gallons of water per day per oyster—and its cultural value within the extensive history of oyster husbandry in nineteenth-century New York. Moreover, oysters were a fundamental part of New York City's economy and culinary culture and also served a major role in the harbor's ecology. The re-establishment of the oyster on the urban waterfront places Oyster-tecture in dialogue with models of trans-species urbanization, such as that framed by Jennifer Wolch. She proposes the zoöpolis, considering animals within the "urban moral landscape" and recognizing "that both people and animals are embedded in social relations and networks with others (both human and non-human) upon which their social welfare depends."[4]

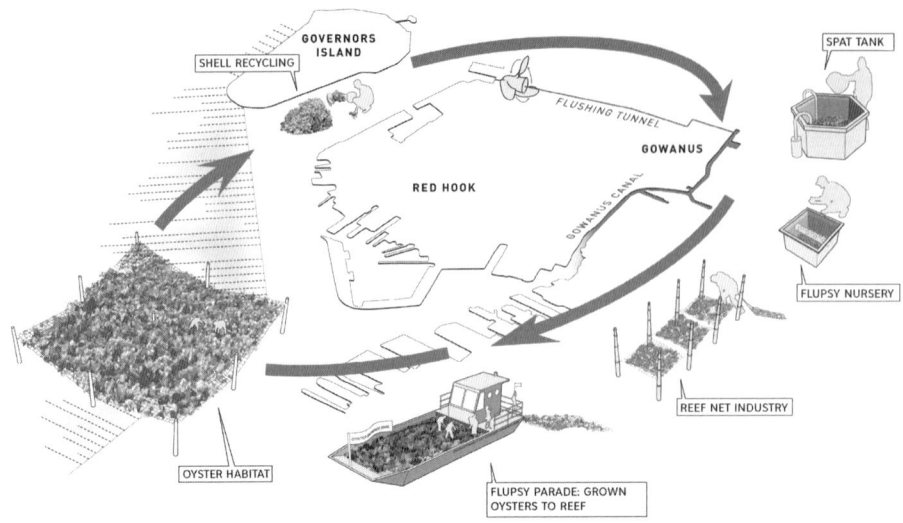

Fig. 25.5 Diagram of Oyster-tecture lifecycle (courtesy of SCAPE).

Understanding this network of interdependency as a new urban paradigm, SCAPE proposes a marine-animal infrastructure to remediate water quality and the effects of rising sea levels. The phased process of oyster growth ties to a gradual process of community-based development along the remediated canal. The proposal animates the canal edge with a string of FLUPSY (floating upwelling system) rafts for the growth of spats (oysters in the larval stage) that also provide water access for people. The spats are seeded out in the shallow waters of the Bay Ridge flats onto an armature, which becomes transformed over time into an aquatic park with a mosaic of intertidal zones with mussel growth, subtidal areas with young oysters, and sandy, grassy shoals for people and birds. A fuzzy rope-shellfish assemblage becomes the building material for a new reef: oyster-seeded patches are subsequently reattached to the grid of piles that provides the initial armature for a reef to be created south of Governors Island. While Oyster-tecture's shellfish-centric dimension might raise concerns, especially in the context of a cosmopolitan approach that explicitly values the productive friction of competing views (and species), SCAPE proposes a phased system in which keystone species—oysters along with mussels and eelgrass—can anchor a reef ecosystem. Attracting a full spectrum of species, the reef evolves to become a wave-attenuating structure that protects the coast from its rising waters.

Emphasizing that "there is a latent, forgotten connection to the water that could be rebuilt as part of urban culture,"[5] SCAPE integrates water as an overlooked component of urban cultural life. Reef-development becomes community development to create what Orff calls a new "reef culture:" programs that extend from the Gowanus Canal to Governors Island in an aquatic network that functions both as ecological sanctuary and public recreation space. This new type of aquatic park establishes a cultural and culinary experience founded on oyster husbandry and

Lourie Harrison

recalls the oyster's historical role in New York harbor. Reef culture also unfolds the complex system of oyster farming as an educational and recreational experience. SCAPE's renderings underscore this intertwined set of programs: a long section places water taxi stations around oyster hatcheries, diving stations, a "canal school," and new Gowanus oyster bars. Yet one might press for a more cosmopolitan representation of the varied social and cultural practices—including Brooklyn's diverse street cultures or programs embracing its Hispanic, Chinese, and Indian communities, for example—to demonstrate the project's integration of urban politics, which must also be considered a component of a cosmopolitan ecology. As Matthew Gandy demonstrates in *Concrete and Clay*, Brooklyn's grassroots environmental activism during the 1990s paved the way for the area's environmental benefits programs which facilitated public participation in environmental policy; these in turn contribute to a contemporary understanding that "scientific knowledge acquired through actual participation becomes a part of a people's culture, no longer an alien product to be accepted as an article of faith."[6] Oyster-tecture's reef culture works towards a cosmopolitan consciousness by intertwining public programs with those led by experts: "we worked with the help of a range of scientists from NY/NJ Baykeeper, enthusiasts from the Gowanus Dredgers, the New York Harbor School, and smaller independent groups."[7]

Perhaps the most palpable demonstration of eco-cosmopolitanism's goal of bridging global ecological perspectives with local implementation (i.e. making "concrete"), SCAPE has developed Oyster-tecture from a visionary 2010 exhibition into a schematic design for a current pilot project in the Brooklyn Marine Terminal at Sunset Park's 30th Street Pier. And what began in Orff's terms as a "self-initiated 'design development'

Fig. 25.6 Oyster-tecture model, Museum of Modern Art, New York (courtesy of SCAPE).

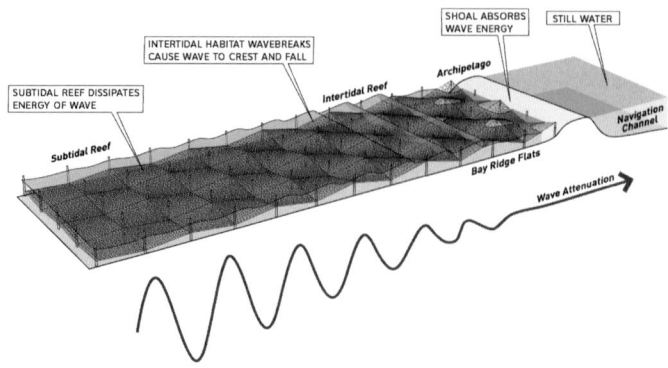

Inside the diagram, the following labels appear:
SUBTIDAL REEF DISSIPATES ENERGY OF WAVE
INTERTIDAL HABITAT WAVEBREAKS CAUSE WAVE TO CREST AND FALL
SHOAL ABSORBS WAVE ENERGY
STILL WATER
Archipelago
Intertidal Reef
Navigation Channel
Subtidal Reef
Bay Ridge Flats
Wave Attenuation

Fig. 25.7 Wave-attenuation diagram (courtesy of SCAPE).

phase to carry this project through in non-conventional ways," led to SCAPE's pilot project at the SIMS Metal Management Municipal Recycling industrial waterfront, a site for processing a portion of the metal, glass and plastic collected by the New York City Department of Sanitation.[8] Conceived to complement SIMS' expanding plastics processing facilities, SCAPE's pilot project addresses a one hundred foot portion of the pier designated for SIMS's barge mooring and its adjacent bulkhead. It is important to stress that this is a working industrial site, for which SCAPE proposes a range of marine habitat enhancing techniques that can coexist with SIMS's industrial waterfront activity.

The pilot project extends the collaborative network developed in Oyster-tecture to implement a biologically remediative strategy at the 30th Street Pier. Working with the Israeli marine environmental consulting firm SeaArc, SCAPE is exploring ways to retrofit the existing pier infrastructure with components made from SeaArc's ECOncrete, a concrete matrix hospitable to species recruitment. The goal of the materials research is to create "habitat hubs" for marine ecosystems without interfering with working industrial piers. Material research with SeaArc has also led SCAPE to a number of recycled polyethylene products that can provide habitats for mussels, barnacles, and sponges, yet accommodate SIMS' industrial requirements as well as the need for periodic pier inspections.[9] Both of these material strategies address a multi-species eco-system, broadening what was initially conceived as a shellfish-centric project. The fuzzy rope concept presented in Oyster-tecture has similarly expanded in its applications during the research for this pilot project: frayed polyethylene rope proves successful for mussel cultivation, and with this in mind, the pilot project integrates mussels (which also have a significant filtering capacity and are better able to survive in contaminated water) into the Brooklyn Marine Terminal pilot. SCAPE proposes a range of fuzzy-rope attachments, from wrapped wharf piles to hanging networks of rope providing habitats for mussels, algae, and barnacles. Humans, too, are added to this mix in SCAPE's vision of a "public fuzzy rope knitting project," among educational programs planned for the site.[10] Another important actor in this network is SIMS itself. SCAPE integrates the existing usage patterns of an active industrial waterfront site into its understanding of an ecological program.

Lourie Harrison

Treating SIMS as a part of the ecology, SCAPE's pilot project provides strategies by which SIMS' industrial activity can contribute to the site's remediation. For example, the pilot proposes using recycled glass as the substrate for its intertidal pools, attracting diverse species while advertising SIMS recycling.

This pilot project thus harbors large environmental implications: ecosystem revitalization need not be confined to post-industrial sites, such as the Hegewisch marsh of the Ford Calumet Environmental Center. Instead, SCAPE's project extends biological remediation to an active industrial site, offering a precedent for ways to integrate remediation in sites that are not designated preserves. This approach embodies a cosmopolitan understanding of the environment as a matrix of interconnected actors, avoiding a priori exclusion by type. SCAPE's "shellfish map," a collaboration with the NY/NJ Baykeeper organization, begins to synthesize information on ongoing shellfish restoration projects yet seems likely to locate many new opportunities for coastal remediation.

The eco-cosmopolitan aspect of this design occurs on multiple levels if we trace the manner in which Oyster-tecture combines ecological, cultural and industrial forces in proposing an extensive biological network for the New York harbor. Oyster-tecture proposes a local and small-scale remediative process that addresses climate change biologically rather than relying on large scale (and capital-intensive) initiatives. In a similar vein, the community-based development triggered by its proposed oyster hatchery and "reef culture," weaves an ecological awareness into the everyday rhythms of the city. The SIMS pilot project envisions a further integration of environmental remediation into an existing industrial fabric. The benefits of such small-scale environmental actions are incremental yet the cumulative power of this "Oyster-tecture process"—from polemical vision to pilot projects to diverse partnerships—stages local implementation in the framework of community-based actions, which may in fact provide the most durable means to engage an "urbannature" as a critical product of our Anthropocene period.

NOTES:
1. Kate Orff, "Cosmopolitan Ecologies," in GATEWAY: Visions for an Urban National Park (New York: Princeton Architectural Press, 2011), 71.
2. Ursula Heise, Sense of Place, Sense of Planet: the Environmental Imagination of the Global (New York: Oxford University Press, 2008), 10.
3. Heise, Sense of Place, 62.
4. Jennifer Wolch, "Zoöpolis," in Animal Geographies, Ed. Jennifer Wolch and Jody Emel (London: Verso Press, 1998).
5. Kate Orff, "Q&A," in Rising Currents: Projects for New York''s Waterfront (New York: Museum of Modern Art, 2011), 98.
6. Matthew Gandy, Concrete and Clay (Cambridge, MA: MIT Press, 2003), 219.
7. Kate Orff, "Interview," Harvard Design Magazine 33, (Fall/Winter 2010–11): 22.
8. Orff, "Interview," 22. Pilot project information courtesy of SCAPE (discussion with Gena Wirth on 3/7/2012).
9. The species anticipated in the SeaArc habitat hubs include blue mussel, Eastern Oyster, Bay Barnacle, Bugula simplex, Hard Tube Worm, Red Beard Sponge and Knotted thread hydroid. Pilot project information courtesy of SCAPE (3/8/2012).
10. Pilot project information from discussion with SCAPE's Gina Wirth on 3/7/2012).

Fig. 26.1 Third floor, professor's deck, Ruin Academy (courtesy of M. Casagrande).

Ruin Academy
Casagrande Lab

Architect:
Marco Casagrande and C-Lab

Site: Taipei, Taiwan

Date: 2010–present

Size:
500 square meters
Five stories (20 m x 5m)

Program:
Educational

Conceptualized and constructed by the Finnish architect Marco Casagrande and his collaborators in Casagrande Lab (C-Lab), the Ruin Academy in Taipei is an independent architectural research institution and an unusual public space for cross-disciplinary exchanges. Its title is descriptive of its lodging an institution within an abandoned shell of a building and is also a metaphor for the desired ruin of academia's fortified mentality. Gathering many disciplines around the ecological needs of the rapidly changing city of Taipei, Ruin Academy advances a projective idea of the ruin as the anticipated demise of hermetic thinking. The urban ruin recalls the marginal spaces of Gilles Clément's *third landscape*, spaces that can harbor biological diversity and political value because of a marginal position outside of the city's financial regime. C-Lab's design for Ruin Academy builds on the materiality and metaphor of a garden situated at the margins of the city. This case study will examine several of C-Lab's key terms: *anarchist gardener*, *urban compost*, and the *third-generation city*, to frame Ruin Academy's posthuman design and ecological sensibility within the environmental politics delineated by Erik Swyngedouw and Gilles Clément.

Anarchist Gardener
A term devised to align the anarchist's revolutionary urgency with the gardener's ethos of careful cultivation, the anarchist gardener has multiple figurations in C-Lab's work. It is the name of the Ruin

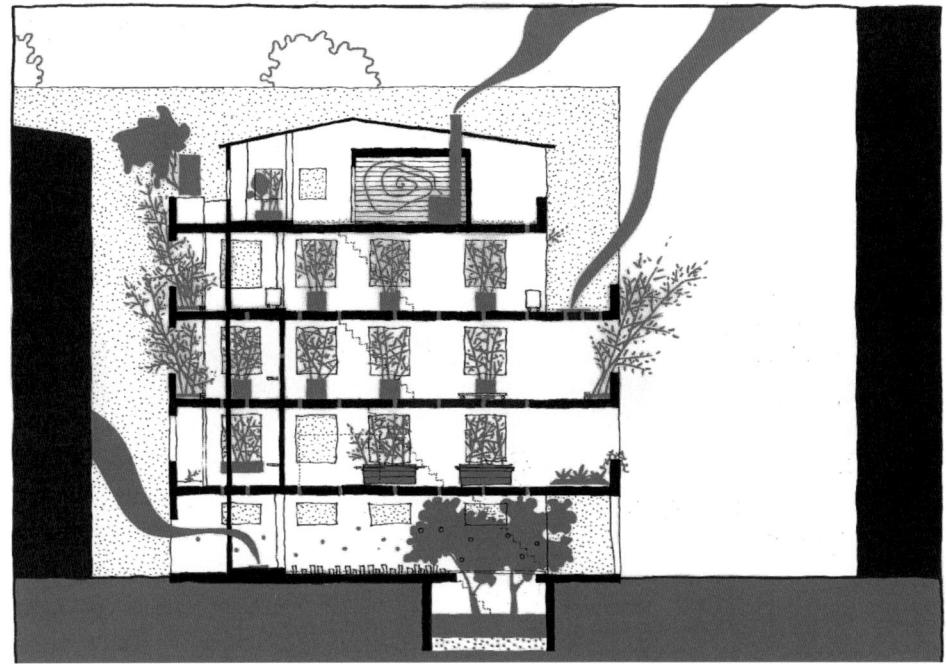

Fig. 26.2 Section north-south,
Ruin Academy (courtesy of
M. Casagrande).

Fig. 26.3 Site plan, Ruin
Academy (courtesy of M.
Casagrande).

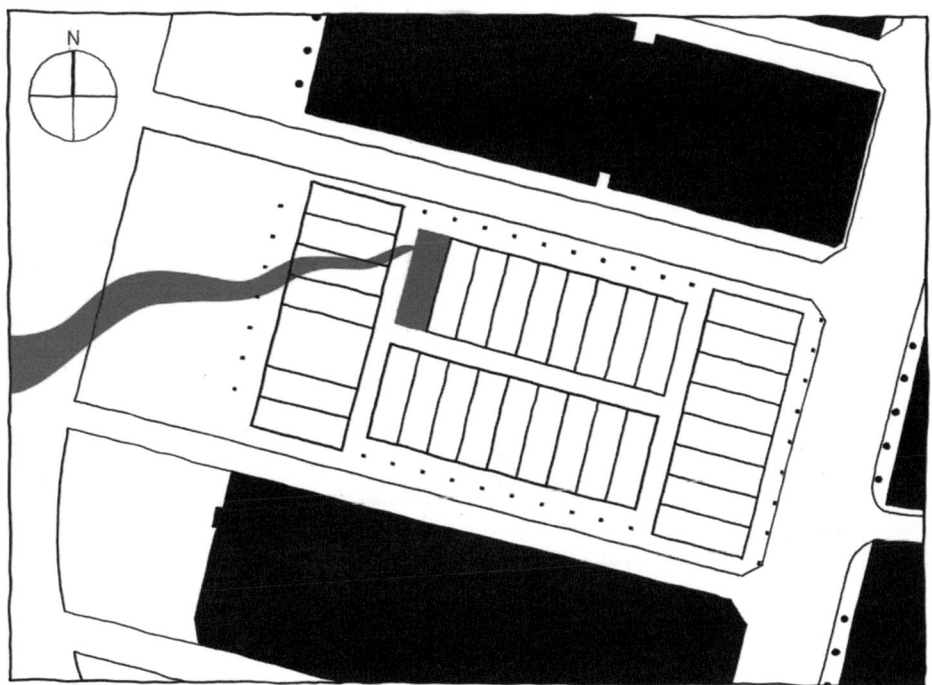

Fig. 26.4 Ground floor, Ruin
Academy (courtesy of M. Casagrande).

Academy's newspaper; it is the title of a series of C-Lab's architectonic interventions in Taipei and San Juan, Puerto Rico; and it
represents a character within C-Lab's performative design installations. In each case, the anarchist gardener manifests the political and
ecological bias in C-Lab's approach to the built environment. This
colorful figure originated from C-Lab's close analysis of the Taipei
basin. Observing that parcels of the Danshui, Xindien and Keelong
River flood-banks were being farmed informally (and perhaps illegally) by elderly neighborhood women, C-Lab appropriated such
"grandmother-dominated community gardens" as a model to define
a range of practices that engage urban ecology and operate outside
of social conventions—and that hence take on an "anarchist" quality.[1]
During urban research workshops undertaken with the National
Taiwan University Department of Sociology, C-Lab discovered that
these informal plots and community farming traditions overlapped
with older formats of land ownership in the city, suggesting that the
anarchist gardener recovers a history of land-use patterns around
Taipei's rivers. C-Lab's anarchist gardener draws on the term's
counter-cultural overtones rather than its politics of violence: sites
for the "anarchist gardener" include urban farms, spontaneous zen
gardens, and other marginal spaces in the city.[2]

A similar ethos animated the *Anarchist Gardener* installations in San
Juan for the Puerto Rico Biennial in 2002. In this instance, Casagrande himself personified this character leading a six-hour pedestrian procession from San Juan's suburbs to its city center. Casagrande's anarchist gardener in this instance disrupted urban flows:
he led a procession that created twelve spontaneous "CityZEN
gardens," protesting the erosion of pedestrian space by the city's

dominant car culture. Each CityZEN garden, composed from industrial waste materials, adopted the size and shape of an automobile's
parking space to mark the citizen's resistance to the privatization of
the city by the automobile. As a broadsheet, the *Anarchist Gardener*
demonstrates the range of C-Lab collaborations in Taipei. The *River
Urbanism* workshop blends sociology, civil engineering, and agriculture in working to return the river's edge to its formerly productive
ecosystem. The *Urban Acupuncture* workshop produces small-scale
but socially catalytic interventions into Taipei's fabric. And perhaps
the most synthetic unit, *Urban Compost,* engages the metaphor and
reality of industrial detritus as potentially useful building material.

Architectural Activism
Casagrande's urban development proposal for Taipei's Treasure Hill
(2003) exemplifies the extent to which performative strategies inform
his understanding of architectural activism. Treasure Hill is an urban
squatter settlement perched on the Guan-Yin hillside of southwest
Taipei, bounded by the Hsin-Dian river and characterized by impro-
vised tiers of terraced dwellings which contrast sharply with the
orderly high rises of metropolitan Taipei. Settled largely by immigrants
and retired veterans, this zone of Taipei was targeted for demolition
to make way for a new urban park. Commissioned by the municipal
government to propose an ecological masterplan for the area, Casagrande found that this settlement, perhaps because of its illegal and
marginal status, had evolved organically to operate according to an
ecological model: recycling and filtering grey water, using minimal
amounts of electricity ("stolen" from the city grid), composting organic
waste, and repurposing Taipei's waste. Casagrande relates his experiences of working on the site:

Fig. 26.5 Ground floor, Ruin
Academy (courtesy of M. Casagrande).

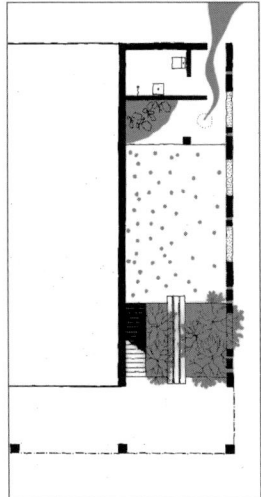

Fig. 26.6 Plan of ground floor,
Ruin Academy (courtesy of M.
Casagrande).

For the ecological urban laboratory I had to do nothing, it was already there. What I did was to construct wooden stairways and connections between the destroyed houses and some shelters for the old residents to play mah-jong and ping-pong.[3]

Going beyond the masterplan, Casagrande chose to protest Treasure Hill's demolition and instead to demonstrate the area's potential as an "environmental art work." He argued that Treasure Hill served as the "attic" of Taipei, containing the urban memory of pre-industrial modes of inhabitation, and that the "attic" contents should be displayed in a manner that was accessible to contemporary Taipei. The ideas for display ranged from a free flea market of scavenged objects to night-time street theater, featuring Casagrande in salvaged veteran's clothing, torchlit and animating the ruins of the riverfront homes already partially destroyed by city mandate. Casagrande advocated that Treasure Hill also be understood as a preserve for matriarchical social structure and "squatter self-sufficiency." Together these two qualities immanent in the site comprised what the architect identified as a localized ecological knowledge.[4]

Casagrande staged a second street performance bringing the "memory theater" into central Taipei as an architectonic installation: steel scaffolds bearing an array of plants and books contributed by Treasure Hill dwellers were wheeled into the city center. This display instigated a barter-like exchange with city bookstores: trading Treasure Hill "memories" for books. That this exchange operates according to barter principles renders the performance work consistent with the vision of the ecological economy described by Clément in "The Emergent Alternative":

> It is time to think about what will, almost mechanically, best accommodate an ecological regime for the planet. The question of what form tomorrow's currency may take is not a matter of which currency will dominate (the dollar, the euro, the yen, the euro-yen!); rather, it is a matter of what philosophy of exchange and sharing is required for the survival of humanity on the planet.[5]

Lourie Harrison

Clément's proposition that ecology represents an alternative material economy, one that draws on the economic theories of Bernard Lietaer and Alain Lipietz, leads us to ask whether such an ecological perspective also describes a posthuman political project. C-Lab's Treasure Hill intervention offers a critique of profit-driven markets by establishing a non-monetary exchange of urban memory. The roving installation gave voice to the marginalized Treasure Hill community through objects that spoke of the ecological efficiency of this community. C-Lab's actual built interventions at Treasure Hill were minimal: stairways, platforms, and bamboo bridges, as well as a water drainage systems and water-filtering gardens. A scaffold for a new farmers' market made of bamboo completed C-Lab's project: a gesture integrating an alternative to profit-driven mechanisms within what Casagrande framed as a paradigm of ecological living. This project, titled Organic Layer Taipei, attracted extensive media attention, an installation at the 2006 Venice Biennale, and sufficient political goodwill from Taipei's municipal powers to preserve the Treasure Hill settlement, albeit as a cultural site and tourist attraction.

Third Generation City

Casagrande's intervention at Treasure Hill illustrates his concept of the *third generation city* as an alternative to aggressive urban development;[6] Ruin Academy's architectural research, workshops and projects seek to implement the ecological principles of the third generation city. If in Casagrande's terms, the first generation city refers to modest urban development respecting the topographical and geological constraints of site, and the second generation city is an industrial city that exploits natural resources to drive its expansion, then the third generation city operates on ecological rather than economic imperatives: "the third generation city becomes the organic ruin of the industrial city."[7] The third generation city is envisaged to be an organic layer that promotes alternative modes of living as well as narratives, or "urban rumors," with the potential to erode the productivist mentality of the industrial city. We can find aspects of the third generation city in the fragmentary organization of community gardens, informal plots managed by "anarchist grandmothers," or the markets of Treasure Hill.

Clément's theoretical propositions for the third landscape provide an important conceptual framework for understanding the implications of Casagrande's third generation city. Clément's *Manifesto on the Third Landscape* stresses the alignment of the concept with that of the Third Estate (the common people as opposed to the nobility or clergy) as an ideal collective. This third estate is mapped onto landscape as an overlooked yet powerful agent of social change. The biological and social diversity implicit in the third landscape echoes the precepts of the third generation city. Casagrande locates evidence for this burgeoning sensibility in the informal community gardens that proliferate in Taipei along river flood banks, in abandoned construction sites and other plots of land the ownership of which is complex or unresolved. He notes that these informal gardens may be transient yet may also represent decades of

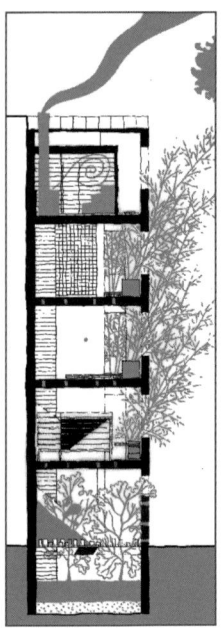

Fig. 26.8 Section east-west, Ruin Academy (courtesy of M. Casagrande).

urban farming traditions, for example on the island between Zhongxiao and Zhongshing bridges. These informal gardens operate outside of official urban planning as the "voids in the urban structure that suck in ad-hoc community actions and present a platform for anarchy through gardening."[8] Casagrande echoes the ecological consciousness described by Clément:"A *planetary consciousness*, born of ecological thought, is dramatically overturning relationships among institutions, and between institutions and individuals."[9]

Performative architecture
C-Lab's architecture creates performative installations out of the tension between urban detritus and the urban grid. In Ruin Academy, a similar performative tension is achieved by playing living organic material against urban structure, operating in many ways like a microcosm of the third generation city. Ruin Academy occupies a five-story apartment building affiliated with Taiwan's JUT Foundation for Arts & Architecture and the Aalto University's SGT Sustainable Global Technologies Center. All of the windows and interior walls have been removed to create an interior space with plentiful natural light to allow vegetation to grow freely within the building. Swathes of living bamboo and taro become the primary spatial dividers. Plant beds with bamboo, taro, Chinese cabbage, passion fruit, *Asplenium nidus* and ferns line the interior walls. The irrigation infrastructure for this organic layer is simple: six-inch cylindrical apertures puncture the walls, ceilings, and floors, opening the building and allowing rainfall to traverse the building section. The needs of vegetation override the conventions of human comfort, in some sense suggesting that the vegetation is the primary inhabitant of the structure. Ruin Academy operates as a metaphorical and physical "hole in the industrial volume;"[10] porosity to the exterior not only services the interior vegetation but also models the program of the space. Programmatic holes include several fireplaces (something of a leitmotif in Casagrande's work) and a public sauna on the fifth floor. These holes issue different atmospheric materialities—smoke, steam, and moisture.

The section of the building provides the most powerful expression of porosity. Each of the five stories of Ruin Academy contains an element that escapes its built enclosure. The basement ceiling is blown open to permit the growth of olive trees. On the first floor, an open terrace gathers sunlight and emits smoke from its small fireplace. The second story dormitory is dotted with vegetable plots, for which the irrigation system involves rainwater streaming in from punctured walls and ceilings. On the professor's deck on the third floor bamboo trees to sprout from unglazed windows. The fourth-floor lounge features another fireplace heat from which helps fuel the sauna on the fifth floor, producing a plume of steam that intermingles texturally with the fireplace smoke. The floor, typically an inert surface in a building, is here refashioned as mahogany bridges, white-pebble zen gardens, light and rainwells, or organic plots: soft and shifting materialities underfoot stimulate the entire body, following a line of enquiry from Architecture Principe in the 1960s, and paralleling that

Lourie Harrison

of Arakawa and Gins at the Bioscleave House. Yet at Ruin Academy, it is organic growth and decay, rather then the oblique surface, that best counters the regimented spaces of modernist rectitude.

Following the example of Treasure Hill, the community of Ruin Academy maintains a minimal environmental footprint with rudimentary work and living spaces. "This is academic squatting," suggests Casagrande; the architect pairs contrasting worldviews—the institutionalizing agenda of academia and the improvisational practice of squatting—to suggest a new avenue for architectural research.[11] Assembling participants from Helsinki University of the Arts and Design, Tamkang University's architecture department, and Taiwan University's sociology department, Ruin Academy's workshops bring an ecological approach to a mapping of the city's informal activities. In this sense, lodging a constructed nature within an architecture of decay dramatizes the incursion of the organic in the city. Ruin Academy establishes a living fragment of the third generation city that counters the modern spaces produced by global technology and standardized construction methods. An event-based program at Ruin Academy draws not only on the PR-logic of contemporary art events, such as pop-up venues and mediatic urban theater, but also on the interpretation of the city as a platform for informal and impermanent programs—from night-markets and street vendors to karaoke and tai-chi stagings—that animate the city. Casagrande suggests in his texts and extensive internet broadcasting that events tap the collective mind of the city: "Something is going on . . . a whole city can be designed by rumors."[12] Ruin Academy, in its form and program, embodies a radical approach to ecological living, challenging the architectural discipline to imagine urban inhabitation as a process of intertwined organic systems and historical architectures, accommodating the flux of rains and rivers as well as the city's changing demographics. Ruin Academy designs a posthuman assemblage shaped by the forces of metabolic urbanization, in Erik Swyngedouw's terms: "Nature and society are in this way combined to form an urban political ecology, a hybrid, an urban cyborg that combines the powers of nature with those of class, gender, and ethnic relations."[13]

NOTES:

1. Marco Casagrande, "Ruin Academy," *Anarchist Gardener*, vol. 1, 2010, 6.

2. Ibid.

3. Marco Casagrande, "Cross-over Architecture and the Third Generation City," *Epifanio* 9, 2008), http://www.epifanio. eu/nr9/eng/cross-over.html, (accessed 2/29/2012).

4. Min Jay Kang, "Confronting the Edge of Modern Urbanity: Treasure Hill, Taipei," *Asian Modernity and the Role of Culture Cities, Asian Culture Symposium*, Gwangju, Korea, December 4–7, 2005: 7.

5. Gilles Clément, "The Emergent Alternative," see Section III of this anthology, 268.

6. Marco Casagrande, "Ultra-Ruin," October 8, 2007. http://casagrandetext.blogspot.com/2007/10/ultra-ruin. (accessed 2/29/2012).

7. Marco Casagrande, "Urban Acupuncture," 2010, http://thirdgenerationcity.pbworks.com/f/urban%20acupuncture.pdf (accessed 2/22/2012).

8. Marco Casagrande, "Taipei Organic Acupuncture," *Anarchist Gardener*, Issue 1 (2010): 6.

9. Gilles Clément, "The Emergent Alternative," see Section III of this anthology, 263

10. Marco Casagrande, "Ruin Academy," *Epifanio* 14 (2011), http://www.epifanio.eu/nr14/eng/ruin_academy.html, (accessed 2/29/2012).

11. Ibid.

12. Ibid.

13. Erik Swyngedouw, "Metabolic Urbanization," see Section II of this anthology, 181.

Notes on Contributors

Credits

Notes on Contributors

Arons en Gelauff (Floor Arons and Arnoud Gelauff) is an Amsterdam based architectural firm specializing in housing developments. The firm has garnered awards including a nomination for the 2006 NAI award for their innovative senior residence, de Plussenburgh. The work of Arons en Gelauff has been exhibited in the 2006 NAI exhibition, *The Best Building Architects in the Netherlands,* and in 2011 at the Shenzhen Biennale, China. Arons and Gelauff have lectured throughout Europe, in China and in the US. They have taught at the German Aachen University, at the Academy for Architecture in Amsterdam and at Delft University.

Denise Bratton is an historian of architecture and urbanism, editor, and translator based in Los Angeles. Her research on the role of the ruin in architectural thought and practice, including its cultural and political implications across time, has led to projects involving marginal spaces as sites of regeneration and the interplay between urban and rural territories. Translations include Françoise Choay's *The Rule and the Model*, André Corboz's *Looking for a City in America*, and the *Manifesto on the Third Landscape* by Gilles Clément (forthcoming). She has taught history of architecture and writing workshops at SCI-Arc in Los Angeles and the Nueva Escuela di Arquitectura (Polytechnic University of Puerto Rico), San Juan, and co-produced the Political Equator in San Diego/Tijuana (2006 and 2007). A protagonist for the journal *Log*, she also serves on the editorial board of *Architectural Design/AD* in London.

Marco Casagrande is a Finnish architect and principal of the Casagrande Laboratory (C-Lab) and WEAK! together with Hsieh Ying-Chun and Roan Ching-Yueh; he was formerly a principal of Casagrande & Rintala. His works have been exhibited in the Venice Architecture Biennale (2000, 2004, and 2006) and in numerous other Biennale (Havana 2000, Florence 2001, Puerto Rico 2002, London 2004, and Hong Kong 2009) and at the Victoria & Albert Museum 2010. His 2010 Ruin Academy was honored at the World Architecture Community Awards (2009). Having taught at the Tokyo University, Aalto University, Helsinki University of Art and Design, and Bergen School of Architecture, Casagrande is a professor of ecological urban planning at Tamkang University in Taiwan, and he runs Ruin Academy in Taipei in cooperation with the Aalto University's SGT Sustainable Global Technologies Centre and the JUT Foundation for Arts & Architecture.

Gilles Clément is a horticultural engineer, landscape designer, botanist, entomologist, educator, writer, and artist. Recipient of the 1998 French national Grand Prix for landscape design in 1998, his public projects include his Garden in Movement and Serial Gardens for the Parc André-Citroën (1986–92; 1992–8), the gardens of the Musée de Quai Branley and L'Arche de la Défense (1991–8) in Paris; Parc Henri-Matisse with Derborence Island, adjacent to the Euralille station (1990–5); and other public and private gardens ranging from Réunion and New Caledonia to Chile, as well as "gardens of resistance" such as the one at Melle, France. He is the author of numerous books including *Élogie des vagabondes: Herbes, arbres et fleurs à la conquête du monde* (2002), *Le Manifeste du Tiers paysage* (2004), *Nuages* (2005), *Où en est l'herbe? Réflexions sur le Jardin Planétaire* (2006), *Le Salon des berces* (2009), *Un brève Histoire du Jardin* (2011). He was invited to compose a series of seven interdisciplinary panel discussions at the Centre Pompidou for the public program *Le monde sélon Gilles Clément* (2010). Clément has taught since 1979 at the École Nationale Supérieure du Paysage (ENSP), Versailles, and held the Annual Chair at the Collège de France in Artistic Creation (2011–2).

Matthew Gandy is a geographer and urbanist. He is Professor of Geography at University College London (UCL) and was Director of the UCL Urban Laboratory from 2005–11. His publications include *Concrete and Clay: Reworking Nature in New York City* (MIT Press, 2002), *The Return of the White Plague* (Verso, 2003) and *Urban Constellations* (Jovis, 2011). His research on urban infrastructure has involved the production of a documentary film, *Liquid City* (2007), that explores the complexity of water politics in Bombay/Mumbai. He is currently working on three themes: urban metabolism (how cities function and the ecological dynamics of urban space); cyborg urbanization (how our bodies are connected to urban space); and cinematic landscapes (how cities and landscapes are represented in moving images).

Studio Gang Architects (Jeanne Gang) is a Chicago-based collective of architects, designers, and thinkers led by architect and MacArthur Fellow Jeanne Gang, FAIA. The firm's projects confront pressing contemporary issues, and their transformative potential is exemplified by such recent projects as the Aqua Tower (the 2009 Emporis Skyscraper of the Year), Northerly Island framework plan, and the Nature Boardwalk at Lincoln Park Zoo. Widely awarded and published, their work has been exhibited most notably at the International Venice Biennale, MoMA, the National Building Museum, and the Art Institute of Chicago. A graduate of the Harvard University Graduate School of Design, Jeanne Gang has taught at Harvard, Yale, Princeton, and IIT. Her first volume on Studio Gang's work and working process is titled *Reveal* (Princeton Architectural Press, 2011).

Madeline Gins is an artist-scientist-poet-procedural architect-philosopher and a co-founder, together with world-renowned artist-scientist-poet-procedural architect-philosopher Arakawa, of Reversible Destiny Foundation. Gins began collaborating with Arakawa in 1963 while earning recognition as a leading poet through such works as *Word Rain: Or, A Discursive Introduction to the Intimate Philosophical Investigations of G,R,E,T,A, G,A,R,B,O, It Says* (1969), *What the President Will Say and Do* (1984), and *Helen Keller or Arakawa* (1994). Arakawa and Gins have produced installations such as *Ubiquitous Site*Nagi's Ryoanji* Architectural Bod*y (1992–24; Nagi Museum of Contemporary Art, Japan), massive landscapes such as Site of Reversible Destiny—Yoro Park (1993–35; Gifu Prefecture, Japan) and multifamily residences such as Reversible Destiny Lofts (2005; Mitaka, Japan). Arakawa and Gins' work has been exhibited widely, with a major retrospective at the Guggenheim Museum in 1997, a 2008 exhibit at the Slought Foundation, and the series of international conferences, *Arakawa and Gins: Architecture and Philosophy* (Paris 2005, University of Pennsylvania 2008, Griffith University 2010). Seminal books by Arakawa and Gins include *Making Dying Illegal, Architecture Against Death* (Roof, 2006), *Architectural Body* (Tuscaloosa, 2002), and *Reversible Destiny: We Have Decided Not to Die* (Guggenheim, 1997).

Francisco González de Canales is Professor of History and Theory of Architecture at the University of Seville. He is also Cultural Coordinator, Unit Master and co-director of the visiting school Politics of Fabrication Laboratory at the Architectural Association of London. His recent publications include *First Works: Emerging Architectural Experimentation of the 1960s and 1970s* and *Net Works: An Atlas of Connective and Distributive Intelligence in Architecture*, both with Brett Steele, and *Experiments with Life Itself*. Apart from England and Spain, he has previously taught architecture in Mexico, Chile, and the US, and published his works in architectural journals such as *AA files*, *Abitare*, *Archithese*, *ARQ, Arquitectos, Arquitectura, Arquitectura Viva, Domus, Journal of Architectural Education, Metalocus* and *RA* among others. He was director of *Neutra* magazine for five years.

Elizabeth Grosz is Professor of Women's and Gender Studies at Rutgers University. She also teaches gender studies at the University of Bergen, Norway, and architecture at the University of Sydney, Australia. She has been a Visiting Professor at University of California, Santa Cruz; University of California, Davis; Johns Hopkins University; the University of Richmond; George Washington University; the University of California, Irvine; and Duke University. She has written widely on the body, sexuality, space, time, and materiality; her books include *Architecture from the Outside: Essays on Virtual and Real Space* (MIT Press, 2001), and *Chaos, Territory, Art: Deleuze and the Framing of the Earth* (Columbia University Press, 2008).

Simon Guy is the Head of School Environment and Development and Director of the Manchester Architecture Research Centre. Drawing upon graduate and post-graduate studies in urban sociology, and previous professional experience as an engineer, Simon's research aims to explore the co-evolution of design and development strategies and socio-economic-ecological processes shaping cities. His numerous publications include *Urban Transitions: Intermediaries and the Governance of Socio-Technical Networks*, (Earthscan, 2011) with W. Medd, S. Marvin, and T. Moss; *Sustainable Architectures: Cultures and Natures in Europe and North America* (Spon, 2005) with S. Moore, *Development and Developers: Perspectives on Property* (Blackwell, 2002) with J. Henneberry, *Urban Infrastructure in Transition: Networks, Buildings, Plans* (Earthscan, 2001) with S. Marvin and T. Moss and *A Sociology of Energy, Buildings and the Environment: Constructing Knowledge, Designing Practice* (Routledge, 2000) with E. Shove.

Ariane Lourie Harrison is a lecturer and critic at the Yale School of Architecture. She is a principal of the design firm Harrison Atelier, whose recent projects include a 2010 performance, *Anchises*, and *Pharmacophore*, a 2011 exhibition at New York's Storefront for Art and Architecture. She is the editor of *Ten Canonical Buildings* by Peter Eisenman (Rizzoli, 2008) and has published articles in *Log, Constructs,* and *Perspecta*. She received her M. Arch from GSAPP, Columbia University and Ph.D. from New York University.

Seth Harrison, MD, is a designer, writer, and biotechnology entrepreneur, having founded numerous companies in the fields of medical devices, drug discovery, and drug development since 1991. He is a principal of the design firm Harrison Atelier, whose recent projects include a masterplan for a Fire Island eco-camp for the National Park Service and performances, *Anchises* (2010) and *Pharmacophore* (2011). He received his MFA, MD and MBA from Columbia University.

N. Katherine Hayles is Professor of Literature at Duke University. She has a background in Chemistry (MS) and English (PhD); she worked as a chemical research consultant before shifting fields to English Literature. Her focus is the relationship between science, literature, and technology. Past teaching positions include Professor of English at UCLA and faculty director of the Electronic Literature Organization (2001–06), an organization that focuses on facilitating electronic literature. Hayles is the author of numerous books, including *How We Think: Digital Media and Contemporary Technogenesis* (University of Chicago Press, 2012); *Electronic Literature: New Horizons for the Literary* (University of Notre Dame Press, 2008); *My Mother Was a Computer* (University of Chicago Press, 2005); and *How We Became Posthuman: Virtual Bodies in Cybernetics, Literature, and Informatics* (University of Chicago Press,1999), for which she won the Rene Wellek Prize.

Ursula K. Heise is Professor of English and faculty member of the Institute of the Environment and Sustainability at the University of California, Los Angeles. She is the author of several books including *Nach der Natur: Das Artensterben und die moderne Kultur* (Suhrkamp, 2010), *Sense of Place and Sense of Planet: The Environmental Imagination of the Global* (Oxford University Press, 2008), and *Chronoschisms: Time, Narrative, and Postmodernism* (Cambridge University Press, 1997). She is currently working on a book called *Where the Wild Things Used To Be: Narrative, Database, and Biodiversity Loss*, which examines cultural representations of the current mass extinction of species in literature, film, photography, videogames, databases, and endangered species laws. She is editor of the series *Literatures, Cultures, and the Environment* (Palgrave) and co-editor of the series *Literature and Contemporary Thought* (Routledge).

Catherine Ingraham is a Professor of Architecture at Pratt Institute and the author of numerous books and essays on contemporary history and theory in architecture. Dr. Ingraham's current book project, *And the Pursuit of Property*, explores relationships between architecture and property systems. Other books include *Architecture, Animal, Human* (Routledge 2006) and *Architecture and the Burdens of Linearity* (Yale University Press, 1998). Dr. Ingraham was Chair of the Graduate Architecture program at Pratt Institute from 1998–2006. She has lectured widely and has taught as a visiting professor at Harvard, Princeton, and Columbia University. Dr. Ingraham was an editor of the critical journal *Assemblage* from 1991–98.

Natalie Jeremijenko is an artist, engineer, and Associate Professor of Visual Art at New York University, where she directs the xDesign Environmental Health Clinic (httpxdesign.nyu.edu). Previously she was on the visual arts faculty at UCSD and the faculty of engineering at Yale. Jeremijenko's projects explore socio-technical change and have been exhibited in museums and galleries including the 2006 Whitney Biennial of American Art, the Cooper Hewitt Smithsonian Design Triennial 2006–7, MassMOCA, and the Postmasters Gallery, NY.

Bruno Latour is a philosopher, anthropologist, and theorist in Science and Technology Studies. He is currently a professor at L'Institut d'études Politique (IEP) in Paris, associated with the Centre de Sociologie de Organisations, where he also serves as Vice President for Research. He is the author of numerous books and articles including *Reassembling the Social* (Oxford University Press, 2005), *Politics of Nature* (Harvard University Press, 2004), *We have Never Been Modern* (Harvard University Press, 1993), *Science in Action* (Harvard University Press, 1987), and *Making Things Public* with Peter Weibel (2005).

The Living (David Benjamin and Soo-in Yang) is an architectural practice based in New York City founded in 2004. The practice emphasizes open source research and design, with each project representing an iteration of research connected to other experiments to form an eco-system of design. Benjamin graduated from Harvard with a BA in Social Studies and played in the rock band Push Kings. Yang graduated from Yonsei University with a BE in Architectural Engineering and managed the construction of apartment complexes in Seoul. Benjamin and Yang both received Master of Architecture degrees from Columbia University. They currently teach at Pratt Institute and at Columbia Graduate School of Architecture, Planning and Preservation, where they are co-directors of the Living Architecture Lab, founded in 2005.

Minifie van Schaik (Paul Minifie and Jan van Schaik) is a Melbourne-based architectural practice. The firm's projects include a display case veterinary hospital for Australian wildlife, a colorful student hub for RMIT University students, a luxury hotel in Bangkok, a Centre for Ideas at the Victorian College of the Arts, a chain of confectionery stores, apartments in Melbourne's central business district, a house for Mildura's celebrity chef and a ten storey retail/multiple residential building in Grocon's Carlton Brewery "New City Living" development. The firm has received awards from The Australian Institute of Architects for the Victorian College of the Arts Centre for Ideas, Southbank in 2004, and for the Australian Wildlife Centre, Healesville Sanctuary in 2006 which subsequently received the Premiere's Award for Cultural Architecture at the 2009 State of Design Festival.

William J. Mitchell, Professor of Architecture and Media Arts and Sciences at MIT, held the Alexander W. Dreyfoos, Jr. (1954) Professorship and directed the Media Lab's Smart Cities research group. He was formerly Dean of the School of Architecture and Planning and head of the Program in Media Arts and Sciences, both at MIT. His recent books include *Placing Words: Symbols, Space, and the City* (MIT Press DATE), *Me++: The Cyborg Self and the Networked City* (MIT Press, 2003), *e-topia: Urban Life, Jim—But Not As We Know It* (MIT Press, 1999), and *City of Bits: Space, Place, and the Infobahn* (MIT Press, 1995). These books explore the new forms and functions of cities in the digital electronic era and suggest design and planning directions for the future.

Matteo Pasquinelli is an Amsterdam-based writer and researcher at the Queen Mary University of London and has an activist background in Italy. He is the author of *Animal Spirits: A Bestiary of the Commons* (Nai Publishers, 2008). He edited the collection *Media Activism: Strategies and Practices of Independent Communication* (Derive Approdi, 2002) and co-edited *C'Lick Me: A NetPorn Studies Reader* (Institute of Network Cultures, 2007). Since 2000, he has been the editor of *Rekombinant*. Together with Wietske Maas he developed the art project Urbanibalism. He is currently writing on the history of the notion of surplus across biology, psychoanalysis, knowledge economy, and the environmental discourse.

R&Sie(n) is a Paris and Bangkok-based architectural firm, founded in 1989 by François Roche and Stephanie Lavaux. R&Sie(n) has exhibited work at institutions around the world, including the Tate Modern in London, the Pompidou Center and Musée d'Art Moderne in Paris, Moca in San Francisco, the Medialab at MIT and others. R&Sie(n) has exhibited for France at the 1990, 1996, and 2000 Venice Architectural Biennale, and they were also featured in the 2000 and 2004, 2008, 2010 international selection. François Roche has been a guest lecturer and professor of architecture at a number of prestigious universities and is currently teaching in the advanced studio at the Graduate School of Architecture, Planning and Preservation, Columbia University.

SCAPE (Kate Orff) is a landscape architecture and urban design office based in Manhattan and founded by Kate Orff. SCAPE's projects range from a 1,000 square foot pocket park in Brooklyn, NY, to a hundred-acre environmental center in Greenville, SC, to a 1,000-acre landfill regeneration project in Dublin, Ireland. SCAPE has exhibited work in the Museum of Modern Art, and the Seoul, Lisbon, and Hong Kong/Shenzhen Bienniale. Orff is a registered landscape architect and an Assistant Professor at the Columbia University Graduate School of Architecture, Planning and Preservation. She is the co-author of *Petrochemical America* (Aperture Foundation, 2012) and co-editor of *Gateway: Visions for an Urban National Park* (Princeton University Press, 2011).

Erik Swyngedouw is Professor of Human Geography at the University of Manchester in its School of Environment and Development. Swyngedouw has authored several major works on political ecology, radical politics, economic globalization, regional development, finance, and urbanization, including *Can Neighbourhoods Save the City?* with eds. Gonzalez, Martinelli and Moulaert (Routledge, 2010), *In the Nature of Cities* with eds. Heynen and Kaika (Routledge 2005), *Social Power and the Urbanization of Water* (Oxford University Press, 2004), *The Globalized City* with Moulaert and Rodriguez, (Oxford, 2003) and *The Urbanization of Injustice* with ed. Merrifield (Lawrence and Wishart, 1996). His forthcoming book will be on *Modernization, Water and Social Power in Spain, 1898–2010* (MIT Press).

Sarah Whatmore is the Statutory Professor of Environment and Public Policy at the University of Oxford. She graduated from University College London in Geography (BA, PhD) and Planning (MPhil). She has authored several works on nature, social theory and the politics of techno-science, including *Hybrid Geographies: Natures Cultures Spaces* (Sage, 2002); *Using Social Theory* (Sage, 2003) with eds. Pryke and Rose; and *Political Matter: Technoscience, Democracy, and Public Life* (University of Minnesota Press, 2010) with ed. Braun. She is an editor of *Environment and Planning, A* (Pion) and of the *Blackwell Dictionary of Human Geography* (5th edition) and a member of the Department of Energy and Climate Change (DECC) Social Science Expert Panel in the UK.

Jennifer Wolch is William W. Wurster Dean and Professor of City and Regional Planning at UC Berkeley's College of Environmental Design. She has authored or co-authored several books, including *Landscapes of Despair: From Deinstitutionalization to Homelessness* (with M. Dear, Princeton, 1987), *The Shadow State: Government and Voluntary Sector in Transition* (Foundation Center, 1990), and *Malign Neglect: Homelessness in an American City* (with M. Dear, Jossey-Bass, 1993), and she has edited or co-edited *The Power of Geography: How Territory Shapes Social Life* (co-edited with M. Dear, Unwin Hyman, 1989), *Up Against the Sprawl: Public Policy and the Making of Southern California* (co-edited with M. Pastor Jr., and P. Dreier, Minnesota, 2004) and *Animal Geographies: Place, Politics and Identity in the Nature/Culture Borderlands* (with J. Emel, Verso, 1998).

Cary Wolfe is the Bruce and Elizabeth Dunlevie Professor of English at Rice University. His books include *Before the Law: Animals in a Biopolitical Frame* (University of Chicago Press, 2012), *Critical Environments: Postmodern Theory and the Pragmatics of the "Outside"* (University of Minnesota Press, 1998), *Animal Rites: American Culture, The Discourse of Species, and Posthumanist Theory* (University of Chicago Press, 2003), the edited collection *Zoontologies: The Question of the Animal* (University of Minnesota Press, 2003), and, most recently, *What Is Posthumanism?* (University of Minnesota Press, 2009). He is founding editor of the series *Posthumanities*, with University of Minnesota Press; recent and forthcoming authors in the series include Donna Haraway, Roberto Esposito, Isabelle Stengers, Michel Serres, and David Wills.

Albena Yaneva is a Reader in Architectural Studies at the University of Manchester, and Co-director of the Manchester Architecture Research Center. She holds a master degree in *Sociology from École des Hautes Etudes en Sciences Sociales* (1997) and a doctoral degree from *École des Mines de Paris* (2001). Her research draws on Actor-Network-Theory to explore fieldworks in architecture, industrial design, contemporary art, and museum studies. She is the author of *Mapping Controversies in Architecture* (Ashgate, 2012), *The Making of a Building: A Pragmatist Approach to Architecture* (Peter Lang, 2009), and *Made by the Office for Metropolitan Design: An Ethnography of Design* (010 Publishers, 2009). She is the guest editor of *Understanding Architecture, Accounting Society*, 2008 (special issue of *Science Studies*) and *Traceable Cities*, 2012 (special issue of *City, Culture & Society*). In 2010 she received the RIBA President's Award for Outstanding University-located Research.

Text Credits

All previously published texts are credited to the individual authors, firms and organization unless otherwise noted. The editor and publishers would like to thank the authors that gave permission to reproduce material in the book. Every effort has been made to contact and acknowledge copyright holders. The publishers would be grateful to hear from any copyright holder who is not properly acknowledged here and will undertake to rectify any errors or omissions in future printings or editions of the book.

Gandy, Matthew. "Zones of Indistinction: Bio-political Contestations in the Urban Arena," *Cultural Geographies* 13, no. 4, (2006): 497–516. Reprinted with author's permission and with the permission of Hodder Arnold Journals.

Gonzàlez de Canales, Francisco. "Approaching a New Biotope," *The International Journal of the Arts in Society 2*, no. 2, (2007), 31–6. © Francisco Gonzalez de Canales, Reprinted with author's permission.

Grosz, Elizabeth. *Architecture from the Outside: Essays on Virtual and Real Space* (Cambridge, MA: MIT Press, 2001), 49–52, © 2001 Massachusetts Institute of Technology, by permission of The MIT Press. Reprinted with author's permission.

Guy, Simon. "Pragmatic Ecologies: situating sustainable building," *Architectural Science Review* 53 (2010): 21–8. Reprinted with author's permission and with the permission of Routledge.

Hayles, N. Katherine. "Unfinished Work: From Cyborg to Cognisphere," *Theory, Culture & Society* 28, no. 7–8, (2006): 159–66. © N. Katherine Hayles, Reprinted with author's permission.

Heise, Ursula K. "Risk, Globalization, and the Cosmopolitan Imaginary" *Sense of Place and Sense of Planet: the Environmental Imagination of the Global* (New York: Oxford University Press, 2008), 150–159. Reprinted with the author's permission and the permission of Oxford University Press, Inc.

Ingraham, Catherine. "Post-Animal Life," *Architecture, Animal, Human: The Asymmetrical Condition* (New York: Routledge, 2006), 81–90. © Catherine Ingraham. Reprinted with author's permission and with the permission of Routledge.

Latour, Bruno and Albena Yaneva. "Give me a Gun and I Will Make All Buildings Move: An ANT's View of Architecture" in *Explorations in Architecture: Teaching, Design, Research*, ed. Reto Geiser (Basel: Birkhäuser, 2008), 80–90. © Bruno Latour and Albena Yaneva. Reprinted with authors' permission.

Mitchell, William J. *Me++: The Cyborg Self and the Networked City* (Cambridge, MA: MIT Press, 2003), 159–68, © 2003 Massachusetts Institute of Technology, by permission of The MIT Press.

Pasquinelli, Matteo. "The Biosphere of Machines: Enter the Parasite," *Animal Spirits: a Bestiary of the Commons* (Rotterdam: NAI Publishers, 2008), 54–67. © Matteo Pasquinelli, Reprinted with author's permission and the permission of NAI Publishers.

Swyngedouw, Erik. "Metabolic Urbanization: the Making of Cyborg Cities," in *In the Nature of Cities,* Eds. Nik Heynen, Maria Kaika and Erik Swyngedouw (New York: Routledge, 2006), 20–39. © Erik Swyngedouw. Reprinted with author's permission and with the permission of Routledge.

Whatmore, Sarah. "Hybrid Cartographies for a Relational Ethics," *Hybrid Geographies: Natures, Cultures, Spaces* (London: Sage Publications, 2002), 159–67. Reprinted with author's permission and with the permission of Sage Publications.

Wolch, Jennifer. "Anima Urbis," *Progress in Human Geography* 26 (2002): 721–45. Reprinted with author's permission and with the permission of Hodder Arnold Journals.

Wolfe, Cary. "Lose the Building: Systems Theory, Architecture, and Diller + Scofidio's BLUR," *PostModern Culture* 16 no. 3 (May 2006). © Cary Wolfe. Reprinted with author's permission and with the permission of The Johns Hopkins University Press.

Image Credits

All figures are credited to the individual authors, firms and organization unless otherwise noted. The editor and publishers would like to thank the individuals and organizations that gave permission to reproduce material in the book. Every effort has been made to contact and acknowledge copyright holders. The publishers would be grateful to hear from any copyright holder who is not properly acknowledged here and will undertake to rectify any errors or omissions in future printings or editions of the book.

Cover Credit: The Living, Living Light Pavilion, Seoul, Korea.
Section Break Credit: R&Sie(n)
Fig. 1.1 Credit: Courtesy of Eléonore de Lavandeyra Schöffer)
Fig. 1.2 Credit: Courtesy of Eléonore de Lavandeyra Schöffer)
Fig. 1.3 Credit: pneumastudio
Fig. 1.4 Credit: Coop Himmelb(l)au © Gertrud Wolfschwenger, Wien
Fig. 1.5 Credit: OMA, © Hans Werlemann
Section Break Credit: Bioscleave House © Ariane Harrison
Fig. 3.1 Credit: OMA © Hans Werlemann
Fig. 3.2 Credit: OMA © Hans Werlemann
Fig. 7.1 Credit: Bioscleave House © Ariane Lourie Harrison
Fig. 7.2 Credit: Bioscleave House © Ariane Lourie Harrison
Fig. 7.3 Credit: Bioscleave House © Ariane Lourie Harrison
Fig. 7.4 Credit: Bioscleave House © Ariane Lourie Harrison
Fig. 7.5 Credit: Bioscleave House, courtesy of Arakawa and Gins
Fig. 7.6 Credit: Bioscleave House © Ariane Lourie Harrison
Fig. 7.7 Credit: Bioscleave House © Ariane Lourie Harrison
Fig. 7.8 Credit: Bioscleave House © Ariane Lourie Harrison
Fig. 7.9 Credit: Bioscleave House © Ariane Lourie Harrison
Fig. 7.10 Credit: Bioscleave House © Ariane Lourie Harrison
Fig. 7.11 Credit: Bioscleave House © Ariane Lourie Harrison
Fig. 7.12 Credit: Bioscleave House, courtesy of Arakawa and Gins
Fig. 8.1 Credit: Arons en Gelauff
Fig. 8.2 Credit: Arons en Gelauff
Fig. 8.3 Credit: Arons en Gelauff
Fig. 8.4 Credit: Arons en Gelauff © Jeroen Musch
Fig. 8.5 Credit: Arons en Gelauff © Jeroen Musch
Fig. 8.6 Credit: Plussenburgh © Ariane Lourie Harrison
Fig. 8.7 Credit: Arons en Gelauff
Fig. 8.8 Credit: Arons en Gelauff
Fig. 8.9 Credit: Plussenburgh © Ariane Lourie Harrison
Fig. 8.10 Credit: Arons en Gelauff
Fig. 8.11 Credit: Arons en Gelauff © Jeroen Musch
Fig. 9.1 Credit: R&Sie (n)
Fig. 9.2 Credit: R&Sie (n)
Fig. 9.3 Credit: R&Sie (n)
Fig. 9.4 Credit: R&Sie (n)
Fig. 9.5 Credit: R&Sie (n)
Fig. 9.6 Credit: R&Sie (n)
Fig. 9.7 Credit: R&Sie (n)
Section Break Credit: Minifie van Schaik © Peter Bennetts
Fig. 10.1 Credit: Étienne–Jules Marey, "Photographic Rifle," *La Nature* (April 22 1882), 289, Engraving by Louis Poyet (courtesy of La BIU Santé, Université Paris Descartes
Fig. 11.1 Credit: Diller, Scofidio and Renfro
Fig. 11.2 Credit: Diller, Scofidio and Renfro
Fig. 16.1 Credit: Minifie van Schaik © Peter Bennetts
Fig. 16.2 Credit: Minifie van Schaik © Peter Bennetts

Fig. 16.3 Credit: Minifie van Schaik
Fig. 16.4 Credit: Minifie van Schaik © Peter Bennetts
Fig. 16.5 Credit: Minifie van Schaik
Fig. 16.6 Credit: Minifie van Schaik © Peter Bennetts
Fig. 16.7 Credit: Minifie van Schaik
Fig. 16.8 Credit: Minifie van Schaik
Fig. 16.9 Credit: Minifie van Schaik © Peter Bennetts
Fig. 17.1 Credit: The Living
Fig. 17.2 Credit: The Living
Fig. 17.3 Credit: The Living
Fig. 17.4 Credit: The Living
Fig. 17.5 Credit: The Living
Fig. 17.6 Credit: The Living
Fig. 17.7 Credit: The Living
Fig. 17.8 Credit: The Living
Fig. 17.9 Credit: The Living
Fig. 18.1 Credit: © Studio Gang Architects
Fig. 18.2 Credit: © Studio Gang Architects
Fig. 18.3 Credit: © Studio Gang Architects
Fig. 18.4 Credit: © Studio Gang Architects
Fig. 18.5 Credit: © Studio Gang Architects
Fig. 18.6 Credit: © Studio Gang Architects
Fig. 18.7 Credit: © Studio Gang Architects
Fig. 18.8 Credit: © Studio Gang Architects
Fig. 18.9 Credit: © Studio Gang Architects
Section Break Credit: The Living
Fig. 24.1 Credit: SCAPE
Fig. 24.2 Credit: SCAPE
Fig. 24.3 Credit: SCAPE
Fig. 24.3 Credit: SCAPE
Fig. 24.4 Credit: SCAPE
Fig. 24.5 Credit: SCAPE
Fig. 24.6 Credit: SCAPE
Fig. 24.7 Credit: SCAPE
Fig. 25.1 Credit: The Living
Fig. 25.2 Credit: The Living
Fig. 25.3 Credit: The Living
Fig. 25.4 Credit: The Living
Fig. 25.5 Credit: The Living
Fig. 25.6 Credit: The Living
Fig. 25.7 Credit: The Living
Fig. 25.8 Credit: The Living
Fig. 26.1 Credit: Marco Casagrande
Fig. 26.2 Credit: Marco Casagrande
Fig. 26.3 Credit: Marco Casagrande
Fig. 26.4 Credit: Marco Casagrande
Fig. 26.5 Credit: Marco Casagrande
Fig. 26.6 Credit: Marco Casagrande
Fig. 26.7 Credit: Marco Casagrande
Fig. 26.8 Credit: Marco Casagrande
Section Break Credit: Marco Casagrande

Index

war, 270; against disease, 52-60; science wars, 252
Whatmore, Sarah, 31, 188, 249-57
Wiener, Norbert, 6
Wigley, Mark, 11, 21
Willis Faber Headquarters (Foster and Partners), 18
Wikipedia, 40
Wolch, Jennifer, 31, 188, 227-48, 294
Wolfe, Cary, 29, 115-37
Wolfram, Stephen, 41
World Cup Soccer Stadium, Seoul, 194-5
World Wide Web, 159

Yaneva, Albena, 28-9, 107-14

Žižek, Slavoj, 118-9
Zitouni, Benedikte, 178
zoning, 159, 238-41
zoo, 15, 18, 65, 182, 184, 186, 188, 234, 238;
    Adeleide zoo, 294, 299;
zoology, 229; of machines, 78
zoögeography, 228-31
zoomorphism, 75
zöopolis, 244, 299